Keynote™
fast&easy™

Lisa A. Bucki

SVP, Retail and Strategic Marketing Group: Andy Shafran

Publisher: Stacy L. Hiquet

Senior Marketing Manager: Sarah O'Donnell

Marketing Manager: Heather Hurley

Manager of Editorial Services: Heather Talbot

Associate Marketing Manager: Kristin Eisenzopf

Retail Market Coordinator: Sarah Dubois

Packager and Project Editor: Justak Literary Services, Inc.

Technical Reviewer: Brian Proffitt

Interior Layout: Bill Hartman

Cover Designer: Mike Tanamachi

Indexer: Sharon Hilgenberg

Proofreader: Barbara Potter

ISBN: 1-59200-129-7

Library of Congress Catalog Card Number: 2003108456

Printed in the United States of America

03 04 05 06 07 BH 10 9 8 7 6 5 4 3 2 1

Premier Press, a division of Course Technology
25 Thomson Place
Boston, MA 02210

To my husband, Steve, who has taught me a lot about communication.

Acknowledgments

Many fine people associated with Premier Press provided the impetus for this project and deserve recognition. Thank you, Stacy Hiquet and Kevin Harreld, for having confidence in me and signing me to write this book. Project editor and book packager Marta Justak brought her superior expertise to bear, assembling a fine team to help her produce the finished book. Marta, I appreciate your efforts to ensure a smooth process and quality outcome. I extend my thanks to technical editor Brian Proffitt and proofreader Barbara Potter, both of whom reviewed every word and every step to ensure the clarity and accuracy of the text and illustrations. Thanks as well to the production team, Bill Hartman, and indexer, Sherry Massey for providing the art and science to turn a collection of data files into a finished book.

About the Author

An author, trainer, and publishing consultant, **Lisa A. Bucki** has been involved in the computer book business for more than 12 years. She wrote *iTunes 4 Fast & Easy, Mac OS X Version 10.2 Jaguar Fast & Easy, FileMaker Pro 6 for the Mac Fast & Easy, iPhoto 2 Fast & Easy, Adobe Photoshop 7 Fast & Easy, Adobe Photoshop 7 Digital Darkroom,* and *Managing with Microsoft Project 2002* for Premier Press. She also has written or contributed to dozens of additional books and multimedia tutorials, as well as spearheading or developing more than 100 computer and trade titles during her association with Macmillan. Bucki currently also serves as a consultant and trainer in western North Carolina.

Contents at a Glance

Contents

Introduction

Keynote is a presentation graphics program created by Apple. With Keynote, you can create and deliver impressive slideshows, even if you are not a computer whiz. And because Keynote costs only $99—a steal for a business computing application these days—the program makes it affordable for professionals in all environments to upgrade their printed and spoken communications. Plus, Keynote takes full advantage of the Quartz Extreme graphics handling capabilities built into Mac OS X. This means that Keynote provides crisp, smooth, responsive presentation playback, no matter how many multimedia elements you build in.

This *Fast & Easy* book from Premier Press covers the essential features of Keynote. Even if you still draw all your overheads by hand or rely on presentation materials from other sources, you can achieve success with Keynote and *Keynote Fast & Easy*. This book zeros in on the key skills you need to know, making each skill accessible with concise steps and clear illustrations.

Keynote Fast & Easy teaches the steps that will enable you to navigate the Keynote interface; create slides with text, graphics, charts, and tables; format slides and text; and manage your slideshow files. You also learn to revise text and change slide order; include transitions, animations, and multimedia elements in a presentation; deliver a slideshow onscreen; and print a slideshow.

If you want to start developing and delivering impressive speeches and presentations, Keynote, your Mac, and this book provide everything you need.

Who Should Read This Book?

This book is geared for novices who are new to Keynote. Users of other presentation graphics programs who have switched to Keynote also can benefit from this book because it presents the features that are unique in Keynote.

Because nearly every step in this book includes a clear illustration, you won't have to struggle to learn a process or find the right tool onscreen. The non-technical language also helps smooth the transition from newbie to comfortable user.

With each task clearly identified by a heading, you'll also find it easy to use the table of contents to find the steps you need. So, whether you want to work through the book from beginning to end or find just the tricks that you need, this book will accommodate your style and enhance your results.

Added Advice to Make You a Pro

Once you get started, you'll notice that this book presents many steps, with little explanatory text to slow you down. Where warranted, however, the book presents these special boxes to highlight a key issue:

- **Tips** give shortcuts or hints so you learn more about the ins and outs of the software.
- **Notes** offer more detailed information about a feature, food for thought, or guidance to help you avoid problems or pitfalls in your work.
- **Cautions** alert you to pitfalls and problems you should avoid.

An appendix at the end of the book highlights how to install Keynote. Finally, the glossary explains key terms that you need to understand to work effectively in Keynote.

Whether or not you have used Keynote before, you'll have fun as you dive in now with *Keynote Fast & Easy*!

PART I

Introducing Keynote

1

Getting Started with Keynote

Use Apple's Keynote application to develop attractive presentations on paper or for the screen. Keynote enables you to present your ideas in a variety of formats, including charts, clip art, and animated elements to drive your message home. But before you fire up the projector, take a few minutes to master the program basics. In this chapter, you will learn how to:

- Understand slideshow basics.
- Start Keynote and make a blank slideshow.
- Tour the parts of the Keynote application.
- Adjust the view in Keynote.
- Use the Inspector.
- Get help in Keynote.
- View and learn from the example presentation.
- Quit Keynote.

Learning Key Slideshow Features

When you want to communicate results, ideas, or product details, use the Keynote presentation graphics program. With Keynote, you can transform a basic presentation into an impressive slideshow. When you build the slideshow, you choose a theme to set the overall presentation design; the theme specifies a background and text formatting for the presentation. Divide the presentation content into individual pages or slides. Apply a master slide to design each slide's layout.

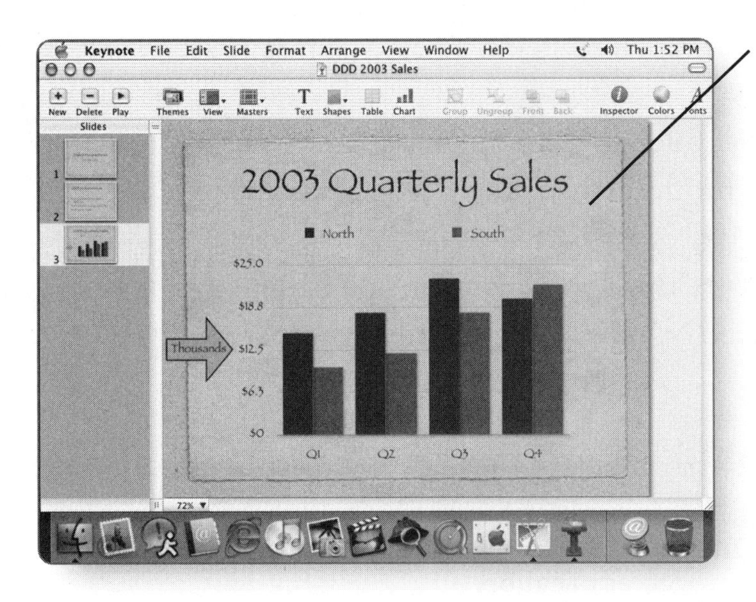

Slides can hold text, bulleted lists, tables, charts, graphic images, drawn shapes, movies, and animations. You also can include speaker notes to prompt you to discuss additional information about a slide while you're delivering the presentation. You have total control over positioning and formatting slide elements. You can even animate objects like bulleted lists to ensure a lively presentation. Keynote offers easy-to-use, yet powerful, tools so that you build a professional slideshow every time.

Once you've built your presentation, Keynote offers a variety of methods for sharing the presentation content. You can print individual slides on paper or on transparency film, print slide pages with speaker notes, or print a slideshow outline. You can play back the presentation on your computer screen, or even on a second monitor or projector attached to your system.

Starting Keynote and Creating a New Slideshow

When you install the Keynote application, the Installer program creates an icon for Keynote in the Applications folder of your Home folder in Mac OS X. Starting the Keynote application loads it into your Mac's RAM so that you can begin working. Unlike many other programs, however, Keynote by default prompts you to create a new slideshow file. You can choose a theme to serve as the background for your new file, saving you the work of adding a number of design elements to the slideshow. The following steps assume that you have installed Keynote to the default location within the Applications folder on your system.

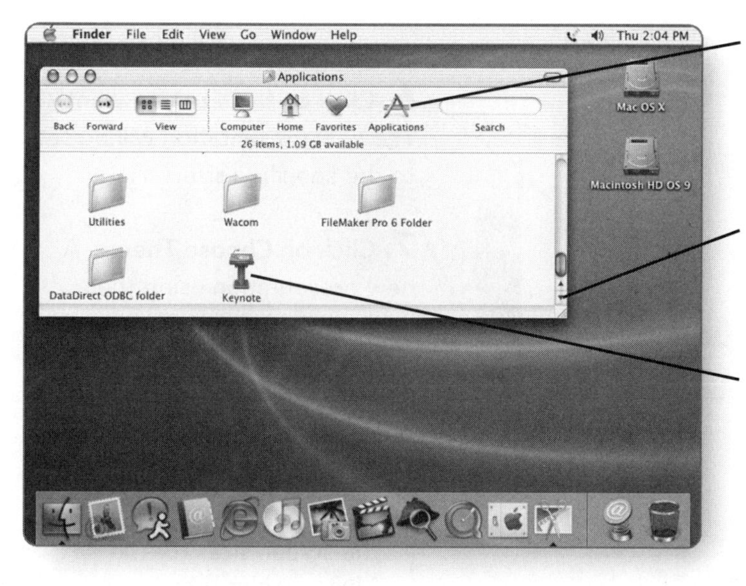

1. **Click** on **Applications** on a Finder window toolbar. The Applications folder contents will appear in the Finder window.
2. **Click** on the **down scroll arrow** as needed. The Keynote icon will appear.
3. **Double-click** on the **Keynote icon**. Keynote will launch and display a sheet for you to choose a slideshow theme.

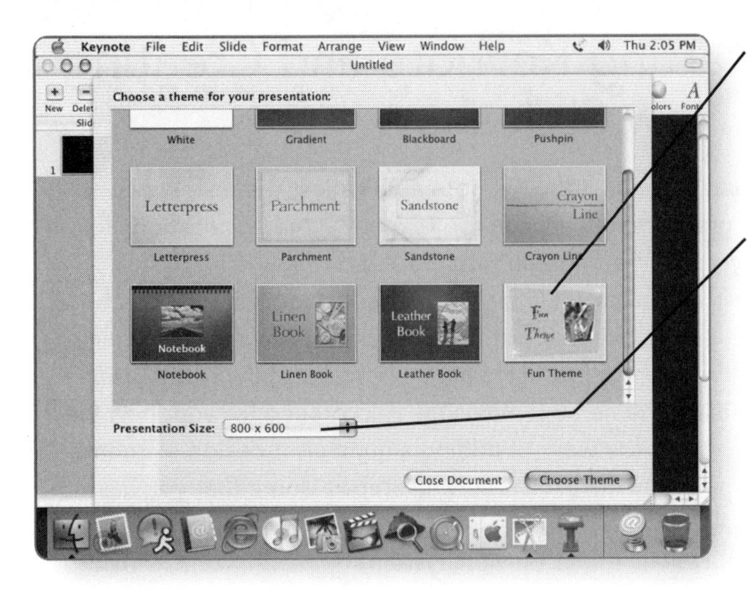

4. Scroll down, if needed, and then **click** on the **theme you want**. The theme will be highlighted in the list.

5. Click on the **Presentation Size pop-up menu**. The menu choices will appear.

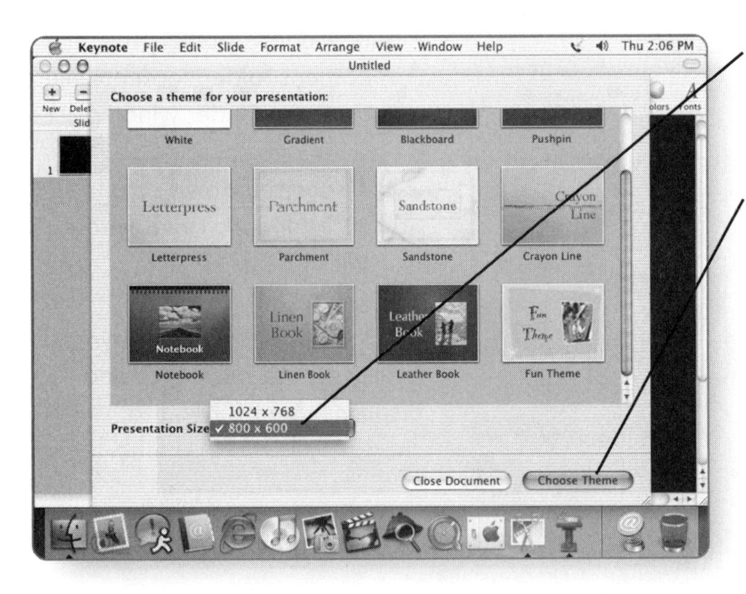

6. Click on the **size you want.** The new presentation will be set to the specified size.

7. Click on **Choose Theme**. A new presentation using the designated theme will appear.

> **NOTE**
>
> To display a slideshow using a projector, check the screen sizes for the Mac to which you'll connect the projector. Many projectors require an 800 x 600 resolution. If so, build your slides using the 800 x 600 presentation size for best results.

The new presentation will include a single slide using the Title & Subtitle master slide. The master slide (or layout) determines what elements appear on a particular slide and includes placeholders for each of those elements. Chapter 2, "Starting a Slideshow," will show you how to work with slideshow placeholders to build slide content. Chapter 5, "Working with Slideshow Files," explains how to save and open slideshow files that you've created.

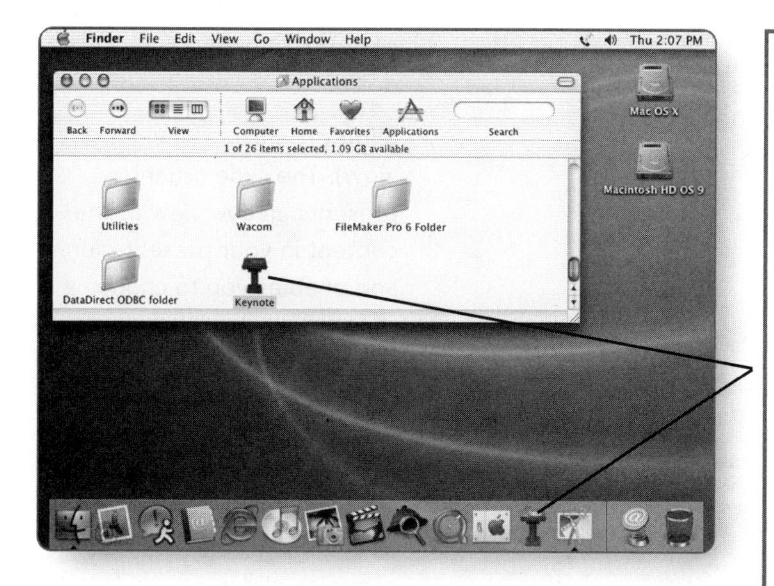

SHORTCUTS FOR STARTING KEYNOTE

If you've recently started Keynote, you can start it again by choosing FileMaker Pro 6 from the Recent Items submenu of the Apple menu.

You also can add an icon for Keynote to the Dock. To do so, open the Applications folder, and drag the Keynote icon onto the Dock. Alternately, Control+click on the Keynote icon, and then click on Make Alias. Drag the alias icon onto the Desktop, where you can then double-click on it to start Keynote.

Looking at the Keynote Application

Within Keynote, each slideshow file you create or open appears in its own window. Most of the elements for working with slides appear within the presentation window itself, as detailed here.

- **Menu bar.** The Keynote menu bar loads when you start the program. The menu bar organizes available commands, with each menu listing several related commands.
- **Toolbar.** Keynote includes a toolbar for easy access to certain actions and commands, such as choosing another theme or an alternate slide layout. You can customize the icons available on the toolbar. The section called "Customizing the Toolbar" in Chapter 14 explains how to do so.
- **Slide organizer (Navigator view).** The slide organizer presents an overview of the content in your presentation and enables you to choose a slide to work on. In the Navigator view, the slide organizer presents a thumbnail of each slide. You can drag the slide thumbnails to perform operations such as changing slide order or grouping slides.

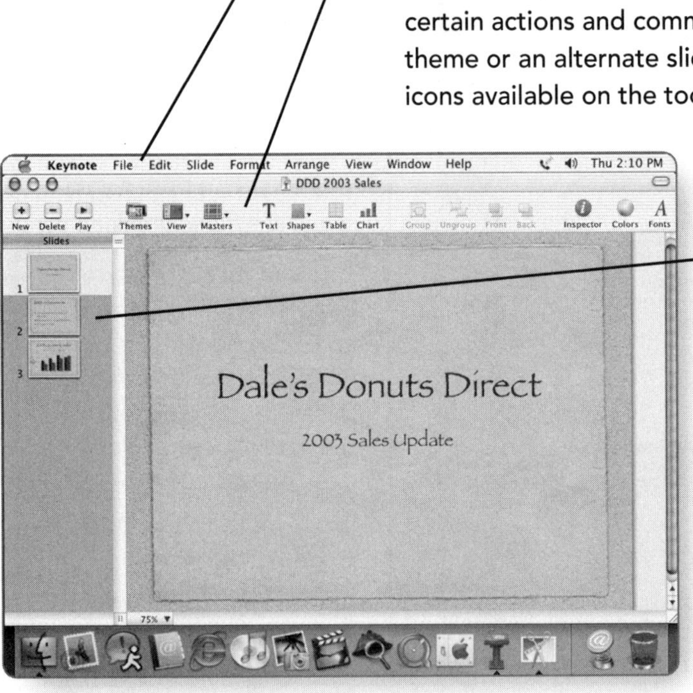

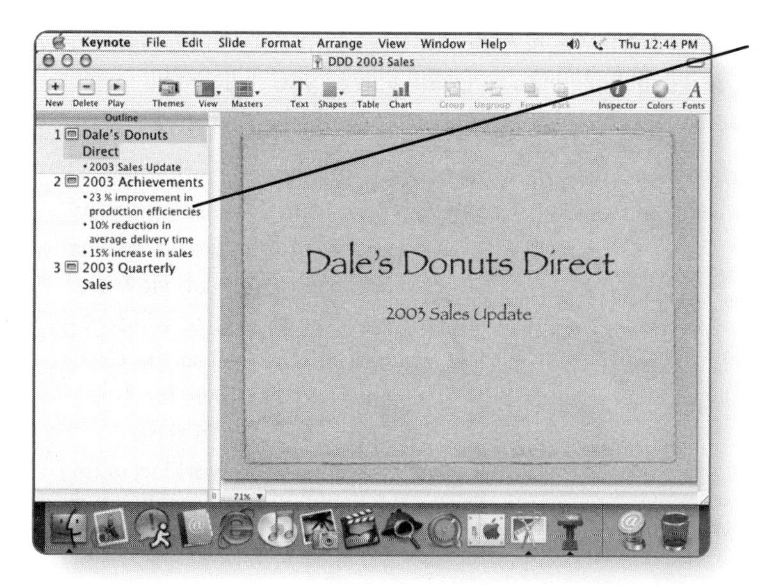

- **Slide organizer (Outline view).** When you change to the Outline view, the slide organizer shows the title and subtitle or bulleted text for each slide, along with a small icon for each slide. You can not only change slide order, but also edit slide text when using the slide organizer in Outline view.

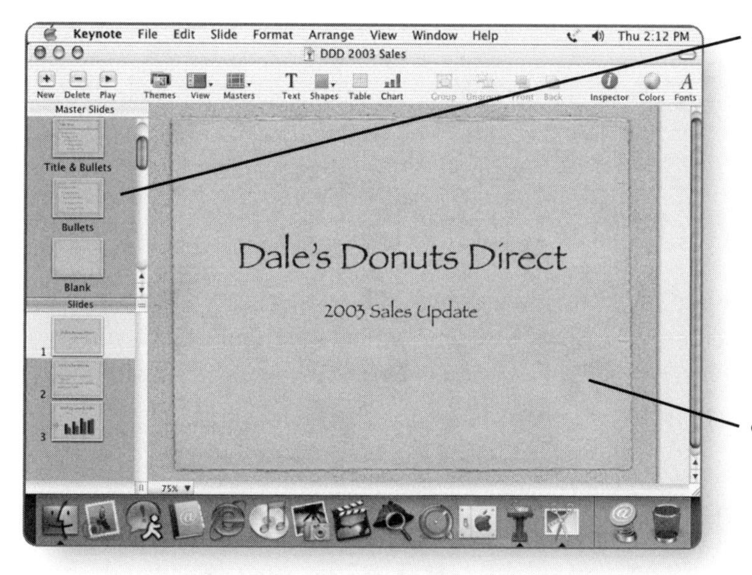

- **Master slides.** You can drag down the divider bar at the top of the slide organizer to reveal the master slides. Select a master slide thumbnail to edit the master, or drag a master to a slide in the slide organizer to apply the master to the selected slide.
- **Slide canvas.** This area shows the selected slide in a large size so that you can work with the elements on the slide.

- **Notes field.** You can display the notes field if you want to write speaker notes to guide you as you deliver the presentation.
- **Inspector and other windows.** The Inspector offers a variety of panels for changing formatting and settings for slides, graphics, text, tables, and more. You can view and hide the Inspector window as needed, as well as the Colors and Text windows for applying color to slide elements and working with spacing , color, and alignment settings for text.
- **Zoom pop-up menu.** Open this menu to change the zoom setting for the slide canvas.

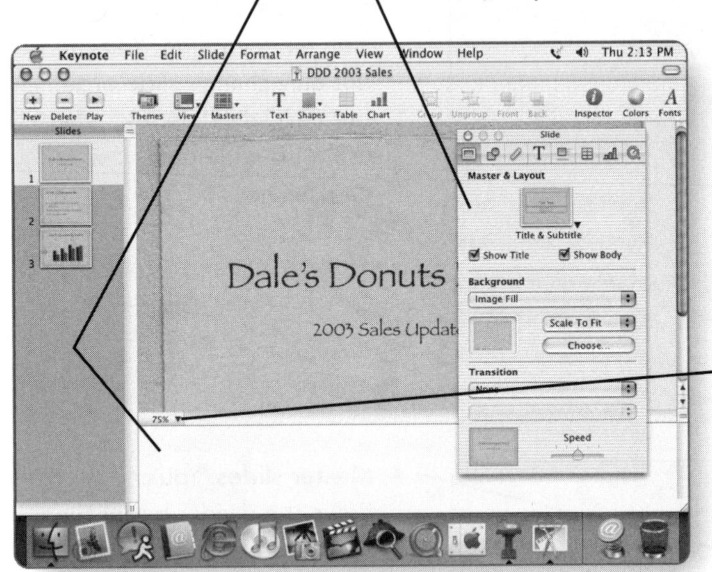

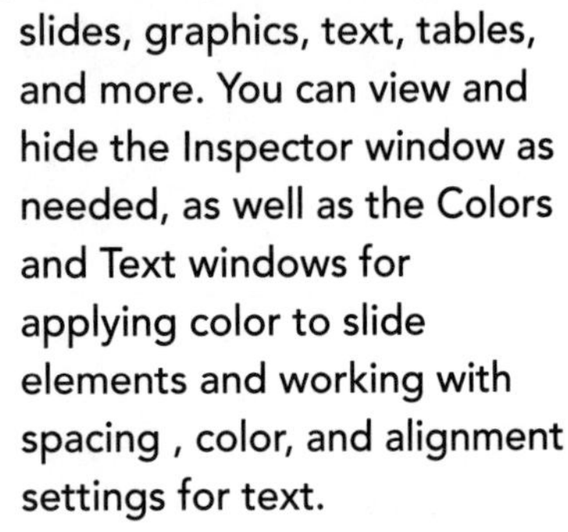

Working with the View

You can adjust several aspects of how Keynote appears onscreen, and what tools and features are available to you at any given time. This section shows you how to work with the screen features in Keynote.

Changing the View

Keynote offers three views that you can use to build and refine a slideshow:

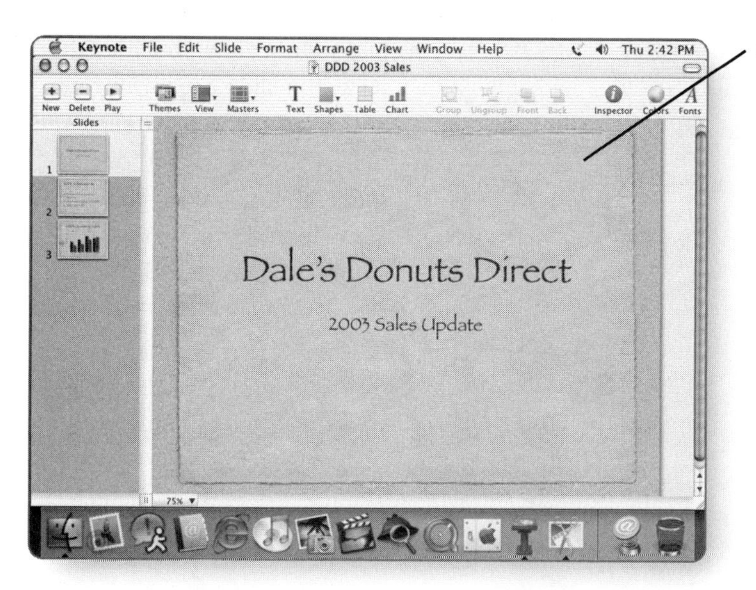

- **Navigator view.** In this view, Keynote displays a thumbnail for each slide in the slide organizer, as well as a larger view of the selected slide in the slide canvas. This view in essence provides a preview of how the slideshow will flow. It also enables you to easily reorder slides in the slide organizer.

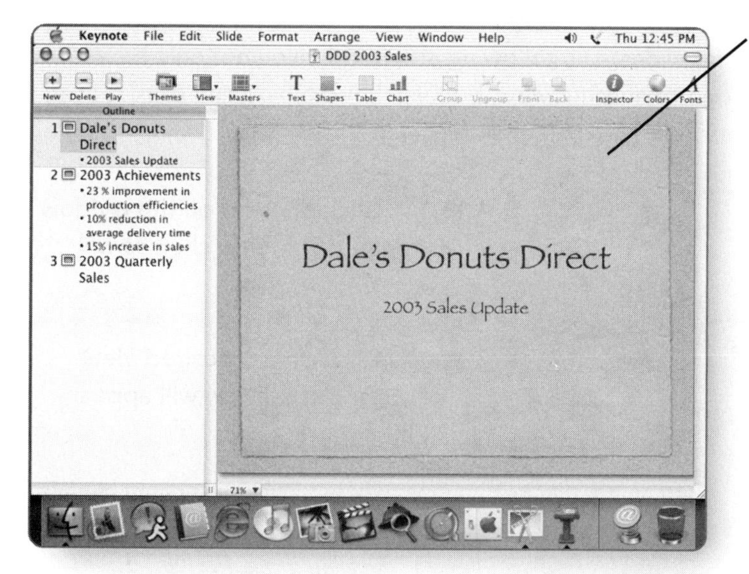

- **Outline view.** In this view, Keynote displays slide text (titles, subtitles, and bulleted lists) in the slide organizer, and again a larger view of the selected slide in the slide canvas. You can use this view to edit and enhance the text more quickly within the slide organizer.

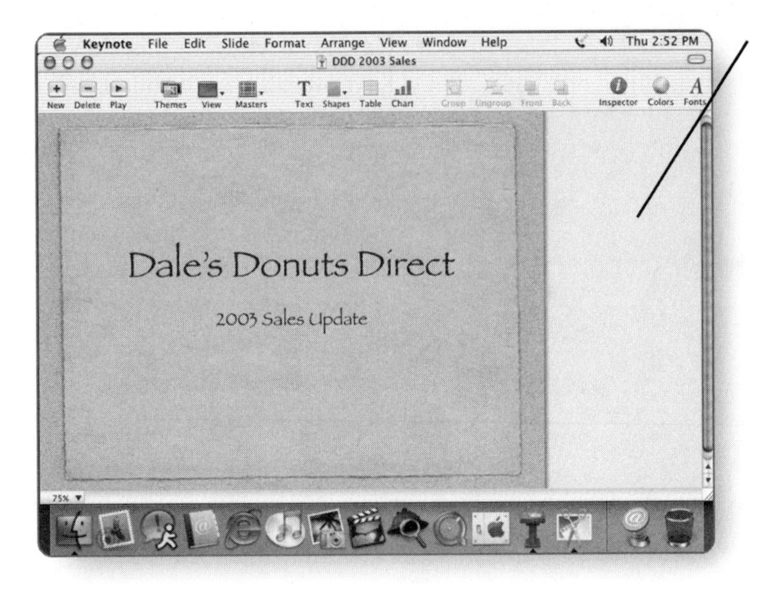

- **Slide Only view.** In Slide Only view, the slide organizer does not appear. This view allows more room onscreen for the slide canvas, making the view convenient for making enhancements to individual slides.

In combination with any of the above views, you can display and hide two additional elements: the notes field and the master slides. The following steps show you not only how to change to another view, but also how to hide and display the notes field and master slides.

1. **Click** on **View** on the window toolbar. The View choices will appear.

2. **Click** on the **desired view**. The specified view will appear in Keynote.

> **TIP**
>
> You also can use choices on the View menu to change the view and display and hide other screen elements.

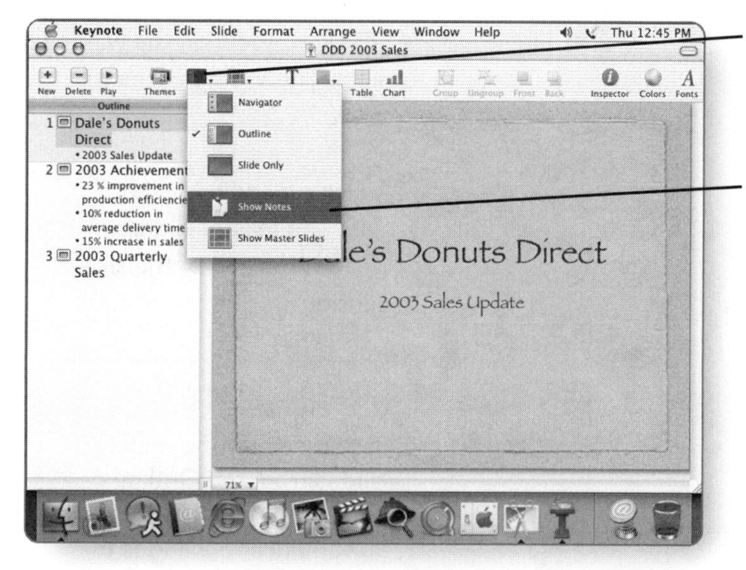

3. Click on **View** on the window toolbar. The View choices will appear.

4. Click on **Show Notes**. The notes field will appear below the slide canvas in the current view.

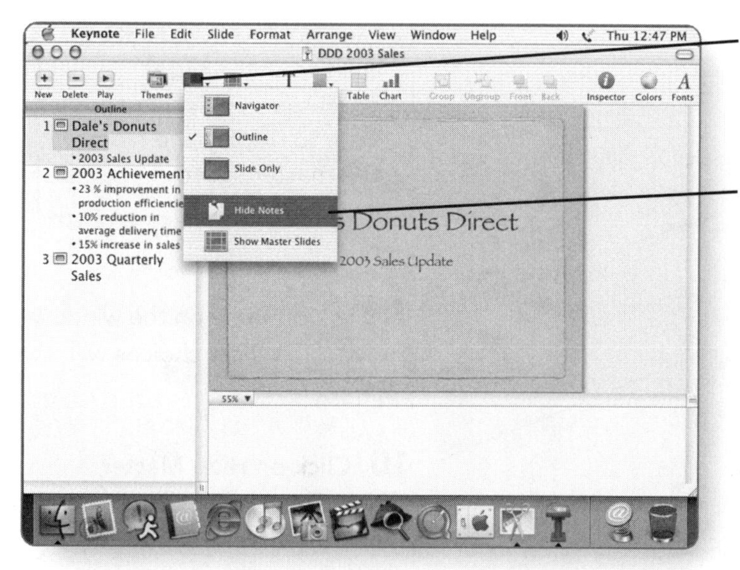

5. Click on **View** on the window toolbar. The View choices will appear.

6. Click on **Hide Notes**. The notes field will close.

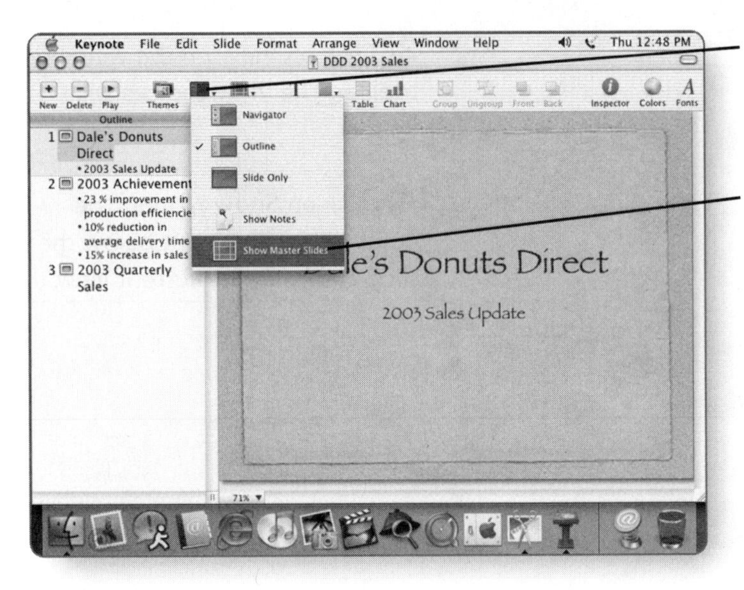

7. Click on **View** on the window toolbar. The View choices will appear.

8. Click on **Show Master Slides**. The master slides will appear at the top of the slide organizer.

> **NOTE**
>
> If you display the master slides from the Outline or Slide Only view, Keynote automatically changes to Navigator view. Also, note that you can display and hide the master slides by dragging the bar at the top of the slide organizer in Navigator view to display and hide the master slides.

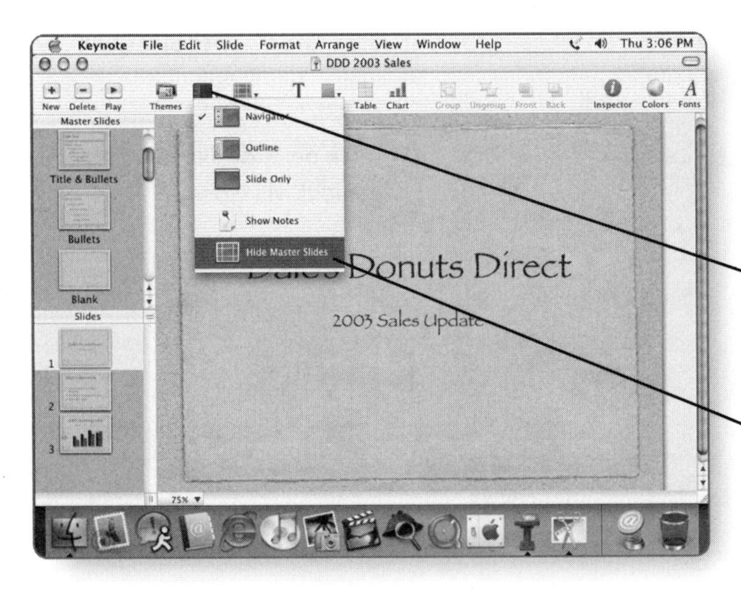

9. Click on **View** on the window toolbar. The View choices will appear.

10. Click on **Hide Master Slides**. The master slides area above the slide organizer will close.

Changing the Zoom

You can change the zoom level of the slide shown on the slide canvas using either the zoom pop-up menu in the bottom-left corner of the slide canvas or the Zoom submenu of the View menu. You can change the zoom level in any of Keynote's three views. For example, you may want to zoom in to position overlapping objects with greater precision, or zoom out to see an entire slide.

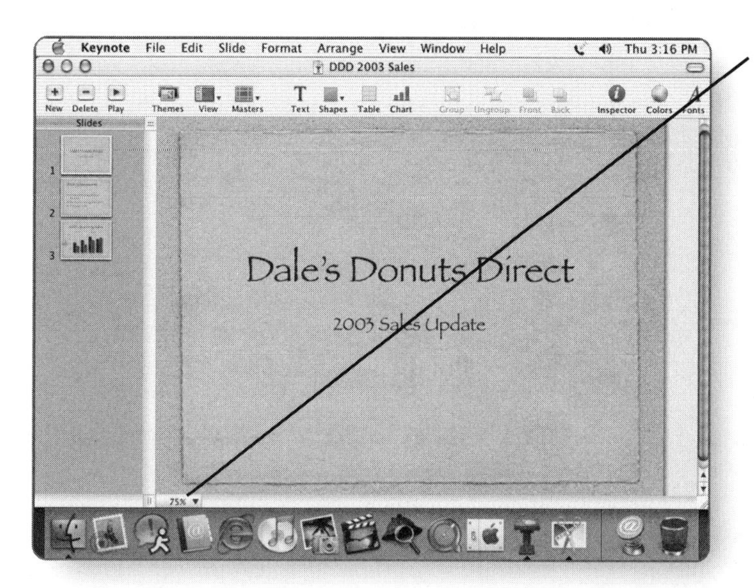

1. Click on the **zoom pop-up menu**. The zoom level choices will appear.

NOTE

Sometimes the zoom pop-up menu will display only a few zoom levels, with a down-pointing triangle below them. Drag the mouse down in this case to display the rest of the zoom levels.

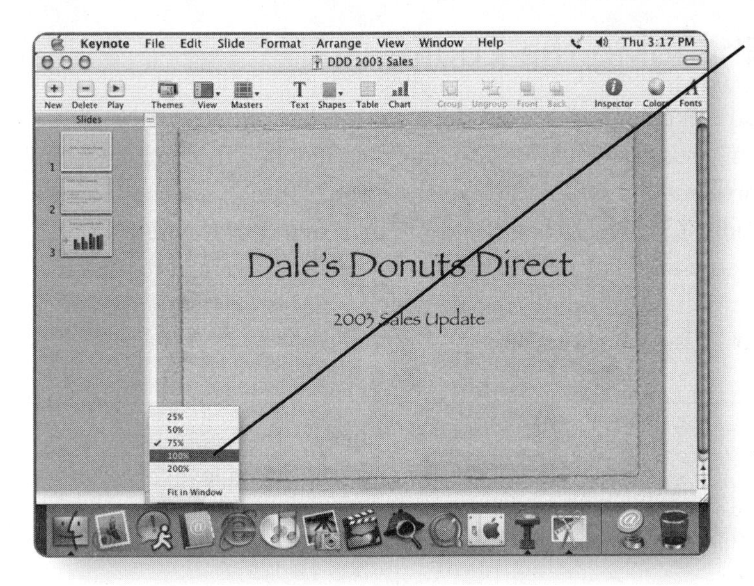

2. **Click** on the **desired zoom level**. The slide will zoom on the slide canvas.

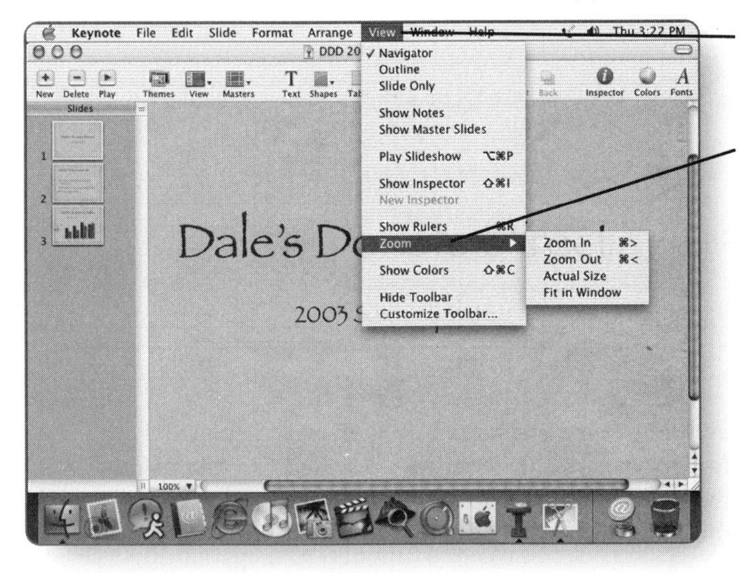

3. **Click** on **View**. The View menu will appear.

4. **Point** to **Zoom**. The Zoom submenu will appear.

5. Click on the **desired zoom choice**:

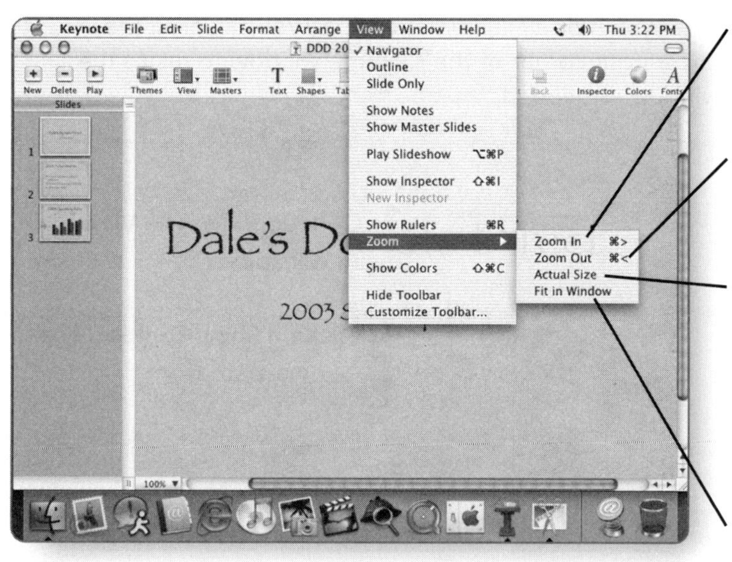

- **Zoom In.** Zooms in by one zoom level, from 75% to 100%, for example.
- **Zoom Out.** Zooms out by one zoom level, from 100% to 75%, for example.
- **Actual Size.** Zooms to show the slide at actual size, as determined by the presentation (slide) size you chose when you created the presentation.
- **Fit in Window.** Zooms to the percentage that allows Keynote to display the entire slide in the slide canvas.

Viewing and Hiding the Toolbar

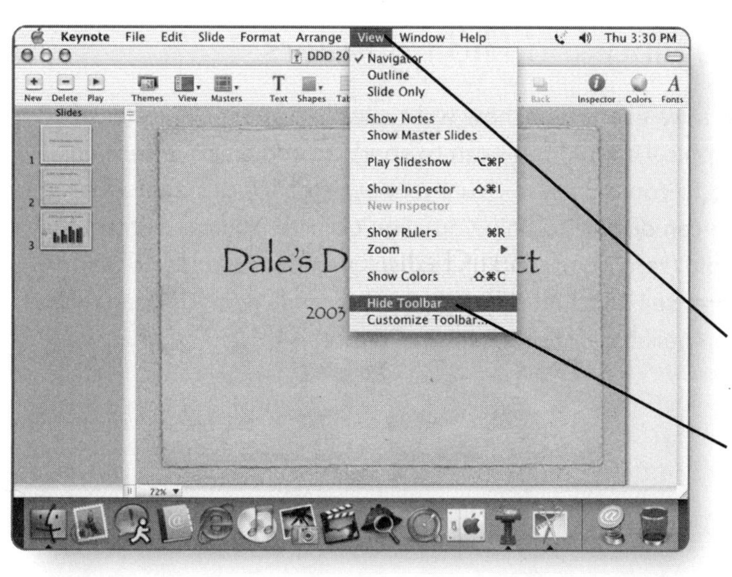

If you prefer, you can hide the toolbar when you're not using it in order to allow more room for viewing the presentation in the slide canvas and slide navigator. Here's how to hide and redisplay Keynote's toolbar.

1. Click on **View**. The View menu will appear.

2. Click on **Hide Toolbar**. The toolbar will no longer appear in the window, causing the window to shrink.

TIP

After you hide or show the toolbar, you can drag the lower-right corner of the Keynote window to resize the window as needed.

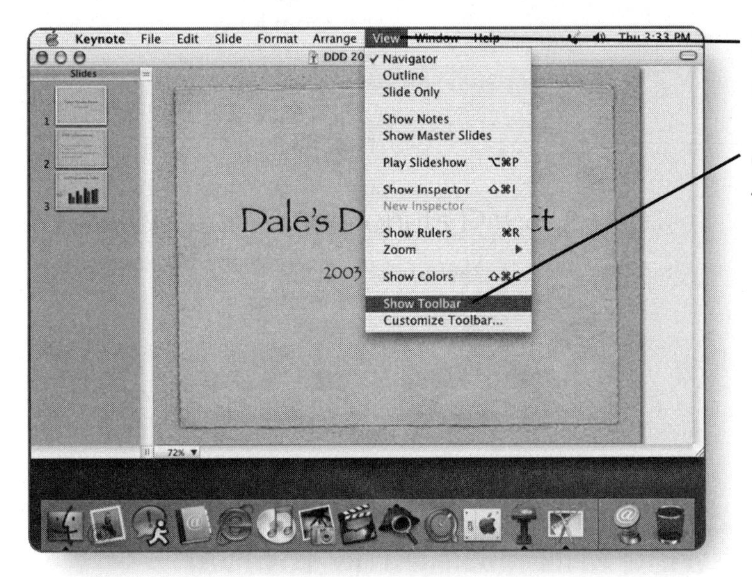

3. **Click** on **View**. The View menu will appear.

4. **Click** on **Show Toolbar**. The toolbar will reappear.

Viewing and Hiding Rulers

Because every slideshow will typically contain a number of graphical elements—both to spark an audience's attention and to communicate visually—Keynote includes rulers that you can display to help you align objects. You can control the origin (zero point) and units displayed on the ruler. To learn more, see "Setting Keynote Preferences" and "Understanding the Available Preferences" in Chapter 14.

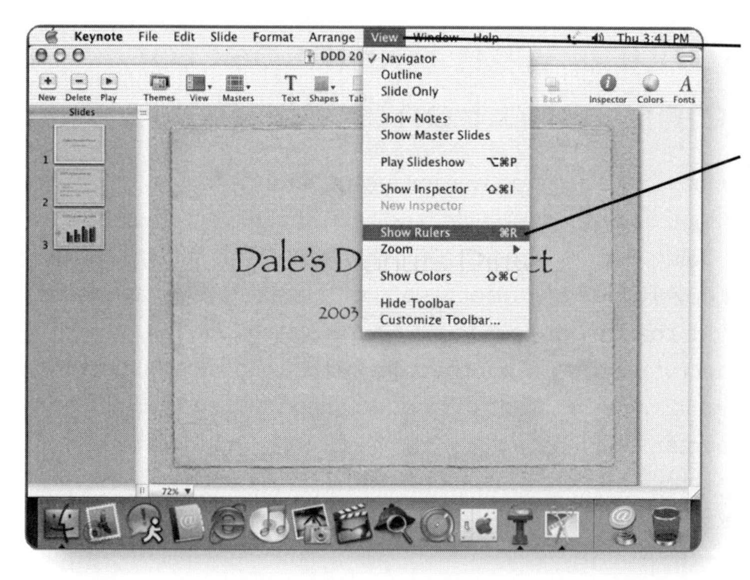

1. **Click** on **View**. The View menu will appear.

2. **Click** on **Show Rulers**.

The vertical ruler will appear along the left side of the slide canvas, and the horizontal ruler will appear across the top of the slide canvas.

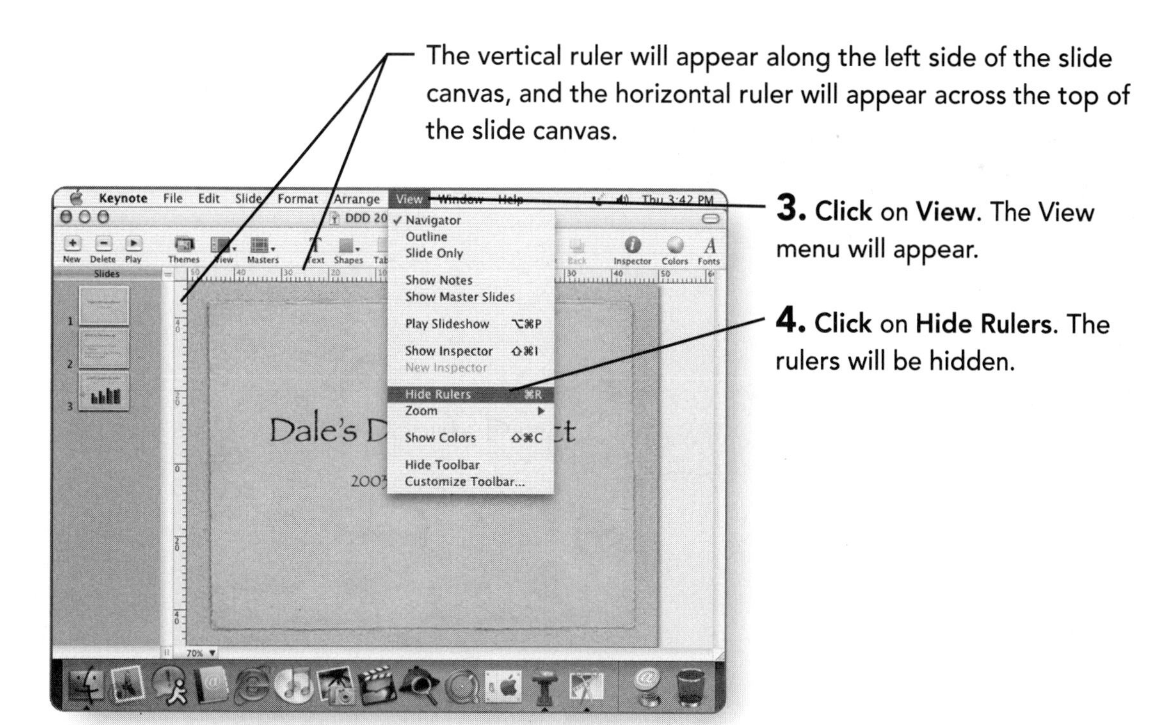

3. **Click** on **View**. The View menu will appear.

4. **Click** on **Hide Rulers**. The rulers will be hidden.

Working with the Inspector, Colors, and Fonts Windows

Keynote includes three windows with settings for manipulating slides, objects, and text: the Inspector window, the Colors window, and the Fonts window. This section shows you how to hide and display each of these windows, as well as how to change between the various Inspectors in the Inspector window. The Inspectors include the Slide Inspector, Graphic Inspector, Metrics Inspector, Text Inspector, Build Inspector, Table Inspector, Chart Inspector, and Media Inspector. Later chapters explain how to use each of these windows to format a selected object on a slide.

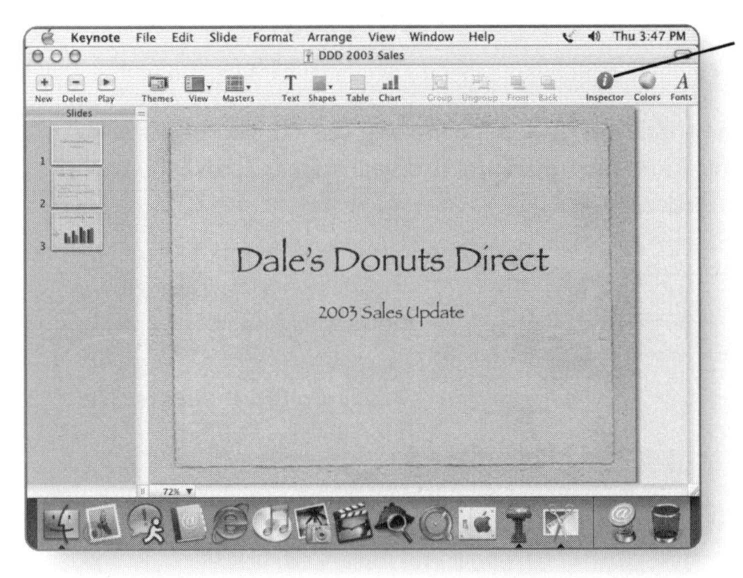

1. **Click** on **Inspector** on the window toolbar. The Inspector window will open.

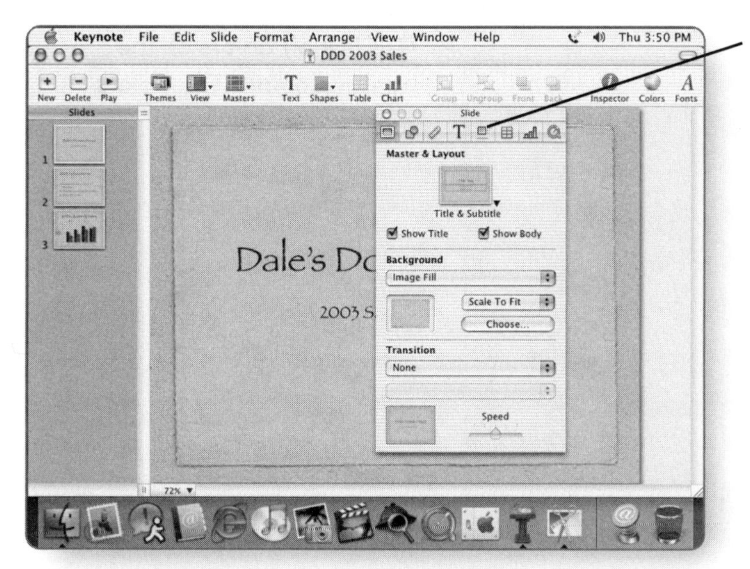

2. Click on the **desired Inspector button.**

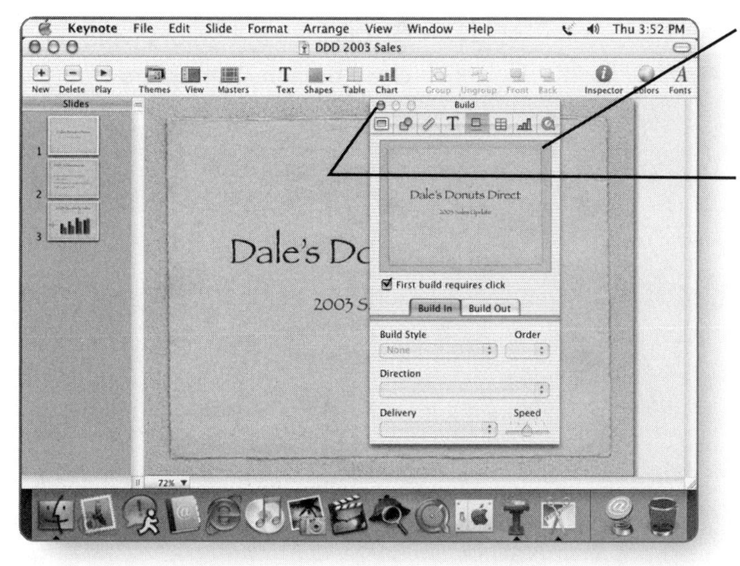

The specified Inspector's choices will appear in the Inspector window.

3. Click on the **Inspector window close button**. The Inspector window will close.

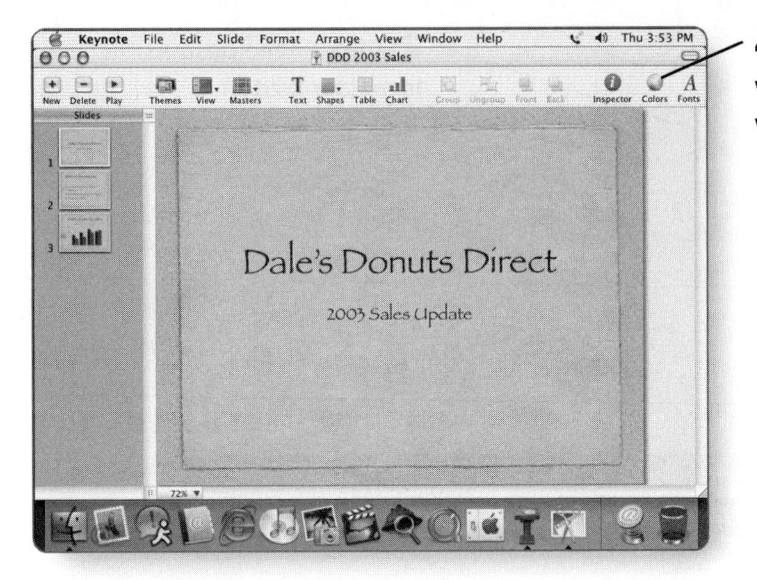

4. Click on **Colors** on the window toolbar. The Colors window will open.

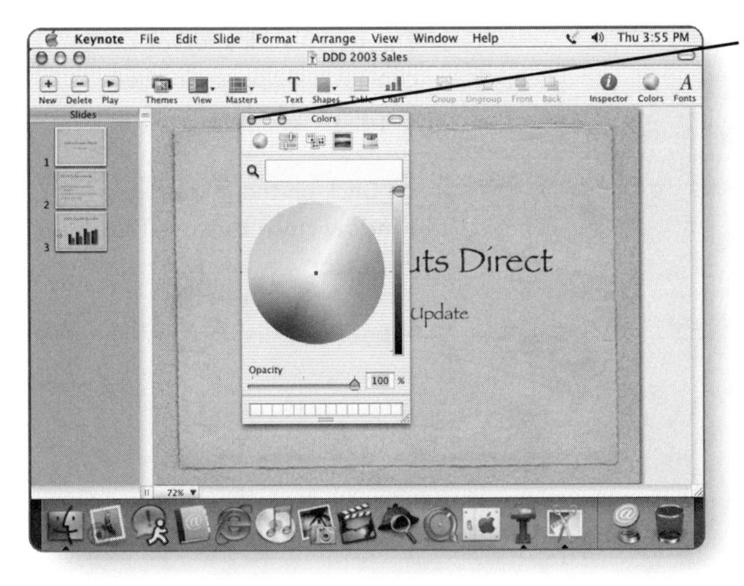

5. Click on the **Colors window close button**. The Colors window will close.

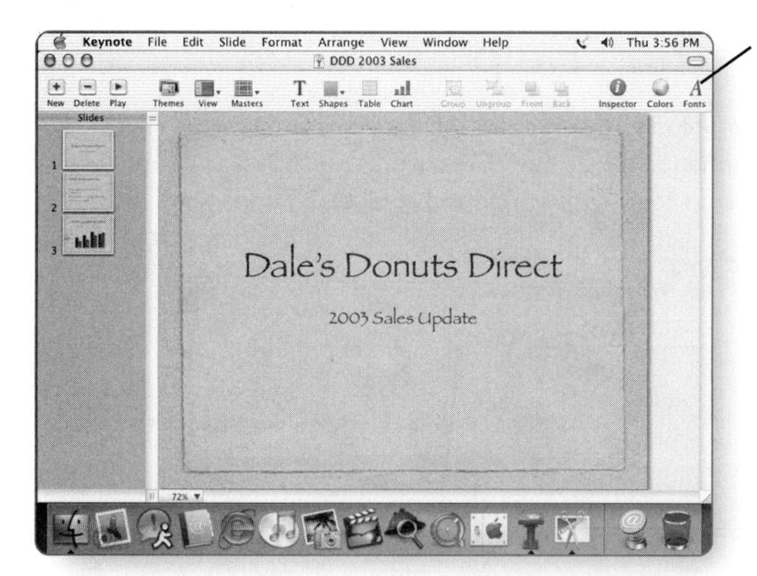

6. Click on **Fonts** on the window toolbar. The Fonts window will open.

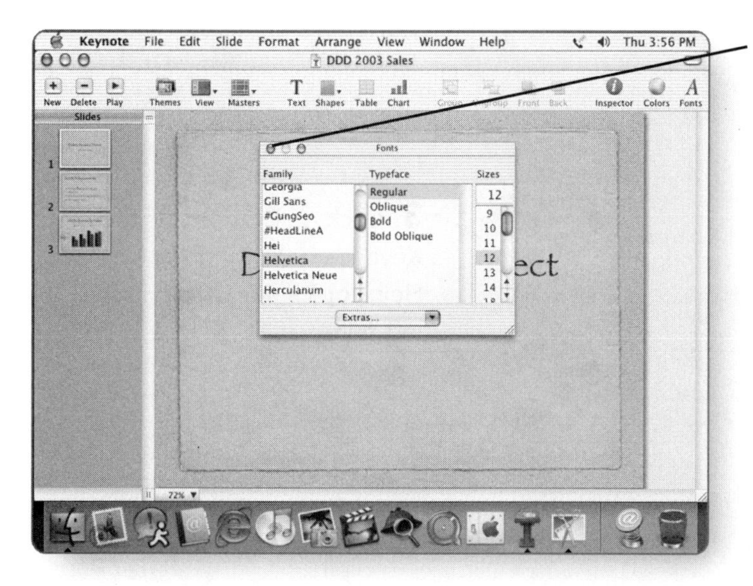

7. Click on the **Fonts window close button**. The Fonts window will close.

Getting Help

Keynote uses the Mac OS X Help Viewer to present Help information. The Help Viewer works much like a Web browser. Click on topic links (formatted in blue and underlined by default) to navigate to the Help topic you need. The following steps show a basic Help navigation, but keep in mind that some Help Viewer links may take you to an online site or a search location.

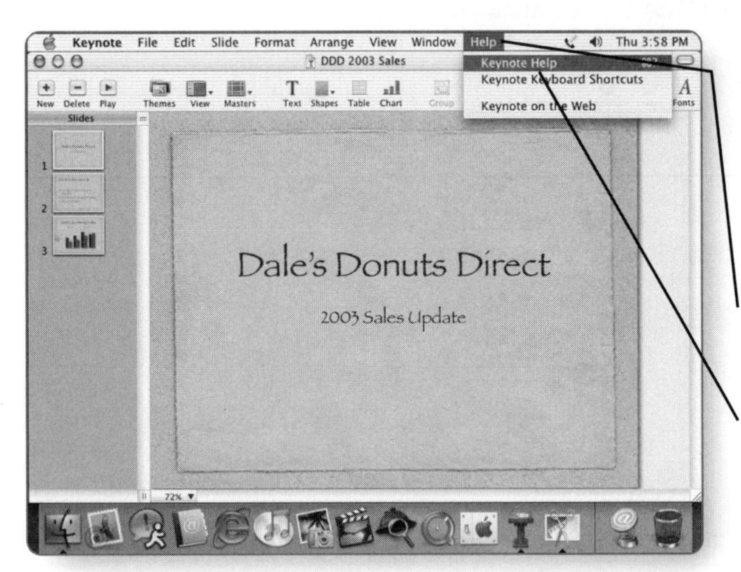

1. **Click** on **Help**. The Help menu will appear.

2. **Click** on **Keynote Help**. Help Viewer will open.

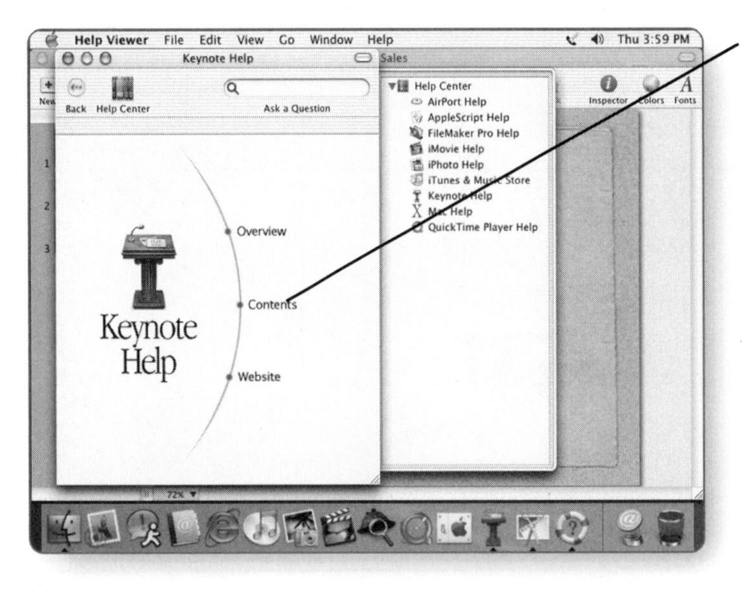

3. **Click** on **Contents** in the Keynote Help window. A list of Help topics will appear in the left pane.

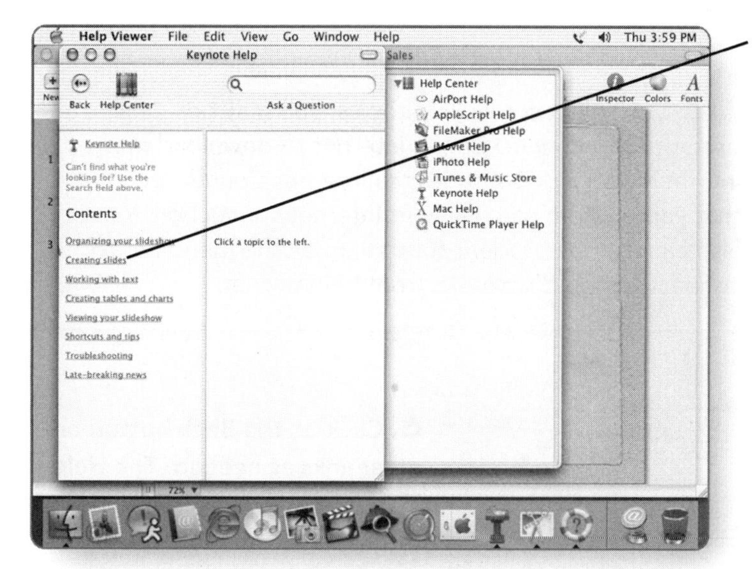

4. Click on the **topic you want.** A listing of more specific Help topics will appear in the right pane of the Keynote Help window.

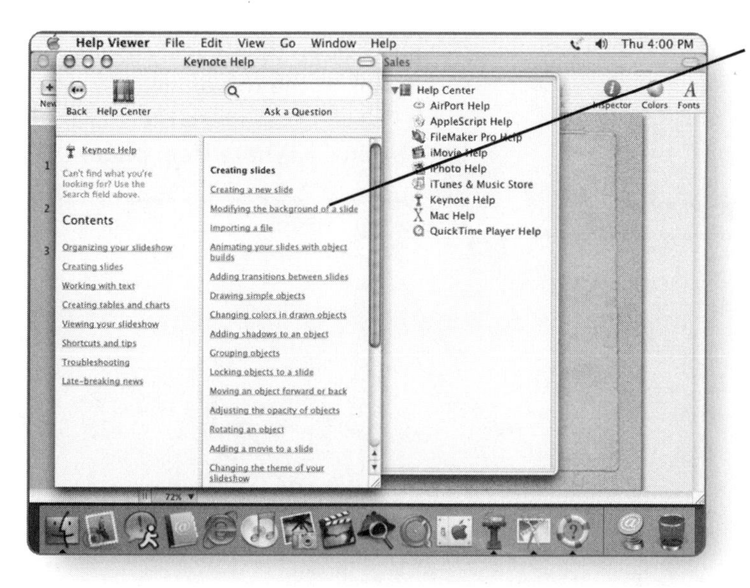

5. Click on the **topic of interest**. The topic will appear in the Keynote Help window. Use the Pg Up and Pg Dn keys to scroll the Help information as needed.

NOTE

When you select some Help topics, you may be prompted to connect to the Internet to download more information. Click OK to launch Internet Connect so that your system can dial your Internet connection. You also can use the modem status icon on the menu bar to connect to and disconnect from the Internet.

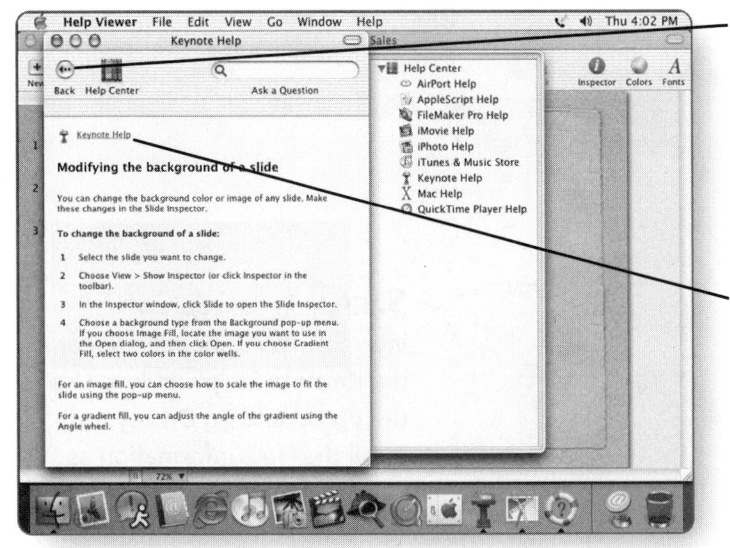

6. Click on the **Back button** or other links as needed. The Help Viewer window will navigate to the appropriate page.

NOTE

Click on the Keynote Help link at the top of any page to return to the initial Keynote Help page.

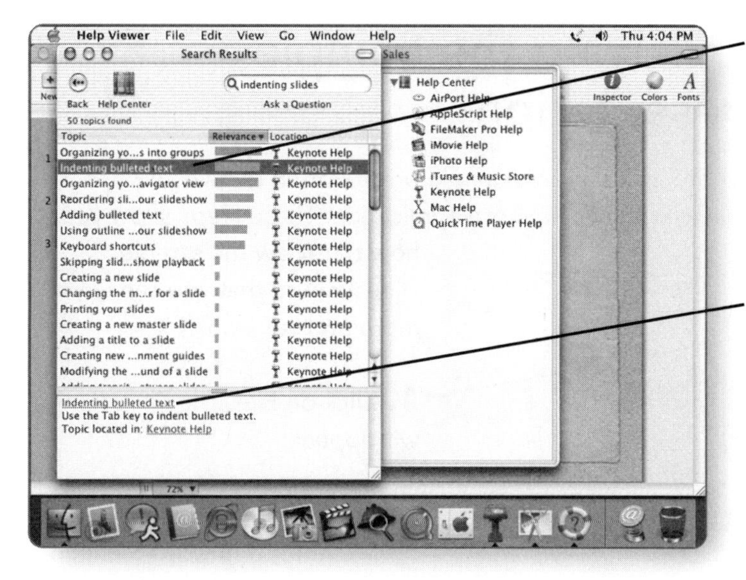

7. If you click on a Tell me more link and see a list of topics like this, **click** on the **topic you want** in the top pane. A preview of the topic will appear in the bottom pane.

8. Click on the **topic link** in the bottom pane. The Help Viewer will display the specified page.

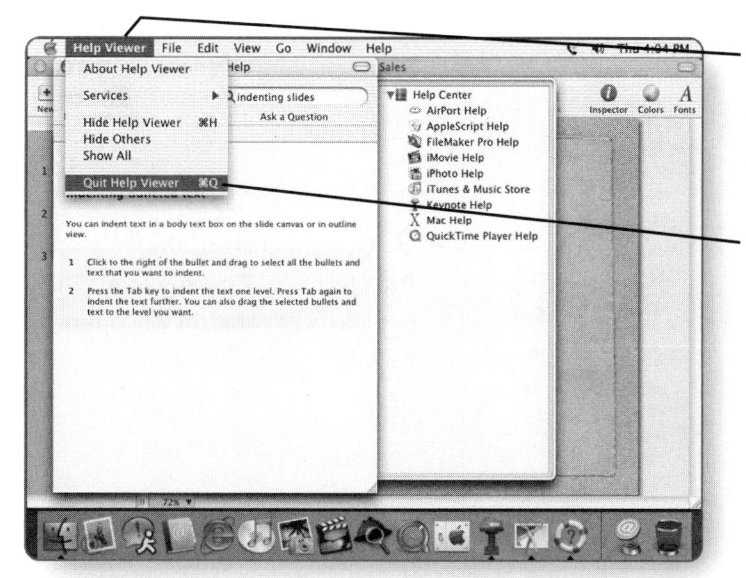

9. When you've finished viewing Help, **click** on **Help Viewer**. The Help Viewer menu will appear.

10. Click on **Quit Help Viewer**. Help Viewer will close.

Reviewing the Sample Presentation

Keynote includes an example presentation to give you tips for working with the Keynote application. These steps show you how to review the sample slideshow so that you can learn more on your own.

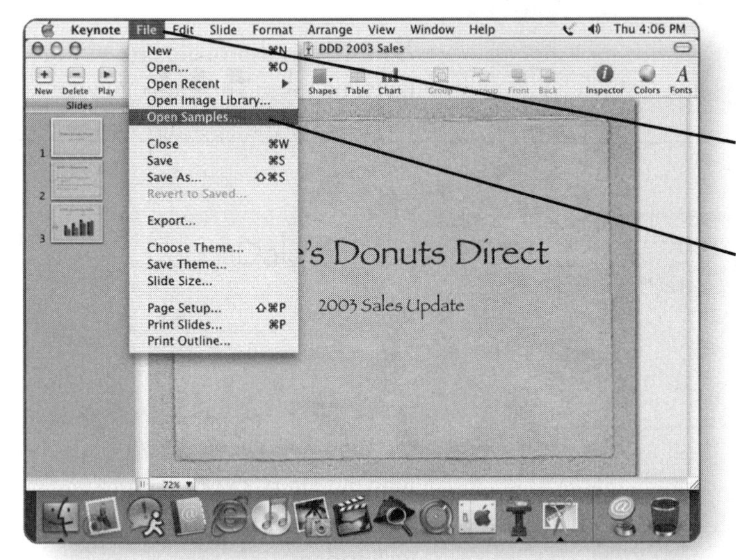

1. **Click** on **File**. The File menu will appear.

2. **Click** on **Open Samples**. A Finder window holding the icon for the sample presentation file will open.

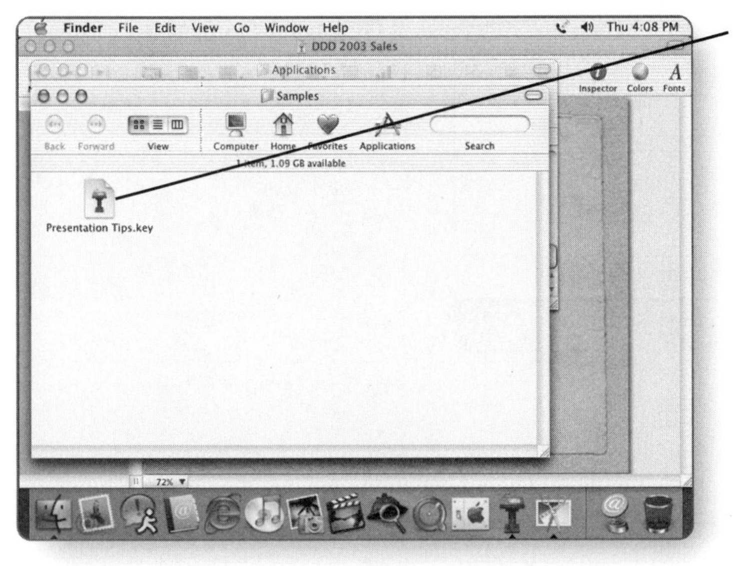

3. **Double-click** on the **Presentation Tips.key icon**. The sample presentation will open in Keynote.

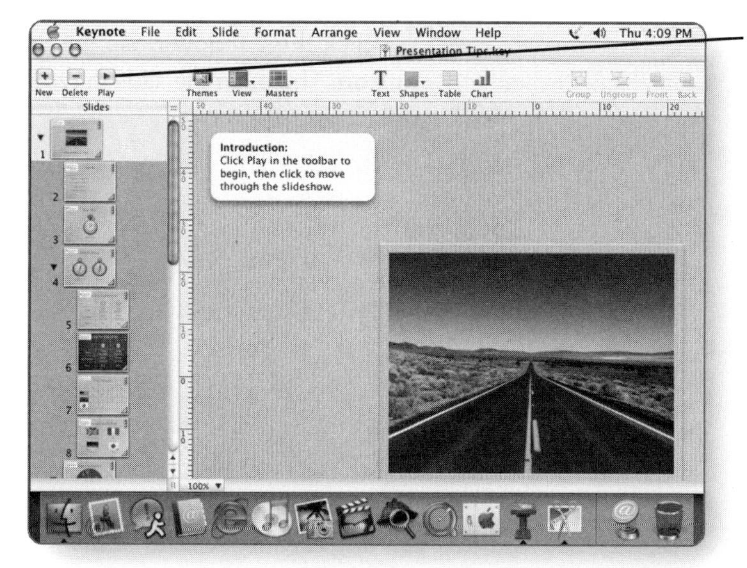

4. Click on **Play** on the toolbar. The slideshow will start onscreen.

5. Click the mouse or **press Spacebar** to move to the next slide. The slideshow will advance. You can continue clicking or pressing Spacebar to view the entire slideshow, or press Esc at any time to quit the slideshow. When the slideshow finishes, the Keynote window will reappear.

6. Click the window close button. The example slideshow will close.

TIP

You can select an object on a particular slide in the sample presentation window and use the Inspector window to see what settings have been applied to the object. For example, on slide 12, you can select one of the circle objects and then review the settings for it in the Build Inspector.

Quitting Keynote

You can quit the Keynote application at any time to finish working and free up RAM in your system. Note that there's no need to save your playlist before quitting. If you have unsaved work, you will be prompted to save it.

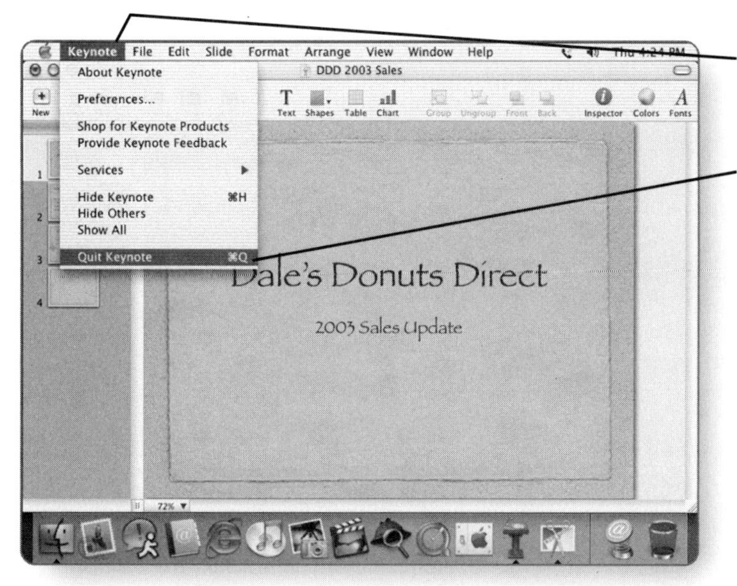

1. **Click** on **Keynote**. The Keynote menu will appear.
2. **Click** on **Quit Keynote**. If you have made changes to your presentation and have not saved them, Keynote will prompt you to do so.

> **NOTE**
>
> If multiple slideshow files are open, a message box will ask whether you want to review changes. Click on the Review Changes button. After you do, Keynote will prompt you to save each open file.

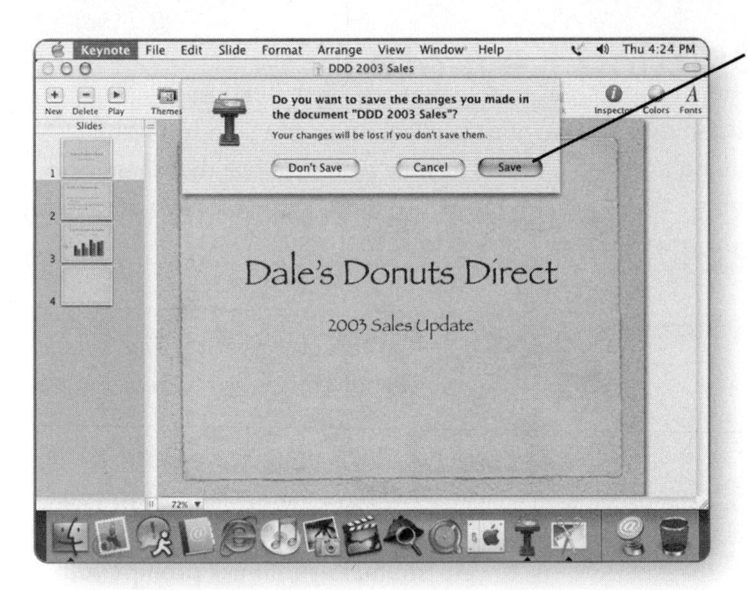

3. Click on **Save**. If you haven't previously saved and named the presentation, a sheet will appear so that you can specify a file name and folder in which to save the file. See "Saving a File" in Chapter 5 to learn more about saving files.

2

Starting a Slideshow

Keynote provides you with all the tools you need to create a terrific presentation. You can add content either by adding slides or working with the outline. Once you've sketched out the presentation, you can delete or move slides at will to improve the flow. In this chapter, you will learn how to:

- Make a new slideshow file.
- Fill in the title slide.
- Add other types of slides that include text, photos, tables, or charts.
- Select a slide.
- Move or delete a slide.
- Group, hide, and redisplay slides.
- Build a slideshow outline.

Creating a New Slideshow

Chapter 1 taught you that each time you start the Keynote application, by default it prompts you to create a new slideshow file. You also can create a new slideshow file at any later time. When you do so, you once again choose a presentation theme (look). Keynote creates a slideshow with a single title slide, waiting for your text.

1. **Click** on **File**. The File menu will appear.

2. **Click** on **New**. Keynote will display a sheet for you to choose a slideshow theme.

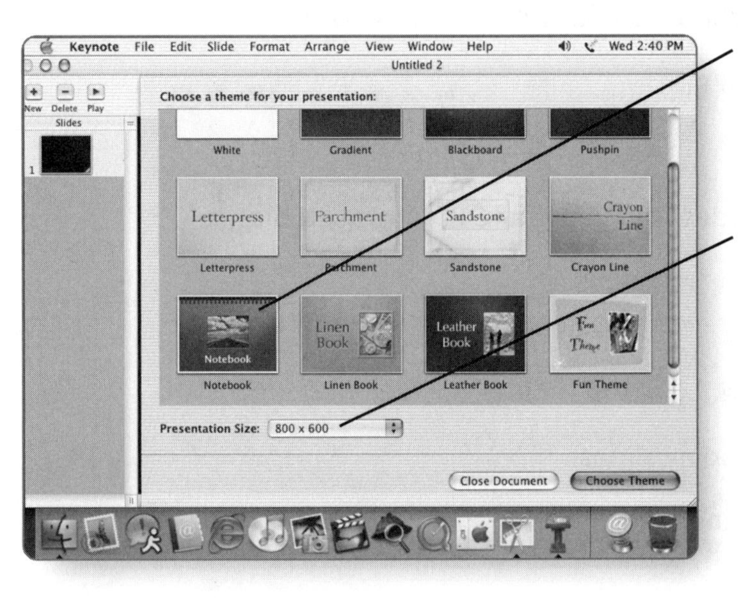

3. Scroll down, if needed, and then **click** on the **theme** you want. The theme will be highlighted in the list.

4. **Click** on the **Presentation Size pop-up menu**. The menu choices will appear.

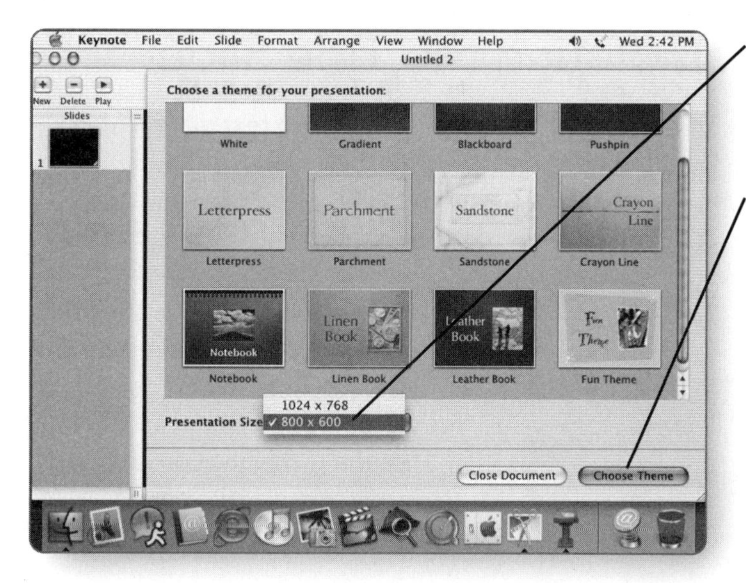

5. **Click** on the **size** you want. The new presentation will be set to the specified size.

6. **Click** on **Choose Theme**. A new presentation using the designated theme will appear.

The new presentation will include a single slide using the Title & Subtitle master slide. Keynote assigns a temporary name, *Untitled X*, to the slideshow file. You will replace that placeholder name when you save the file at a later time, as described in Chapter 5, "Working with Slideshow Files."

Completing the Title Slide

The Title and Subtitle master includes two text placeholders: one for the slide title and one for the slideshow subtitle. Keynote applies this master to the first slide of a new presentation because traditionally, the first slide includes the presentation name and a subtitle (which may include the presenter's name or the date instead). To fill in the placeholders on a title slide, you use the technique you use to fill in any text placeholder, as demonstrated next.

1. **Double-click** on the **top (title) placeholder**. The placeholder text will disappear, and a blinking insertion point will replace it.

2. **Type** the **desired text**. The text you type will appear.

> **TIP**
>
> When adding text to a title or subtitle place-holder, press Return to start a new line.

3. **Click outside** the **place-holder**. Keynote will accept your entry and deselect the place-holder.

4. Double-click on the **bottom (subtitle) placeholder**. The placeholder text will disappear, and a blinking insertion point will replace it.

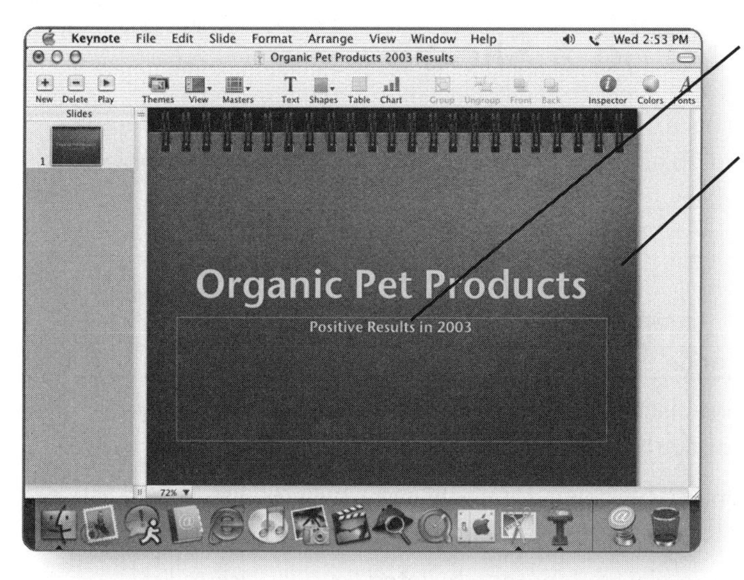

5. Type the **desired text**. The text you type will appear.

6. Click outside the **placeholder**. Keynote will accept your entry and deselect the placeholder.

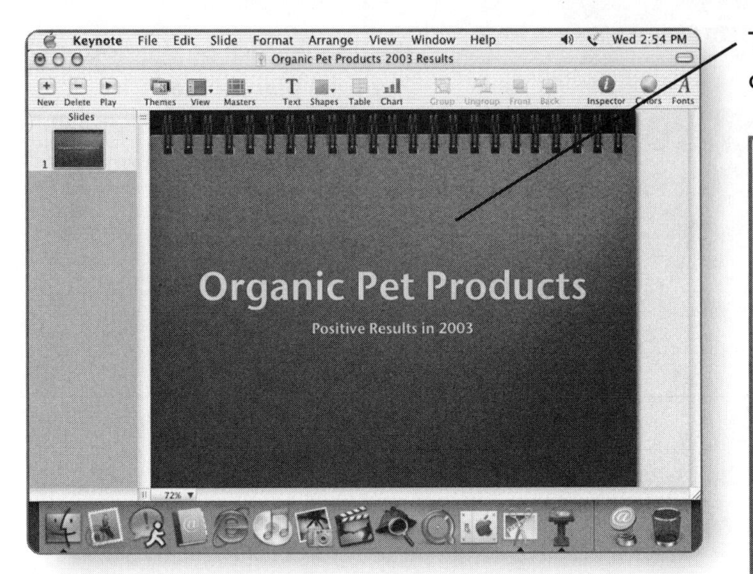

The completed slide remains onscreen.

NOTE

By default, all slides in a slideshow use a horizontal (*landscape*) orientation. To format the slide with a vertical (*portrait*) orientation, you must change the slide dimensions manually. See "Changing Slide Size" in Chapter 3 to learn more.

Adding a Slide

Keynote offers 12 different masters that combine different slide objects. The following table describes the available slide masters.

Slide Masters in Keynote

Name	Description
Title & Subtitle	Contains placeholders for title and subtitle text. Typically used for the first slide in the presentation.
Title & Bullets	Contains placeholders for a title and a bulleted list. Use to list points to cover in the presentation.
Bullets	Contains a placeholder for a bulleted list only. Use to list points to cover in the presentation.
Blank	Contains no placeholders. Use for a slide to which you want to add a table or chart, or other graphic element.

Slide Masters in Keynote (continued)

Name	Description
Title-Top	Contains a title placeholder located at the top of the slide. Use for a slide to which you want to add a table or chart, or other graphic element.
Title-Center	Contains a title placeholder centered on the slide. Use when you want the slide to include a title only.
Photo-Horizontal	Contains a photo frame with a title placeholder below it.
Photo-Vertical	Contains title and subtitle placeholders on the left and a photo frame on the right.
Title, Bullets, & Photo	Contains a title placeholder at the top, a bulleted list placeholder at the left, and a photo placeholder at the right.
Title & Bullets-Left	Contains a title placeholder at the top and a bulleted list placeholder at the left, with blank space at the right for you to insert additional elements.
Title & Bullets-Right	Contains a title placeholder at the top and a bulleted list placeholder at the right, with blank space at the left for you to insert additional elements.

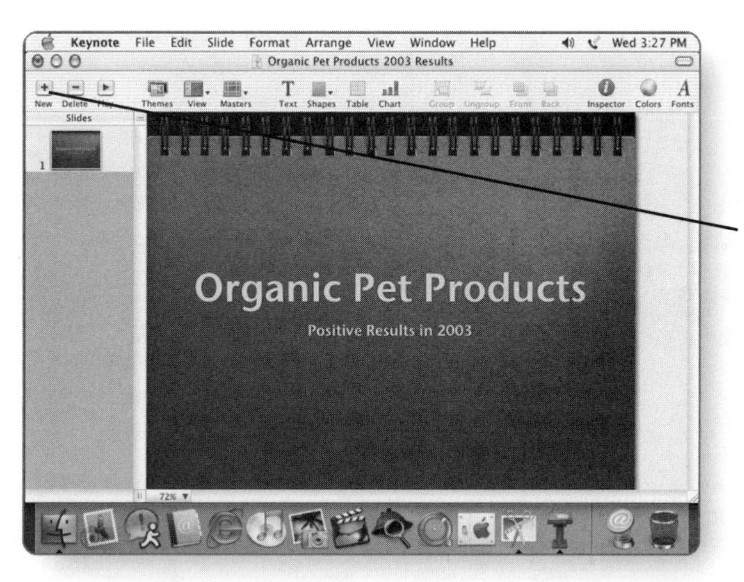

No matter what type of slide you want to add into your slideshow, the initial steps are the same.

1. Click on the **New button** on the toolbar. The new slide will appear after the current slide in the slide organizer.

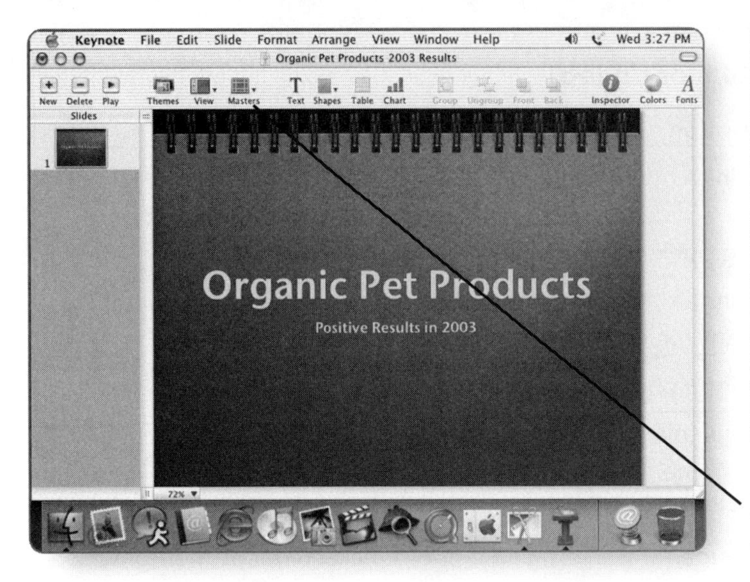

TIP

To place a slide after a specific slide in the presentation, you must first select the slide after which you want to insert the new slide. See "Moving Between Slides" later in the chapter to learn how.

2. Click on **Masters** on the toolbar. A menu of the available masters will appear.

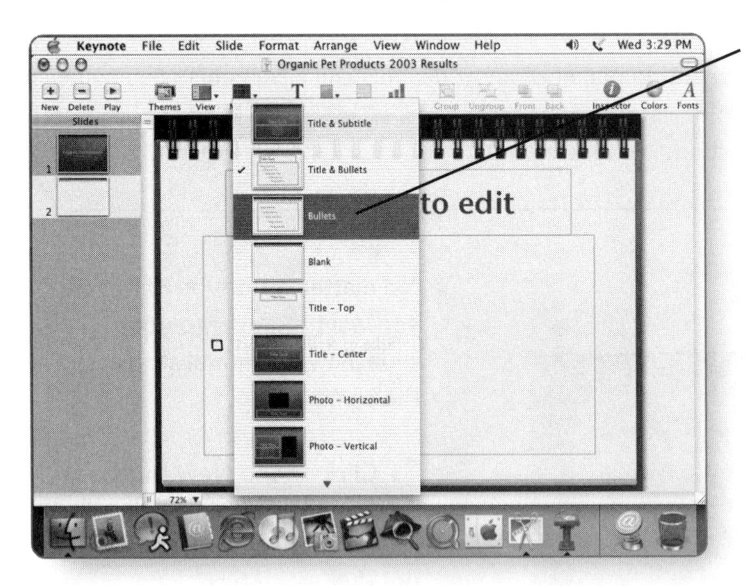

3. Click on the **desired master**. The specified master will be applied to the new slide.

TIP

If you see a triangle at the bottom or top of a toolbar menu, that means some menu choices are hidden. Drag the mouse over the triangle to reveal the hidden menu choices.

4. Complete the **slide** using the techniques described next. The new slide content will appear.

Adding a Text Slide

A number of the masters include a placeholder for a bulleted list. If you selected one of these masters, here's how to fill in its text.

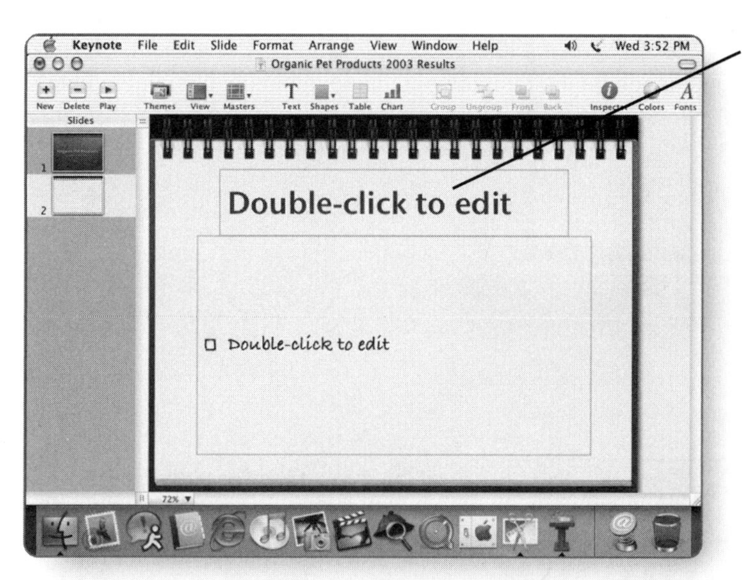

1. **Double-click** on the **title placeholder**, if present. The placeholder text will disappear, and a blinking insertion point will replace it.

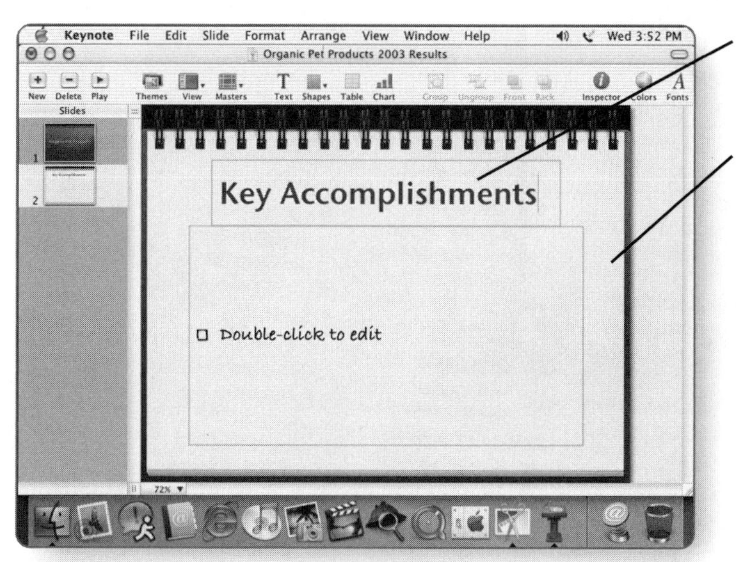

2. **Type** the **desired text**. The text you type will appear.

3. **Click outside** the **placeholder**. Keynote will accept your entry and deselect the placeholder.

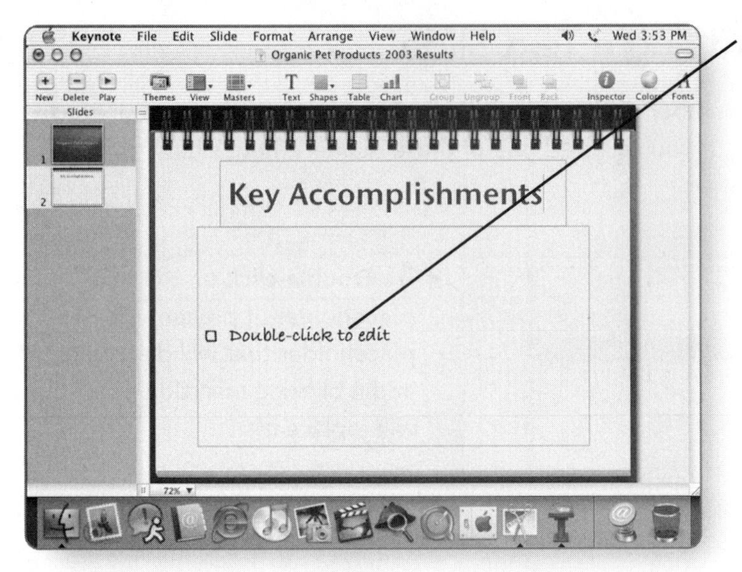

4. Double-click on the **bulleted list placeholder**. The placeholder text will disappear, and a blinking insertion point will replace it.

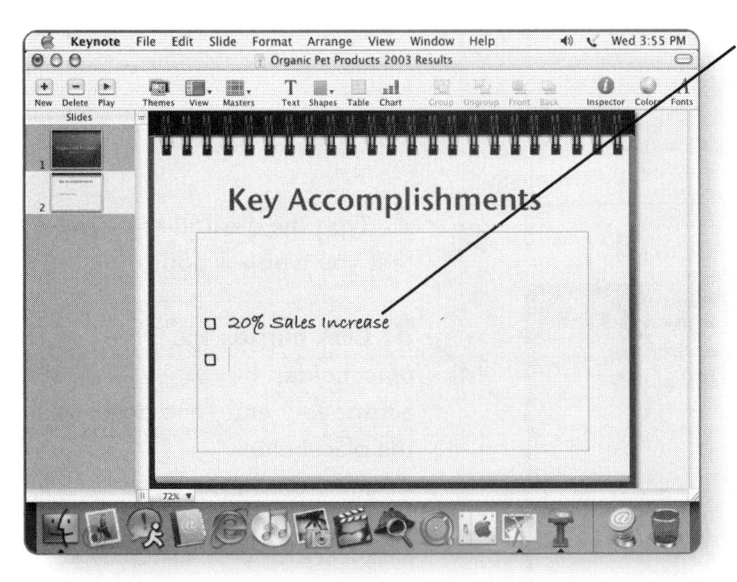

5. Type text for **one list item** and then **press Return**. The bullet item will appear, along with a bullet for the next item in the list.

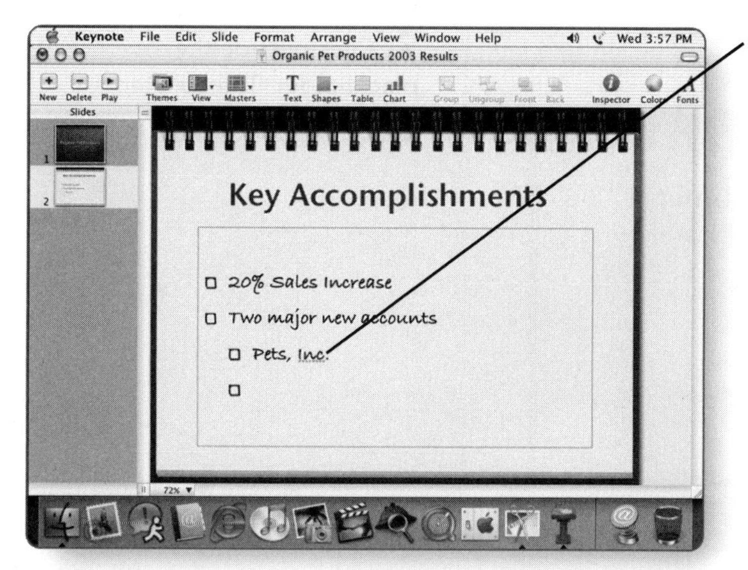

6. To create a sub-bullet, **press Tab, type the item text,** and then **press Return**. The indented bullet item will appear, along with a bullet for the next indented item in the list.

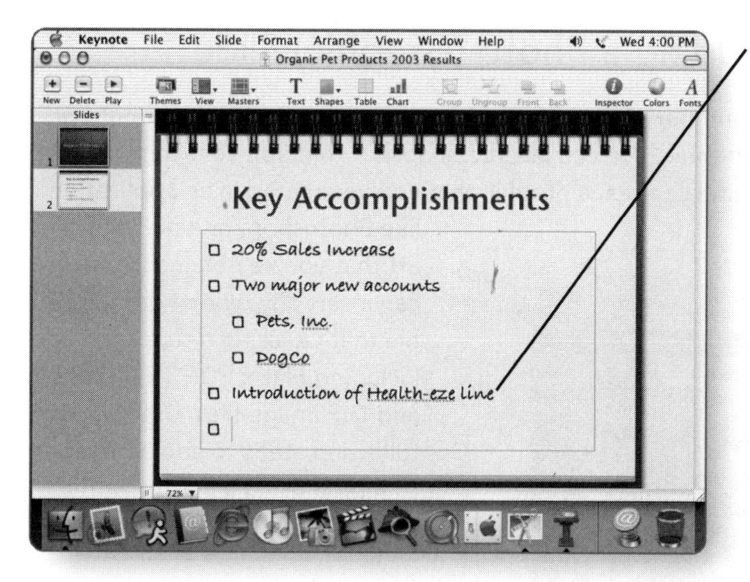

7. To return to the top bullet level, **press Shift+Tab, type** the **item text,** and then **press Return**. The bullet item will appear, along with a bullet for the next indented item in the list.

8. Repeat Steps 5 through 7 in any needed combination to build the list content. The bulleted list items will appear as you add them.

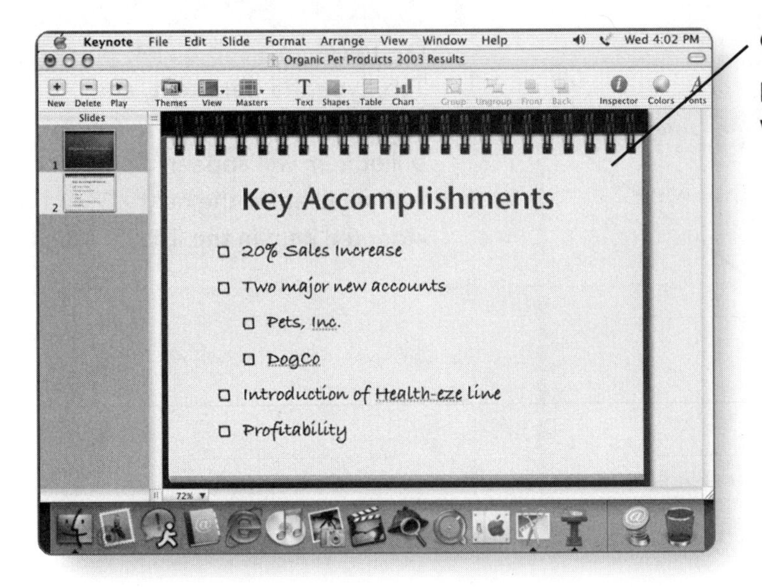

9. Click outside the **placeholder**. The bulleted list will be deselected.

Adding a Photo (Graphic) Slide

A number of the masters include a placeholder for a photo or a graphic. You can insert a snapshot that you've taken with a digital camera, a graphic that you've created in an application like Photoshop, or a piece of clip art that you've obtained. You can insert any type of graphic file that QuickTime supports, including Flash, PDF, TIFF, JPEG, and GIF image files. Use the following steps to add a picture to a slide using a master with a picture frame (*placeholder*).

1. Control+click on the **photo frame (placeholder)**. A contextual menu will appear.

2. **Point** to **Place**. A submenu will appear.

3. **Click** on **Choose**. A sheet will open so that you can choose the picture to insert.

4. **Navigate** to the **folder** holding the **desired picture**, if needed. The picture file will appear in the sheet.

5. **Click** on the **desired picture**. A preview icon for the picture will appear in the sheet.

6. **Click** on **Place**. The sheet will close, and the graphic will appear on the slide.

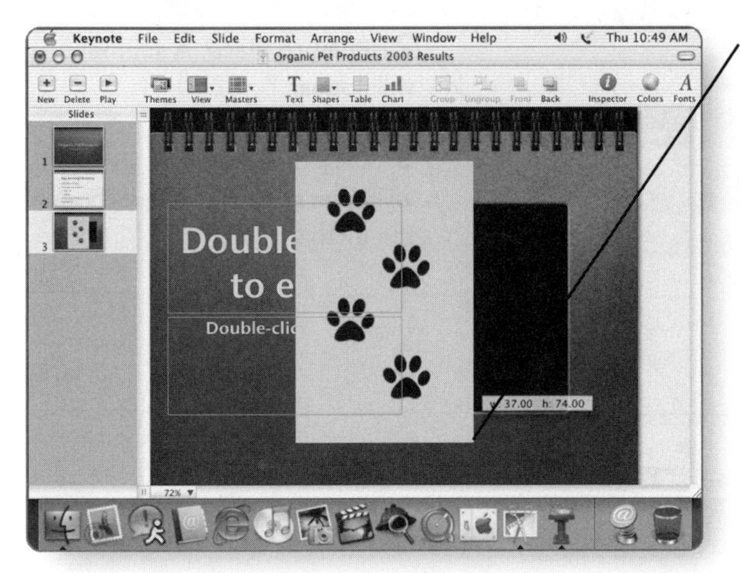

7. Drag a corner of the **graphic** to size it as desired. When you release the mouse button, the graphic will assume the new size.

8. Drag the **graphic over** the **placeholder**. When you release the mouse button, the graphic will assume the new position.

9. **Click** on **Arrange.** The Arrange menu will appear.

10. **Click** on **Send to Back.** The graphic will move behind the frame formed by the picture placeholder.

> **TIP**
>
> At this point, you can fine-tune the graphic's size and placement by dragging a corner handle or dragging from the center of the graphic.

11. **Finish the slide** by adding text to text placeholders as desired. The text will appear in the placeholders.

K.I.S.S.

When you're delivering a presentation, keep in mind that you're using a communication medium that's quite different from an e-mail message, a memorandum, or a report. One key to an effective presentation is to simplify the presentation content by keeping these pointers in mind:

- Keep your bulleted lists short and sweet. Three or four main points per slide should do it.
- Limit the amount of data included in any table or chart. In particular, if a chart becomes too complex and overloaded with data, it tends to confuse rather than clarify key data. While the amount of data that will work will vary depending on the chart type, about three series (sets of related data) per chart is a good guideline.
- Don't let clutter obscure your message. Don't feel like you have to put a picture or drawn object on every slide. Use such elements only when they enhance your message.
- Cross-check your content to make sure slides present consistent information. I have a client company that's absolutely hung up on flow charts. The problem is that most of the company's flow chart graphics have become dated, typically making them inconsistent with text included elsewhere in the presentation.
- If in doubt, leave it out. If you have data that's incomplete or of questionable accuracy, don't include it. Instead, include a speaker note about it in case a related question comes up. Otherwise, if you hand out copies of the slideshow contents to your audience, they'll be walking away with that potentially wrong information.
- Give any complicated word or phrase a test run. Say it out loud a few times. If you stumble over it repeatedly, revise the text to use simpler language.

Adding a Table Slide

As in a word processing document, a table on a slide helps organize information into neat rows and columns. None of the slide masters include a placeholder for a table. So before starting this process, apply the Blank or Title-Top master to a new slide you've added to the presentation.

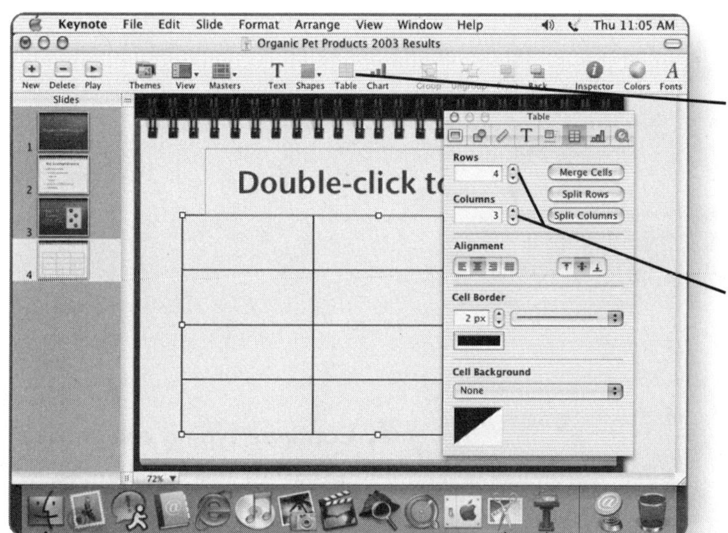

1. **Click** on **Table** on the toolbar. A table grid will appear on the slide, and the Table Inspector will open.

2. **Click** on **spinner buttons** to change the number of **Rows** and **Columns** in the table as desired. The table grid will adjust to include the specified number of rows and columns.

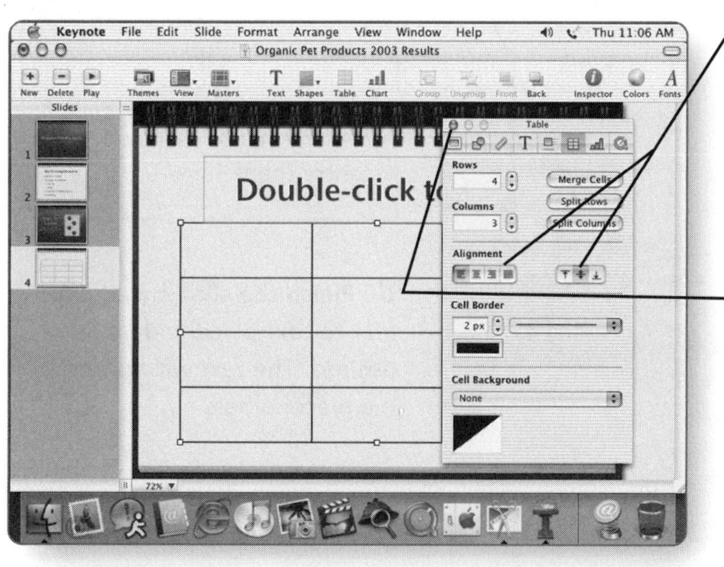

3. **Click** on the desired **horizontal** and **vertical Alignment** settings. When you add text to the table, the text will use the specified alignments.

4. **Click** on the **Table Inspector close button.** The Table Inspector will close.

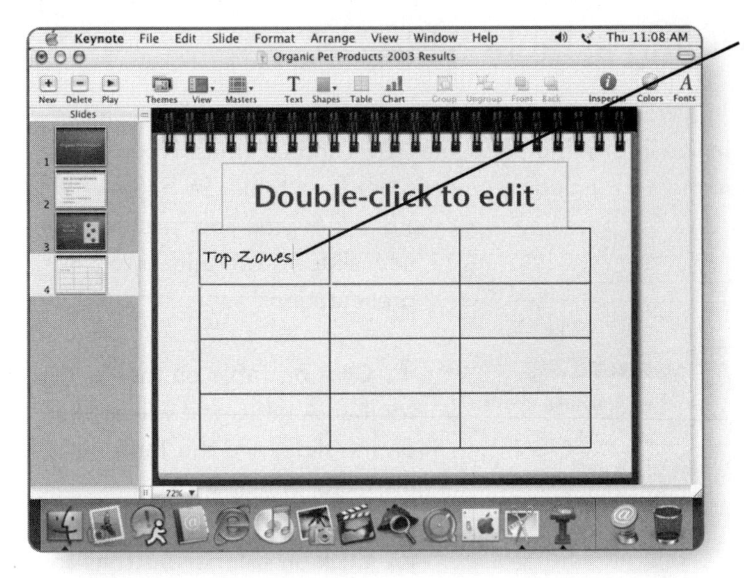

5. **Click** on the **upper-left table cell** and **type** the **desired text**. The text will appear in the cell.

6. **Press Tab**. The selection highlight will move to the next cell.

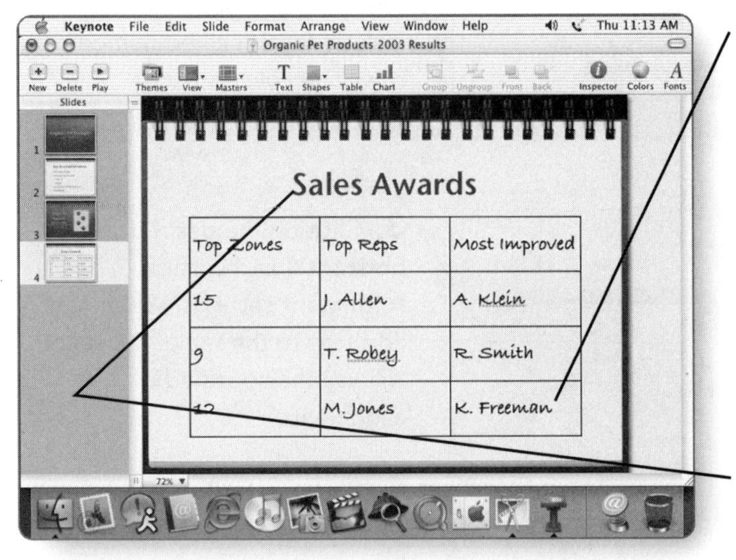

7. **Continue typing cell entries and pressing Tab** to fill in the cells. The text will appear in the table.

> **TIP**
>
> You also can click directly on any cell to make an entry there.

8. **Finish the slide** by adding text to text placeholders as desired. The text will appear in the placeholders.

Adding a Chart Slide

Charts present data in graphical format. Keynote offers eight different chart types: Column, Stacked Column, Bar, Stacked Bar, Line, Area, Stacked Area, and Pie. Each chart contains one or more *series* of information, with each series consisting of a group of related data points, such as all the data about a particular product line or year. A Pie chart contains only one data series.

When you add a chart to a slide, the Slide Inspector appears automatically so that you can choose the desired chart type and formatting settings. ("Formatting a Chart" in Chapter 6 will provide more details about working with all the elements in a chart.) The Chart Data Editor window also opens so that you can enter the data for your chart. As you did for a table slide, apply the Blank or Title-Top master to a new slide you've added to the presentation before using the following steps.

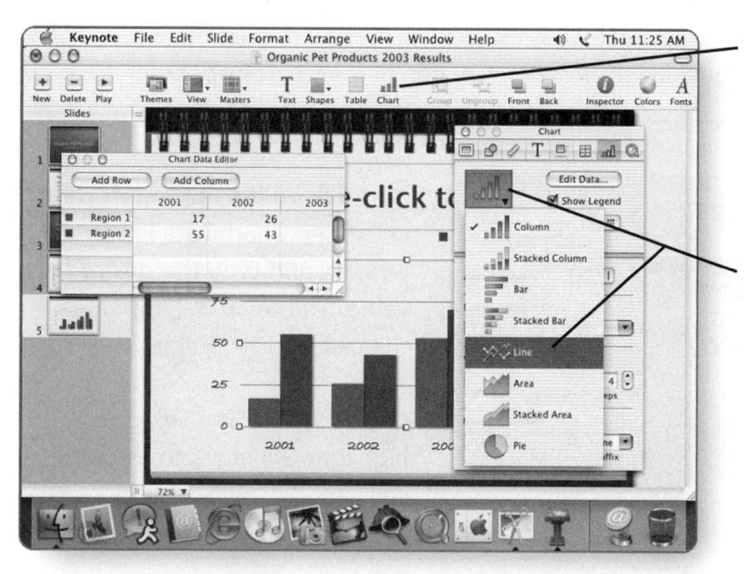

1. **Click** on **Chart** on the toolbar. A default chart will appear on the slide, and the Chart Inspector and Chart Data Editor windows will open.

2. **Click** on the **chart type button** in the Chart Inspector, and then **click** on the **desired chart type**. The default chart will immediately display the new chart type.

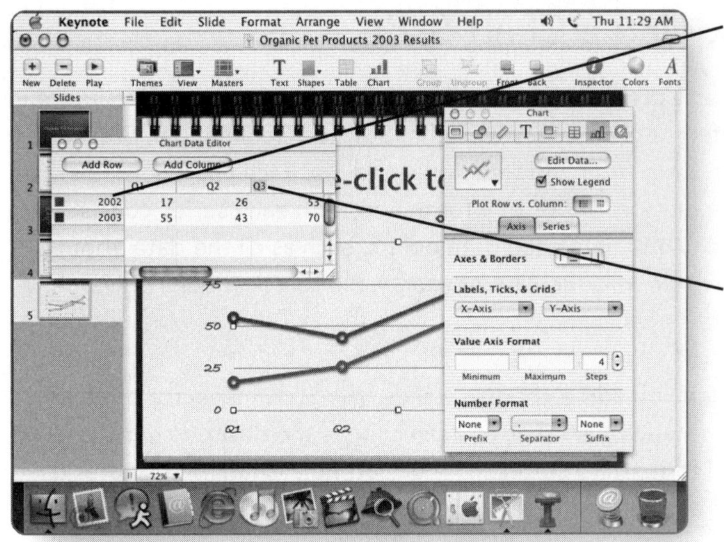

3. Edit the **series names** in the Chart Data Editor. To change each name, double-click on it, type a new name, and press Return. The revised series names will appear.

4. Edit the **column (data point) names** in the Chart Data Editor. To change each name, double-click on it, type a new name, and press Return. The revised names will appear.

NOTE

By default, each row in the Chart Data Editor holds a single series, and each column holds a single data point or value (often for a specific period of time) for each series entry. To reverse this, click on the right button beside Plot Row vs. Column in the Chart Inspector.

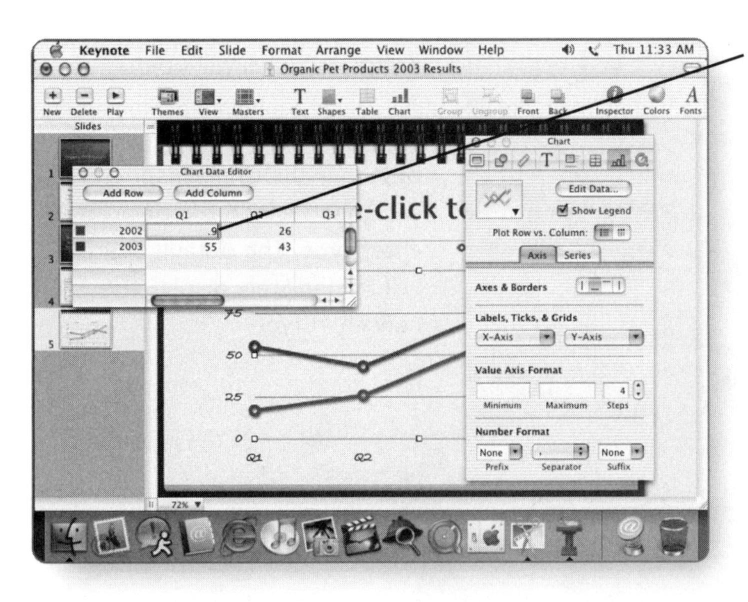

5. Click on the **upper-left data cell** in the Chart Data Editor window and **type** the **desired value.** The value will appear in the cell.

6. Press Tab. The selection highlight will move to the next cell.

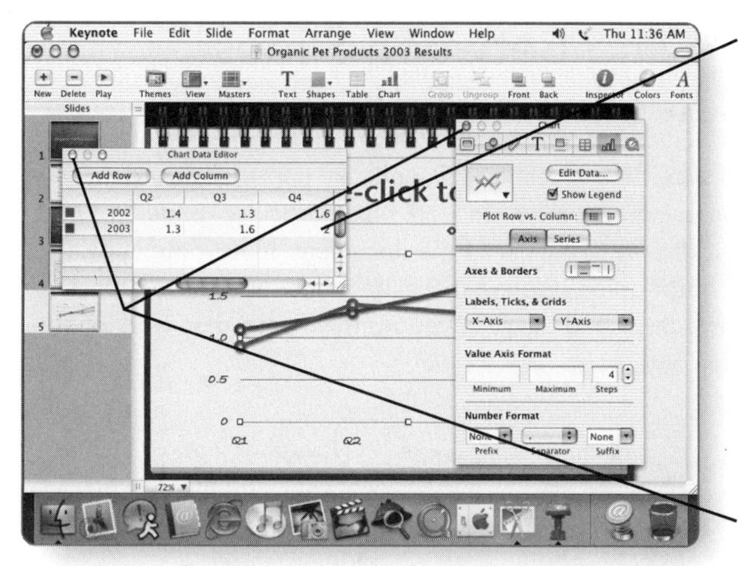

7. **Continue typing cell entries** and **pressing Tab** to fill in the cells. The table will redraw to reflect your entries.

TIP

You also can click directly on any cell, such as the first cell on the next row, to make an entry there.

8. **Click** on the **Chart Inspector** and **Chart Data Editor windows close buttons**. The windows will close.

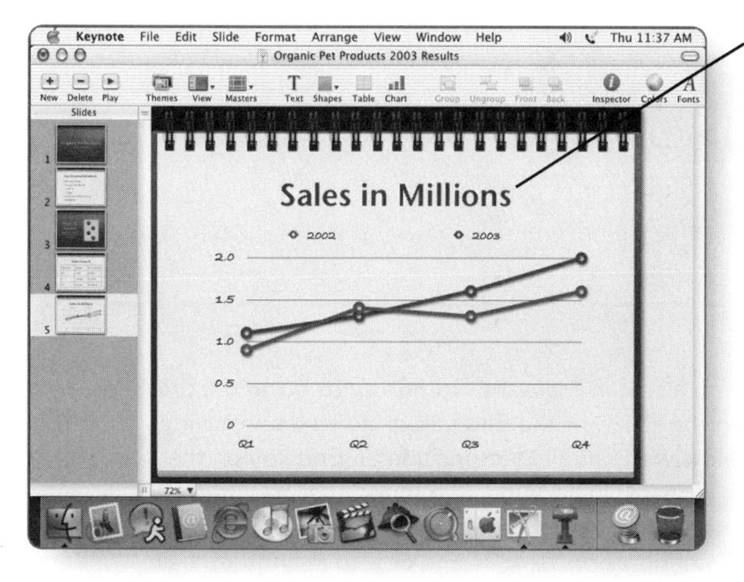

9. **Finish the slide** by adding text to text placeholders as desired. The text will appear in the placeholders.

Moving Between Slides (Selecting a Slide)

The slides in a slideshow file work like pages in a word processing document. To work on a particular "page," you must display that page of the document. In Keynote, moving to another slide displays that slide in the slide canvas. Once you've displayed the slide you want, you can then work on the slide contents.

- In Navigator view or Outline view, click on the desired slide icon or thumbnail in the slide organizer.
- In any of the views, press Pg Up to display the previous slide, or Pg Dn to display the next slide.

NOTE

You also can press the Home key to go to the first slide in the show, or the End key to go to the last slide. However, not all Macs include an End key on the keyboard. In addition, I've found that this method works best for some reason in the Slide Only view. Sometimes pressing Home or End in another view doesn't work as it should.

Moving a Slide in the Show

Chances are your presentation content will not spring from your brain in the perfect order, especially if you like to do a brain dump first and organize information afterwards. You can use the slide organizer to move a slide to a new position in the presentation at any time in Keynote. You must work in the Navigator or Outline view to move a slide to a new location.

> **TIP**
>
> You can select multiple slides to move in the slide organizer. Use Shift+click to select multiple adjacent slides, or ⌘+click to select non-adjacent slides.

- In Navigator view, click on the thumbnail for the slide to move, and then drag it to a new position in the slide organizer. When you release the mouse button, the slide will move to the new position indicated by the blue arrow and line.

- In Outline view, click on the icon for the slide to move, and then drag it to a new position in the slide organizer. When you release the mouse button, the slide will move to the new position indicated by the blue arrow and line.

> **CAUTION**
>
> When moving a slide in the Outline view, be sure that the blue arrow appears as far left as possible, directly in line with the icons for other slides. If you instead drag a bit to the right, the moved slide will be inserted as bullet points within the slide above it, not as a separate slide. If this happens, you can use Shift+Tab to reinstate the slide (see "Building Slideshow Content in Outline View" at the end of the chapter), but you may have to reapply the desired master and reinsert any pictures, tables, or charts.

Deleting a Slide

Revising presentation content may include deleting slides that no longer suit the presentation message. For example, you may decide to delete a slide that's wordy and makes the presentation too long. Or you may decide to copy a slide with a chart, try different chart formatting on the copied slide, and delete the one you like least.

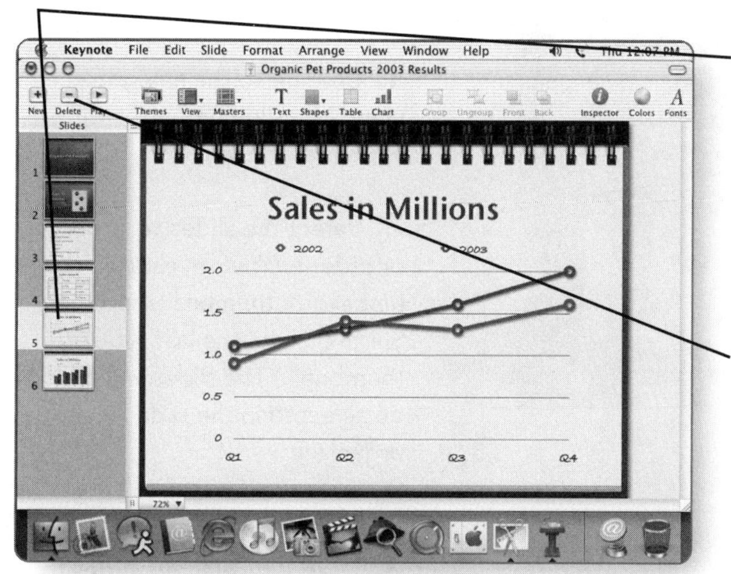

1. **Display** or **select** the **slide to delete**. The slide will appear on the canvas. If you're working in the Navigator or Organizer view, the slide thumbnail or icon will also be selected in the slide organizer.

2. **Click** on **Delete** on the toolbar. The slide will be removed from the presentation.

CAUTION

Keynote doesn't prompt you to verify the slide deletion. If you mistakenly delete a slide, click on the Edit menu, and click on Undo Delete.

Grouping (Indenting) Slides

When you have a lengthy presentation with dozens of slides, it becomes tougher to find a slide that you want to review or edit. To help you better navigate in a presentation file, you can *group* slides with similar content. Grouping slides enables you to hide and redisplay them in the slide organizer, as described in the next section.

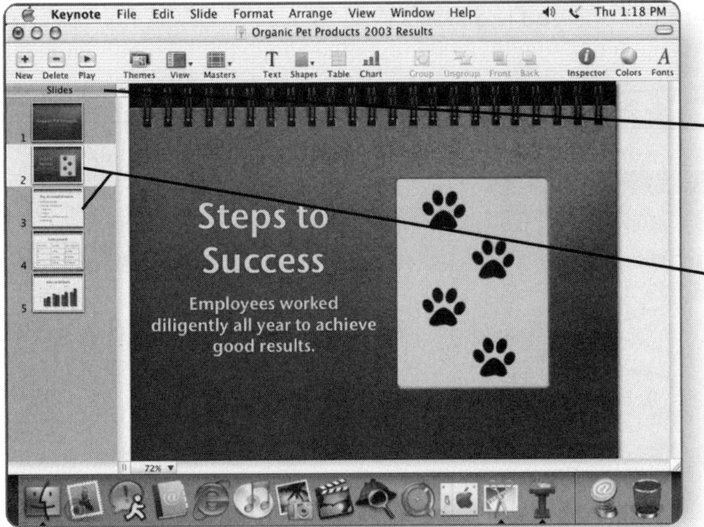

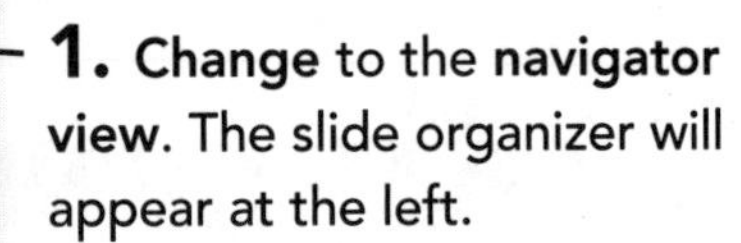

1. **Change** to the **navigator view**. The slide organizer will appear at the left.

2. **Select** the **slides to group** or **indent**. (You can click on the first slide's thumbnail, and then Shift+click on the last slide's thumbnail.) The slides will also be selected in the slide organizer.

3. **Drag** the **selected slides** to the **right** until the blue triangle appears to specify the next indent level. When you release the mouse button, the selected slides will be grouped below the slide above them. A *disclosure triangle* will also appear beside the slide at the top of the group.

Hiding and Redisplaying Slides

Once you've created a group of slides, you can hide or display the group at any time. Note that the slides will not be hidden from the on-screen slideshow or any presentation printout. They will be hidden only in the slide organizer to facilitate slideshow navigation during editing.

1. **Click** on the **down disclosure triangle**. The slides in the group will be hidden in the slide organizer.

2. **Click** on the **right disclosure triangle**. The slides in the group will be redisplayed in the slide organizer.

Building Slideshow Content in Outline View

Content still reigns as king in all forms of communication, including slideshows. If you prefer to nail down the overall content first rather than worrying about slide layouts and graphics, you can use the Outline view to add slides to your presentation, and then use the techniques described in later chapters to choose a master and add various slide elements. After you've created a new presentation file and have specified a master, use the following steps to add slides to the presentation in Outline view.

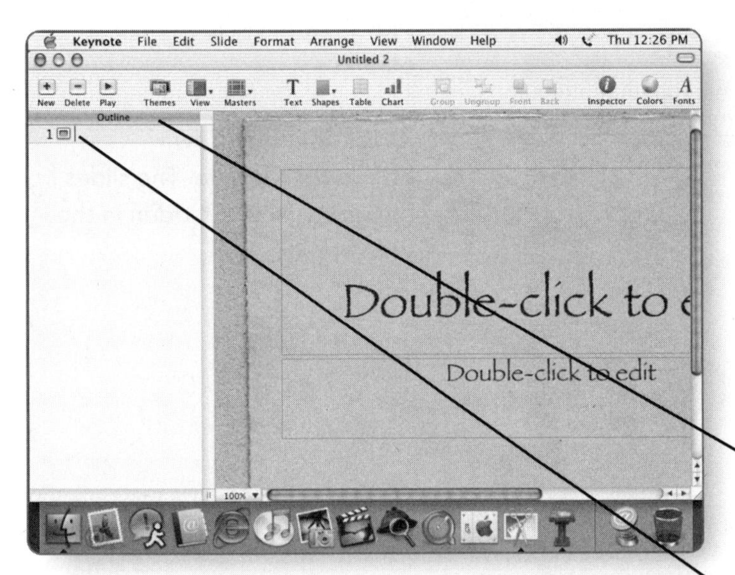

1. **Change** to the **Outline view.** The slide organizer will appear at the left.
2. **Click beside** the **slide icon** in the slide organizer. A blinking insertion point will appear.

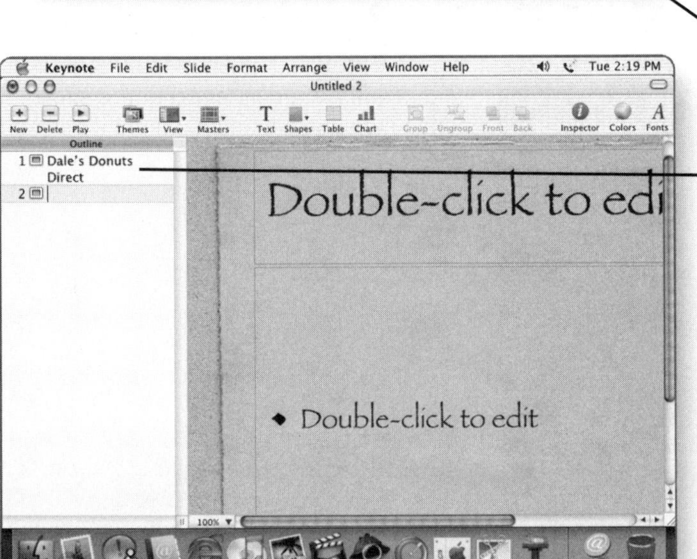

3. **Type title text** for the **first slide,** and then **press Return.** The title will appear, along with an icon for a new slide.

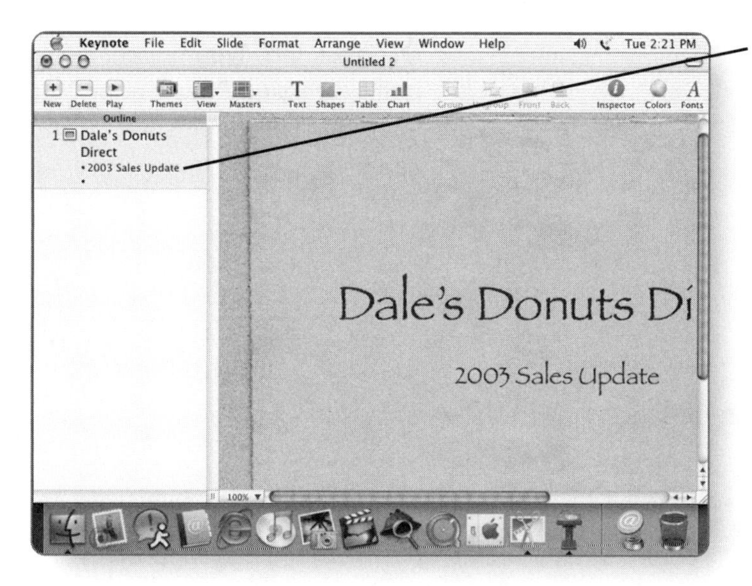

4. Press Tab, type the **subtitle** for the **first slide,** and then **press Return**. The indented subtitle will appear, along with another indented bullet.

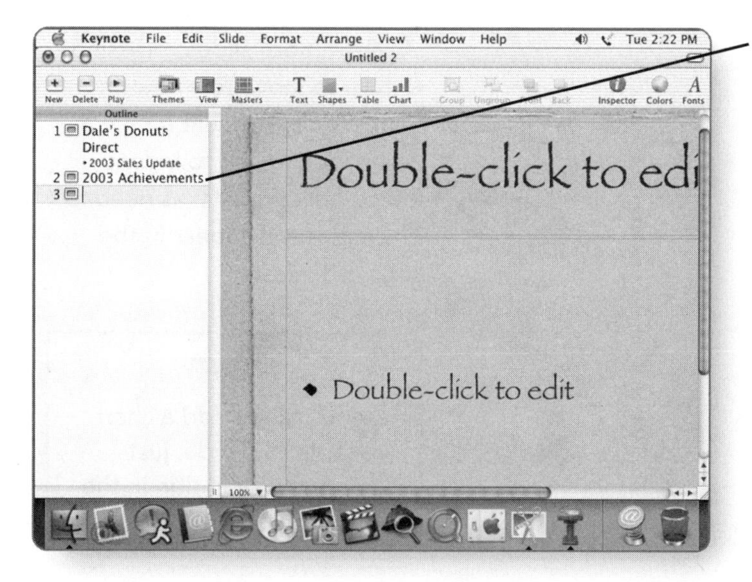

5. To create a new slide instead of another bullet item, **press Shift+Tab, type the slide title,** and then **press Return**. The slide title will appear, along with an icon for a new slide.

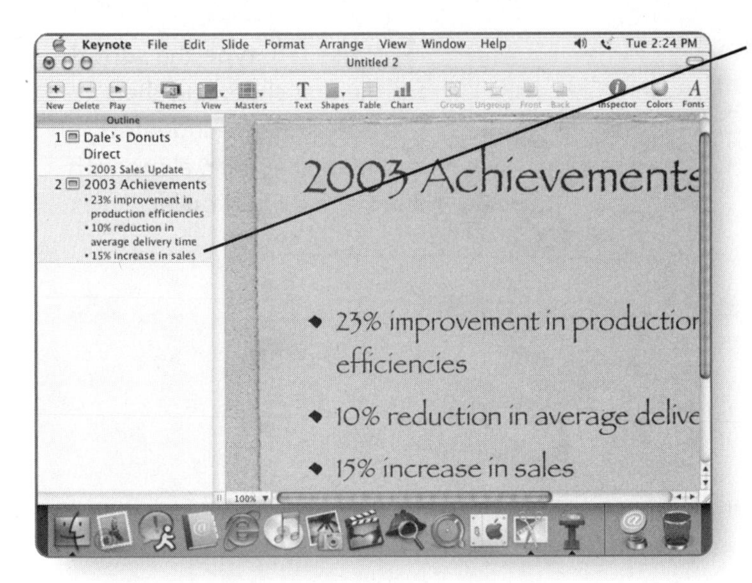

6. Press Tab. Type bullet items, pressing Return after each. The bullet items will appear.

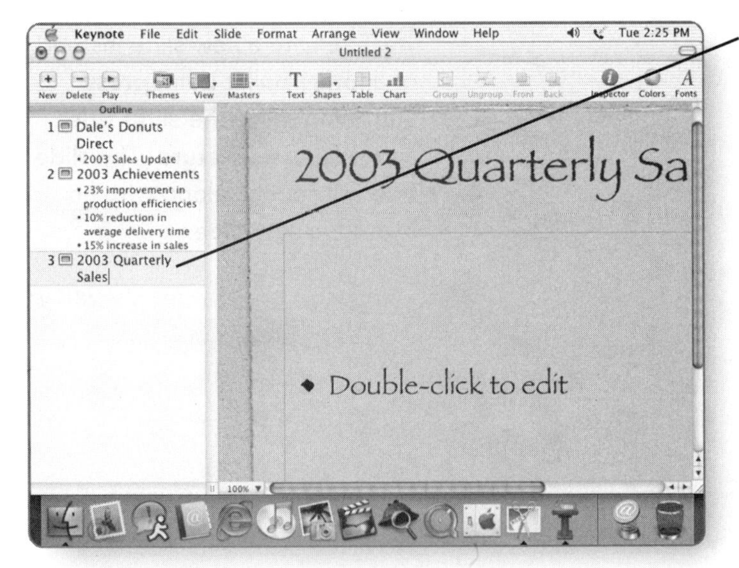

7. Add more slides, pressing Return to move to a new line, Shift+Tab to outdent (make a new slide), or Tab to indent (make bullet points) as needed. The slides will appear in the slide organizer.

NOTE

If you plan to add a chart or table to a slide, just create the slide title in the Outline view.

Enhancing Slides

When you design your slides, you aren't bound to the layouts defined by the slide masters. You can position any number of additional elements on each slide, such as additional graphics or shapes that you draw. This chapter teaches you how to enhance slides with additional objects and more, including how to:

- Specify a new size for slides.
- Select and deselect objects.
- Add text and shapes.
- Add tables and charts.
- Insert a graphic from iPhoto or another source.
- Use Undo to remove changes.

Changing Slide Size

When you create each presentation file, you not only select a theme but you also choose a size for the slides in the presentation. As was noted in "Creating a New Slideshow" in Chapter 2, choosing a slide size at the starting point helps optimize the presentation for a particular display, such as your monitor or a projector, but the choices are limited. You may instead want to set your presentation to a truly custom size, such as 320 x 240 for a very small presentation size, or 600 x 800 for a portrait layout. You can change slides to any size that you need and prefer.

NOTE

Keynote measures slide sizes in *pixels*. If your Mac's display resolution is set to 800 x 600, then setting presentation slides to 400 x 300 yields a slide size that fills about half the screen.

The catch is that if you specify a slide size that's not the same as the display resolutions (typically 800 x 600 and 1024 x 768) available for your Mac, elements on the slides and masters do not resize and correctly position themselves automatically. So if you choose a truly custom size for your slides, you'll have to position all slide elements manually, as described in "Moving Objects" and "Resizing Objects" in Chapter 6.

1. **Click** on **File**. The File menu will appear.

2. **Click** on **Slide Size**. Keynote will display a sheet for you to specify a new slideshow size.

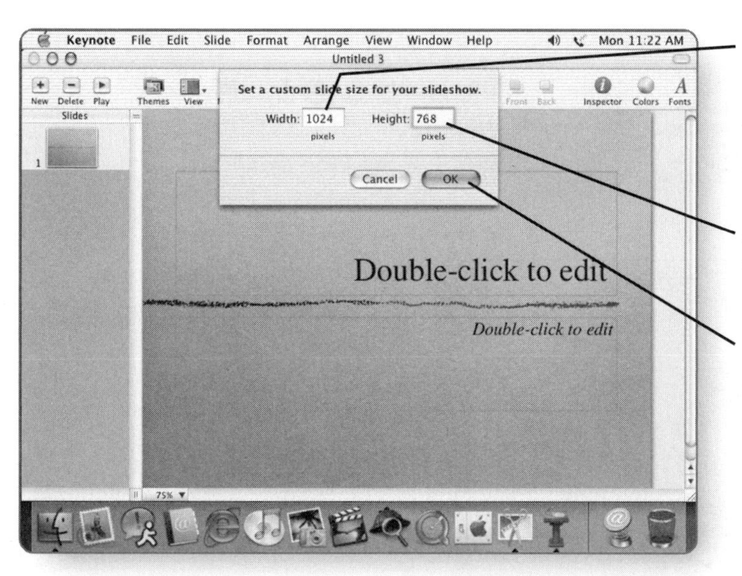

3. **Type** the desired **Width**, and **press Tab**. The specified width will appear, and the Height text box entry will be selected.

4. **Type** the desired **Height**. The specified height will appear.

5. **Click** on **OK**. Keynote will display the slideshow slides in the new size.

Selecting and Deselecting Slide Objects

You can select any type of object on a slide, including a text box, table, chart, drawn object, or inserted picture. Selecting an object enables you to move, resize, and format it, as described in several later chapters. Use the following techniques to select and deselect objects.

- Click on a single object to select it.

- Shift+click on additional objects to select them, as well.

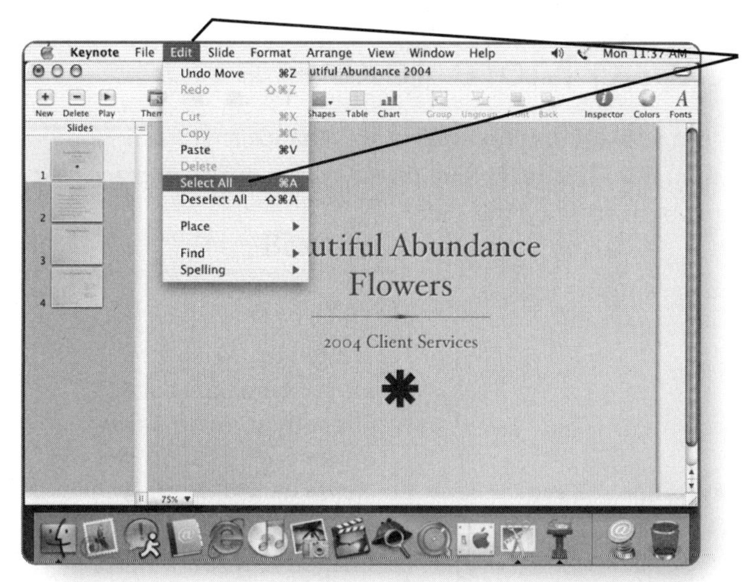

- Click on Edit, and then click on Select All or press ⌘+A to select all objects on a slide.

- Click outside any selection to remove the selection.

Adding More Text

You can add another text object to enhance any slide in a presentation. This technique gives you the ability to place text wherever needed on the slide.

NOTE

It's fun to create a medallion or starburst effect by layering a text object over a shape or image on a slide. (See "Layering Objects" in Chapter 6 to learn how.)

1. Click on **Text** on the toolbar. The text object will appear at the center of the slide.

2. Drag the **text object** to the desired location. When you release the mouse button, the text will remain in the specified location.

3. Double-click on the **text object**, and then **type** the **desired text**. The text will appear in the text box.

4. Click outside the **text object**. The object will be deselected.

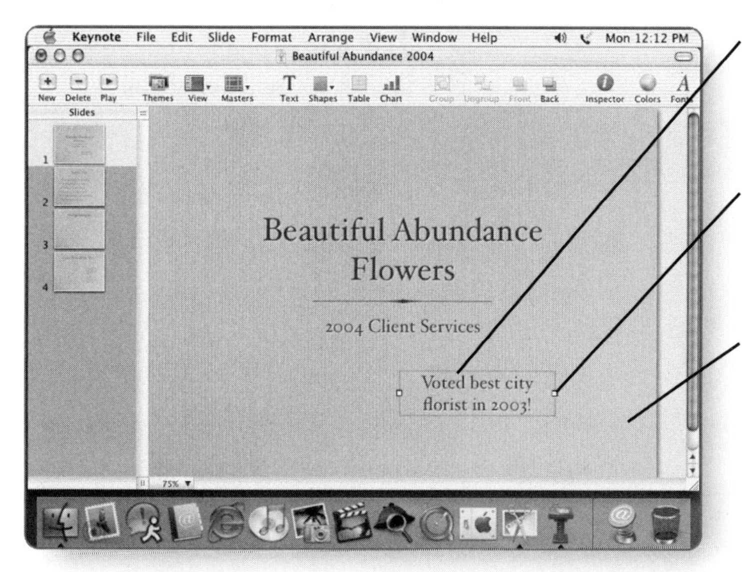

5. Click on the **text object**. White selection handles will appear.

6. Drag a handle to the desired location. The text box will resize.

7. Click outside the **text object**. The object will be deselected.

Adding a Shape

You can draw one of six shapes (line, rectangle, oval, triangle, right triangle, and arrow) on any slide. You can add shapes for interest, or layer them with other objects you add onto a slide.

> **TIP**
>
> You can use the choices on the Edit, Place submenu to insert the objects described in this chapter.

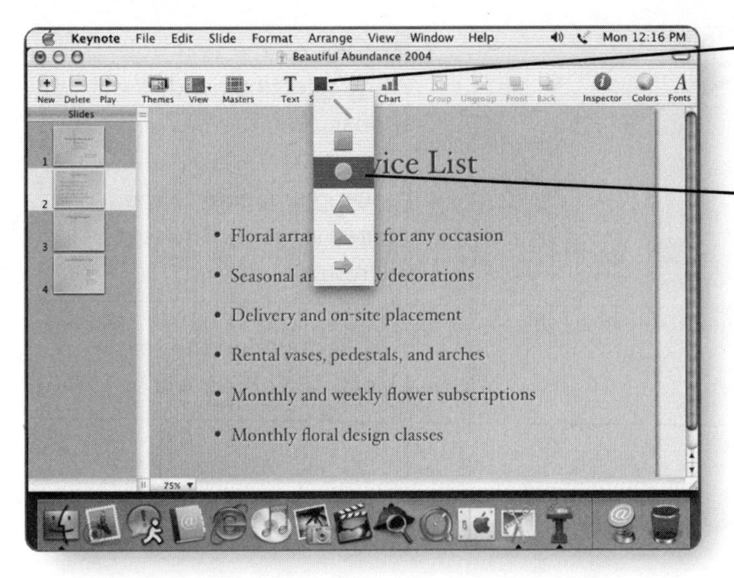

1. **Click** on **Shapes** on the toolbar. A menu of shape choices will appear.

2. **Click** on the **desired shape**. The shape will appear at the center of the slide.

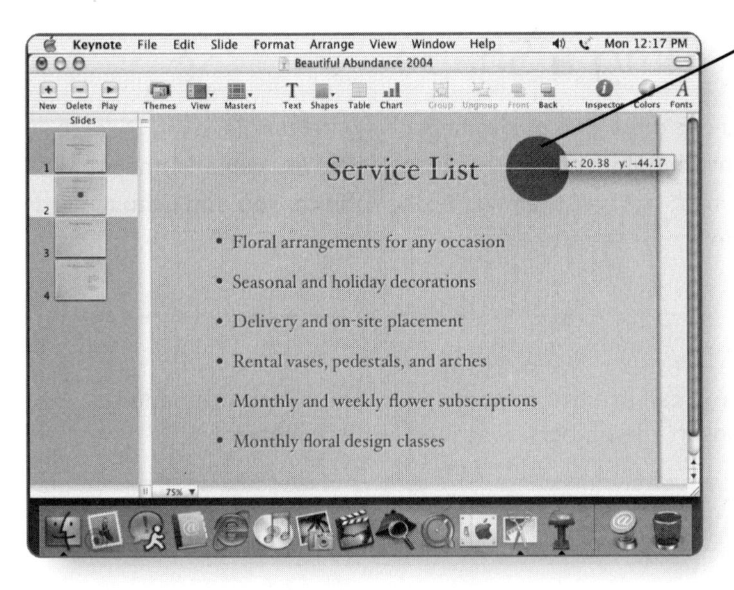

3. **Drag** the **shape** to the desired location. When you release the mouse button, the shape will remain in the specified location.

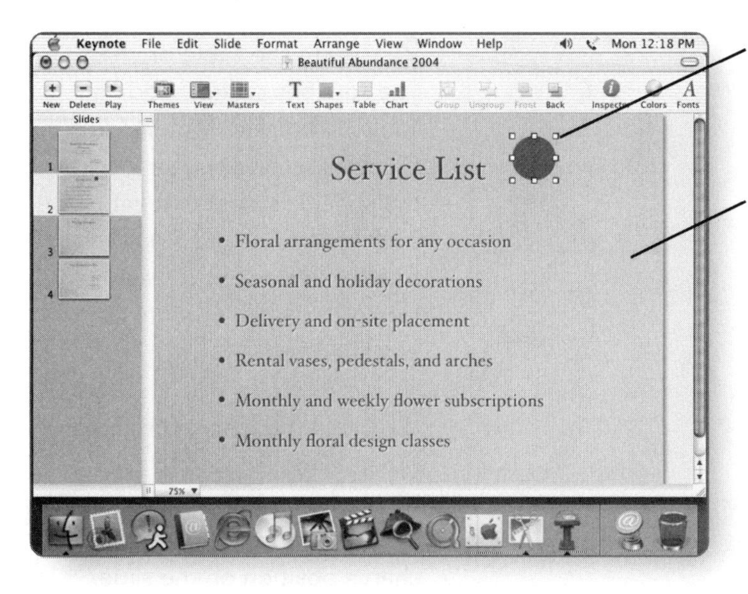

4. **Drag a handle** to the desired location. The shape will resize.

5. **Click outside** the **shape**. The object will be deselected.

Adding a Table or Chart

You can add a table or chart to any slide, no matter the layout. Of course, your table or chart will look better on a slide that allows ample room to allow for a readable size. Here's the overall process for adding a table or chart to a slide:

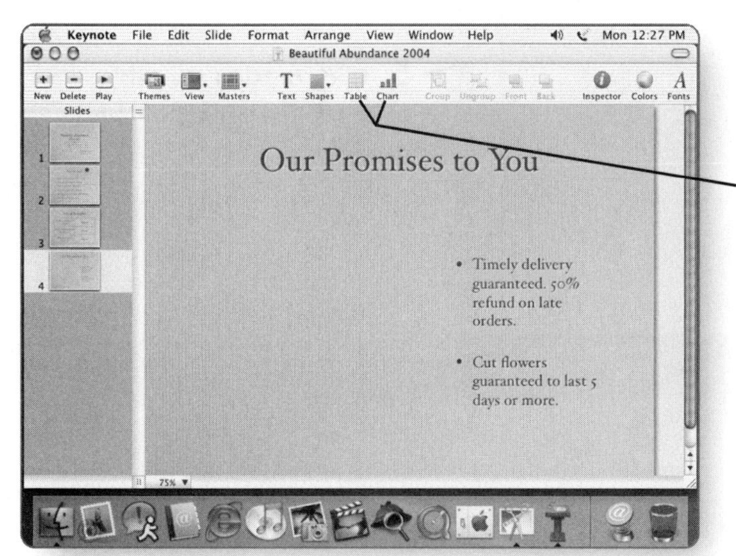

1. **Click** on **Table** or **Chart** on the toolbar. The specified object will appear on the slide.

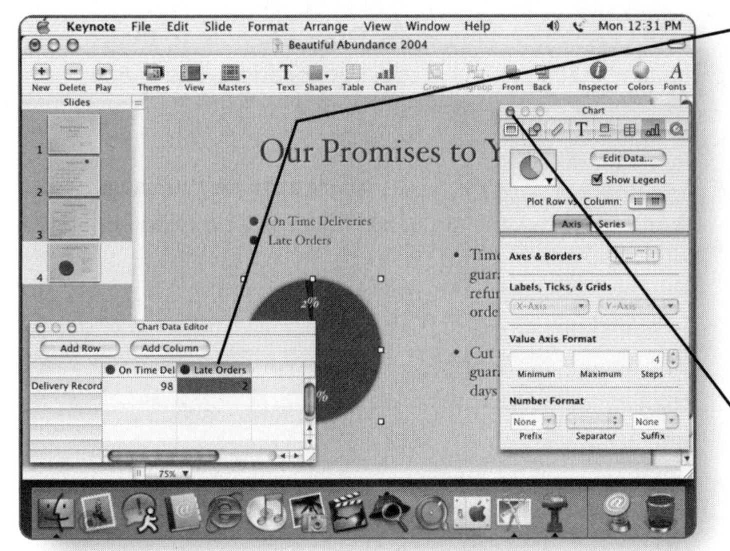

2. **Create** the **table or chart**. The sections called "Adding a Table Slide" and "Adding a Chart Slide" in Chapter 2 cover the specific steps for creating each type of object. The table or chart will adjust to use the formatting and contents that you specify.

3. **Close** the **Inspector** and any other windows used to create the table or chart. You will be able to better see the table or chart's position on the slide. The table or chart will remain selected.

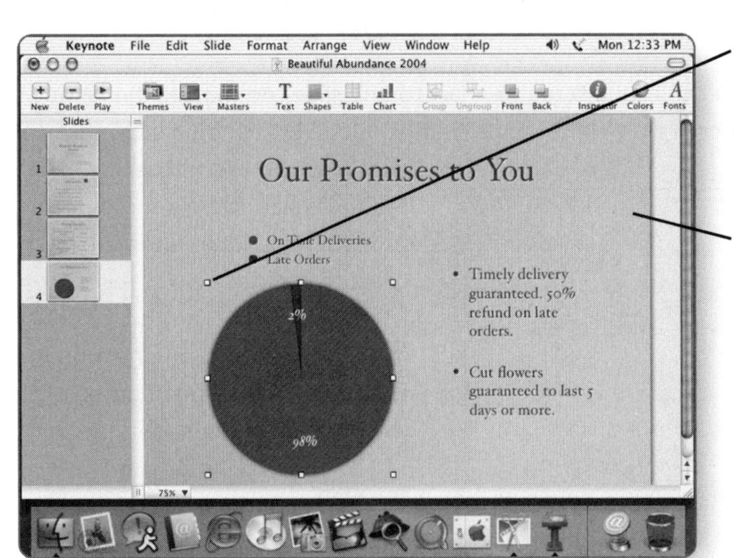

4. **Drag** the **table or chart** or a **selection handle**. The table or chart will move or resize as specified.

5. **Click outside** the **table or chart**. The object will be deselected.

Adding Images

Slideshows have the most visual impact when they include attractive graphics. As was described in Chapter 2, you can add a variety of different graphic files to a slide, including a product snapshot that you've taken with a digital camera, a graphic that you've created in an application like Photoshop, or a piece of clip art that you've obtained. You can insert any type of graphic file that QuickTime supports, including Flash, PDF, TIFF, JPEG, and GIF image files. This section focuses on inserting graphics from various sources onto any slide.

Using Image Library Files

Keynote includes several Image Library presentation files. Each file holds example graphic images that you can copy and paste onto a slide in your presentation. The following steps demonstrate how to insert a graphic from an Image Library file.

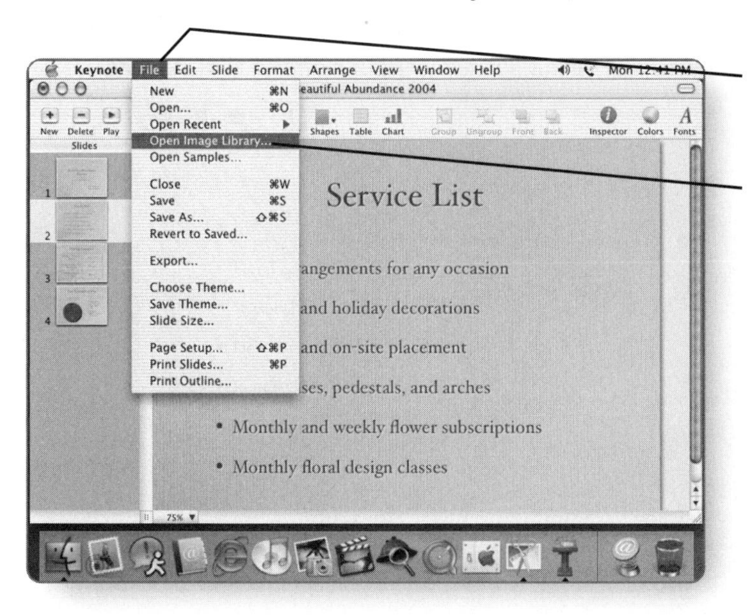

1. **Click** on **File**. The File menu will appear.

2. **Click** on **Open Image Library**. Keynote will open a Finder window for the folder holding the Image Library files.

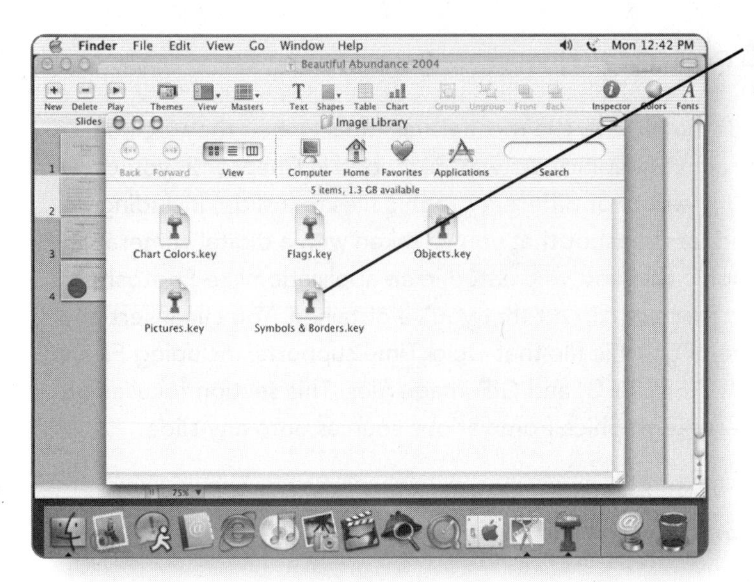

3. **Double-click** on the **desired file**. The file will open in Keynote.

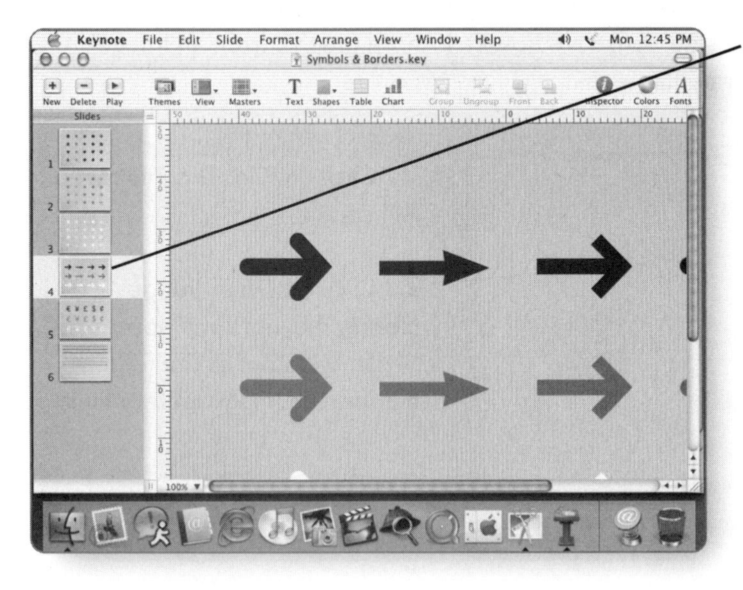

4. **Click** on the **slide** holding the **desired graphic** in the slide organizer. The slide contents will appear on the slide canvas.

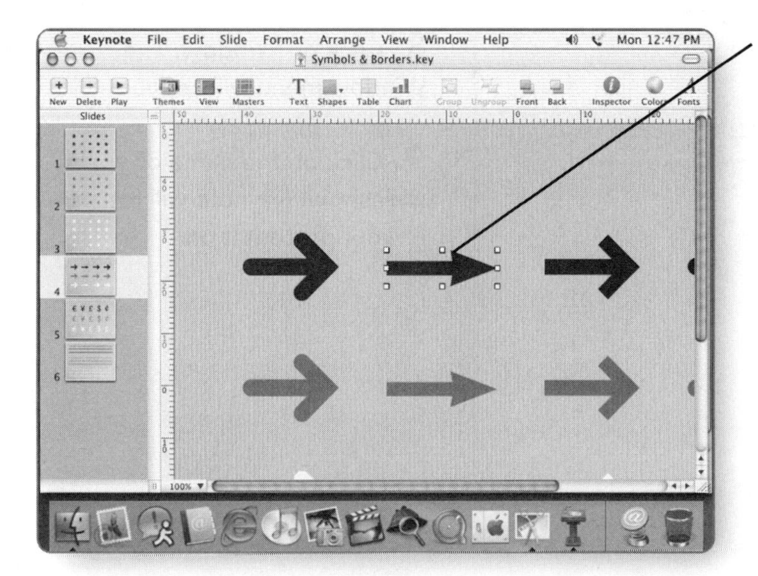

5. **Click** on the **desired graphic**. Selection handles will appear.

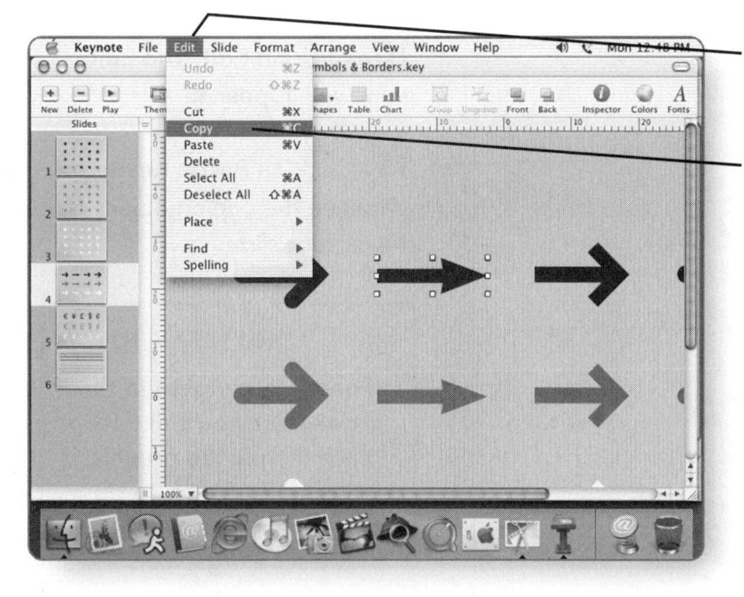

6. **Click** on **Edit**. The Edit menu will appear.

7. **Click** on **Copy**. Keynote will copy the object to the Clipboard, a temporary holding area in your Mac's memory.

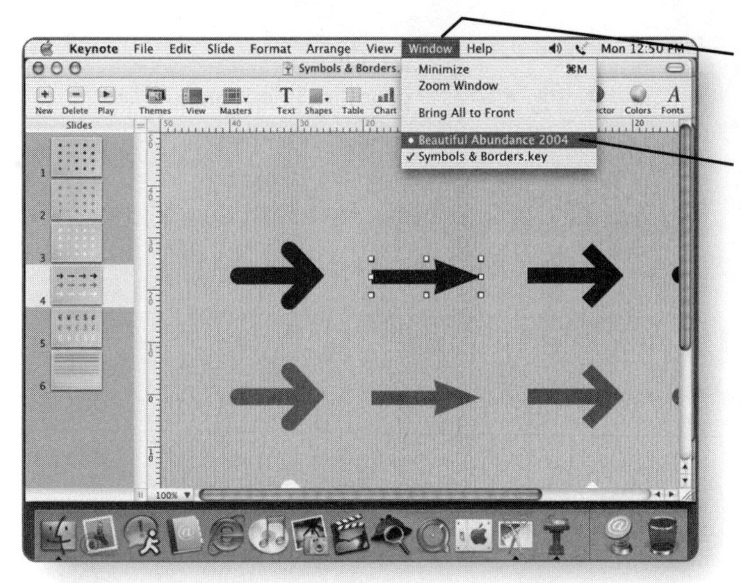

8. **Click** on **Window**. The Window menu will appear.

9. **Click** on the **name of your slideshow**. Keynote will return to your presentation.

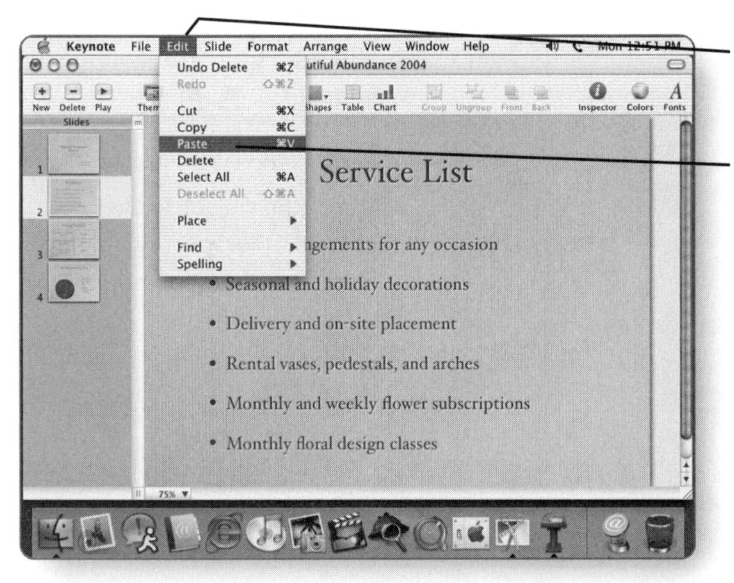

10. **Click** on **Edit**. The Edit menu will appear.

11. **Click** on **Paste**. Keynote will place the copied object on the current slide.

> **NOTE**
>
> If needed, navigate to the slide where you'd like to place the pasted graphic by using Pg Dn or Pg Up or by clicking on the slide in the slide organizer.

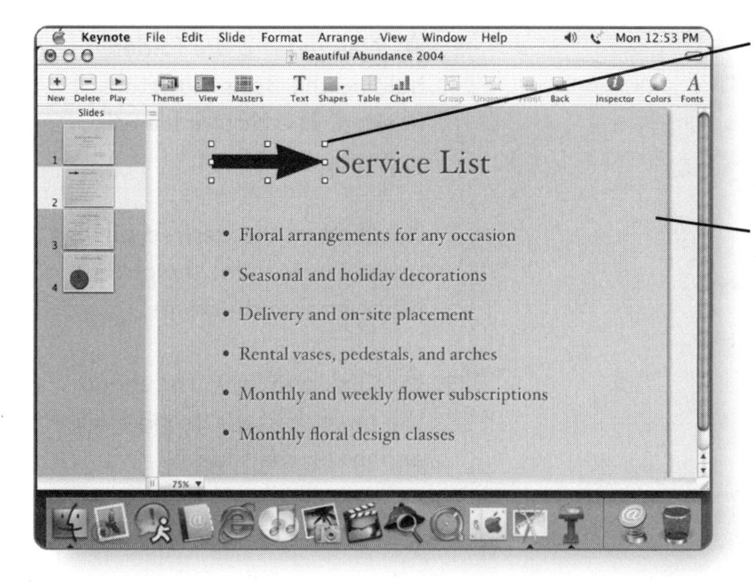

12. **Drag** the **graphic object** or a **selection handle**. The object will move or resize as specified.

13. **Click outside** the **graphic**. The object will be deselected. You can then use the Window menu to switch back to the Image Library file and close that file.

Using Your Own Graphics

You can use a command on the Edit, Place submenu to insert a graphic file that you've scanned, snapped with a digital camera, or created in a graphics program onto any slide.

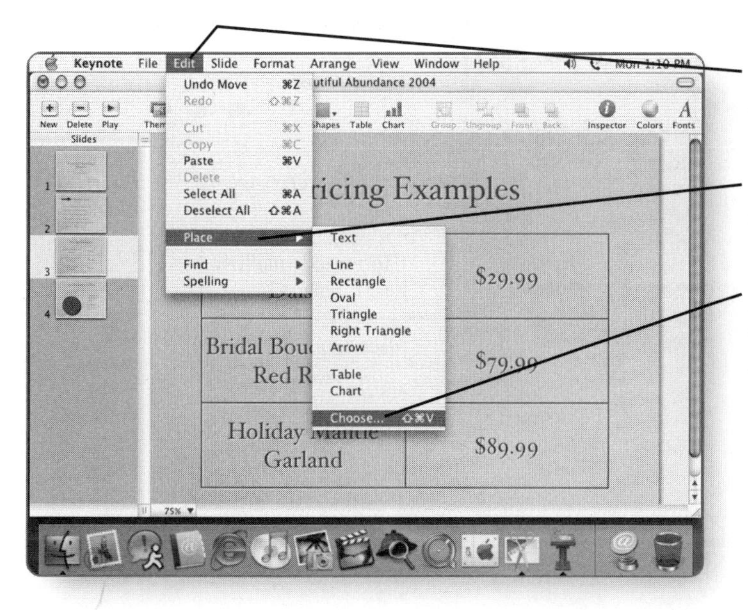

1. **Click** on **Edit**. The Edit menu will appear.

2. **Point** to **Place**. A submenu will appear.

3. **Click** on **Choose**. A sheet will open so that you can choose the picture to insert.

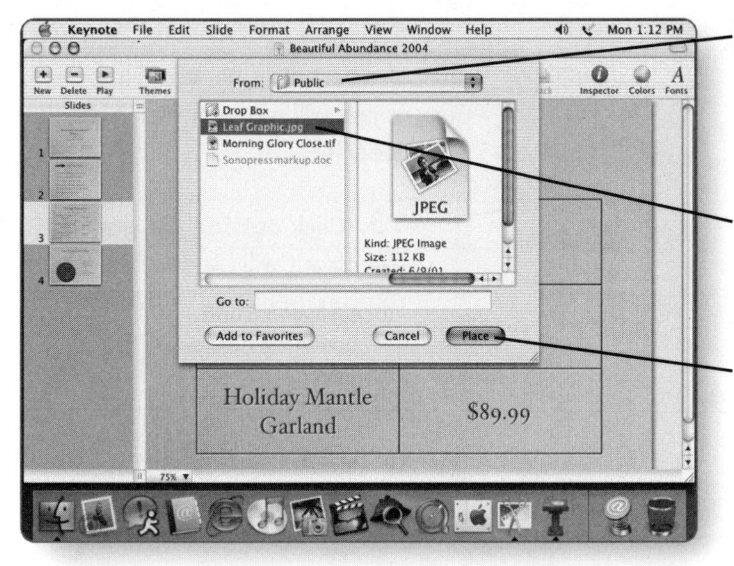

4. **Navigate** to **the folder** holding the **desired picture**, if needed. The picture file will appear in the sheet.

5. **Click** on the **desired picture**. A preview icon for the picture will appear in the sheet.

6. **Click** on **Place**. The sheet will close, and the graphic will appear on the slide.

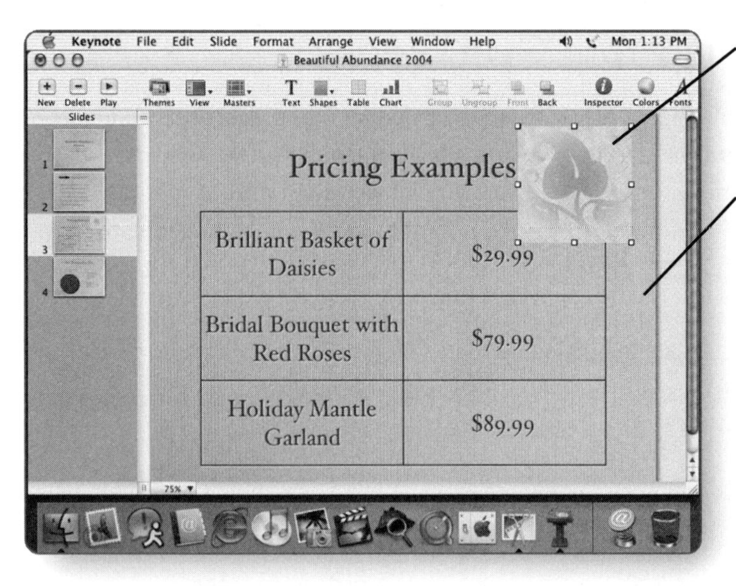

7. **Drag** the **graphic object** or a **selection handle**. The object will move or resize as specified.

8. **Click outside** the **graphic**. The object will be deselected.

Using iPhoto Images

If you've already imported images from a digital camera into iPhoto, you can drag any image from the iPhoto window and drop it directly onto a slide in Keynote.

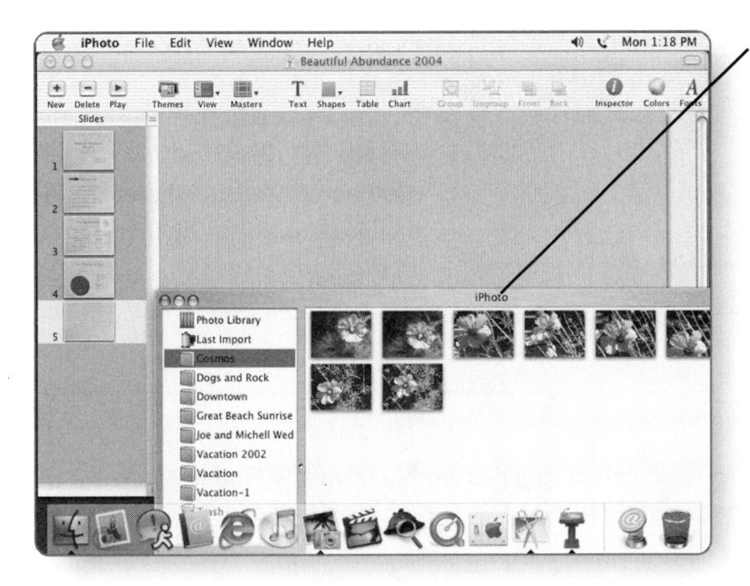

1. Start iPhoto, select the album holding the **desired photo**, and **position** the **iPhoto window** so that Keynote is visible. Your screen will resemble this example.

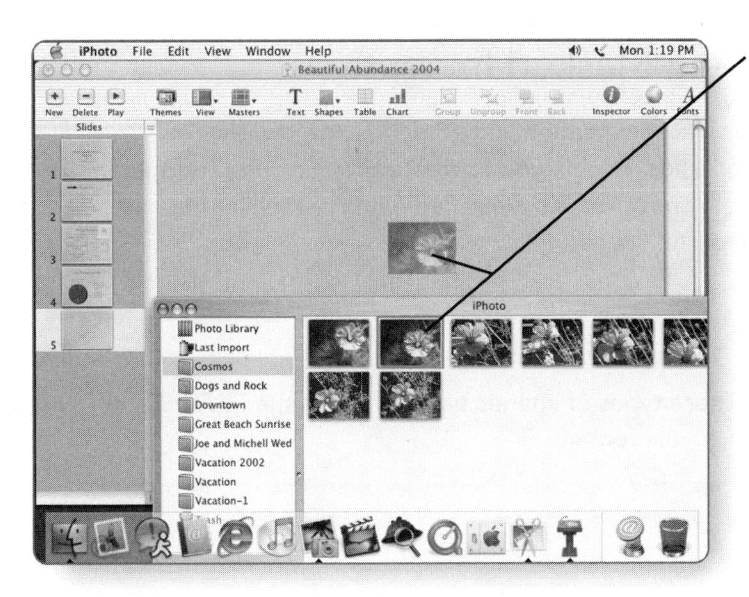

2. Drag the **desired photo onto the slide** in Keynote. When you release the mouse button, the photo will appear on the slide.

3. **Click** on the **Keynote icon** on the Dock. Keynote will become the active application.

4. **Drag** the **image** or a **selection handle**. The object will move or resize as specified.

5. **Click outside** the **graphic image**. The object will be deselected. You can then use the Dock to switch back to iPhoto and close it.

> **TIP**
>
> You also can drag a picture file from any Finder window onto a slide to place the graphic on that slide.

Using Masked Images

Some image creation and editing programs, such as Photoshop, enable you to create graphics with transparent areas. These images are called *alpha channel* or *masked images*.

> **TIP**
>
> These types of images typically are in the PDF, PSD, or TIFF file format.

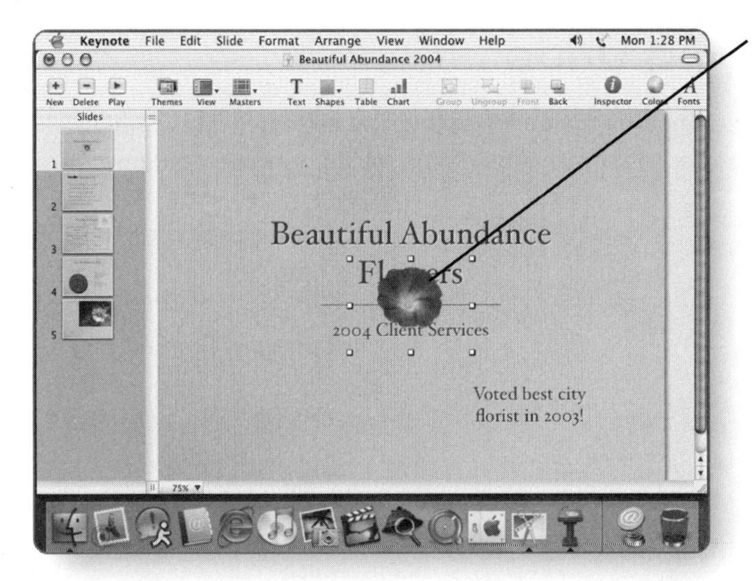

- Insert a picture with transparent areas just as you would any other graphic, by using one of the techniques just presented.

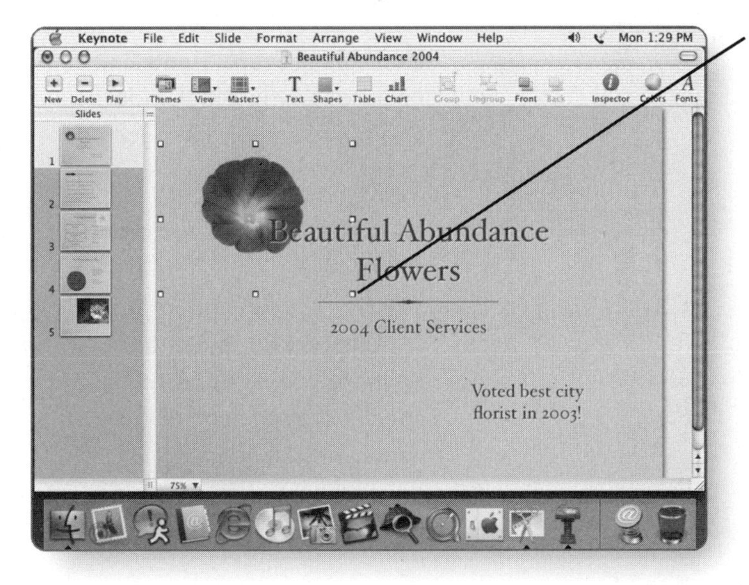

- Move and resize the graphic as desired. If needed, use the Arrange, Send to Back command to move the graphic behind text or another object. As shown here, the transparent areas in the graphic remain transparent and do not cover objects in Keynote, such as the slide background.

Using Undo

Keynote offers the ability to undo an action you just completed or to redo an action that you've previously undone. Actually, you can undo several previous actions and then redo them as desired.

1. **Click** on **Edit**. The Edit menu will appear.

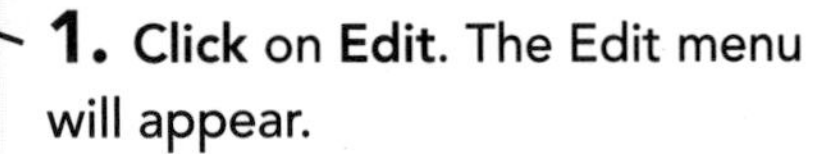

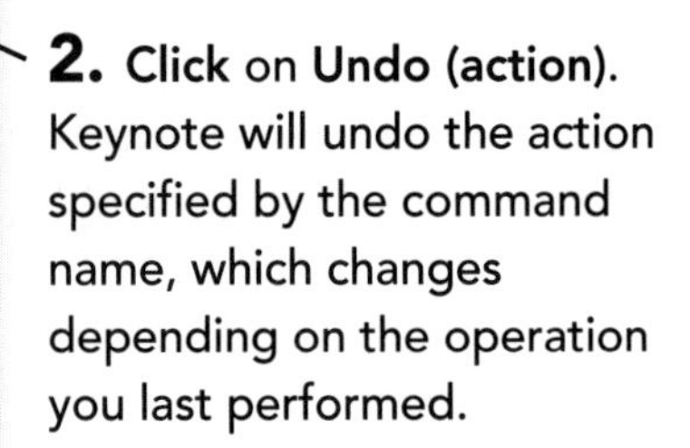

2. **Click** on **Undo (action)**. Keynote will undo the action specified by the command name, which changes depending on the operation you last performed.

3. **Repeat Steps 1 and 2** as needed. Keynote will undo additional actions as specified.

4. **Click** on **Edit**. The Edit menu will appear.

5. **Click** on **Redo (action)**. Keynote will redo the action specified by the command name, which changes depending on the operation you last undid.

4

Working with Slideshow Text

If you're working with a particular presentation graphics program for the first time, it's tempting to get caught up in all the stylish designs and fun effects. You must keep the substance of your presentation in mind, as well. Clear and accurate text will ensure that your message hits home with your audience. This chapter teaches you how to work with slide text, including how to:

- Make changes to text.
- Write speaker notes.
- Use automatic spell checking.
- Spell check the whole presentation.
- Find and replace text.
- Adjust text alignment and tab settings.

Editing Text

You can use a variety of editing techniques (the same ones used in a word processing program) to make the changes you desire to the text on any slide. Here are the actions you can take to edit text on a slide:

- **Start the process.** Click on the text placeholder that holds the text to edit, and then click again within the text in the placeholder to position the insertion point there.

> **TIP**
>
> To edit text in a table cell, click on the table, and then click in the cell to edit.

- **Insert information.** Press the left or right arrow key to move the insertion point within the text, and then type new information to insert.

- **Replace or delete a word.** Double-click on the word to select it. Press Delete to delete the word, or type new information to replace the word.

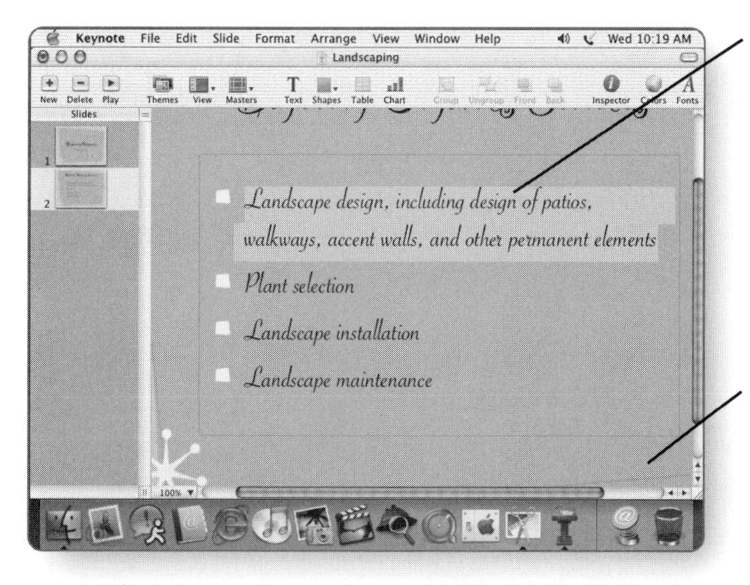

- **Replace or delete the entire entry or bullet item.** Triple-click the text to select all of the placeholder's contents or a specific bullet item in a bulleted list. Press Delete to delete the selection, or type new information to replace the selection.
- **Finish your changes.** Click outside the text placeholder to finish your edits.

TIP

Press ⌘+A to select all the items in a bulleted list. Or drag with the mouse to select a particular phrase or part of a word.

INSERTING SPECIAL CHARACTERS

You can use the Mac OS X Character Palette to insert special characters like arrows, check marks, and stars within a slide's text.

1. Within the text placeholder, position the insertion point where you'd like to insert the special character.

2. Click on Fonts on the toolbar. The Fonts window will open.

3. Click on the Extras pop-up menu in the Fonts window, and then click on Show Characters. The Character Palette window will open.

4. Click on a category in the left side of the Character Palette window. The characters in that category will appear at the right.

5. Click on the character to insert, and then click on the Insert button.

The character will appear in the text, as shown here.

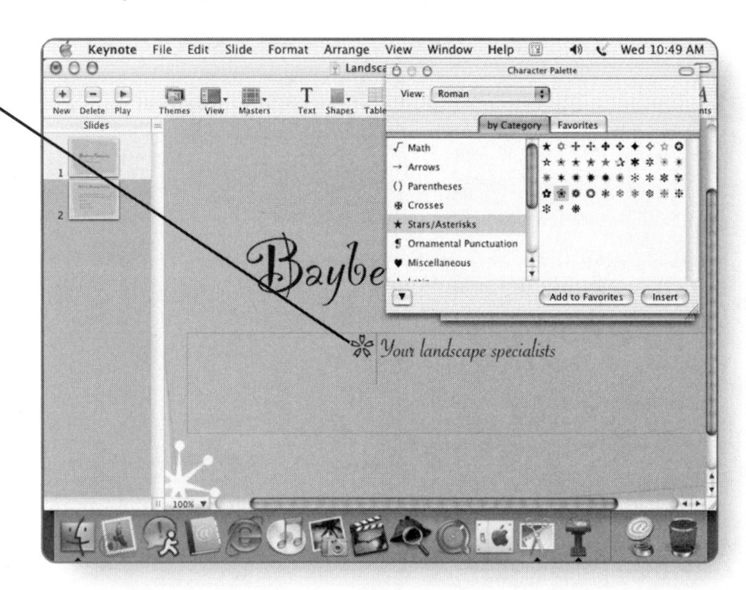

You can then click on the Close button for the Character Palette window and the Fonts window to close them.

To remove the button for the character palette from the menu bar, click on System Preferences in the Dock. Click on International in the System Preferences window, and then click on the Input Menu tab in the International Preferences window. Clear the check box beside Character Palette in the list of layouts. Then choose System Preferences, Quit System Preferences.

Adding Slide (Speaker) Notes

You can add speaker notes for any slide to use as you deliver the presentation. A speaker note might include additional information supporting a key point on the slide, more points to make if time allows, or an anecdote to add color to your delivery. Speaker notes do not appear onscreen when the presentation plays. You can print the slides with speaker notes (or not) as needed. (See Chapter 11, "Printing the Slideshow" to learn more about printing slides and notes.)

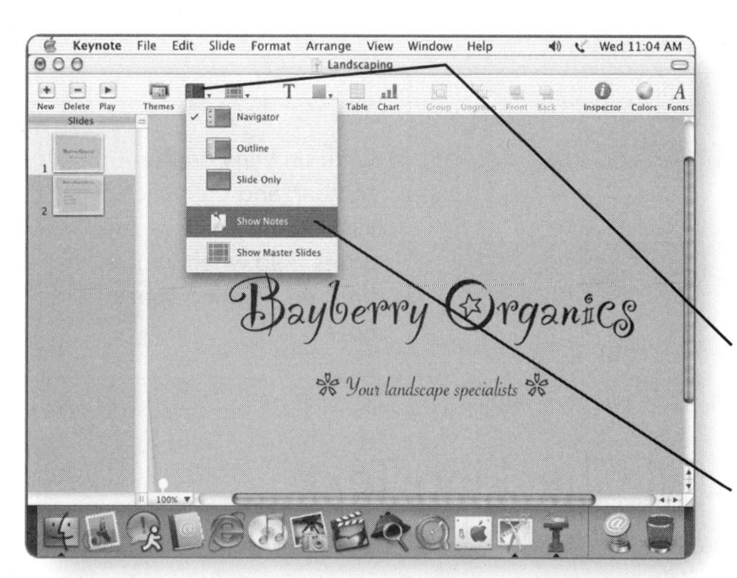

1. **Click** on **View** on the window toolbar. The View choices will appear.

2. **Click** on **Show Notes**. The notes field will appear below the slide canvas in the current view.

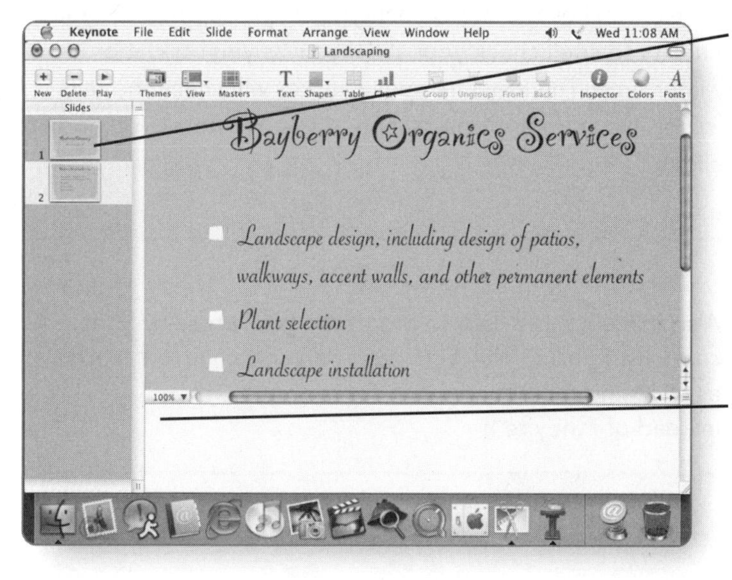

3. **Display** or **select** the **slide for which you want to add notes**. The slide will appear on the canvas. If you're working in the Navigator or Organizer view, the slide thumbnail or icon will also be selected in the slide organizer.

4. **Click** in the **notes field**. The insertion point will appear in the field.

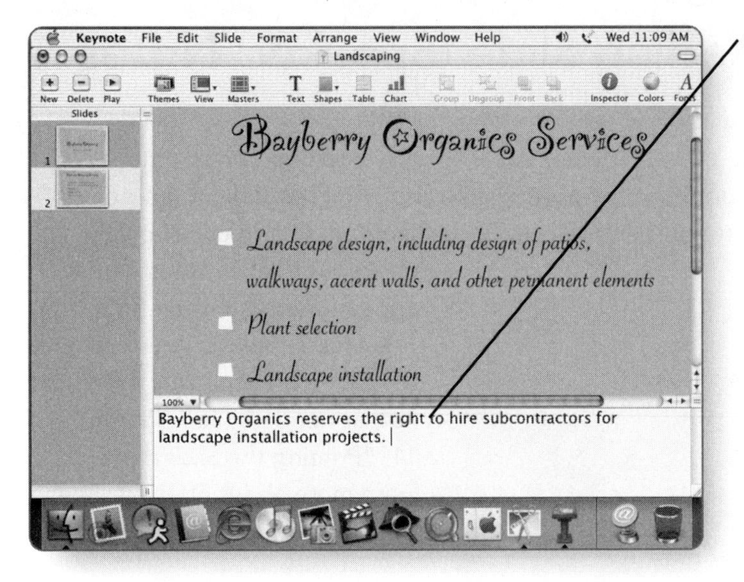

5. Type your notes. The text will appear in the notes field.

6. Repeat Steps 3 through 5 to add notes for additional slides as needed. The insertion point will appear in the field.

> **NOTE**
>
> Click on View on the toolbar, and then click on Hide Notes to close the notes field when you've finished creating speaker notes.

Spell Checking Text

Every businessperson should spell check his or her work before sharing it with others. Even an experienced writer like yours truly makes the occasional typo. Keynote provides you the ability to spell check your slideshow as you build it or at any later time. The Keynote spell checker will check the text on slides, in tables and charts, and in speaker notes you add to slides.

> **CAUTION**
>
> Also make it a practice to proofread your presentations carefully. Spelling checkers can't flag certain errors, such as choosing the wrong word (for example, "there" instead of "they're").

Spell Checking as You Type

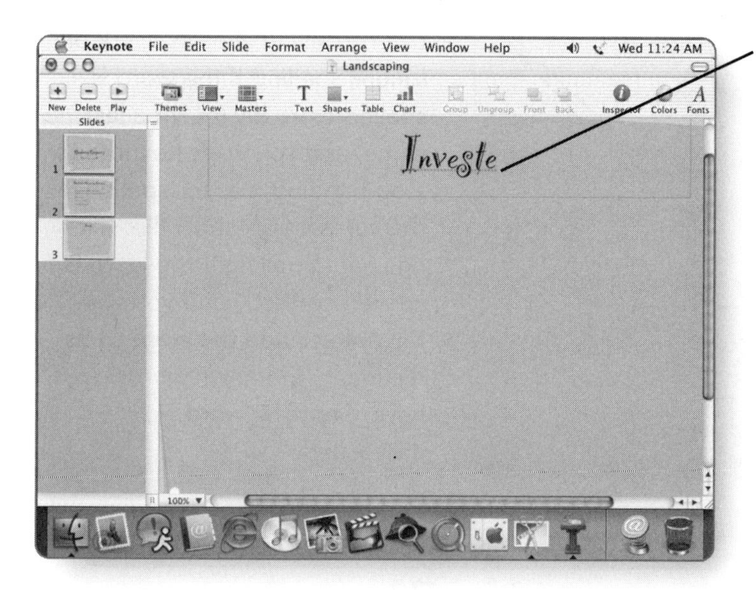

By default, Keynote will check spelling for you as you type text. Whenever you type a word that Keynote doesn't recognize, a red dotted underline will appear below the word.

When that happens and you need to make a correction, use the following steps.

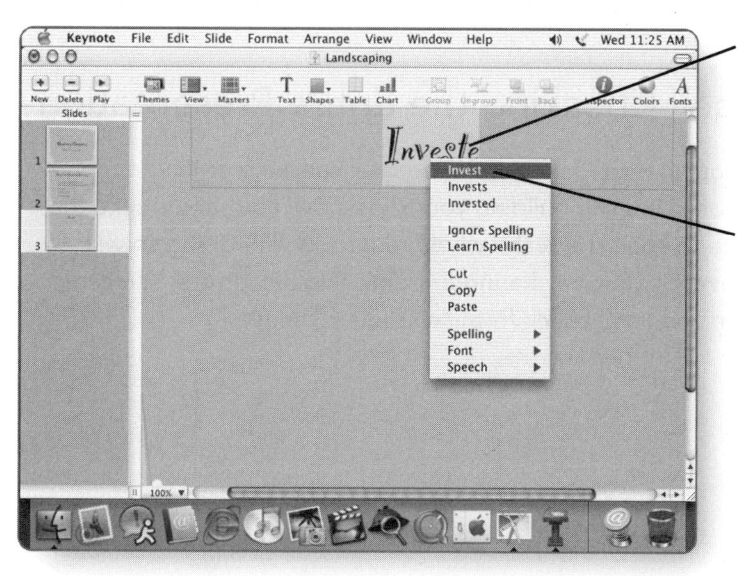

1. **Control+click** on the **underlined word**. A contextual menu with suggested spelling corrections will appear.

2. **Click** on the **desired correction**. Keynote will correct the text.

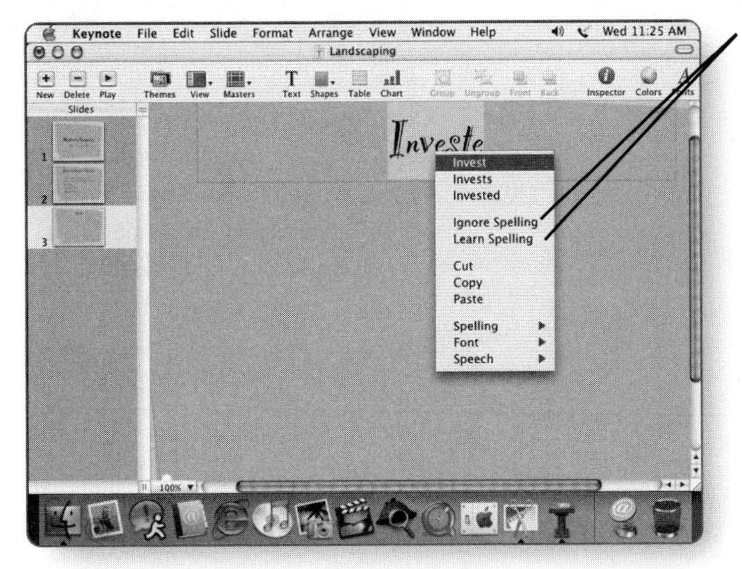

The contextual menu also includes the Ignore Spelling and Learn Spelling choices. Click on Ignore Spelling if the word is spelled correctly (as for a last name) and you want Keynote to stop flagging it as misspelled in the current slideshow file. Click on Learn Spelling if the word is spelled correctly and you want Keynote to add the word to its dictionary of known words, so it never flags the word as misspelled.

TIP

To turn automatic spell checking on or off, choose Edit, Spelling, Check Spelling As You Type.

Spell Checking the Entire Presentation

If you've turned off automatic spell checking or have simply ignored it while building your slideshow, you should take the time to spell check the whole slideshow file. Doing so will prevent you from sharing or publishing any errors. You can start the spell check from any slide in the file.

1. **Click** on **Edit**. The Edit menu will appear.

2. **Point** to **Spelling.** The Spelling submenu will appear.

3. **Click** on **Spelling.** The Spelling window dialog box will open if the spell checker finds a word that may have a spelling error. If the spelling error appears in a chart or speaker note, an additional window or pane may open to show the typo.

> **TIP**
>
> If there are no misspellings, Keynote will simply beep.

4. **Click** on the **appropriate button** to deal with each found word, as follows:

- **Ignore**. If the word is spelled correctly, click on Ignore to stop flagging it.
- **Find Next**. Click on this button to skip the current word and find the next word that may be misspelled.
- **Correct**. Click on the desired replacement word in the Guess list, and then click on Correct.

NOTE

To enter your own guess, type it in the text box below the Guess list, and then click on the Guess button. After you've selected a word in the Guess list, you can click on Learn to add it to the dictionary, or you can click on Forget to remove it from the dictionary.

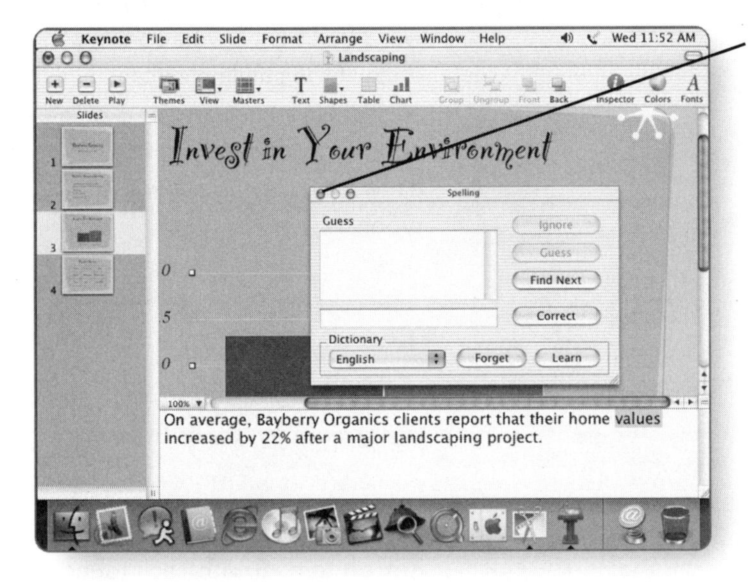

5. **Click** on the **Spelling window close button** when a beep informs you that the spell check is finished.

TIP

To find any misspelled word in the presentation without opening the Spelling window, choose Edit, Spelling, Check Spelling. Keynote will highlight the next misspelled word in the slideshow.

Finding and Replacing Text in a Slideshow

You can find or replace text in a slideshow. Finding text works well when you want to jump to a particular slide, and you know that the slide contains a particular word or phrase. Replacing text makes it faster to substitute one word or phrase for another throughout the presentation. To handle either a Find or a Replace task, start from any slide in the slideshow and use the Find window.

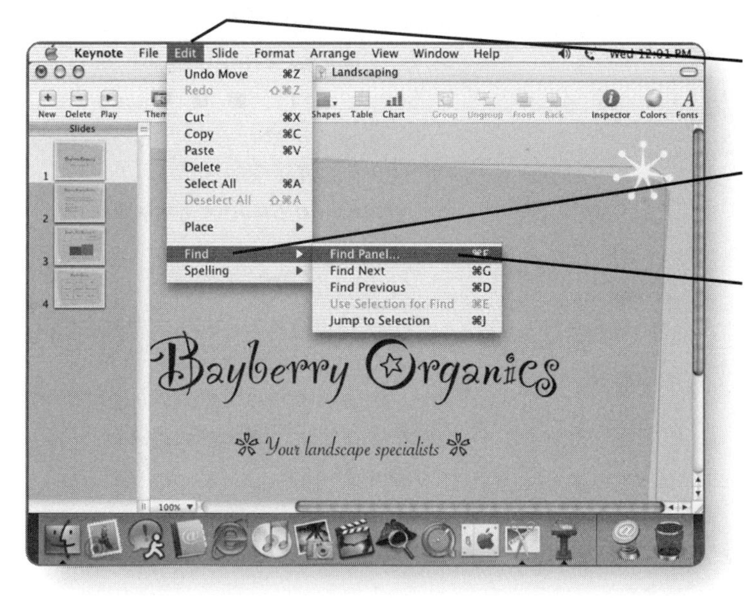

1. **Click** on **Edit**. The Edit menu will appear.

2. **Point** to **Find**. The Find submenu will appear.

3. **Click** on **Find Panel**. The Find window will open.

4. **Type** the **text you want to find** in the Find text box. To simply perform a Find operation, skip to Step 7.

5. **Type** the **replacement text** in the Replace with text box.

6. Choose a **Replace All Scope**. Keynote will replace the Find text in the entire file or the current selection only, depending on your choice.

7. **Choose Find Options.** Depending on which options you check, Keynote will ignore case or find whole words only during the Find or Replace operation.

8. Click on **Next**.

Keynote will display and highlight the first instance of matching text. If you're finding text only, you can close the Find dialog box or click on Next to find the next matching instance of the text.

9. Click on **Replace & Find**. Keynote will replace the first instance of matching text and find the next matching text. Repeat this step as needed to find and replace additional text.

TIP

Click on Replace All to replace all the text matches in the slideshow. Click on Replace to replace the current match without finding the next one.

10. When you finish making replacements as desired, **click** on the Find window **close button**. The Find window will close.

NOTE

To find matching text after you've closed the Find window, choose Edit, Find, Find Next.

Aligning Text

Each text placeholder features default alignment and tab settings for the text within. As you design your slides and edit your text, you may decide to change these alignments and tabs to improve on the design at any time.

Changing Alignment

To change the alignment in a text placeholder, use the Text Inspector. You can choose to apply one of the following horizontal alignments to text in a placeholder: Align Left, Center, Align Right, or Justify. In addition, you can choose a vertical alignment setting: Align Top, Align Middle, or Align Bottom.

> **TIP**
>
> You also can use the Format, Text submenu to change text alignment.

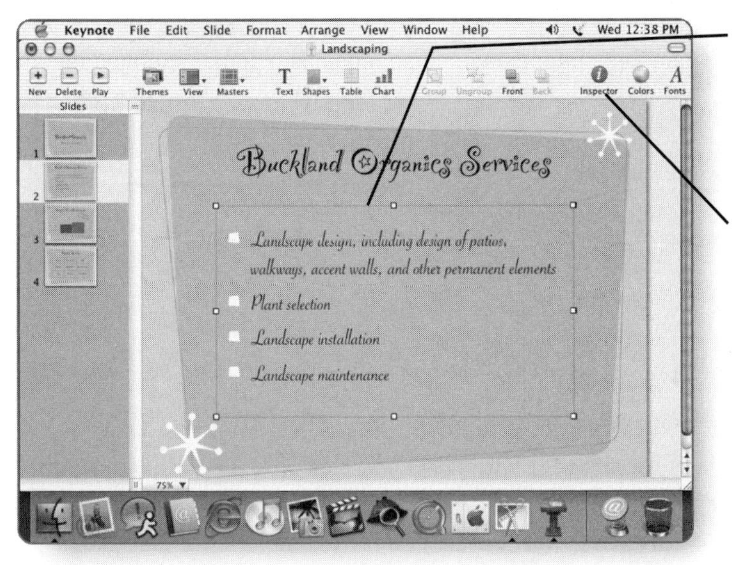

1. **Click** on the **placeholder with the text to realign**. The text placeholder will be selected.
2. **Click** on **Inspector** on the window toolbar. The Inspector window will open.

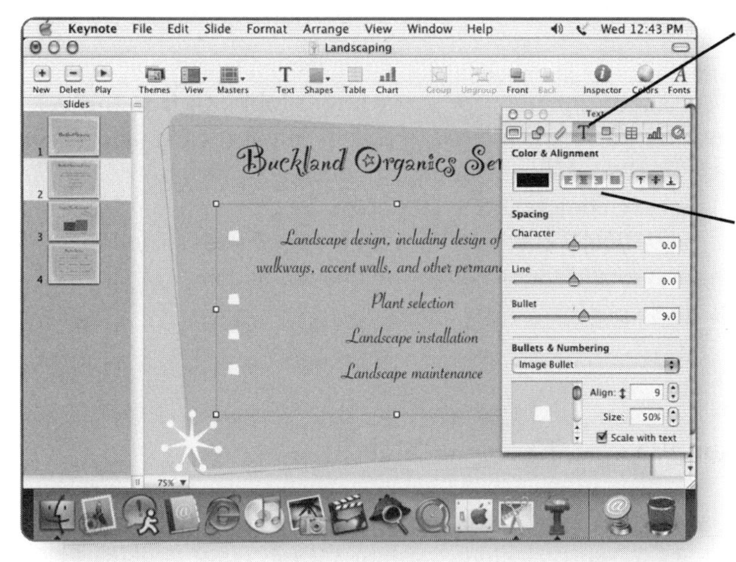

3. **Click** on the **Text Inspector** button in the Inspector window. The Text Inspector settings will appear.

4. **Click** on the **desired horizontal alignment**. The text will realign in the placeholder.

> **CAUTION**
>
> The bullets will not move when you change the horizontal alignment in a bulleted list.

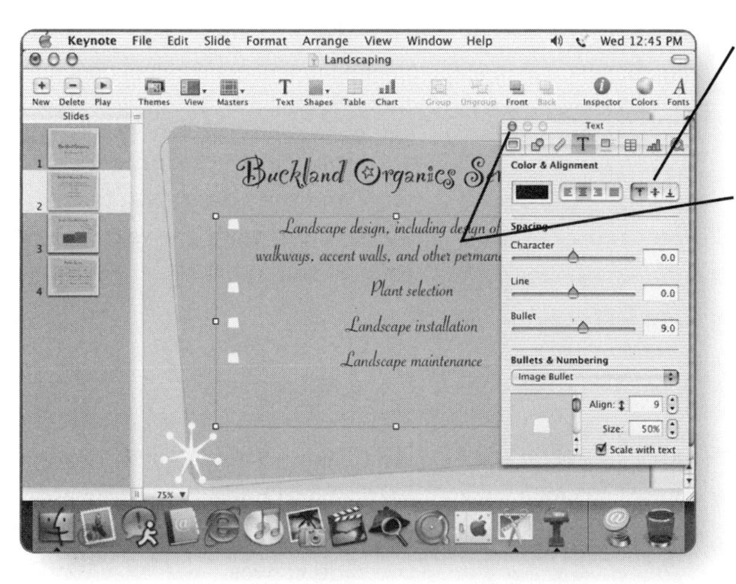

5. **Click** on the **desired vertical alignment**. The text will realign in the placeholder.

6. **Click** on the Inspector window **close button**. (You also could click on Inspector on the toolbar again.) The Inspector will close.

NOTE

To change alignment for text within a table, click on the table to select it. Click on Inspector in the toolbar, and then click on Table Inspector. Choose your new alignment choices in the Inspector. To change alignment for a particular cell only, click on that cell after selecting the table, and then choose the desired alignment in the Table Inspector.

Setting and Using Tabs

If you add text to a placeholder from a slide master, chances are that master will include settings for tab stops. If you add a text box to a slide, on the other hand, you'll need to set up tab stops yourself. In either case, you use the rulers to add and edit tabs for a text box on a slide.

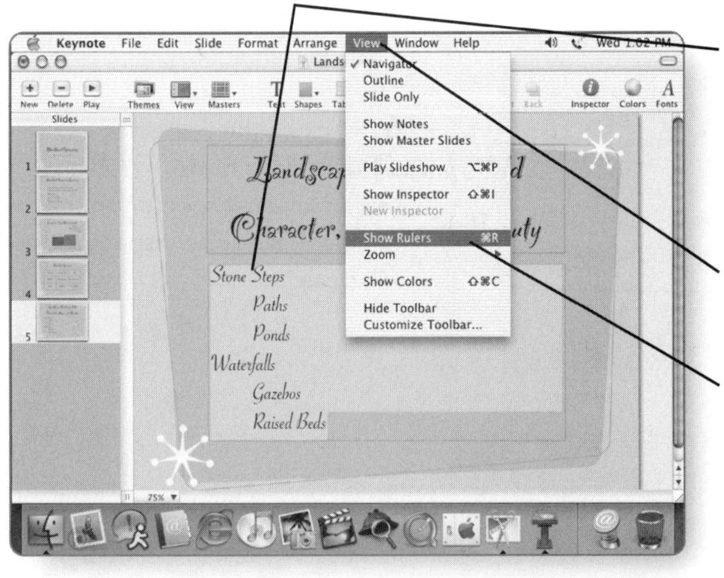

1. **Click** on the **placeholder with the text to realign** with tabs, and then **drag over** the **placeholder text**. The text will be selected.

2. **Click** on **View**. The View menu will appear.

3. **Click** on **Show Rulers.** The vertical and horizontal rulers will appear to the left of and above the slide canvas.

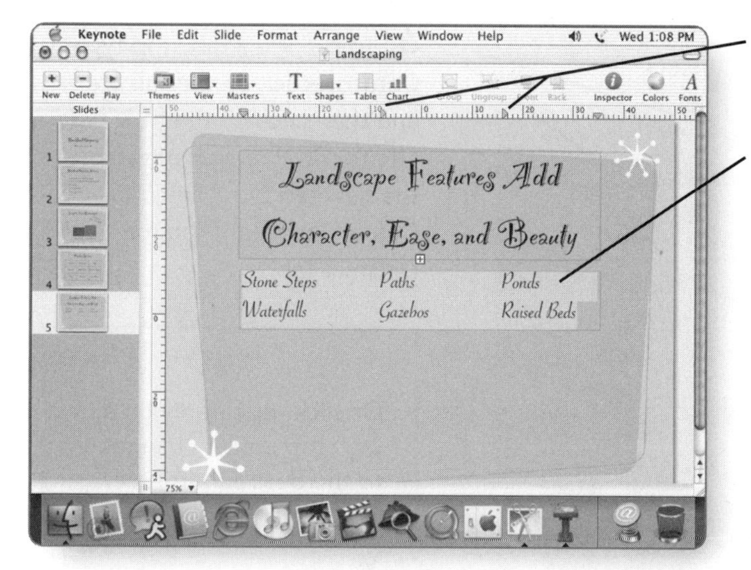

4. To add each tab stop, **click** on the **horizontal ruler**.

If you already typed tab characters into the text, the text will realign according to the new tab stops.

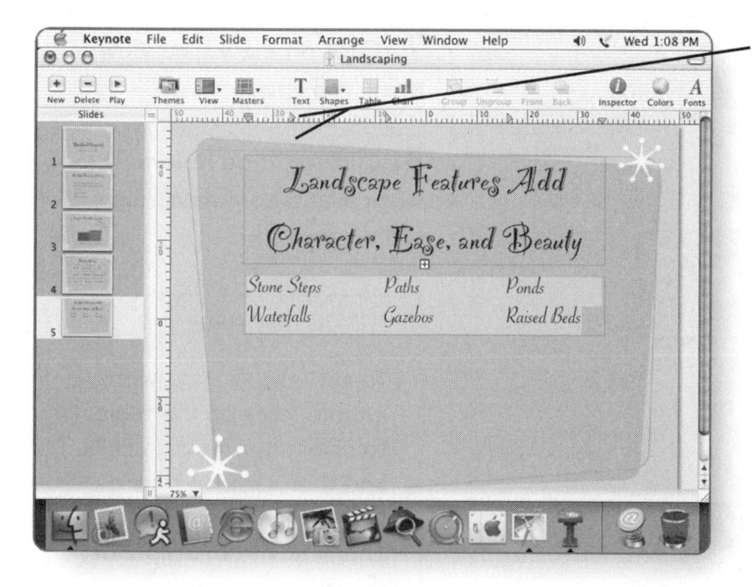

5. To delete a tab stop, **drag it off** the **horizontal ruler**. The tab will disappear, and text will realign if required.

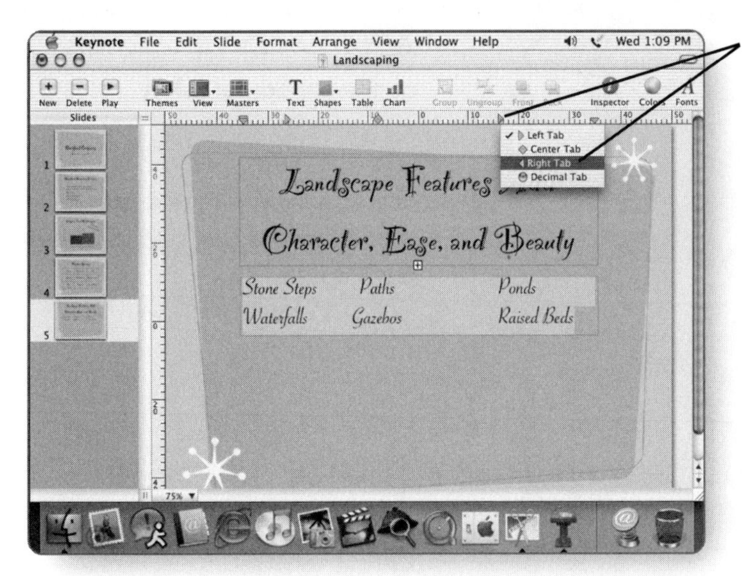

6. To change a tab stop type, **Control+click** on the **tab stop,** and then **click** on the **new type**. The text will realign based on the new tab type: Left Tab, Center Tab, Right Tab, or Decimal Tab.

> **TIP**
>
> Or click repeatedly on a tab stop until it changes to the desired tab type.

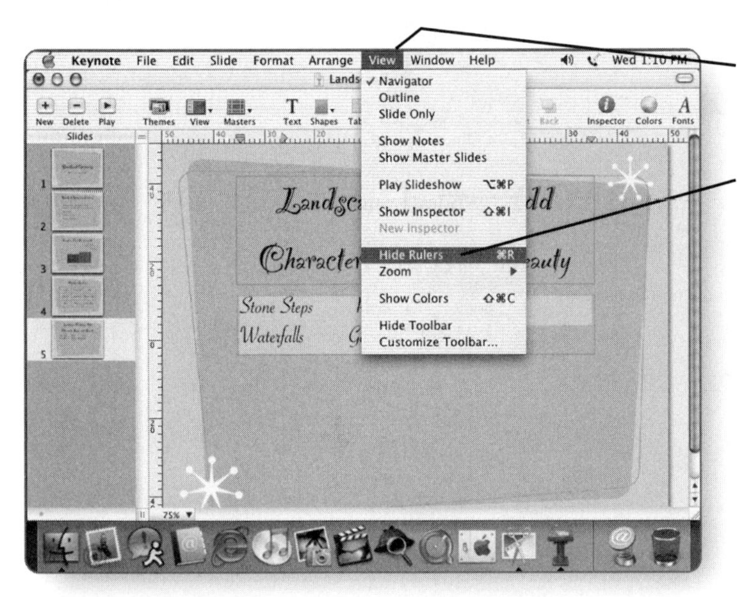

7. Click on **View**. The View menu will appear.

8. Click on **Hide Rulers**. The vertical and horizontal rulers will disappear.

> **NOTE**
>
> To set tabs for text within a table, click on the table to select it, click on a cell, and then click on text within the cell to select it. Then start from Step 2 of the preceding steps.

5

Working with Slideshow Files

Not only does any presentation you build represent a significant investment of your time, but you also typically can reuse a presentation you've developed for several different audiences. Or you may encounter circumstances where you partially develop a presentation, and then need to finish it at a later time. For these reasons and others, you need to know how to manage the slideshow files that you create. In this chapter, you will learn how to:

- Save a slideshow file to a folder.
- Open a slideshow file you saved earlier.
- Open a slideshow file you've used recently.
- Switch to another open slideshow file.
- Copy a slideshow file.
- Return to the previously saved version of a slideshow.
- Close a slideshow file.

Saving a File

To be able to use a slideshow in the future or share a slideshow via e-mail or another medium, you have to save the slideshow file. During the save process, you assign a name for the slideshow file and specify the folder and disk where you'd like to save it.

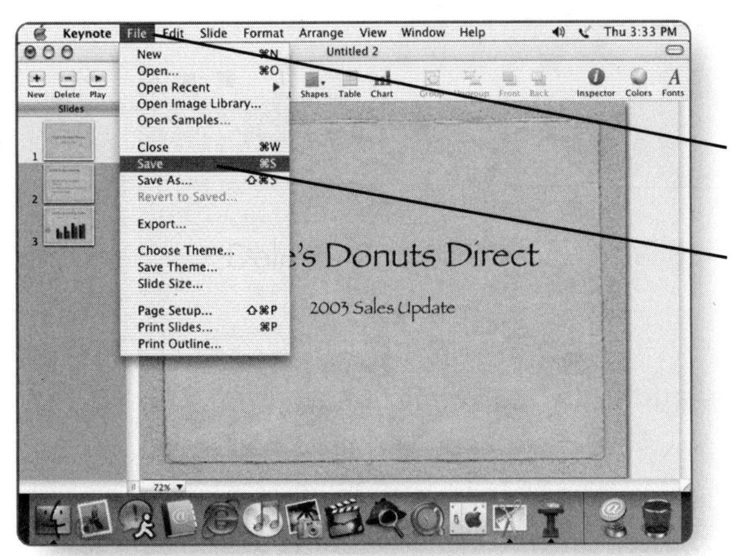

1. **Click** on **File**. The File menu will appear.

2. **Click** on **Save**. A sheet with save options will open.

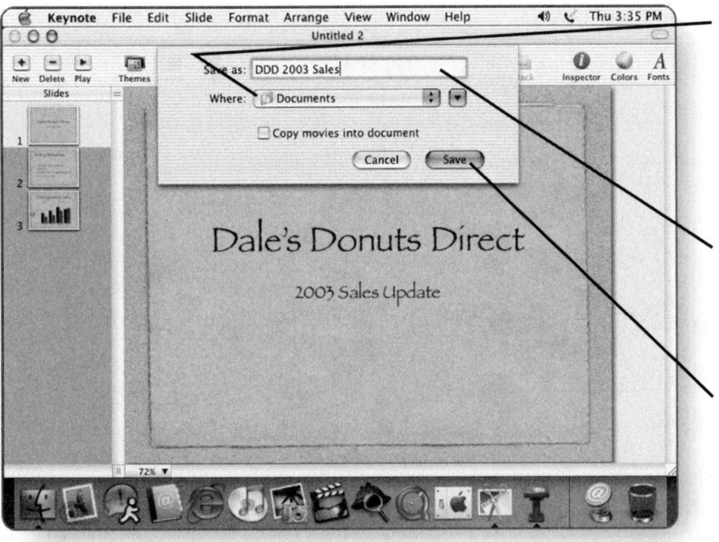

3. **Navigate** to the **disk and folder** where you want to save the slideshow file, if needed. The folder will appear in the Where box.

4. **Type** a **file name** in the Save As text box. The name will appear in the Save As text box.

5. **Click** on **Save**. Keynote will save the file in the location you specified. The file will remain open onscreen.

Opening an Existing File

Once you save and name a slideshow file, it will remain on your system's hard disk or the network drive where you saved it until you delete or move the file. If you need to work on a slideshow or play it onscreen, you have to reopen the slideshow file onscreen. Follow these steps any time you need to open a slideshow file that you've previously created (and closed, as described in the later section called "Closing a File").

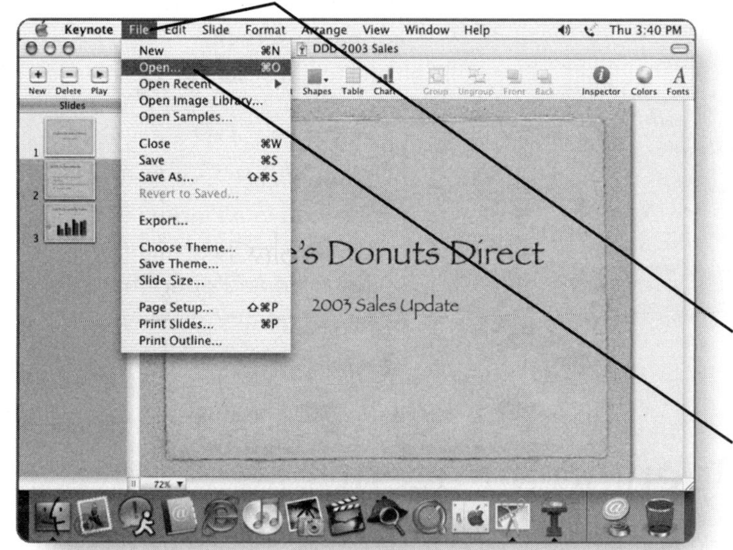

1. Click on **File**. The File menu will appear.

2. Click on **Open**. The Open dialog box will open.

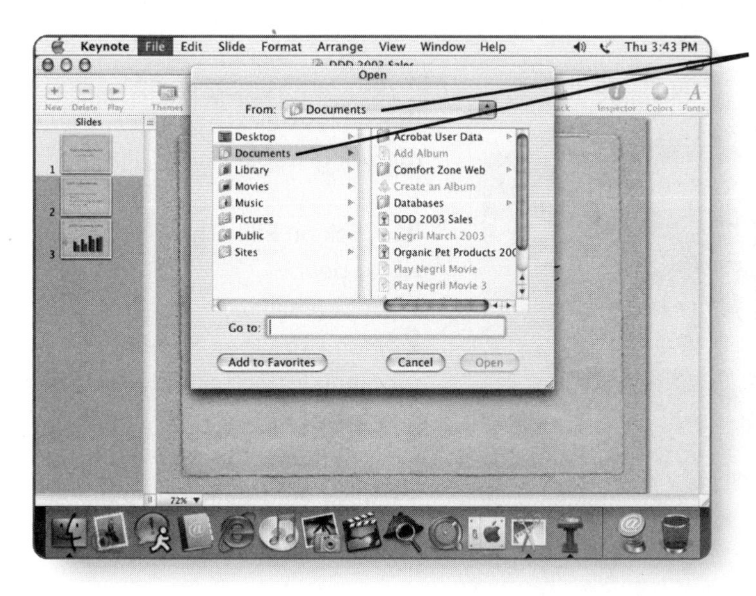

3. Navigate to the **folder** holding the slideshow file you want to open. The file will be displayed in the file list. You may need to do one or more of the following steps to locate the folder:

- Click on the From pop-up menu; then click on the folder that holds the file.
- Click on the scroll arrows below the folder and file list; then click on the desired folder or disk name.

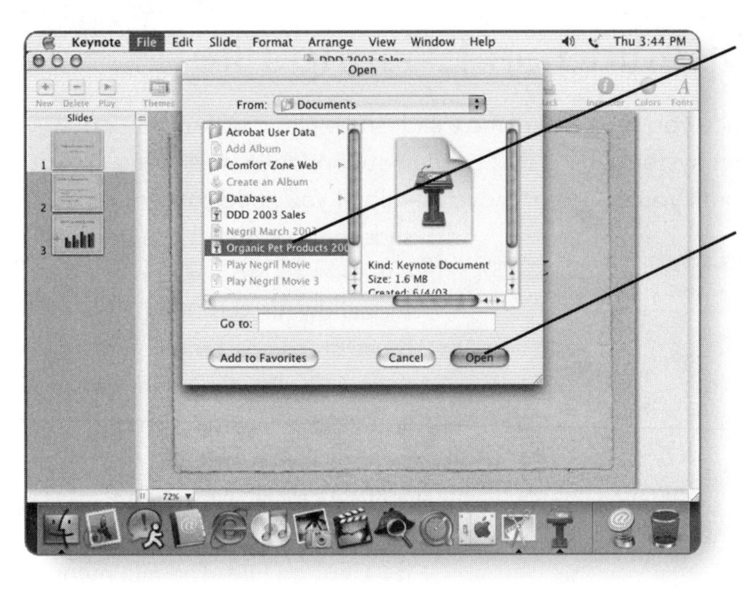

4. Click on the **file** that you want to open. A preview icon will appear at the right side of the Open dialog box.

5. Click on **Open**. The file will appear onscreen.

> **TIP**
>
> Double-click a slideshow file icon in a Finder window to both launch Keynote and open the specified file.

Opening a Recent File

By default, Keynote tracks the last several slideshow files that you've opened.

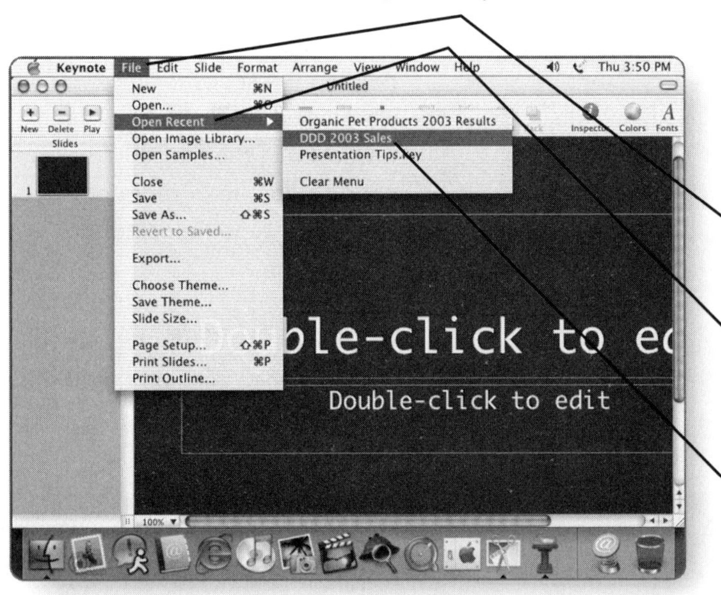

If you want to reopen one of those files quickly, use the following steps.

1. Click on **File**. The File menu will appear.

2. Point to **Open Recent**. The submenu listing recently opened files will appear.

3. Click on the **file to open**. Keynote will open the specified file.

> **TIP**
>
> To clear the list of recently opened files, click on File, point to Open Recent, and then click on Clear Menu.

Moving to Another Open File

Keynote enables you to have multiple slideshow files open at any given time. This means that you can switch between the open slideshow files as needed to verify information and make changes. Only the amount of RAM installed on your system limits the number of files you can open. Use the following process to switch between open slideshow files.

1. **Click** on **Window**. The Window menu will appear, listing open slideshow files at the bottom.

2. **Click** on the **slideshow file** that you want to use. The file will move to the front of other open files onscreen, becoming the current or *active* file.

Saving a Copy of a File

A razzle-dazzle presentation represents a significant investment of your time and other personal or organizational resources. The longer the slideshow and the animations and special elements it contains, the greater the investment. To preserve your investment, you should have a regular backup program in place. If you don't have an application or a system that performs automated backups, you can (and should!) save a copy of each of your slideshow files at regular intervals. Use Keynote's Save As command to create a backup copy of the current slideshow file.

> **TIP**
>
> You also can use this technique when a slideshow you've already developed holds information that you need for a new slideshow. Make a copy of the slideshow file, and then update the copy with any new content that's required.

1. **Click** on **File**. The File menu will appear.

2. **Click** on **Save As**. A sheet with save options will open.

3. **Navigate** to the **disk and folder** where you want to save the slideshow file copy, if needed. The folder will appear in the Where box.

4. **Type** a **file name** in the Save As text box. The name will appear in the Save As text box.

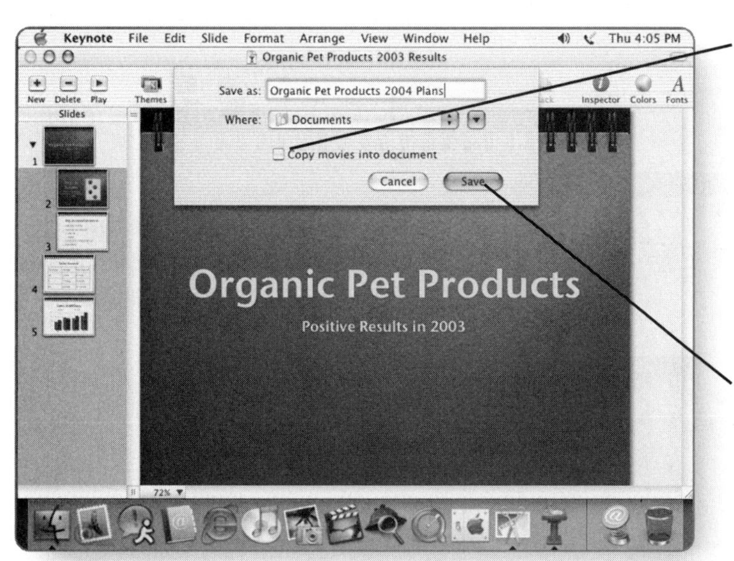

5. If the original slideshow contains inserted movie files, **click** on **Copy movies into document** to check it, if needed. Keynote will copy inserted movies into the slideshow file copy when you check this option.

6. **Click** on **Save**. Keynote will save the file copy in the location you specified. The original file will close, and the new file copy will remain open onscreen.

NOTE

In addition to creating a backup copy of your slideshow files, you should get in the habit of regularly copying those files from your system's hard disk to a backup medium such as CD-ROM.

Reverting a File

Sometimes you may rethink a series of changes that you've made in a slideshow file. Rather than selecting the Undo command repeatedly to backtrack, you can simply *revert* the file to the contents it had the last time you saved it.

> **CAUTION**
>
> You cannot undo a revert operation, so if there's any chance you may need your recent changes to the file, use Save As to create a copy (and preserve the original) instead. The Save As operation will leave the original file as is and save the changes only in the file copy created.

1. **Click** on **File**. The File menu will appear.

2. **Click** on **Revert to Saved**. A sheet prompting you to confirm the revert operation will open.

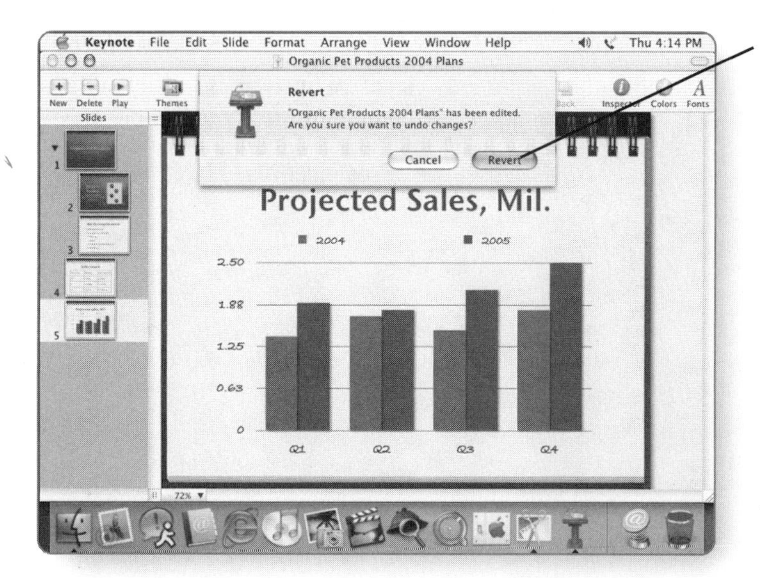

3. Click on **Revert**. The previous version of the file will appear onscreen, and all of your changes will be discarded.

Closing a File

When you finish working with a slideshow file, you should close it to free up RAM and to prevent it from being damaged by any unexpected power or system problems. You can use one of three methods to close the current slideshow file:

- Click on the File menu, and then click on Close.

- Click on the red Close button in the upper-left corner of the file window.
- Press ⌘+W.

Part I Review Questions

1. How do you open the Keynote program? *See "Starting Keynote and Creating a New Slideshow" in Chapter 1.*
2. How do I change the view, zoom, and display other screen features? *See "Working with the View" in Chapter 1.*
3. I need to create a slideshow file. *See "Creating a New Slideshow" in Chapter 2.*
4. What types of slides can I add? *See "Adding a Slide" in Chapter 2.*
5. How do I select and deselect items on a slide? *See "Selecting and Deselecting Slide Objects" in Chapter 3.*
6. I need to add graphics to a slide. Help! *See "Adding Images" in Chapter 3.*
7. Can Keynote find my typos? *See "Spell Checking Text" in Chapter 4.*
8. I want to left align text. How do I do that? *See "Changing Alignment" in Chapter 4.*
9. How do I save a slideshow file? *See "Saving a File" in Chapter 5.*
10. I made changes I don't want. Can I discard them? *See "Reverting a File" in Chapter 5.*

PART II

Editing Your Slideshow

Formatting Slide Elements

Even a businessperson who lacks an artistic side suddenly becomes creative when working with a presentation graphics program. Keynote enables you to format the various elements of each slide until you achieve the appearance that presents your message best. In this chapter, you will learn how to:

- Change text formatting.
- Work with table and chart formatting.
- Reformat drawn objects and inserted graphics.
- Move and resize objects.
- Use other techniques to layer, position, and enhance objects.
- Create interesting effects with opacity settings.

Formatting Text

You may need to make adjustments to the appearance of text for both form and function. You can apply a different *font* (lettering type) that you prefer to text. If text is too small to be readable, you can increase its size. If text is taking up too much area in a slide, you can reduce its size. To format text, work with both the Fonts window and the Text Inspector.

1. Click on the **placeholder for the text to format**. Selection handles will appear.

> **TIP**
>
> You can then drag over text within the placeholder to format only that text.

2. Click on **Fonts** on the toolbar. The Fonts window will open.

3. Click on another **font family** in the Family list. The specified font family will be applied to the text.

4. Click on another **font style** in the Typeface list. The specified typeface style will be applied to the text.

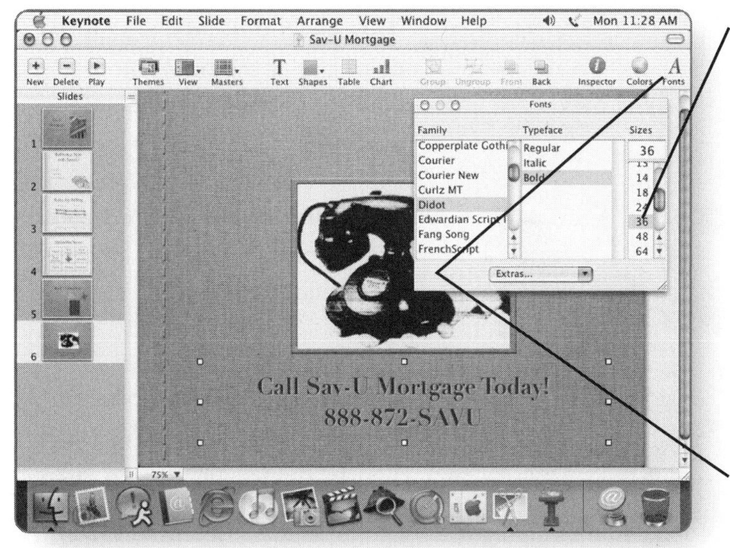

5. Click on another **font size** in the Sizes list. The specified size will be applied to the text.

> **TIP**
>
> You also can enter a specific size in the Sizes text box and press Return.

6. Click on **Fonts** on the toolbar. The Fonts window will close.

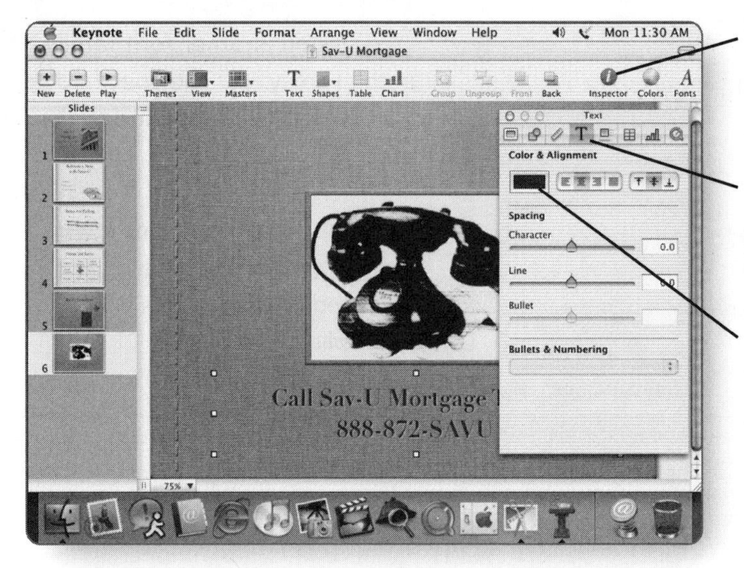

7. **Click** on **Inspector** on the toolbar. The Inspector window will open.

8. **Click** on **Text Inspector**. The Text Inspector settings will appear.

9. **Click** on the **Color box**. The Colors window will open.

10. **Drag** the **slider up** on the color bar at the right. More colors will appear in the color wheel.

11. **Click** on the **desired color** in the color wheel. The color will be applied to the text.

12. **Click** on the **Colors window close button**. The Colors window will close. The Text Inspector will remain open.

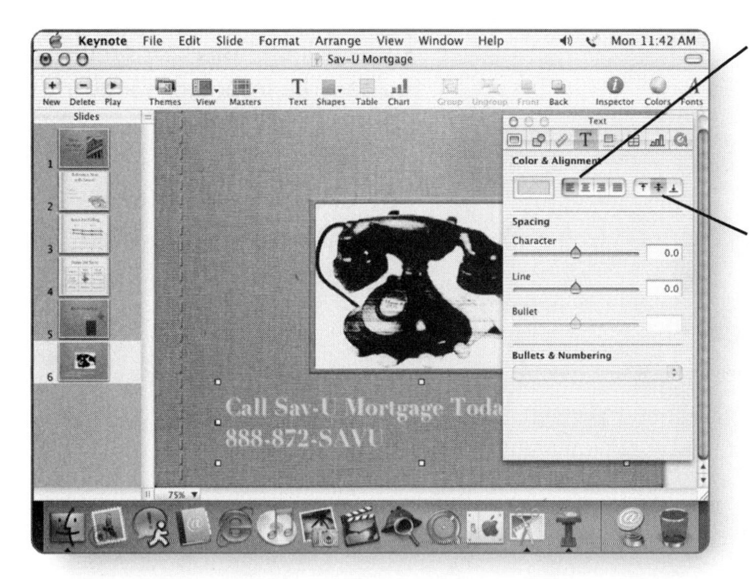

13. Click on the **desired horizontal alignment**. The alignment will be applied to the text.

14. Click on the **desired vertical alignment**. The alignment will be applied to the text.

15. Drag the **Character slider** to specify the spacing between characters. The character spacing will be applied to the text.

16. Drag the **Line slider** to specify the spacing between lines. The line spacing will be applied to the text.

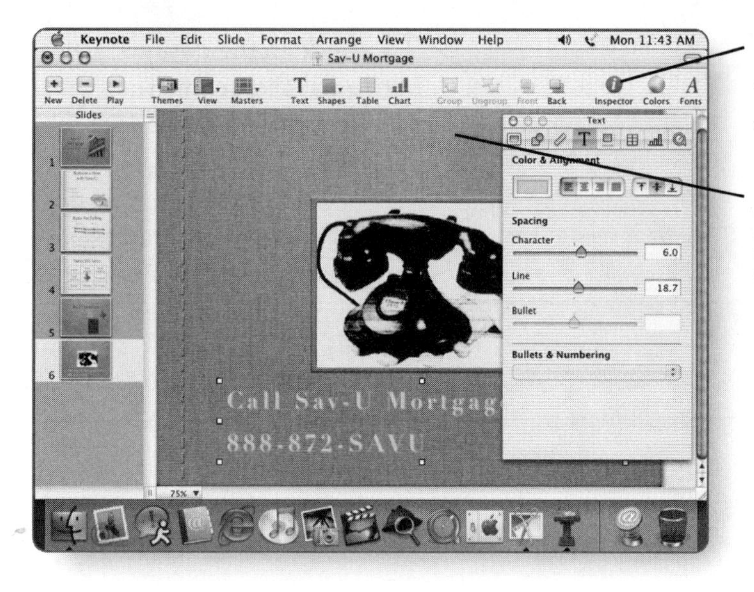

17. Click on **Inspector** on the toolbar. The Inspector window will close.

18. Click **outside** the **text placeholder**. The text will be deselected.

> **TIP**
>
> Avoid using too much different text formatting on a single slide. Remember, your slides must remain readable for audience members. Stick with one or two fonts. Italic text is harder to read, so use it for emphasis only. And make sure that there's enough contrast between the color of the text and the color of the background. Otherwise, the text will tend to blend into the background.

Formatting a Table

Most slideshow themes apply only simple table formatting, including text alignment and a color and weight for the table borders. You can use the Table Inspector to improve on the formatting for any table in your slideshow.

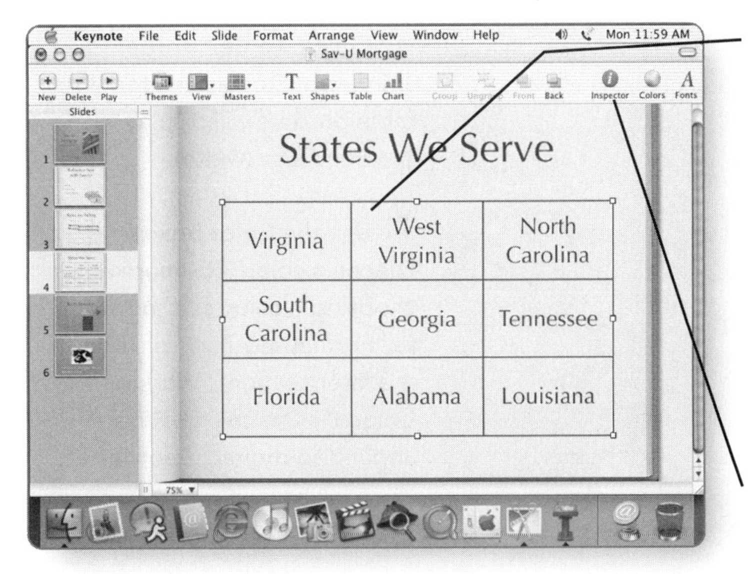

1. **Click** on the **table to format**. Selection handles will appear.

> **TIP**
>
> You can then click on a single cell within the table or drag over multiple cells to select specific cells to format.

2. **Click** on **Inspector** on the toolbar. The Inspector window will open.

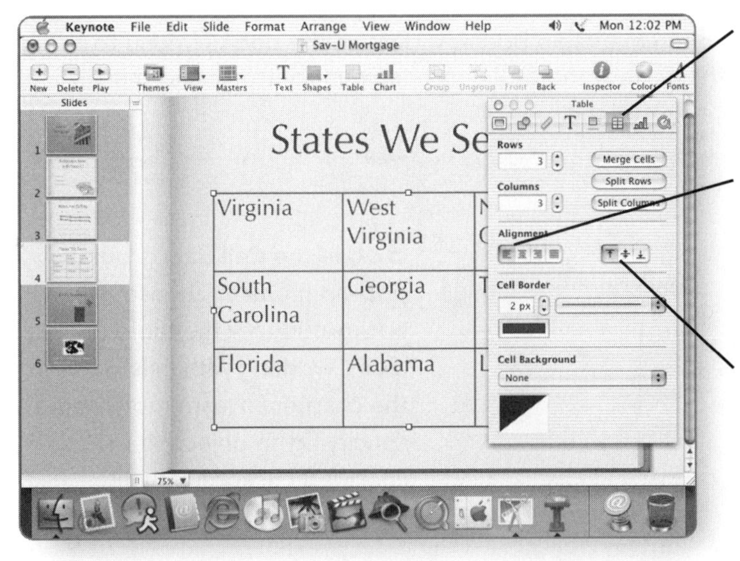

3. **Click** on **Table Inspector**. The Table Inspector settings will appear.

4. **Click** on the **desired horizontal alignment**. The alignment will be applied to the text in the table.

5. **Click** on the **desired vertical alignment**. The alignment will be applied to the text in the table.

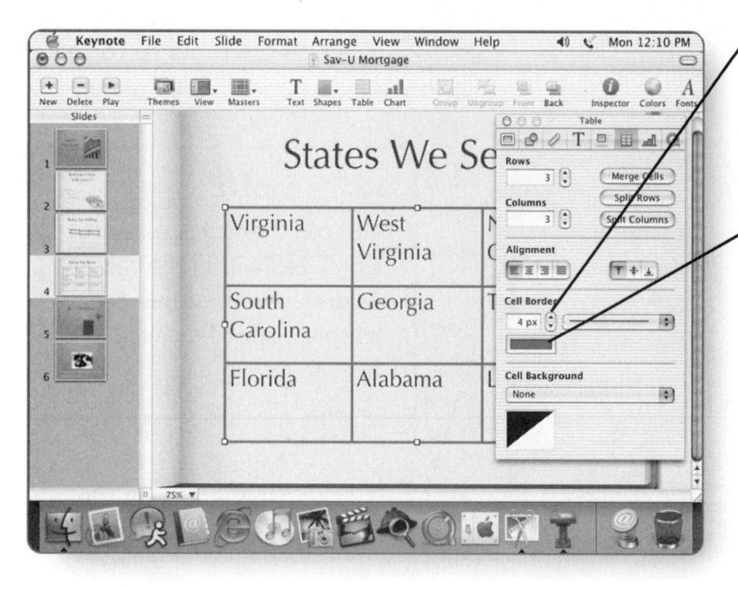

6. Click on a **Cell Border spinner button** as needed. The table borders will display in the specified size (width).

7. Use the **Color box** to choose a color. (For more about choosing a color, see the steps in "Formatting Text" or refer to the later section, "Working with Colors.") The color will be applied to the table borders.

NOTE

To remove table borders, click on the pop-up menu to the right of the Cell Border spinner buttons, and then click on None.

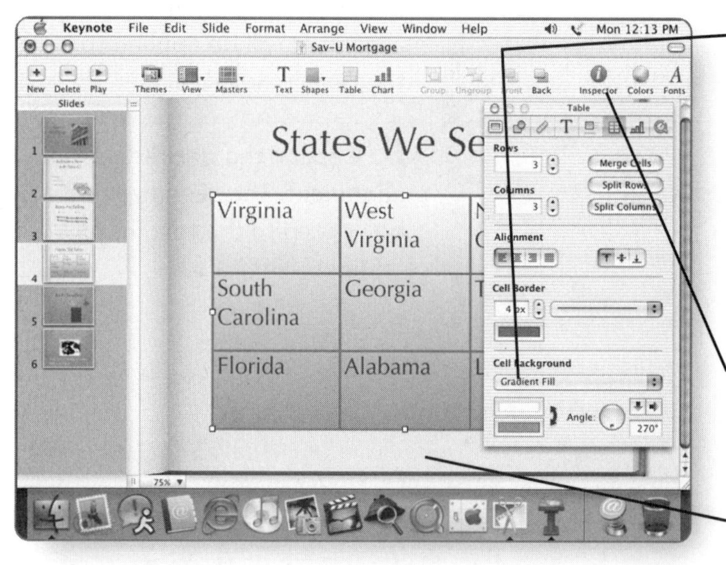

8. Use the **Cell Background pop-up menu** to choose a background for the table cell(s). (See "Working with Fills" later in the chapter to learn more about specifying an object fill.) The specified background will appear in the table.

9. Click on **Inspector** on the toolbar. The Inspector window will close.

10. Click outside the table. The table will be deselected.

> **NOTE**
>
> You can combine cells in a table by selecting those cells and then clicking on Merge Cells in the Table Inspector. You also can split the selected row or column into multiple rows or columns by clicking on the Split Rows or Split Columns buttons in the Table Inspector.

Formatting a Chart

You can make a variety of changes to a chart's formatting by using the Chart Inspector. You can change the chart type, hide and display the chart legend, and work with formatting for other chart elements. The options in the Chart Inspector will vary slightly depending on the type of chart that you're formatting. For example, when you're formatting a pie chart, many of the options on the Axis tab of the Chart Inspector will be disabled.

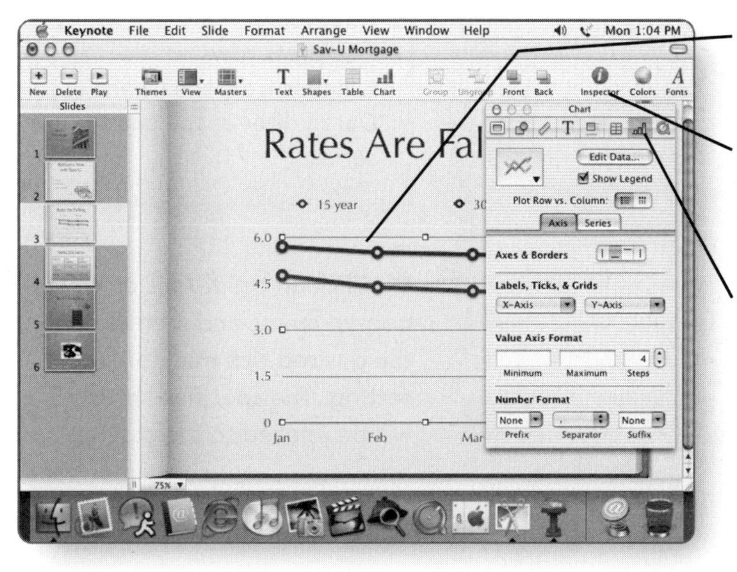

1. **Click** on the **chart to format.** Selection handles will appear.
2. **Click** on **Inspector** on the toolbar. The Inspector window will open.
3. **Click** on **Chart Inspector.** The Chart Inspector settings will appear.

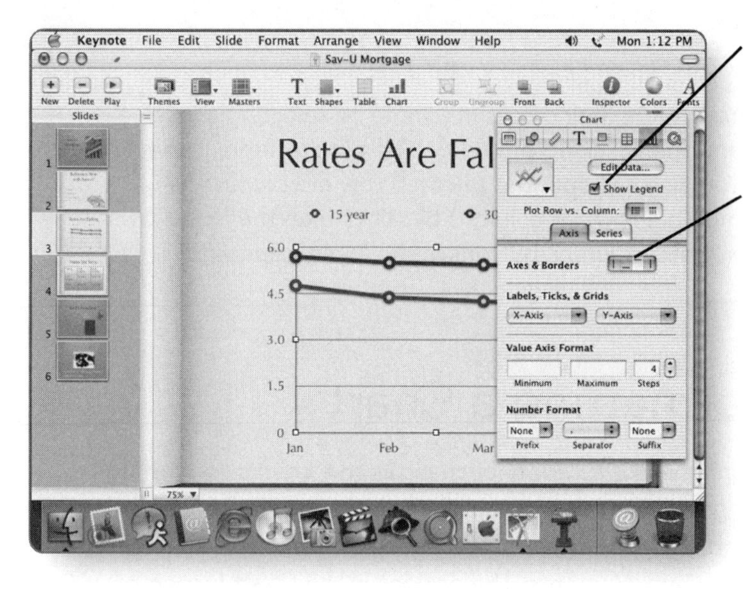

4. **Click** on **Show Legend**. The legend display will toggle on (checked) or off (unchecked).

5. **Click** on **Axes & Borders buttons** as desired. When a button is active (blue), the corresponding border will appear around the chart area.

> **NOTE**
>
> Click on the Edit Data button in the Chart Inspector if you need to make changes to the charted data in the Chart Data Editor window. Click on the desired Plot Row vs. Column button when you need to change whether Keynote interprets rows or columns from the Chart Data Editor as the chart series.

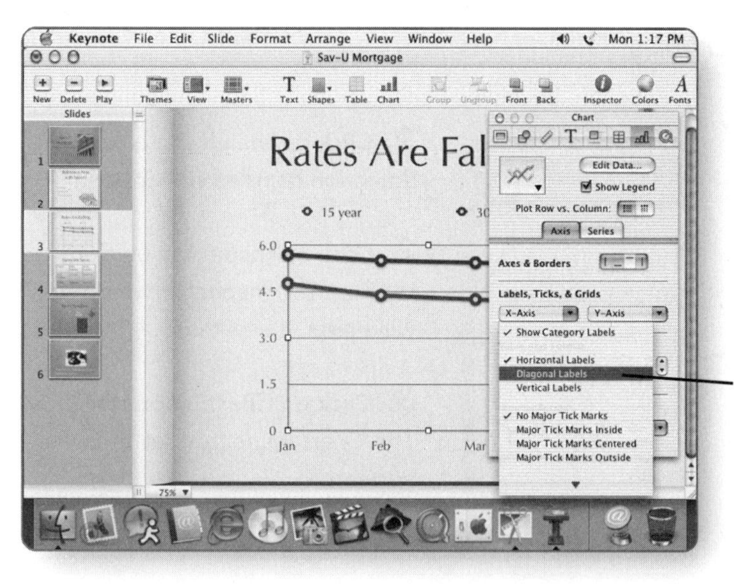

6. **Click** on the **X-Axis** or **Y-Axis** pop-up menu, and then **click** on the **desired tick mark** or **label setting**. The specified setting will be applied to the chart.

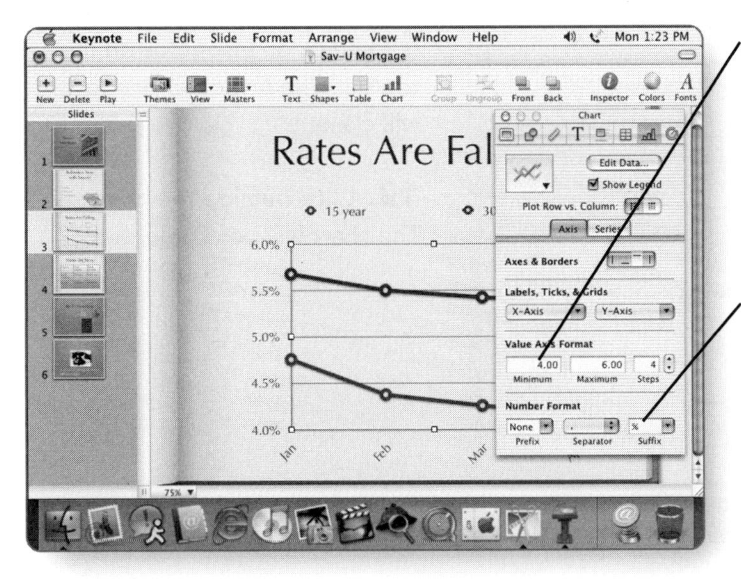

7. Enter Minimum and Maximum value axis values, and **specify** the desired **number of steps** for the value axis. The value axis will adjust as specified.

8. Choose Number Format settings as needed. The number format on the value axis will adjust as specified.

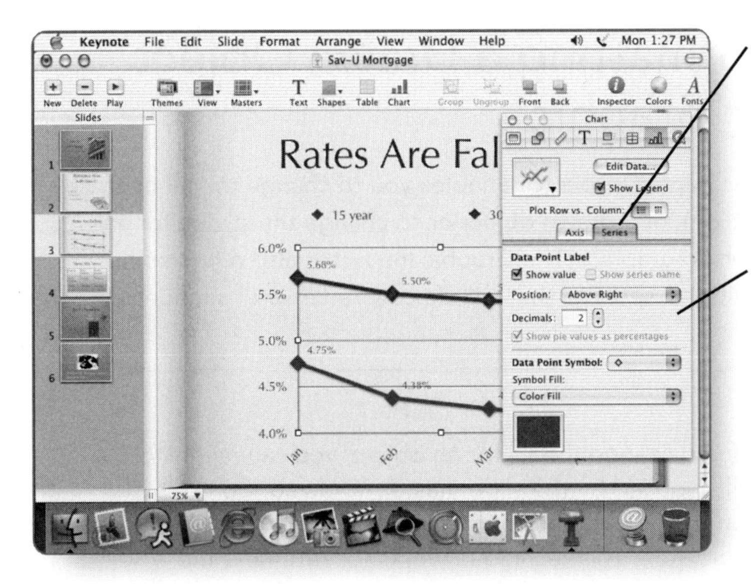

9. Click on the **Series tab**. The settings for formatting data series will appear. These settings will vary greatly depending on the chart type.

10. Choose Series formatting settings as desired. The appearance of the elements used to chart the series will adjust as specified.

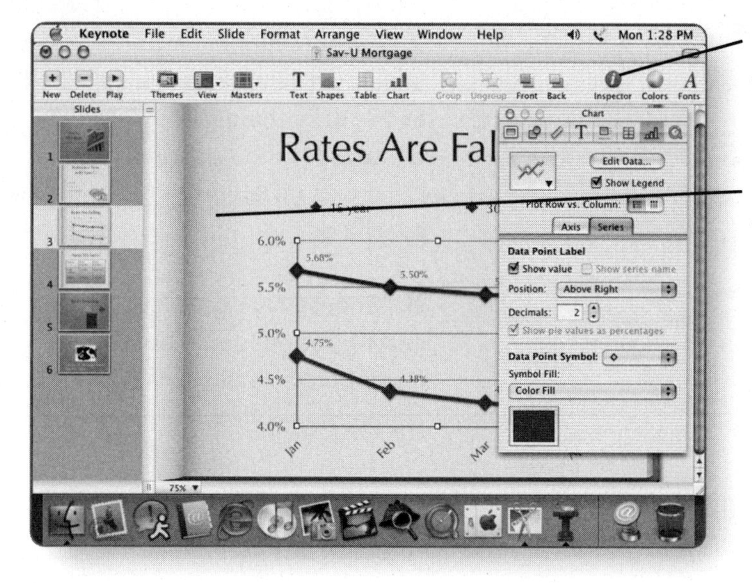

11. **Click** on **Inspector** on the toolbar. The Inspector window will close.

12. **Click outside** the **chart.** The chart will be deselected.

Formatting a Drawn Object or Graphic

The Graphic Inspector enables you to change the fill or *stroke* (outline) for a drawn object or to change the stroke for an inserted graphic. (The Graphic Inspector also offers some additional settings that will be covered in later sections.)

> **TIP**
>
> If you change the fill for an object, you can revert to the fill supplied by the slide master. To do so, Control+click on the object, and then click on Reapply Master to Selection. This technique works for returning the formatting of any slide element to the defaults supplied by the chart master.

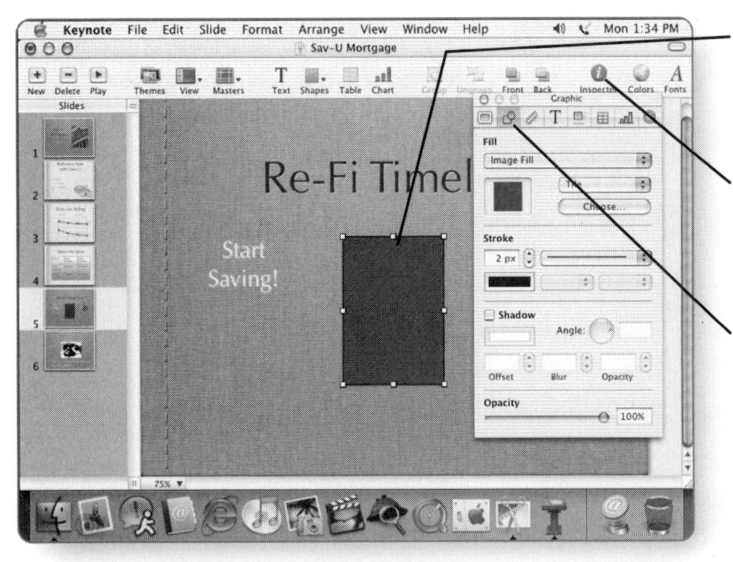

1. Click on the **object to format**. Selection handles will appear.

2. Click on **Inspector** on the toolbar. The Inspector window will open.

3. Click on **Graphic Inspector**. The Graphic Inspector settings will appear.

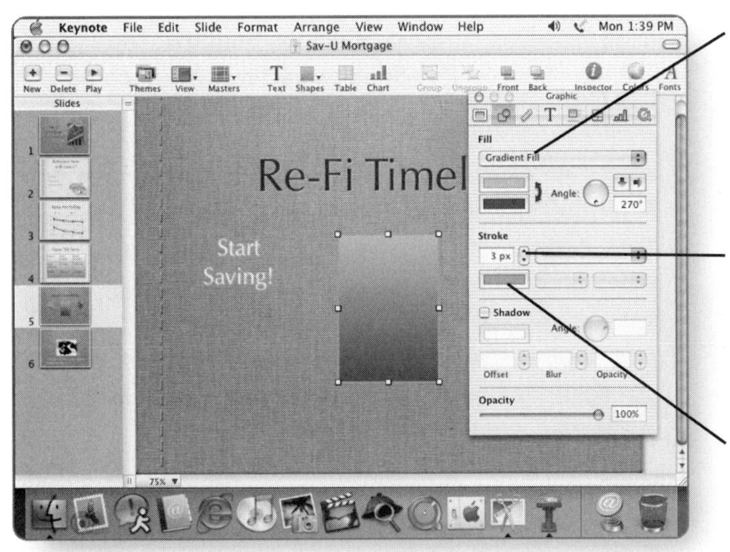

4. **Choose new Fill settings** as desired. (See the later section called "Working with Fills" to learn more about applying fills.) The new fill will appear in the object.

5. Click on a **Stroke spinner button** as needed. The object border will display in the specified size (width).

6. Use the **Color box** to choose a color. (For more information about choosing a color, see the steps in "Formatting Text" or refer to the later section, "Working with Colors.") The color will be applied to the table borders.

7. Click on the **pop-up menu** to the right of the Stroke spinner buttons, and then **click** on the **desired border style**. The border style will be applied to the object.

8. Click on **Shadow**. The Shadow settings will become active.

> **TIP**
>
> You can use the Shadow settings in the Graphic Inspector to apply a graphic to other types of slide elements, such as text or a table.

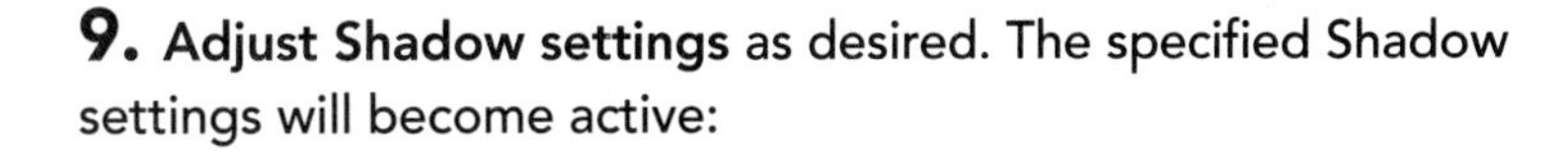

9. Adjust Shadow settings as desired. The specified Shadow settings will become active:

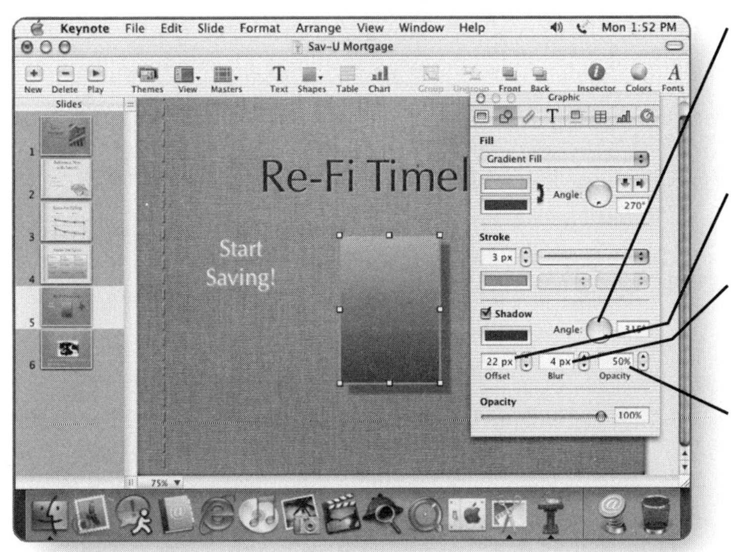

- **Angle.** Controls the shadow direction, relative to the position of the selected object.
- **Offset.** Controls the width of the shadow.
- **Blur.** Specifies how much of the shadow's width to blur or blend.
- **Opacity.** Sets the shadow transparency.

> **TIP**
>
> You also can use the Color box in the Shadow area to change the shadow's color.

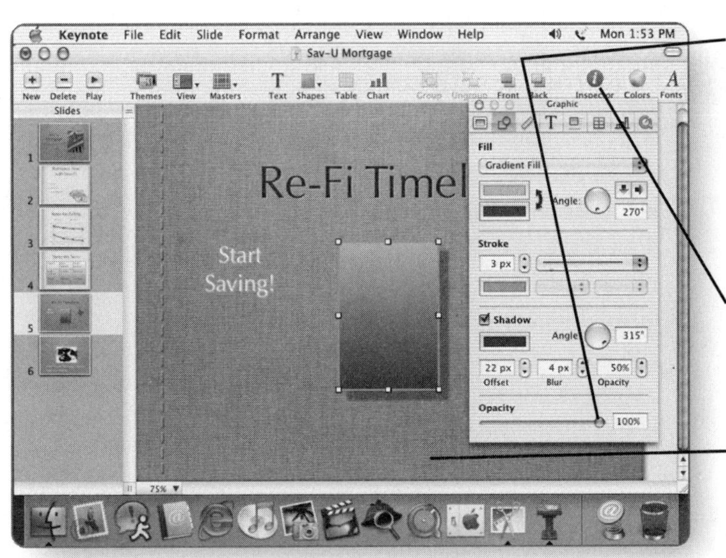

10. Choose an **Opacity setting**. (See "Working with Opacity" later in the chapter to learn more about specifying opacity.) The opacity will be applied to the object.

11. Click on **Inspector** on the toolbar. The Inspector window will close.

12. Click outside the graphic. The object will be deselected.

Working with Positioning

As you build the slides for your presentation, you will often decide that you can improve on a choice you've made previously. In particular, if you've included a lot of graphics and drawn objects to add character to your slides, you will likely need to move, resize, and layer them. This section helps you tackle these key tasks, and some others.

Moving Objects

While you can move an object by dragging it around, this section reveals some additional techniques you can use to position objects with greater precision.

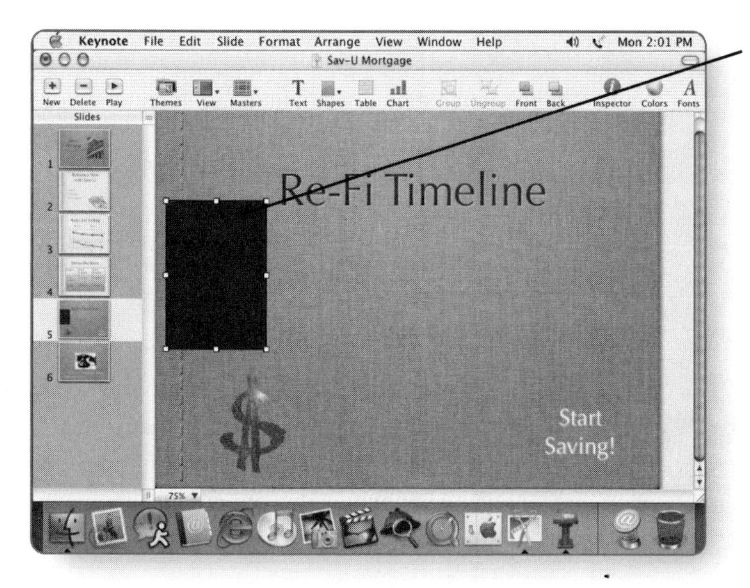

1. **Click** on the **object to move.** Selection handles will appear.

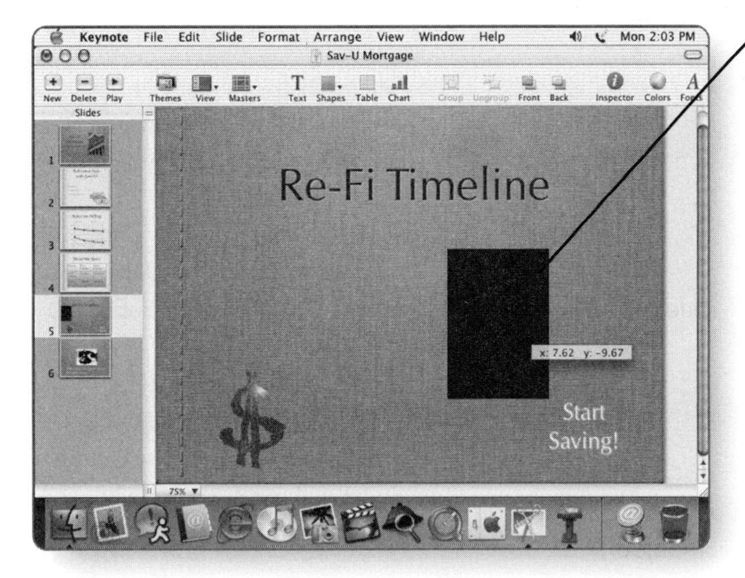

2. **Drag** the **object** to the desired location. When you release the mouse button, the object will stay in that position.

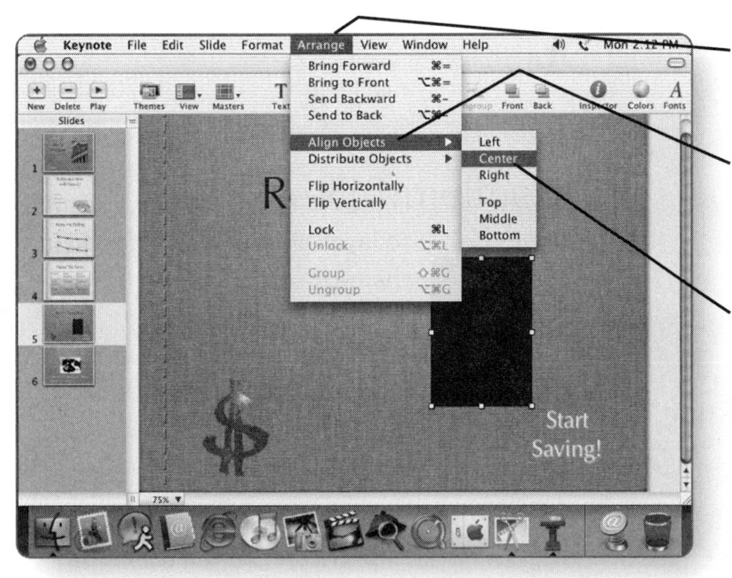

3. **Click** on **Arrange**. The Arrange menu will appear.

4. **Point** to **Align Objects**. The Align Objects submenu will appear.

5. **Click** on the **desired alignment choice**. The selected object will move to the specified position on the slide.

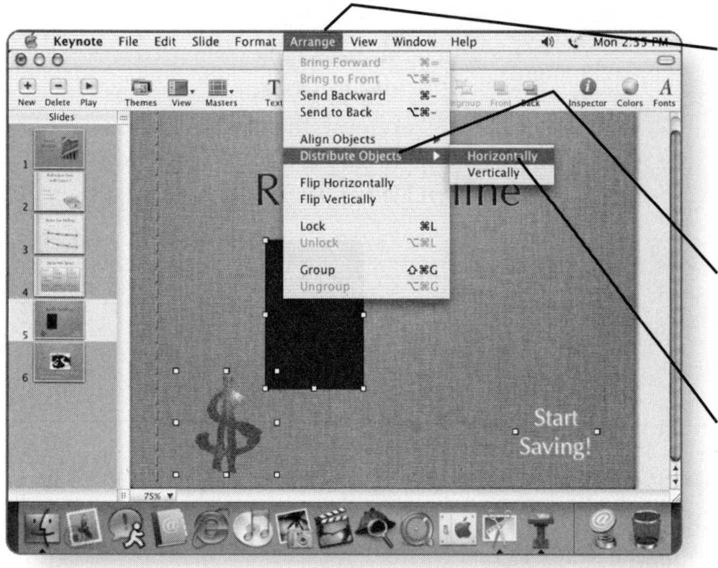

6. If you have multiple objects selected and you want to align them relative to one another, **click** on **Arrange**. The Arrange menu will appear.

7. Point to **Distribute Objects.** The Distribute Objects submenu will appear.

8. Click on the **desired alignment choice.** The selected objects will move to equally spaced positions.

Resizing Objects

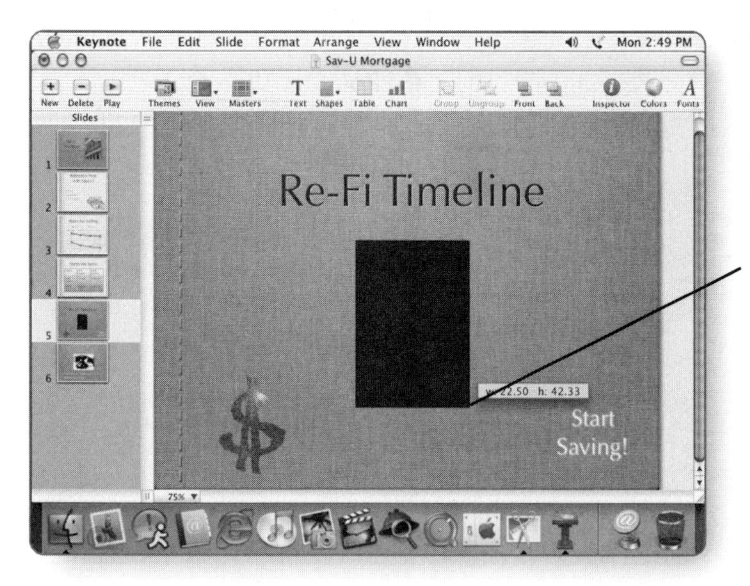

You can resize an object as needed on a slide. Resizing comes in handy when you want to layer objects, as described in the next section.

- To resize any object, click on it, and then drag a selection handle until the object reaches the desired size.
- Press and hold Option+Shift while dragging a handle to resize the object proportionally.

Layering Objects

You can layer individual objects to create a more complex object for a slide. By default, when you drag an object over another object, it appears "in front of" the other object. You can control the order in which the layered objects appear in order to achieve the effect you want, as follows.

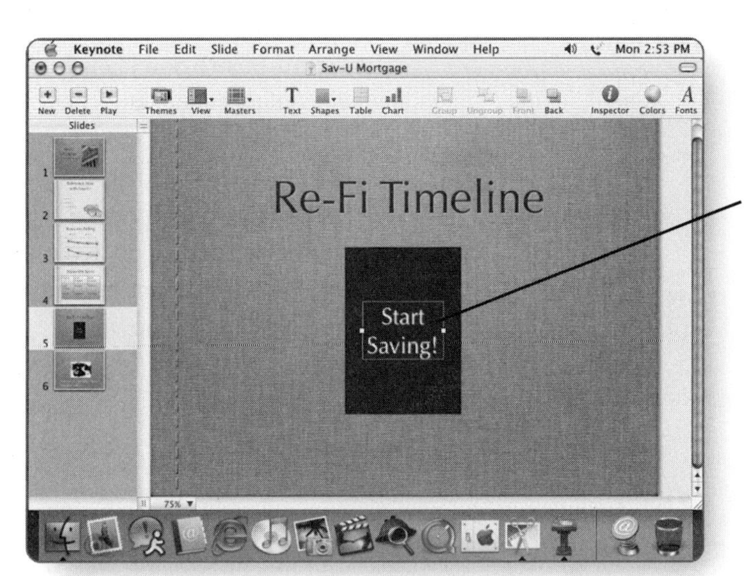

1. **Click** on an **object,** and then **drag** it **over another object**. Repeat this process as needed. The objects will appear *stacked* or layered on one another. By default, text will come to the front layer, or the top of the stack.

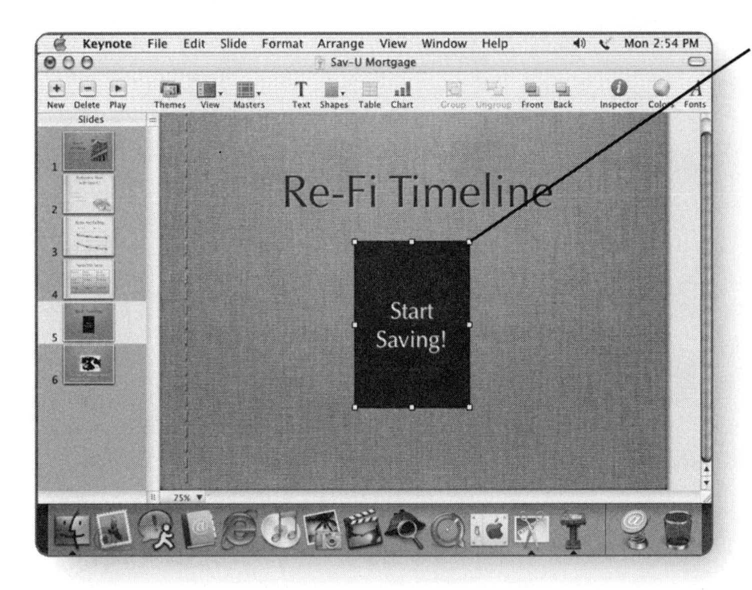

2. When you need to change the layering order, **select** the **object to move**. Selection handles will appear.

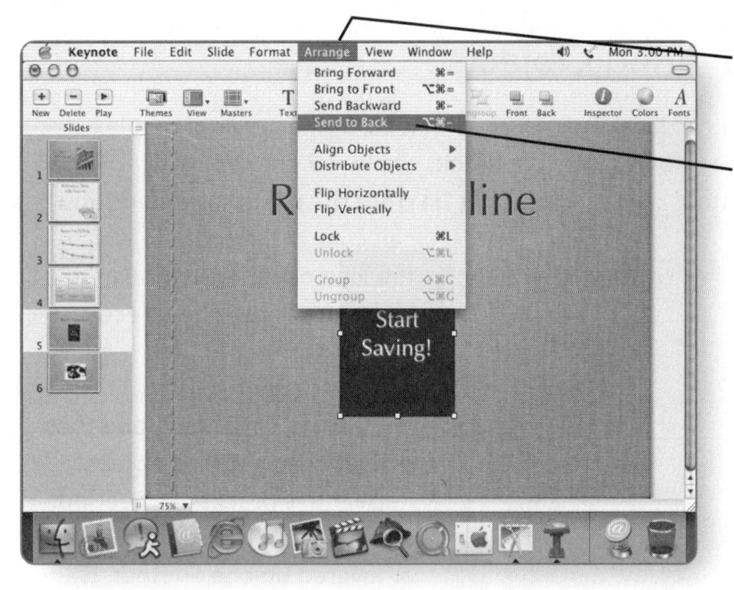

3. Click on **Arrange**. The Arrange menu will appear.

4. Click on the **desired layering choice**. Bring Forward and Send Backward will move the selected object one layer in the specified direction. Bring to Front and Send to Back will move the object to the top (front) or bottom (back) of the pile of objects. Send to Back does not send the object behind the slide background, however.

These layered objects now appear like a single object on the slide.

Grouping and Ungrouping Objects

When you group selected objects, Keynote then treats the group as a single object that you can move and resize. Using a group saves you the trouble of having to move and resize the objects individually. A group can include any type of object on a slide.

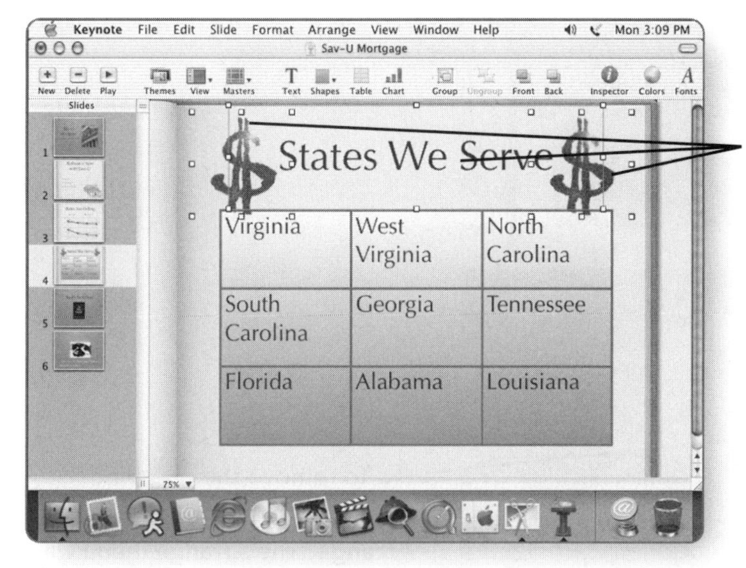

1. **Select** the **objects to group** by using Shift+click. Selection handles will appear around the objects.

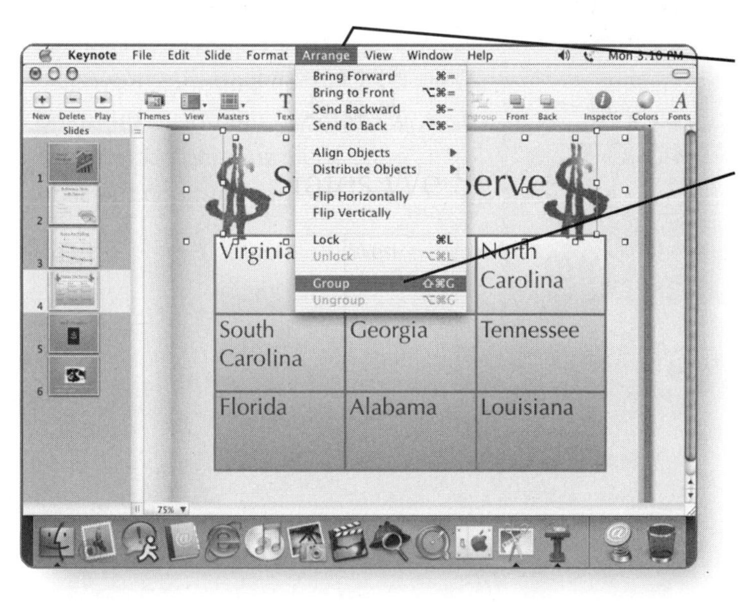

2. **Click** on **Arrange**. The Arrange menu will appear.

3. **Click** on **Group**.

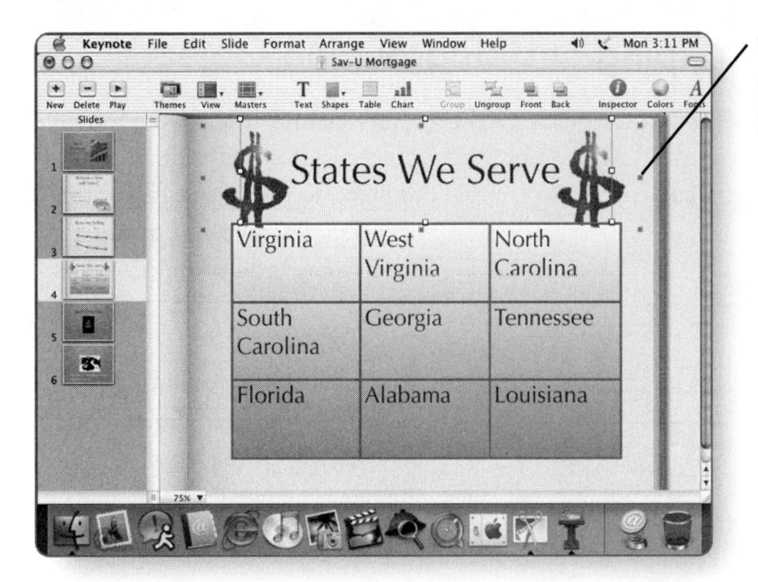

Grayed selection handles will show you that the objects have been grouped.

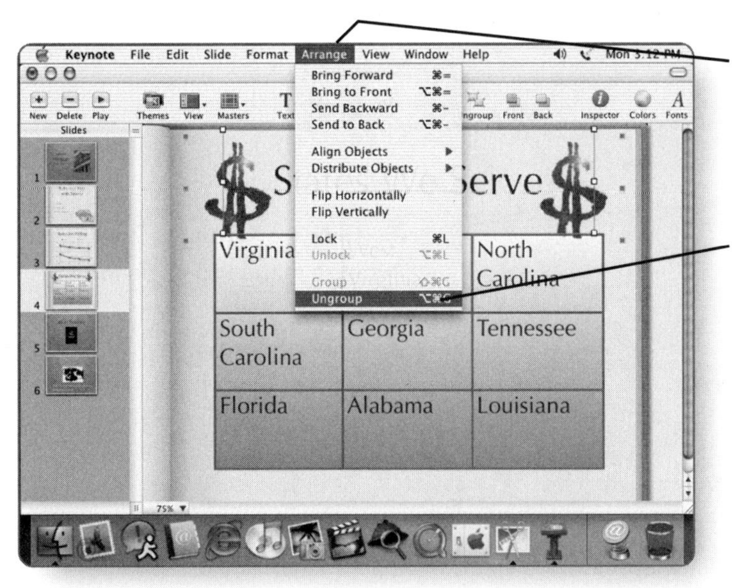

4. To remove the grouping from a selected group, **click** on **Arrange**. The Arrange menu will appear.

5. **Click** on **Ungroup**. Keynote will remove the object grouping, once again treating each object as a separate entity on the slide.

Locking and Unlocking Objects

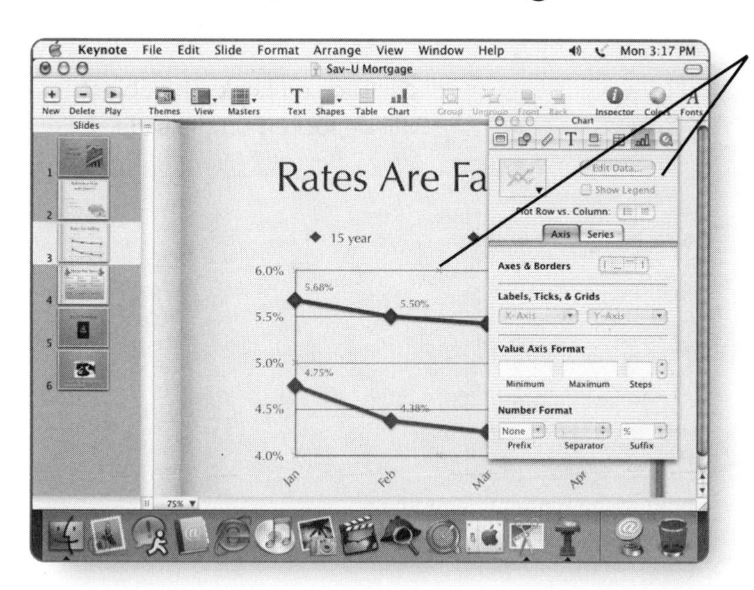

Locking an object freezes its position on the slide. Locking also prevents you from making formatting changes to a slide. As shown here, x handles appear around a locked object, and the Inspector settings are dimmed because the object cannot be formatted.

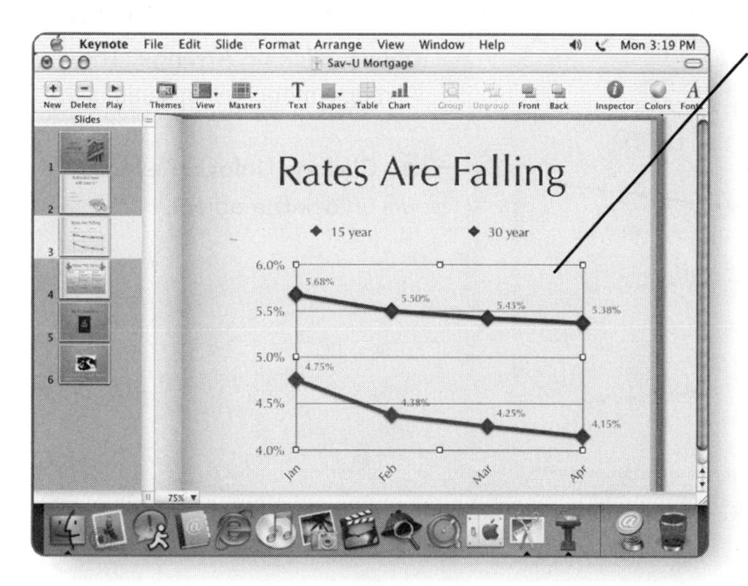

1. Click on the **object to lock**. Selection handles will appear around the object.

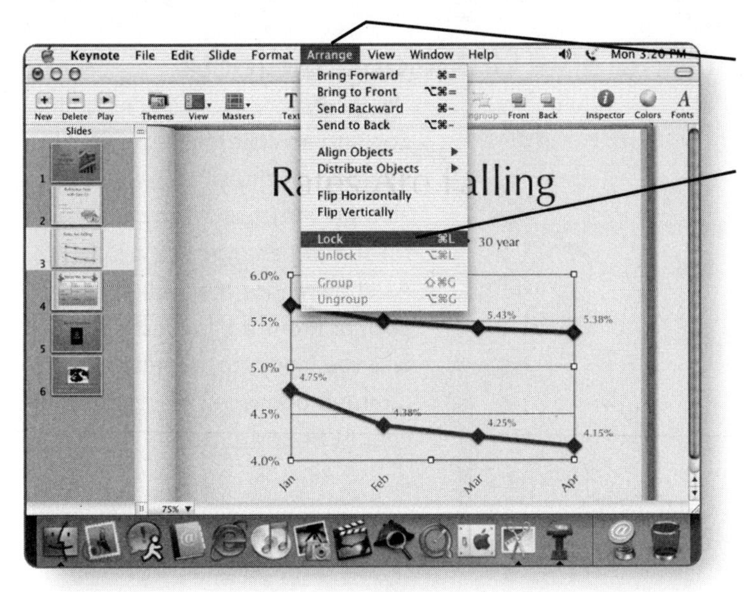

2. Click on **Arrange**. The Arrange menu will appear.

3. Click on **Lock**. The object will be locked on the slide.

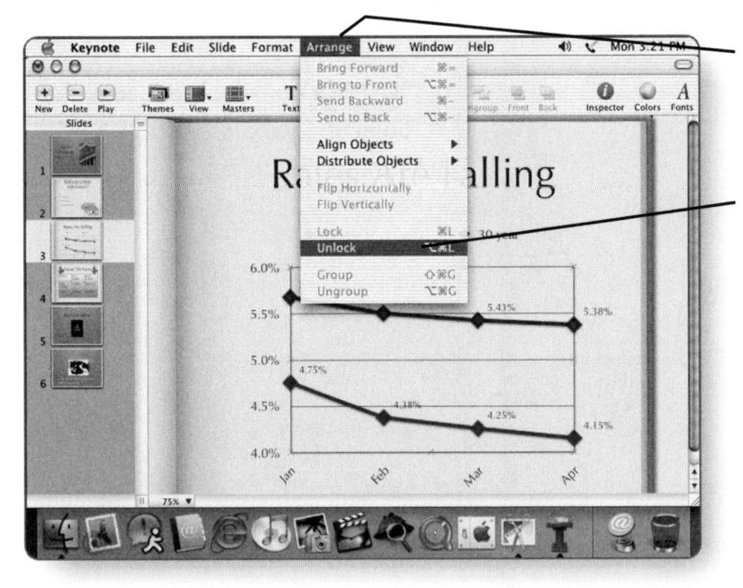

4. To unlock a selected locked object, **click** on **Arrange**. The Arrange menu will appear.

5. Click on **Unlock**. Keynote will unlock the object.

Flipping and Rotating Objects

You can flip any object horizontally or vertically, or you can use a special technique to rotate the object to any angle you desire. In this way, you can control an object's precise appearance and allow for better positioning on a slide.

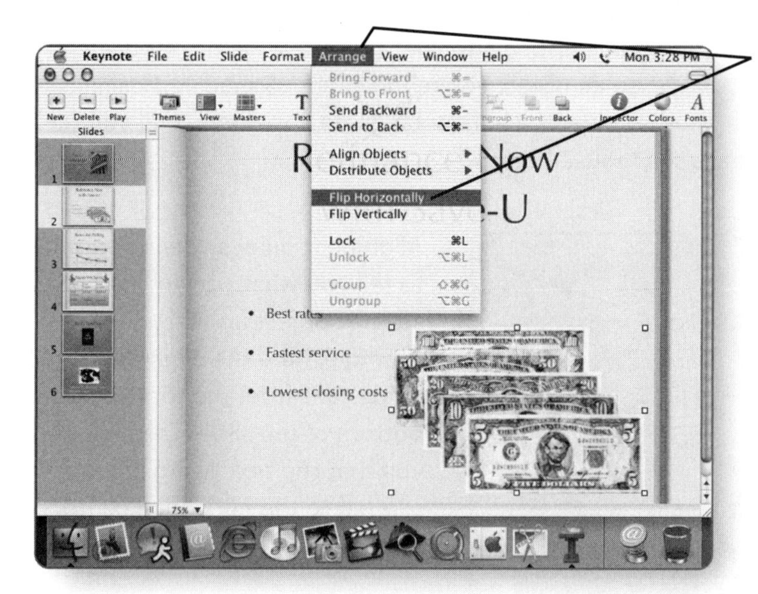

To flip a selected object, click on Arrange. Then click on either Flip Horizontally or Flip Vertically.

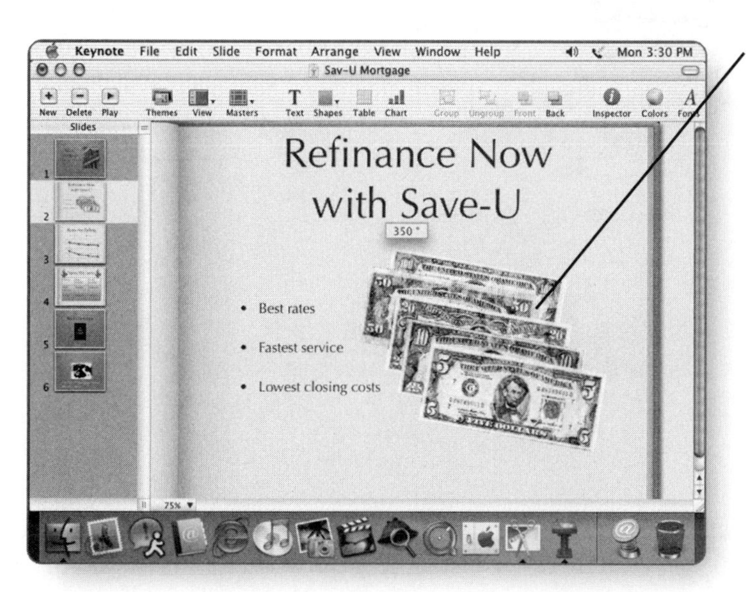

To rotate a selected object, press and hold the ⌘ key while dragging a corner handle for the object. When you release the mouse button, the object will stay in the rotated position.

Using Alignment Guides

When moving objects, you may have noticed that yellow guidelines sometimes appear onscreen. These yellow guidelines are called *alignment guides*, and they help you align objects vertically or horizontally. When an object you're moving is aligned horizontally with another object, a vertical alignment guide appears to cue you to release the mouse button. When an object you're moving is aligned vertically with another object, a horizontal guide appears to cue you to release the mouse button.

Alignment guides vary in length to tell you what you've lined a specific object up with. For example, here the alignment guide runs from the top to the bottom of the slide. This tells you that the text being moved is aligned to the horizontal center of the slide.

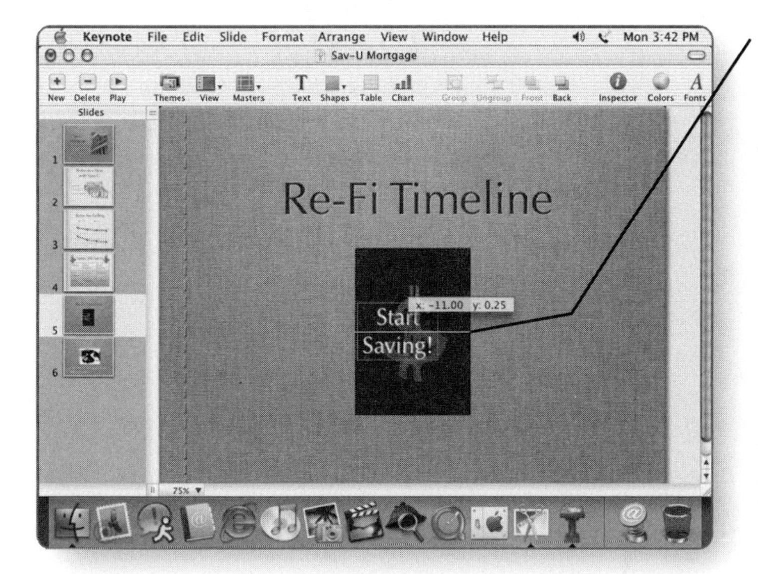

In this case, the alignment guide runs from the left to the right side of the black rectangle. This tells you that the text being moved is aligned to the vertical center of the black rectangle.

If needed, you can add you own alignment guides. The alignment guides you create will appear onscreen while you work, but they will not appear if you play or print the slideshow.

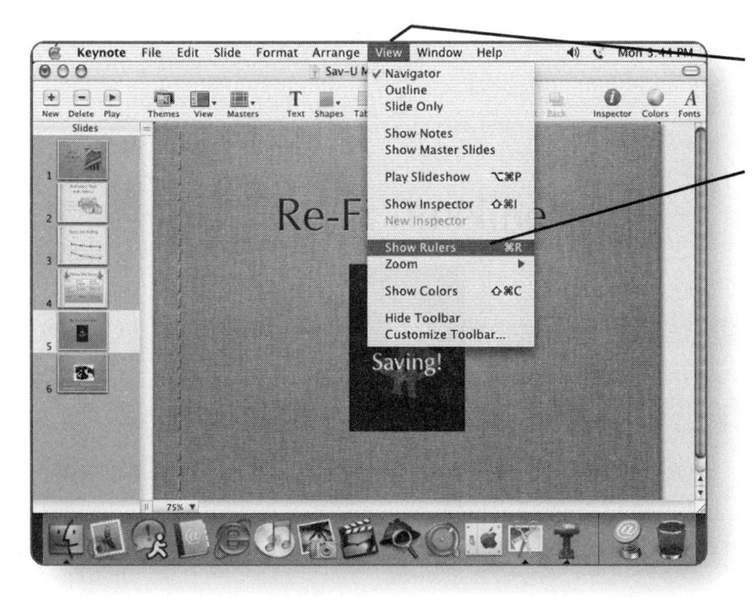

1. **Click** on **View**. The View menu will appear.

2. **Click** on **Show Rulers.** The vertical and horizontal rulers will appear at the left side and top of the slide canvas.

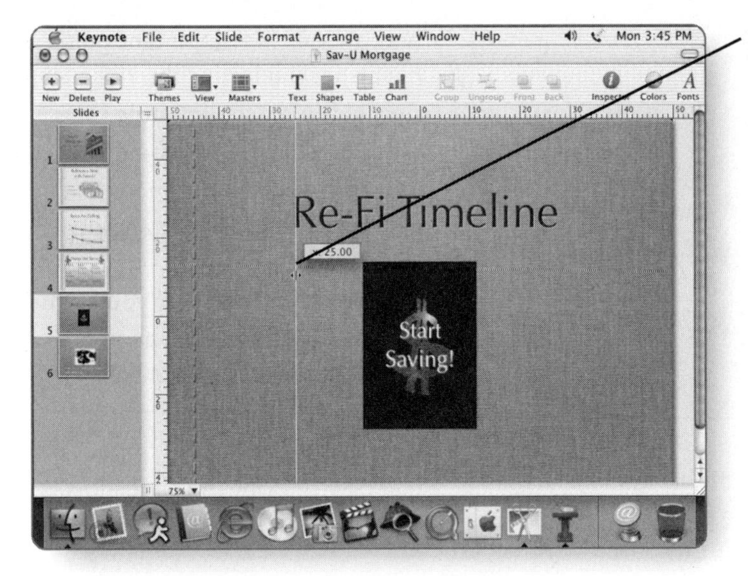

3. Drag from a **ruler**. When you release the mouse button, an alignment guide will appear. You can then drag objects to align them to the alignment guide.

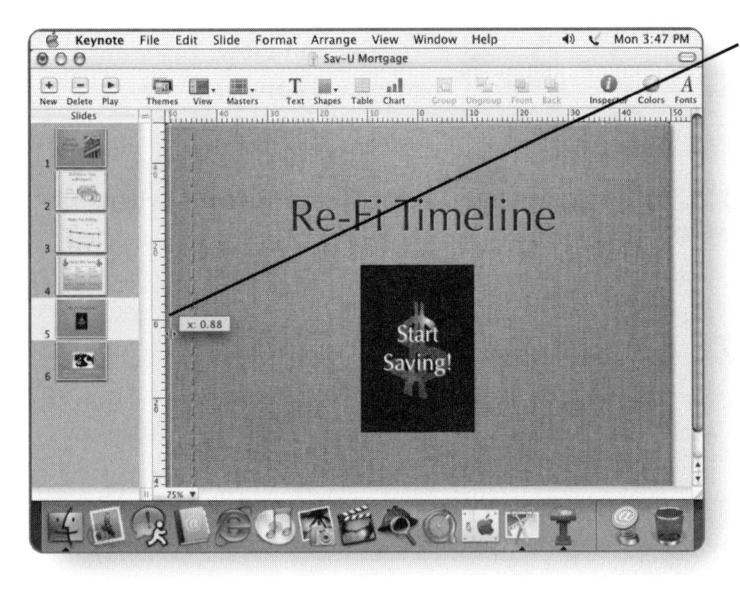

4. Drag an **alignment guide** back to a ruler. When you release the mouse button, the alignment guide will disappear.

Using the Metrics Inspector

Keynote offers one last way to work with the size, positioning, and rotation of any object: the Metrics Inspector.

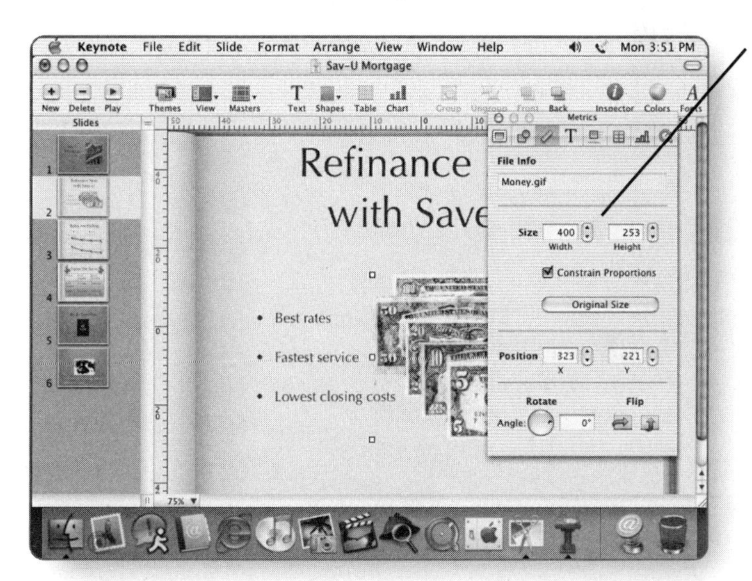

When you click on Inspector on the toolbar and then click on Metrics Inspector, the Metrics Inspector will appear. The Metrics Inspector will tell you the precise Size, Position, and Rotate settings for any selected object. You can change these settings as desired, and then click on Inspector on the toolbar to close the Metrics Inspector.

Working with Fills

If you've tried all the earlier techniques in this chapter, you've seen that several different Inspectors give you the option of applying a new fill to a selected object, such as a table or a drawn object. You actually can apply three different types of fills: a color fill, gradient fill, or image fill. The following steps present an example of using the Graphics Inspector to apply each of these fill types, in turn, to a selected object.

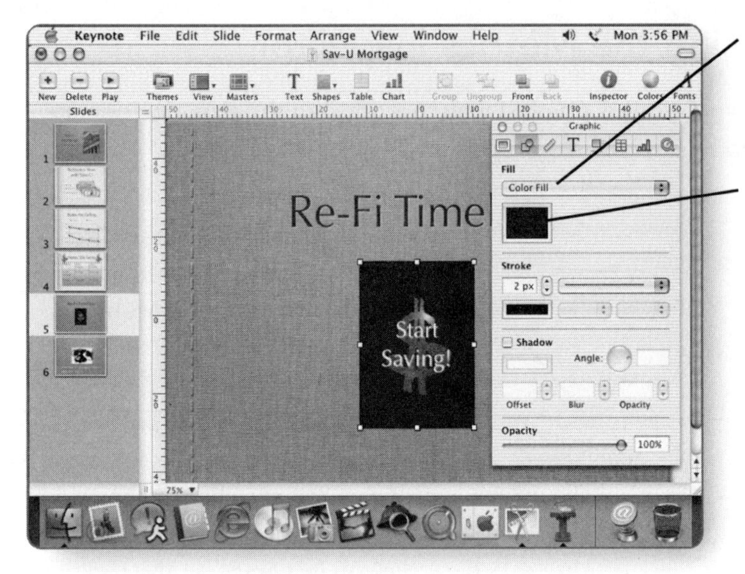

1. Choose Color Fill from the Fill pop-up menu. The Color box will appear.

2. Click on the **Color box**. The Colors window will open.

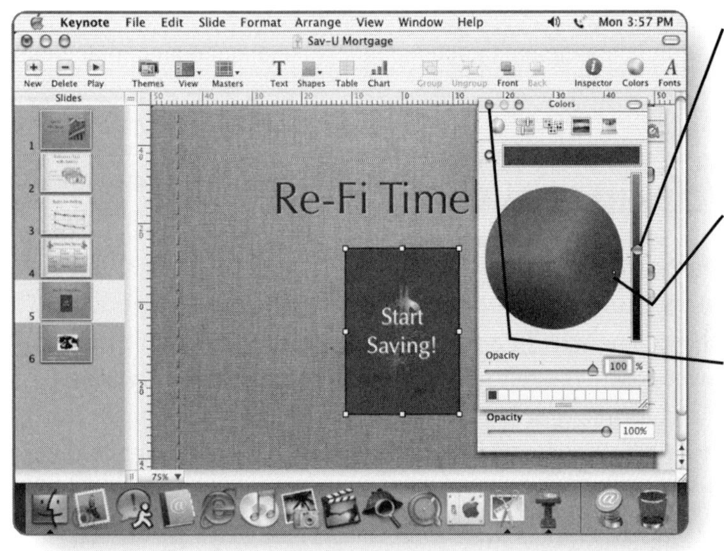

3. Drag the **slider up** on the color bar at the right. More colors will appear in the color wheel.

4. Click on the **desired color** in the color wheel. The color will be applied to the text.

5. Click on the **Colors window close button**.

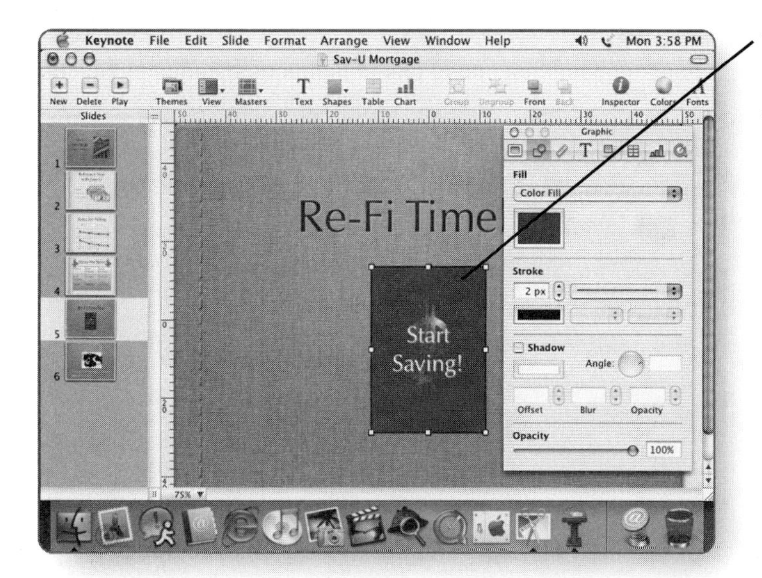

The Colors window will close, and the new fill will appear in the object.

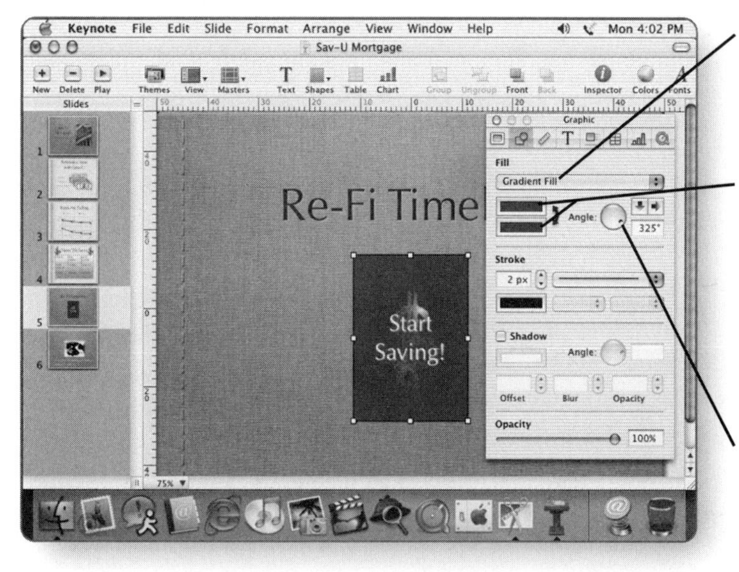

6. **Choose Gradient Fill** from the Fill pop-up menu. The gradient choices will appear.

7. **Click** on each **Color box** and **choose** a **gradient color** from the Colors window. The gradient will use the specified colors, and you can close the Colors window.

8. **Drag** the **Angle button dot**. The gradient will rotate to the specified angle.

> **TIP**
>
> You also can use one of the arrow buttons to specify a top-down or left-right blend of the gradient colors. Or type a precise measurement in the text box beside the angle button.

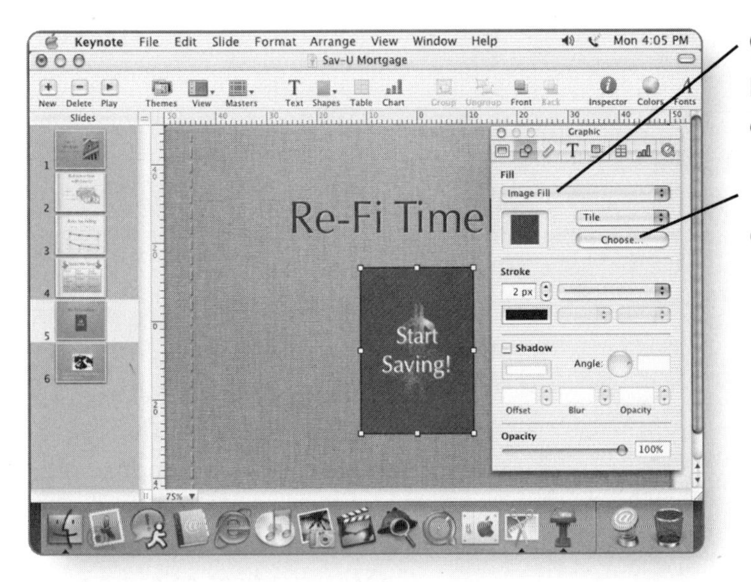

9. **Choose Image Fill** from the Fill pop-up menu. The Image Fill choices will appear.

10. **Click** on **Choose**. The Open dialog box will appear.

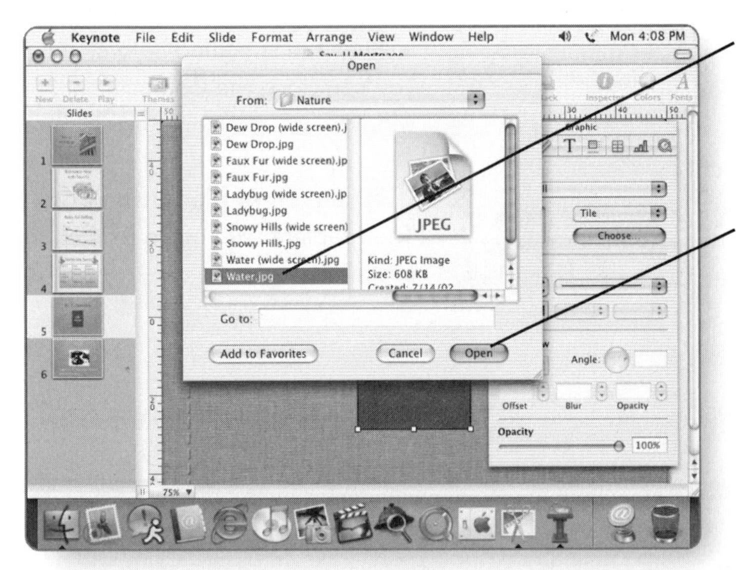

11. **Navigate to** and **click** on the **image to use for the fill**. A preview icon will appear at the right side of the dialog box.

12. **Click** on **Open**. The image will be applied as the object fill.

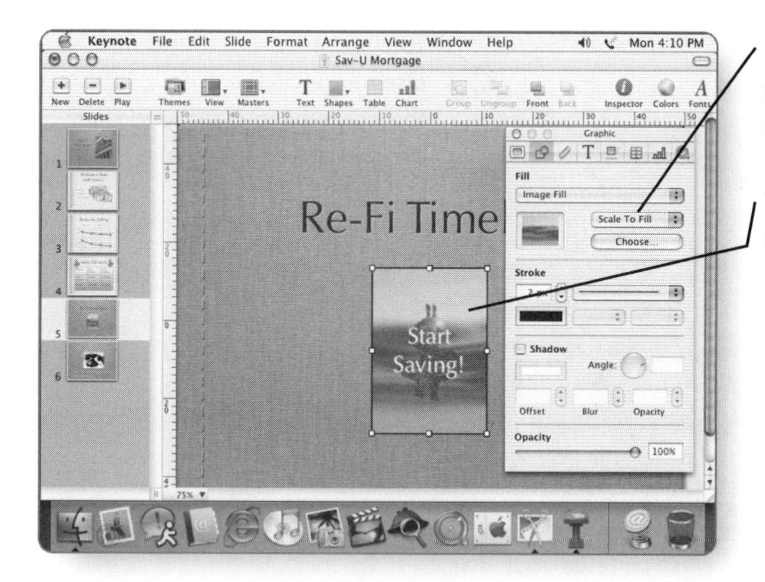

13. Choose the **desired image size** from the pop-up menu above the Choose button.

The Image Fill image will be sized according to your choice.

Working with Colors

As well, several Inspectors present one or more Color boxes that you can click on to open the Colors window. Alternately, you can click on Colors on the toolbar to open the Colors window. While there's not room in this book to give you an exhaustive outline of all the ways you can use the Colors window to choose another color, here are a few pointers to help you work more effectively with the Colors window.

Click on one of the buttons on the Colors window toolbar to choose another color selection method. For example, if you click on the Crayons button at the far right, you can click on one of the crayons that appear to choose a color.

To choose a color found elsewhere on the slide, click on the magnifying glass, and then click on the desired color.

To specify a favorite color to appear at the bottom of the Colors window (no matter which selection method you choose), first choose the color so that it appears in the bar beside the magnifying glass near the top of the Colors window. Then drag the color from that bar to one of the spaces for favorites at the bottom. (Drag a color off one of the favorite spaces if you no longer want to keep it as a favorite.)

Working with Opacity

Finally, you can use the Graphic Inspector to change the opacity setting for selected text, graphics, and drawing objects.

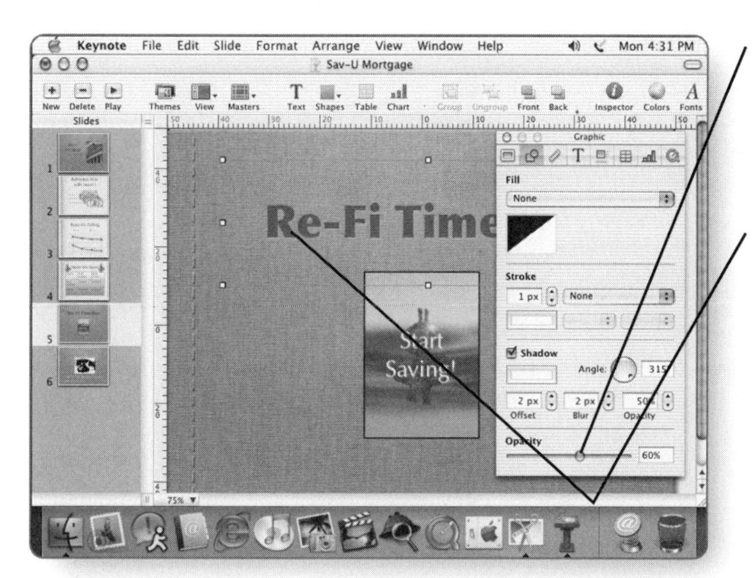

Drag the Opacity slider at the bottom of the Graphic Inspector or enter an opacity setting in the accompanying text box.

The selected object will immediately use the opacity (transparency) setting you specify.

> **CAUTION**
>
> If you plan to export your slideshow file to another format as described in Chapter 12, "Importing and Exporting Presentation Information," use objects with transparency sparingly or not at all because transparency settings don't always export correctly

7

Working with Slide Settings and Design

Although the themes and slide masters available in Keynote accommodate a wide range of styles and information, you are not limited to the designs provided by Keynote or the ones you select initially. You can work with slide backgrounds and make other adjustments to ensure that a slide or your slideshow looks just as you want it to. In this chapter, you will learn how to:

- Reapply a master or apply another master.
- Apply another fill to the slide background.
- Create a bulleted or numbered list on a slide.
- Apply another slideshow theme.
- Obtain other themes online.

Reapplying the Slide Master

You learned in the last chapter how to use the Inspector and other tools to apply various types of formatting to the objects on your slides. If you decide later to remove that formatting from the objects on a slide, it would be time-consuming (and perhaps impossible) to remember all the original formatting settings for all the slide objects. In such a case, you can instead reapply the master to the slide to return to the original formatting settings supplied by the master.

> **TIP**
>
> If a little plus icon appears at the bottom of a text placeholder, it means that you've added more text than can fit in the placeholder according to the slide master. Resize the placeholder to accommodate the text rather than reapply the master.

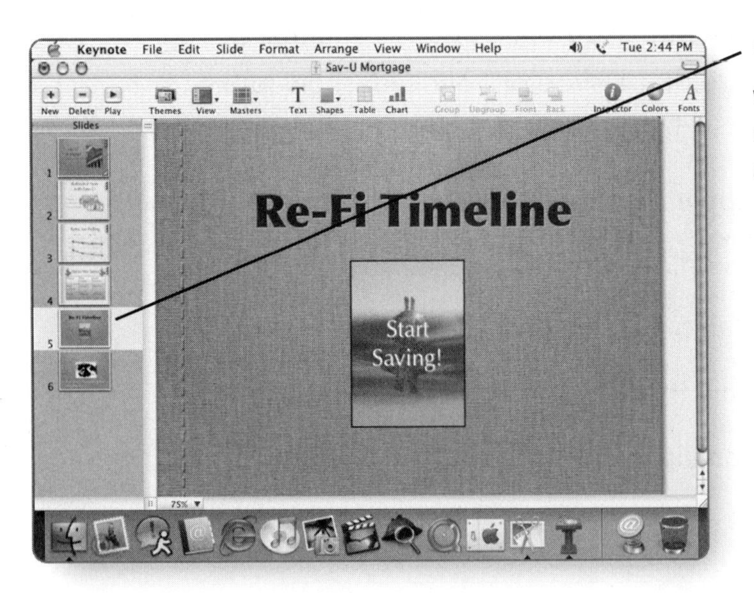

1. **Go to** or **select the slide** to which you want to reapply the master. The slide contents will appear in the slide canvas.

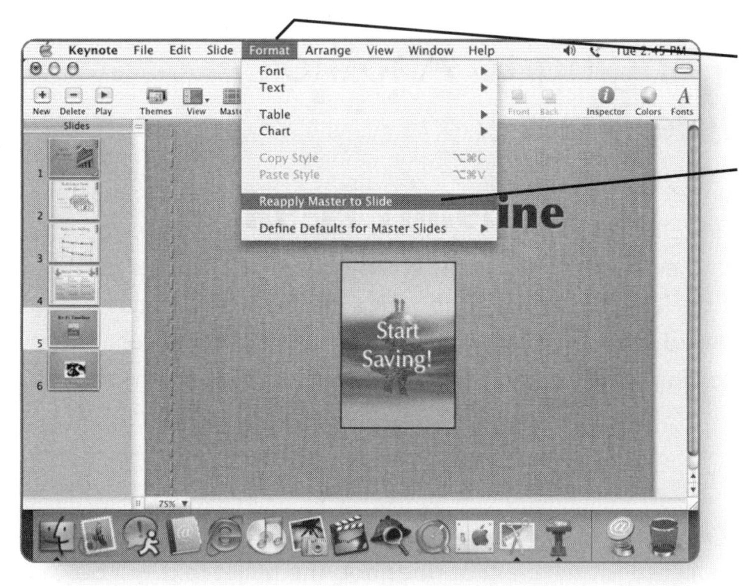

2. **Click** on **Format**. The Format menu will appear.

3. **Click** on **Reapply Master to Slide**. Keynote will reapply the formatting from the slide master.

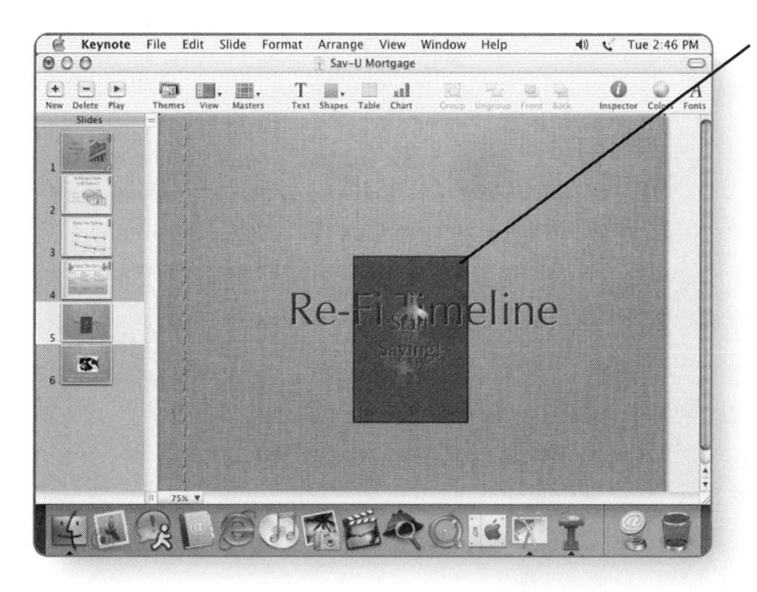

As you can see in this example, Keynote changed the font and placement for the title text. It also changed the fill for a rectangle on the slide. From here, you could adjust the slide elements as needed, undo the change, or try applying a different master to the slide.

Changing to Another Slide Master

You may also decide that you're not satisfied with the master that you've applied to a particular slide. For example, you may create a slide with a graphic list using the Title-Center master, but decide later to jazz it up with a master that includes a bulleted list and a placeholder for a picture. You can use the following steps to apply a new master to a slide at any time.

> **CAUTION**
>
> Of course, if you change from a master that includes a bulleted list to one that does not, the bullet text will be hidden. The bullet text remains in the presentation file, however, until you apply a master with a bulleted list to the slide.

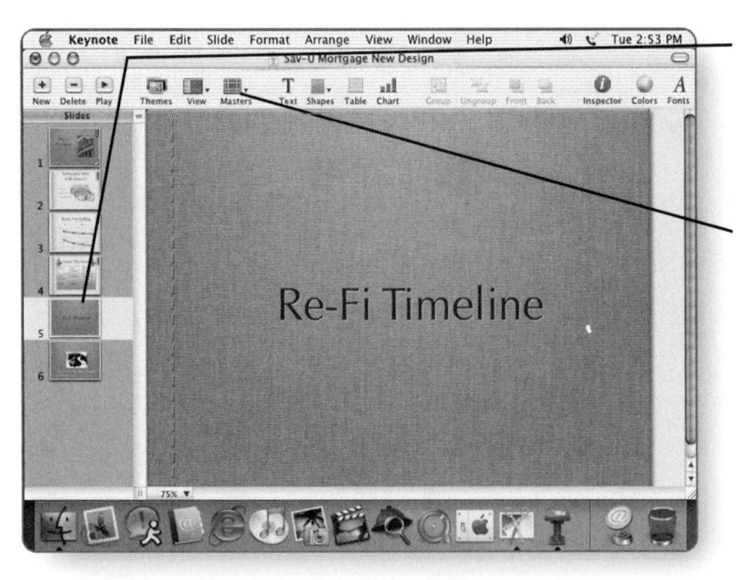

1. **Go to** or **select the slide** to which you want to apply another master. The slide contents will appear in the slide canvas.

2. **Click** on **Masters** on the toolbar. The available masters will appear.

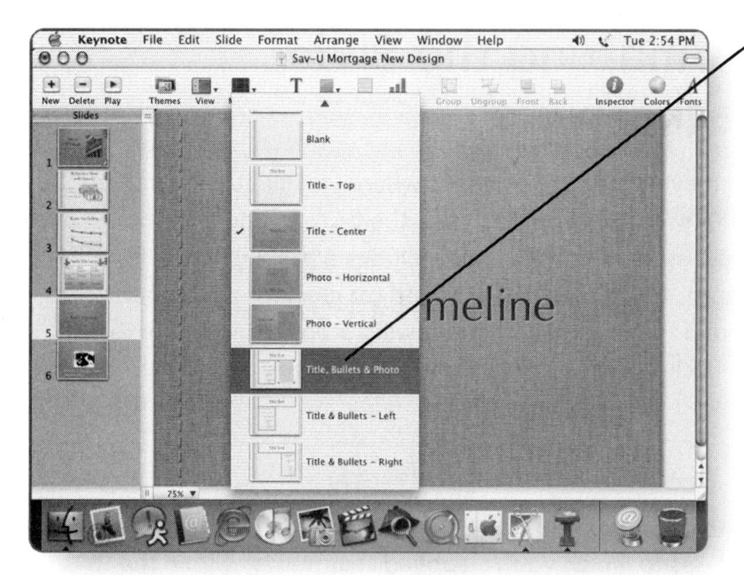

3. Click on the **master to apply**. Keynote will apply the new slide master immediately.

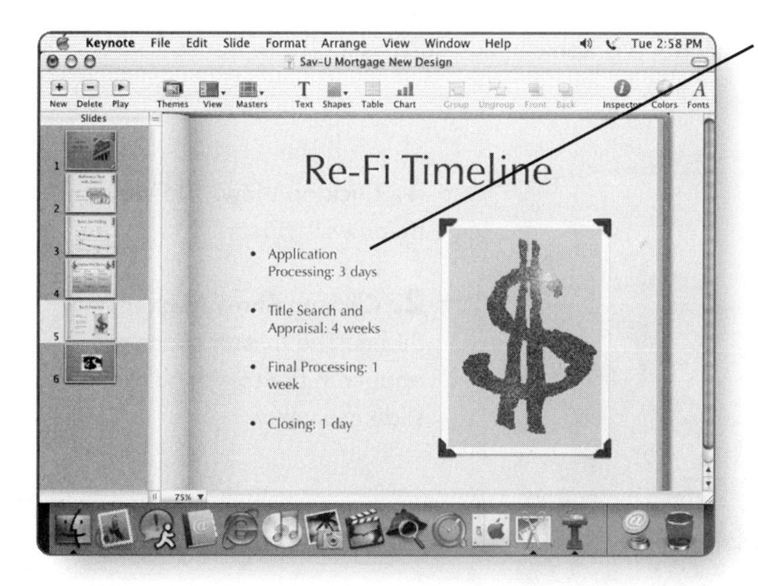

You can then add content to the slide as desired.

Formatting the Slide Background

You may encounter instances where you like the overall layout of the slide, but you don't like the background that the slide uses—especially if the slide includes a graphic frame for a picture, which must be removed for changes to the background to be visible. The following steps explain how to edit the background settings for a slide master.

> **CAUTION**
>
> Any changes you make to the slide master affect all slides to which you've applied that master within the current slideshow file. You can use the Slide Inspector to change the background fill for a selected slide; unfortunately, that doesn't work if the slide master includes a graphic image such as a picture frame.

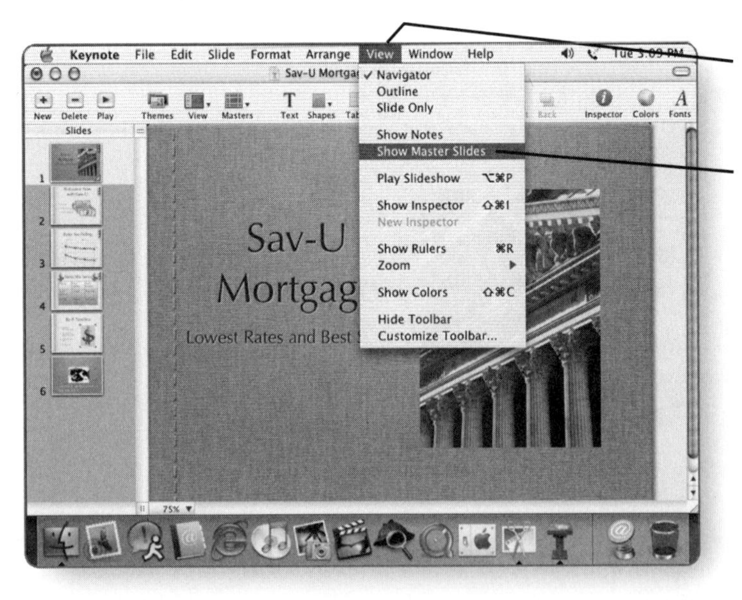

1. **Click** on **View**. The View menu will appear.

2. **Click** on **Show Master Slides.** The master slides will appear in the top pane of the slide organizer.

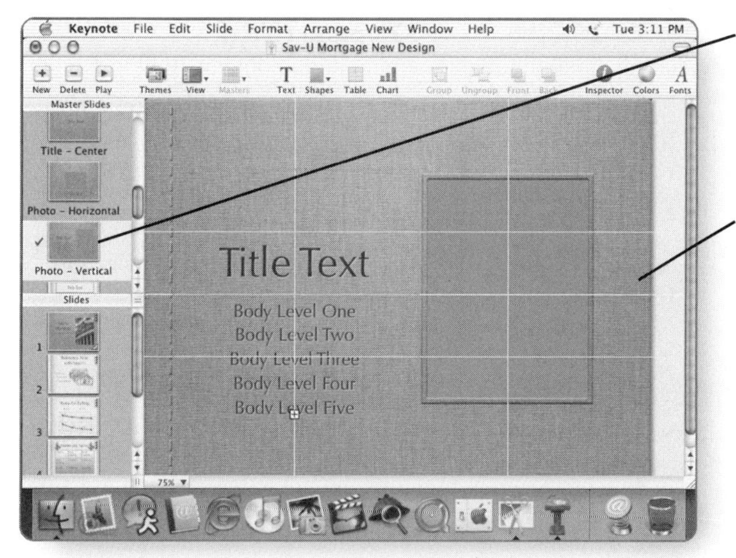

3. Click on the **master to edit** in the slide organizer. The master's content will appear on the slide canvas.

4. Click on the **slide background picture** on the slide canvas. (If the slide doesn't have a background picture, skip to Step 10.) The graphic will be selected, but no handles will appear because graphics in the default themes are locked.

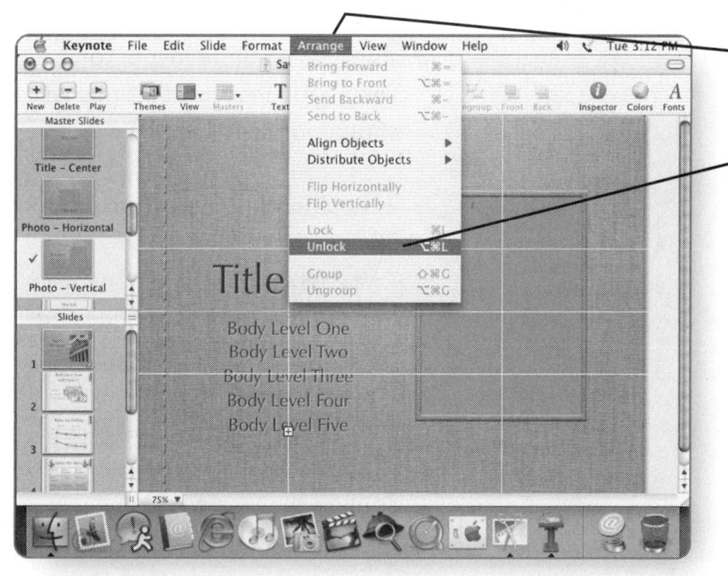

5. Click on **Arrange**. The Arrange menu will appear.

6. Click on **Unlock**. Handles will appear around the background image.

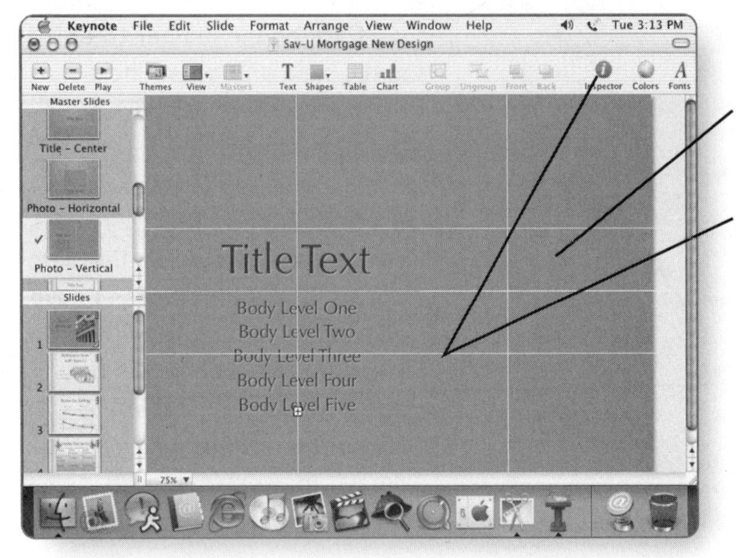

7. Press Delete.

The picture will be deleted from the slide master.

8. Click on **Inspector** on the toolbar. The Inspector window will appear.

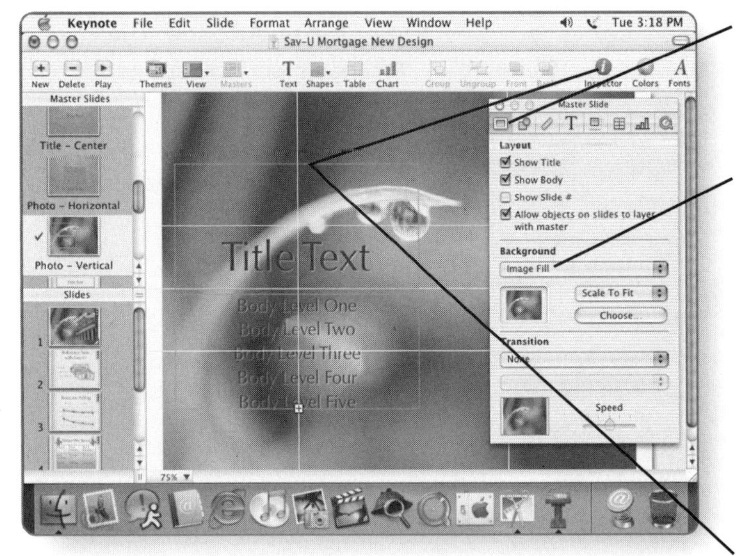

9. Click on **Slide Inspector**. The Slide Inspector settings will appear in the Inspector window.

10. Change the **Background fill** as desired. (Refer to "Working with Fills" in Chapter 6 to learn more about choosing a color, gradient, or image fill.) The new fill will appear immediately on the master and all slides to which you've applied that master.

11. Click on **Inspector** on the toolbar. The Inspector window will close.

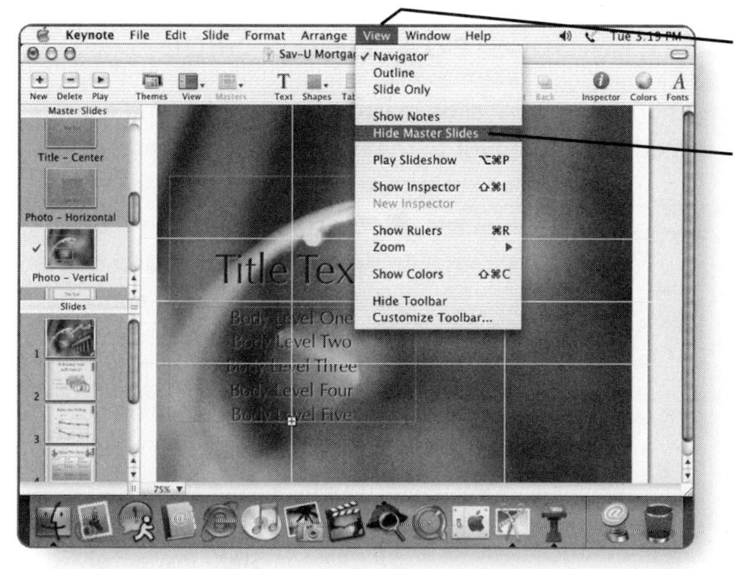

12. Click on **View**. The View menu will appear.

13. Click on **Hide Master Slides**. The master slides pane of the slide organizer will close, and your changes will be applied to the slideshow. You can then click a slide in the slide organizer (change to the Navigator view if needed) to continue working.

> **NOTE**
>
> See "Editing a Master" in Chapter 13 to learn more about adding background objects and working with the content on a master.

Working with Bulleted Lists

Virtually all slideshows contain bulleted lists because such lists offer an effective way to organize thoughts and information for an audience. Indeed, because many of us think in short snippets rather than fully formed paragraphs, a bulleted list format presents information in a format that's easy for an audience member to process. This section shows you how to add a bulleted list to a slide, and how to change the bullet formatting for a bulleted list.

Adding a Bulleted List to a Slide

If you choose the Blank slide master or one with a title only, you can add a bulleted list to that slide with a few easy steps.

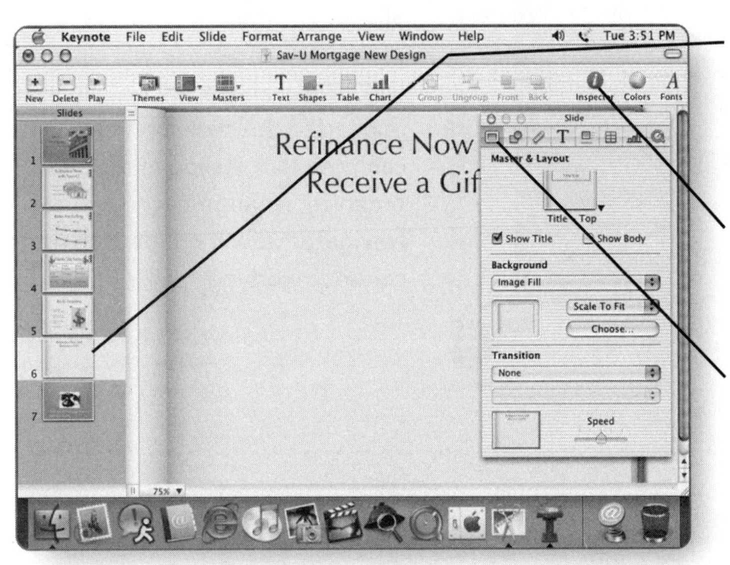

1. **Go to** or **select the slide** to which you want to add a bulleted list. The slide contents will appear in the slide canvas.
2. **Click** on **Inspector** on the toolbar. The Inspector window will open.
3. **Click** on **Slide Inspector**. The Slide Inspector settings will appear.

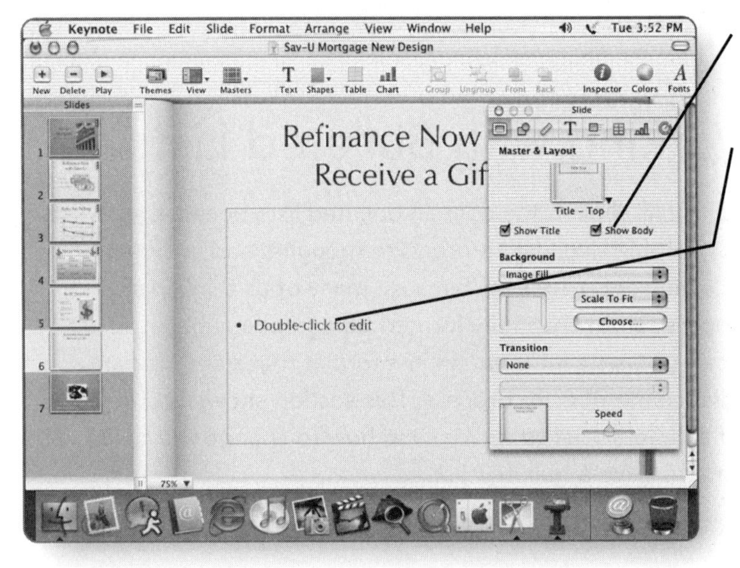

4. **Click** on **Show Body** to check it.

The bulleted list placeholder will appear on the slide.

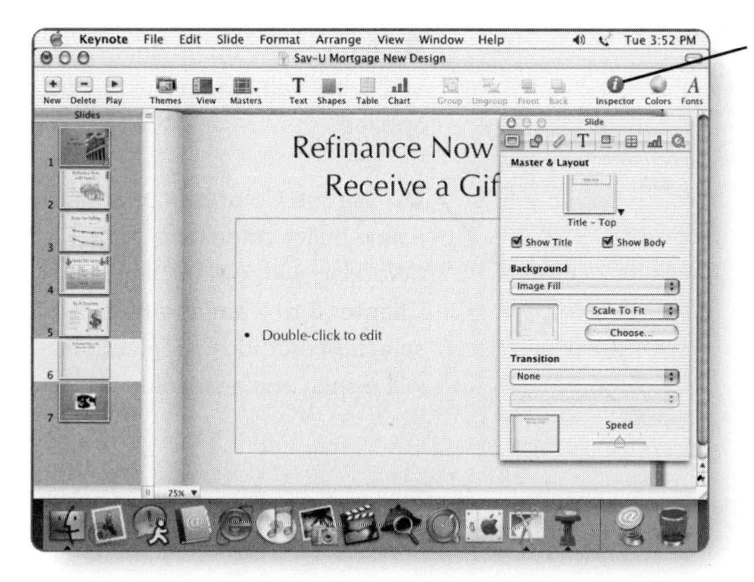

5. Click on **Inspector**. The Inspector window will close.

> **NOTE**
>
> Keynote does not enable you to include multiple bulleted lists on a slide. It also does not allow you to format a text placeholder that you add with bullets, or to add bullets to text within a table.

Using Plain Bullets

Even if you stick with plain old bullets (called *text bullets*) for a bulleted list, you can still make several formatting changes to the bullet appearance.

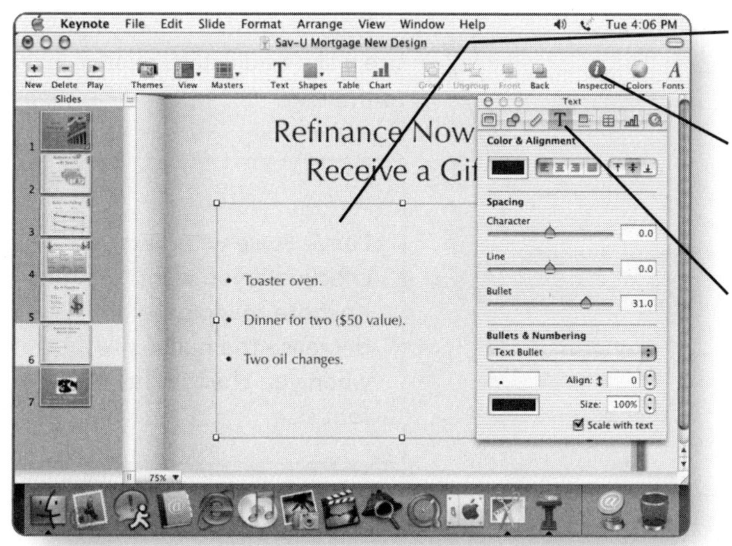

1. Click on the **bulleted list to format**. The list will be selected.

2. Click on **Inspector** on the toolbar. The Inspector window will open.

3. Click on **Text Inspector**. The Text Inspector settings will appear.

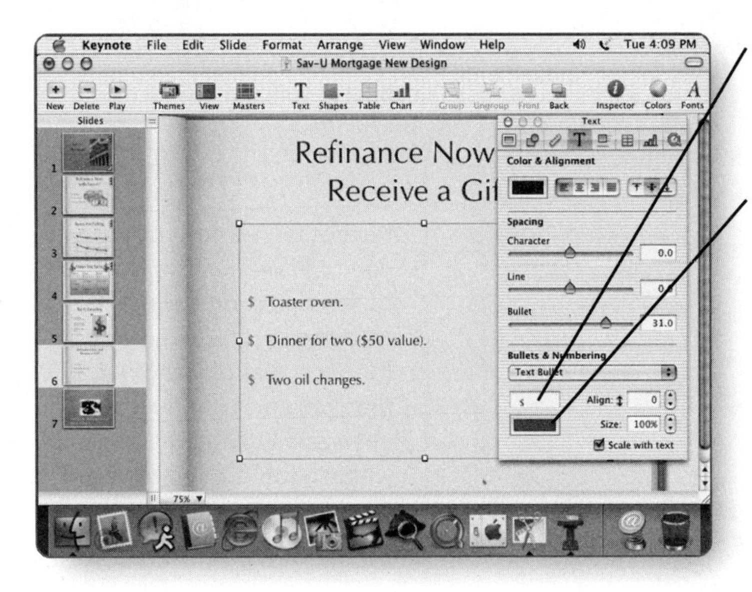

4. **Type** a **new bullet character** and **press Tab**. The bullet will be applied.

5. **Use** the **Color box** to apply a new bullet color. (See "Working with Colors" in Chapter 6 to learn about color selection methods.) The bullets will display the new color.

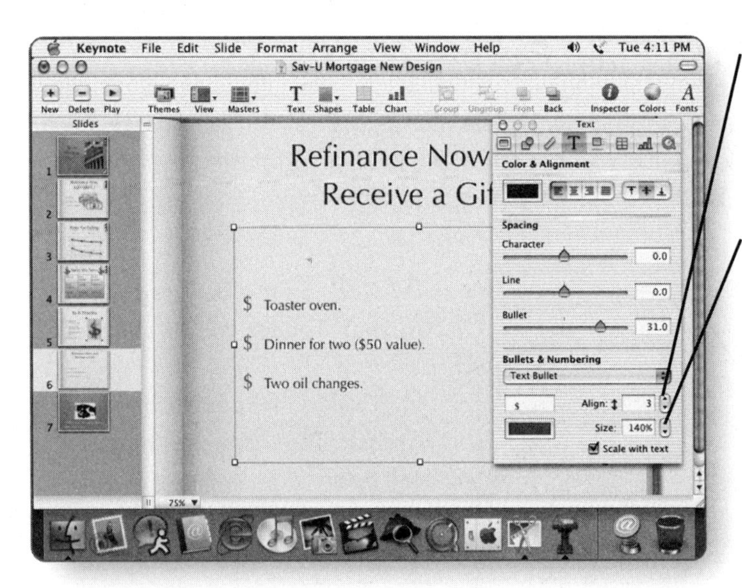

6. **Click** on an **Align spinner button** as needed. The bullet alignment will be adjusted, relative to the text.

7. **Click** on a **Size spinner button** as needed. The bullet size will be adjusted, relative to the text.

> **TIP**
>
> Leave Scale with Text checked if you want Keynote to increase or decrease the bullet size when you change the font size.

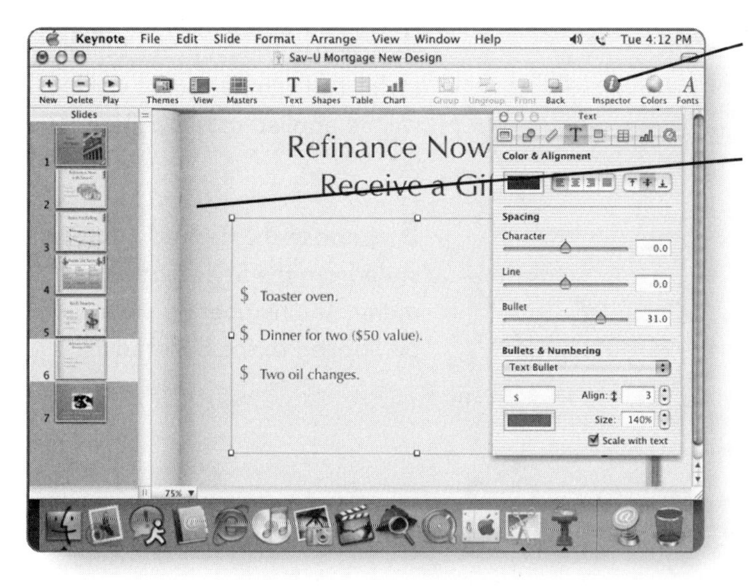

8. Click on **Inspector**. The Inspector window will close.

9. Click outside the **bulleted list**. The list will be deselected.

Using Numbers

You can convert any bulleted list to a numbered list by changing the bullet style. A numbered list can be useful for communicating about the steps in a process, for example.

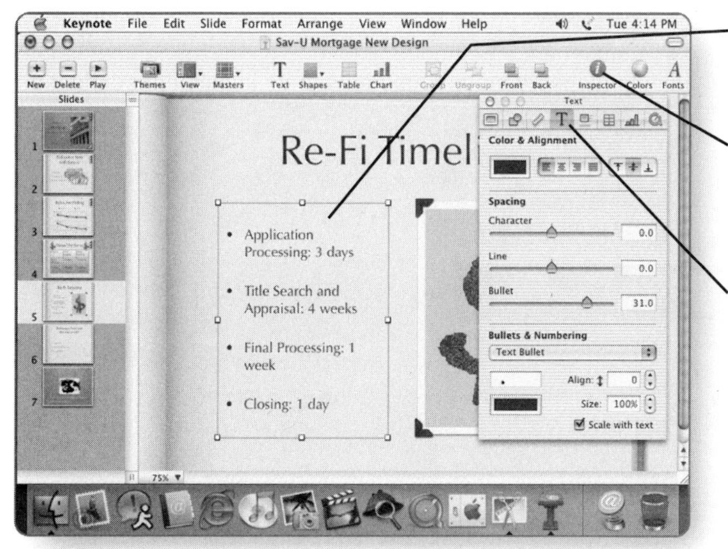

1. Click on the **bulleted list to format**. The list will be selected.

2. Click on **Inspector** on the toolbar. The Inspector window will open.

3. Click on **Text Inspector**. The Text Inspector settings will appear.

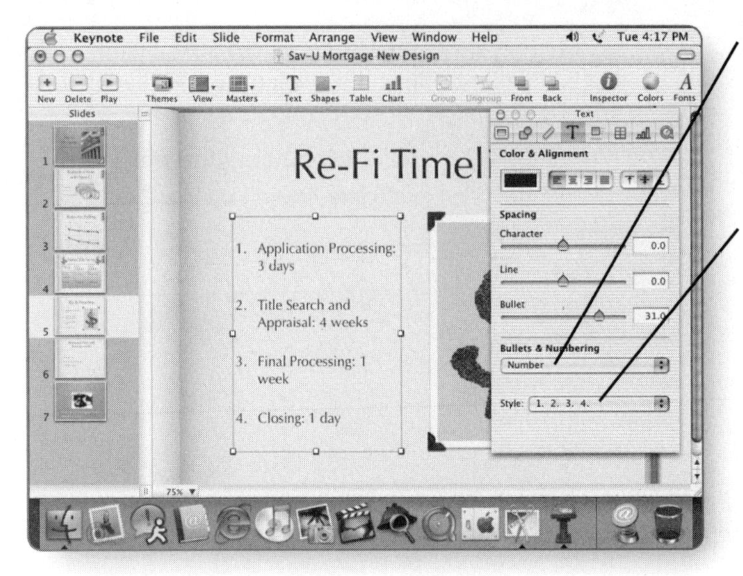

4. Choose the **Number bullet style**. The number bullet style will be applied to the bulleted list.

5. Choose the desired **number style** from the **Style pop-up menu**. The numbering style will be applied to the bulleted list.

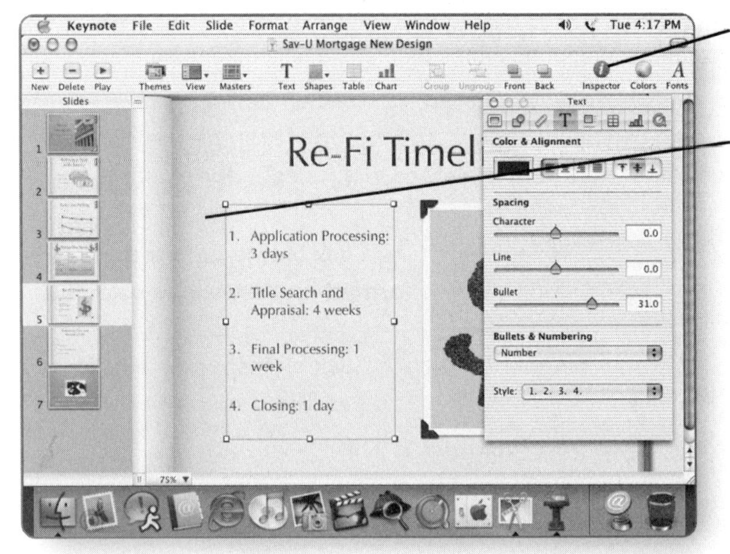

6. Click on **Inspector**. The Inspector window will close.

7. Click outside the **bulleted list**. The list will be deselected.

Using a Custom Image

For the most custom bullet appearance, you can use a graphic file that you have as the bullets for a bulleted list on a slide. Keep in mind that simple, small image files work best in this situation.

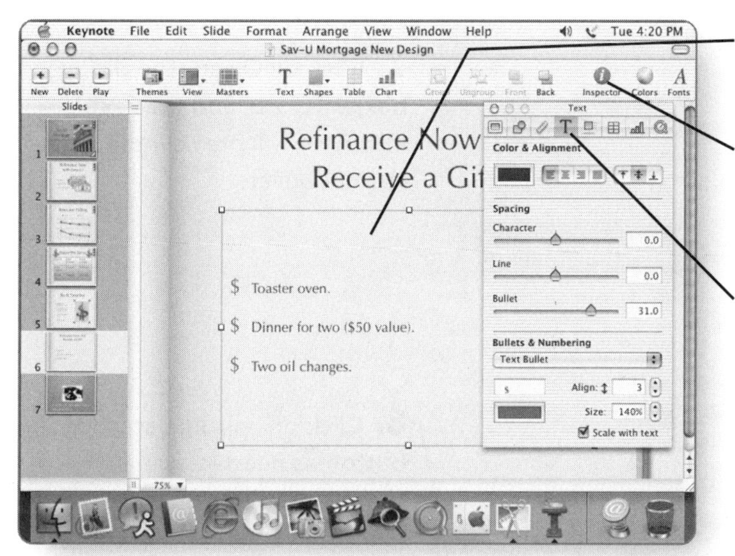

1. **Click** on the **bulleted list to format**. The list will be selected.
2. **Click** on **Inspector** on the toolbar. The Inspector window will open.
3. **Click** on **Text Inspector**. The Text Inspector settings will appear.

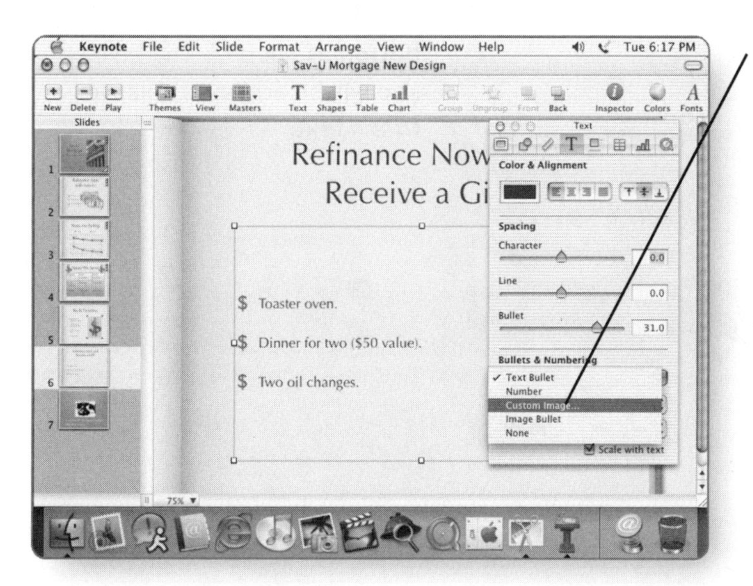

4. **Choose** the **Custom Image bullet style**. The Open dialog box will appear onscreen.

> **TIP**
>
> If you previously selected a custom image bullet but want to change the image used, click on the Choose button below the bullet preview to open the Open dialog box.

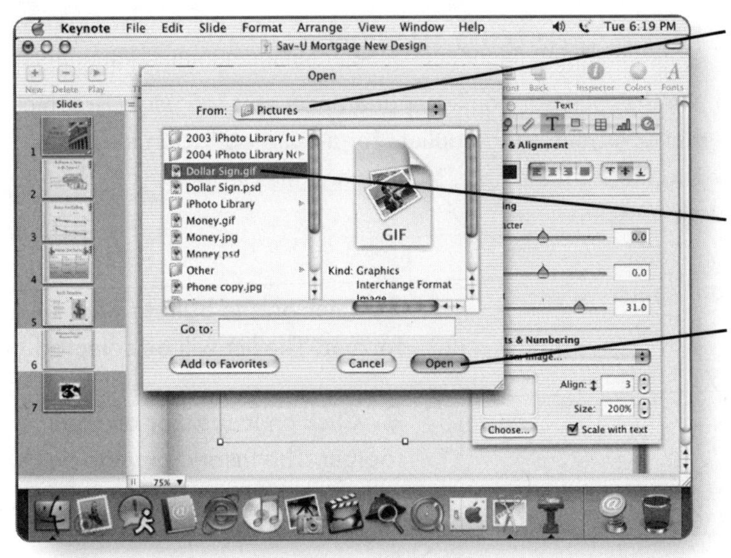

5. **Navigate** to **the folder holding the desired image**, if needed. The graphic file will appear in the dialog box.

6. **Click** on the **desired graphic file**. A preview icon will appear.

7. **Click** on **Open**. The dialog box will close, and the Text Inspector will preview the custom bullet.

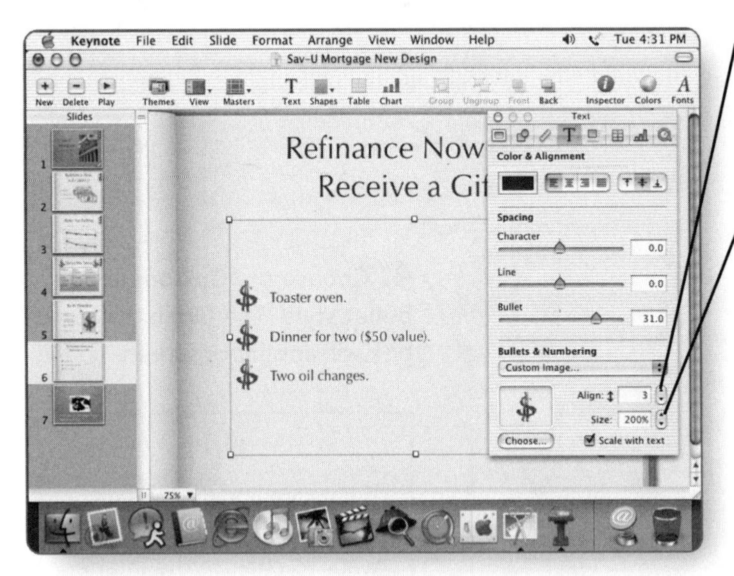

8. **Click** on an **Align spinner button** as needed. The bullet alignment will be adjusted, relative to the text.

9. **Click** on a **Size spinner button** as needed. The bullet size will be adjusted, relative to the text.

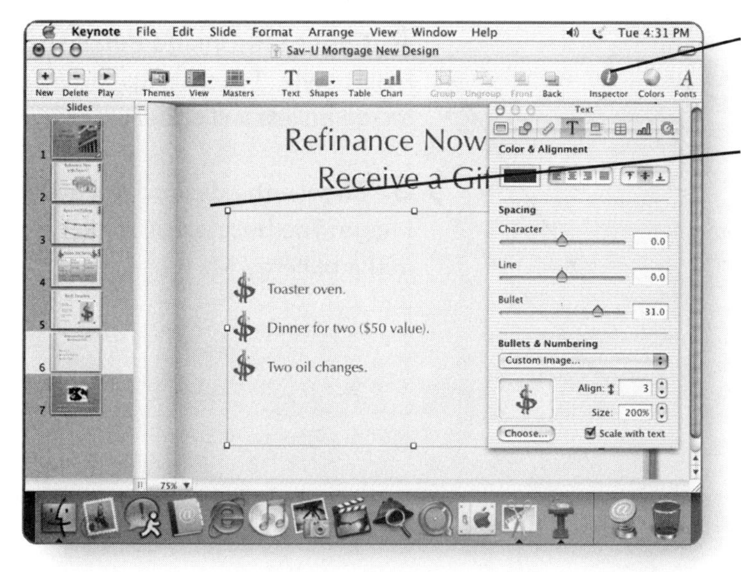

10. Click on **Inspector**. The Inspector window will close.

11. Click **outside** the **bulleted list**. The list will be deselected.

Using an Image Bullet

Keynote also supplies a number of its own images that you can use as bullets in a bulleted list.

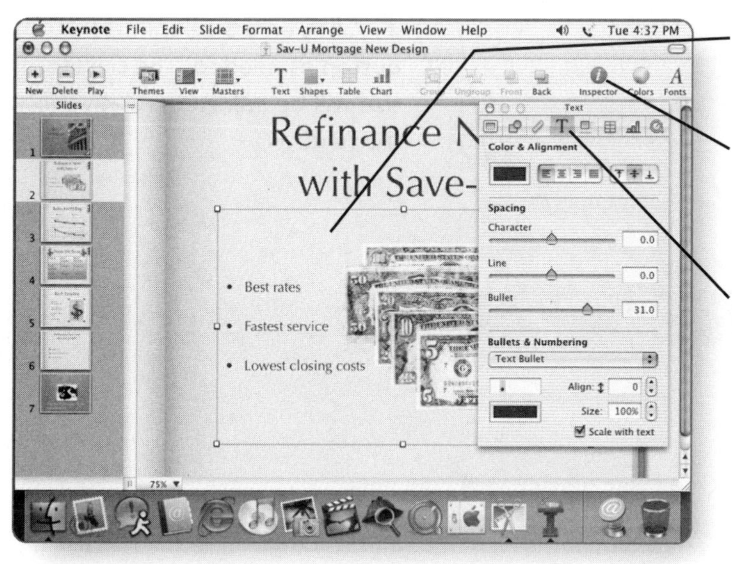

1. Click on the **bulleted list** to format. The list will be selected.

2. Click on **Inspector** on the toolbar. The Inspector window will open.

3. Click on **Text Inspector**. The Text Inspector settings will appear.

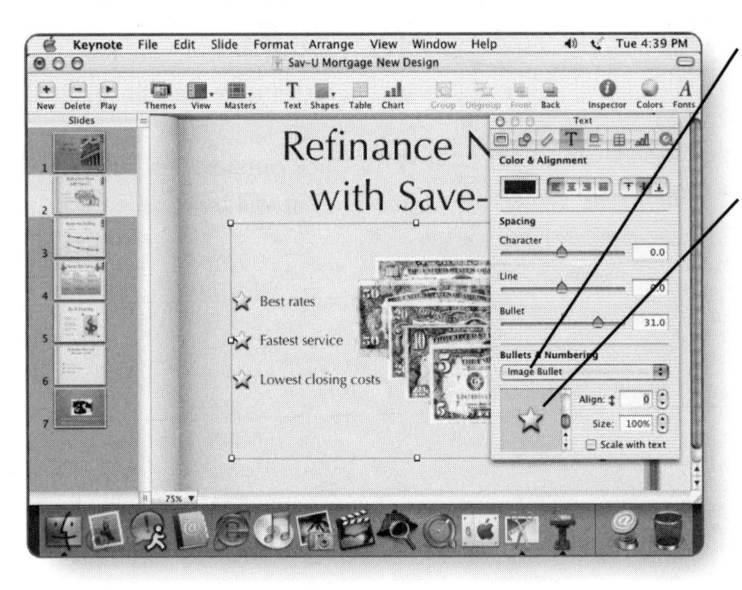

4. Choose the **Image Bullet bullet style**. The settings for image bullets will appear.

5. Choose the **desired bullet image**. The bullets will appear in the bulleted list.

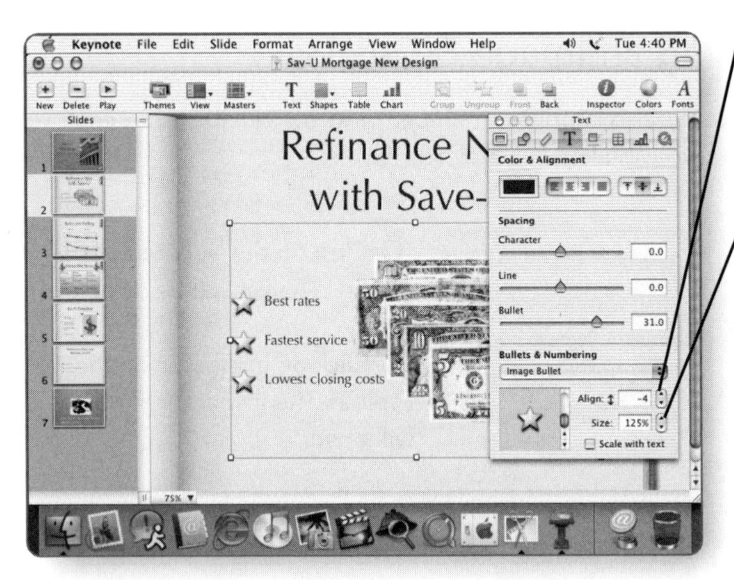

6. Click on an **Align spinner button** as needed. The bullet alignment will be adjusted, relative to the text.

7. Click on a **Size spinner button** as needed. The bullet size will be adjusted, relative to the text.

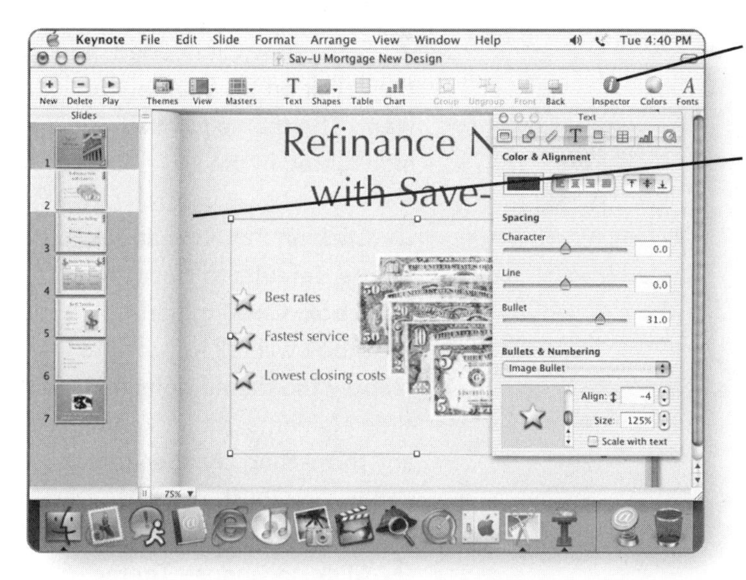

8. **Click** on **Inspector**. The Inspector window will close.

9. **Click outside** the **bulleted list**. The list will be deselected.

Changing the Theme

You can make a more dramatic change to a slideshow by applying another slideshow theme. This process resembles selecting a theme when you create a new slideshow file.

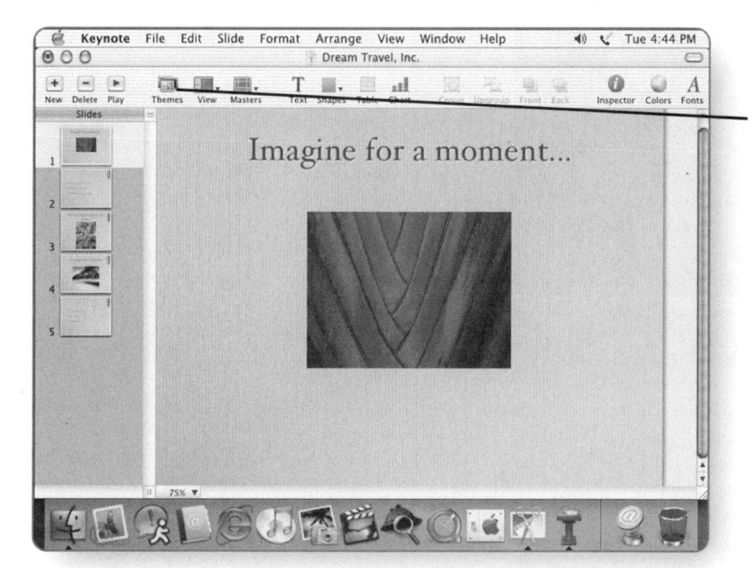

1. **Click** on **Themes** on the toolbar. Keynote will display a sheet for you to choose a slideshow theme.

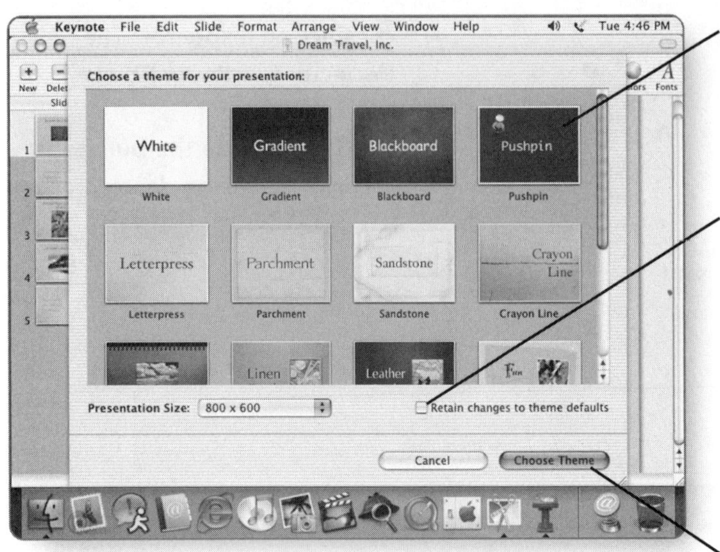

2. Scroll down, if needed, and then **click** on the **theme you want**. The theme will be highlighted in the list.

3. Click on **Retain changes to theme defaults** to clear the checkbox. Clearing that checkbox will tell Keynote to reapply the theme defaults to all slide elements, rather keeping any formatting changes that you've previously applied.

4. Click on **Choose Theme**.

The new theme will be applied to the presentation.

Finding More Themes Online

Keynote by default includes a dozen themes. That's not many if you create numerous presentations in your line of work. As such, a number of third-party companies have begun developing themes that you can download and install on your system. The http://www.apple.com/keynote Web site lists resources for themes. You can visit that page, or you can go directly to the Web site for a theme developer. The sites listed below feature both free and for-sale themes for Keynote.

- **http://www.keynotepro.com.** This site sells professional themes for a modest cost: $20 or so.

- **http://www.keynote-user.com.** This site sells inexpensive themes created by pros, as well as offering a few themes like this for free download.

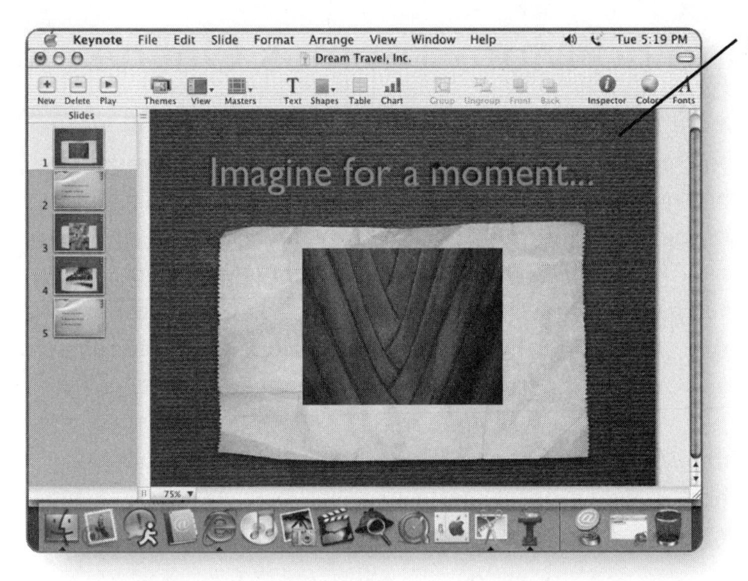

- **http://www.keynotehq.com.** This is the Atlas shareware theme available from Keynote HQ. This site features professionally developed and user-contributed themes.

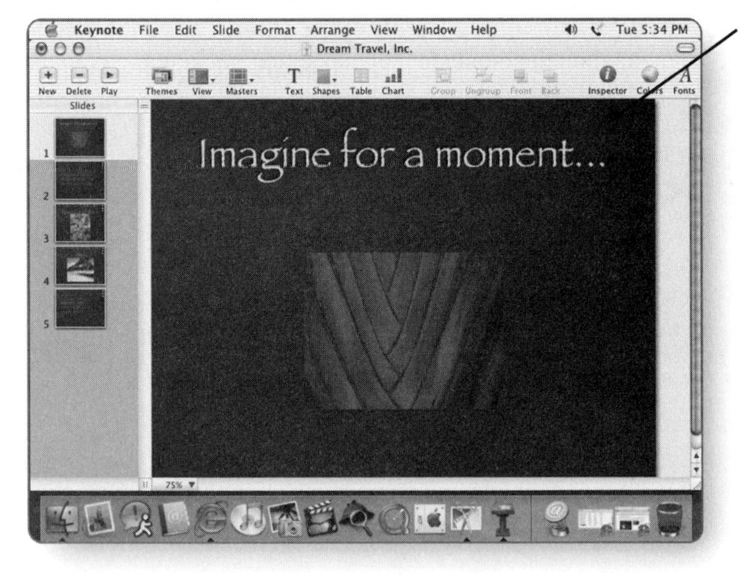

- **http://www.keynotetheme-park.com.** As of this writing, this site primarily sells professionally developed themes, but it does offer one theme (shown here) for free.
- **http://www.keynote-gallery.com.** At $10 or so a pop, the themes on this site are reasonable in price and professional in appearance. Check out the site's Resources link for free downloads, such as a Smiley theme.

TIP

Make sure the slide size for the theme you download or purchase is the same as the slide size that you want to use for your presentation files. Also pay attention to the types of elements included in the theme. Some themes may not include chart defaults, for example.

Once you use your Web browser to download a theme, it should expand automatically if the downloaded file is an archive, such as a .SIT or .PHP file. If the file doesn't expand automatically, use the Stuffit Expander Utility in the Applications:Utilities folder to expand the file. The Keynote .KTH file should appear on the desktop. If the archive file expands to a folder on the desktop, double-click on the folder to see the .KTH file.

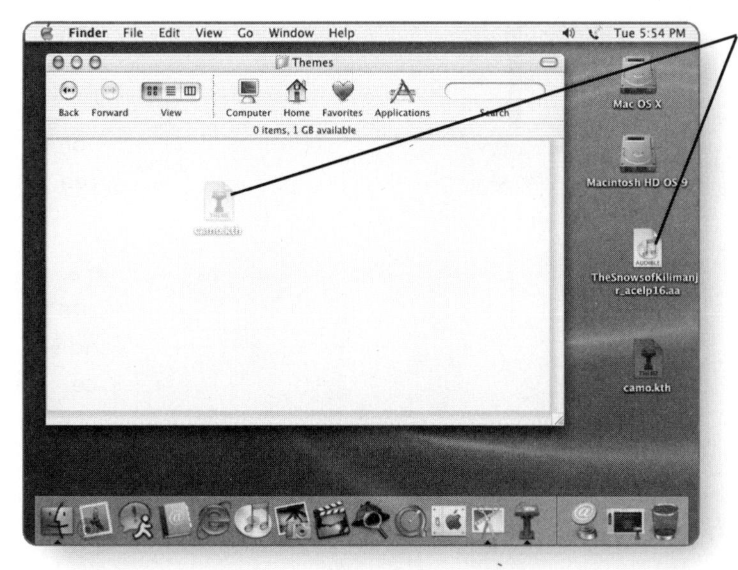

Drag the .KTH file from the desktop into a Finder window for the :Library:Application Support:Keynote:Themes folder on your Mac's hard disk. (You may need to create the Themes folder within the Keynote folder.) This makes the theme available to all users of your system. If you want to make the theme available only when you're logged on to your Mac, drag the .KTH file into the :Library:Application Support: Keynote:Themes folder within your Home folder.

NOTE

More complicated themes may require additional installation steps, such as installing a font distributed with the theme. Consult any Read Me or other documentation file that comes with the theme to ensure you're following all the installation instructions.

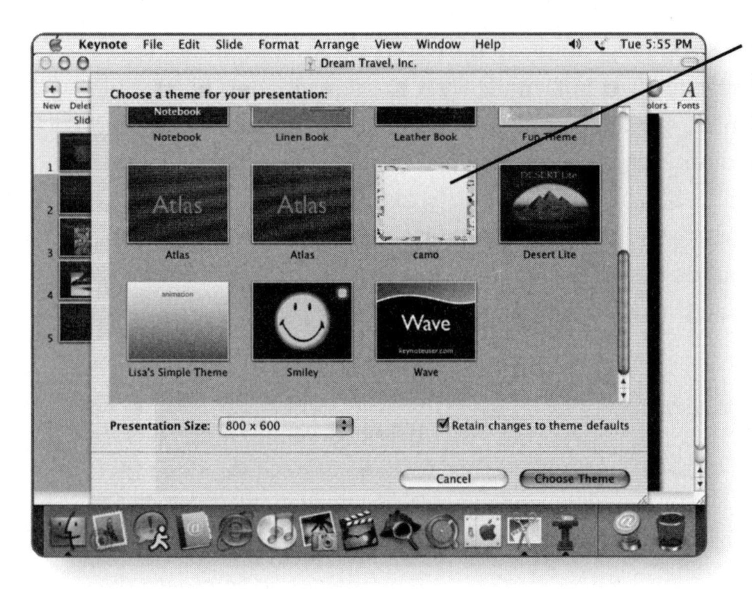

In Keynote, the newly added theme will be available to apply to any new or existing slideshow.

Working with Slideshow Animation

Because a slideshow plays back onscreen, it need not be static, like printed slides or overheads. You can add transitions, animation, and builds to make your on-screen slide show come alive. In this chapter, you will learn how to:

- Apply a transition to a slide.
- Animate an object on a slide.
- Create a build effect for a bulleted list, table, or chart.
- Control the animation order.

Specifying a Slide Transition

A slide transition specifies how the whole slide will appear on the screen during the on-screen slideshow. By default, each slide simply appears when you move to that slide in the slideshow. For increased drama, you can have a slide dissolve onto the screen, appear cube by cube, or wipe the screen. Use the Slide Inspector to apply a transition to the current slide.

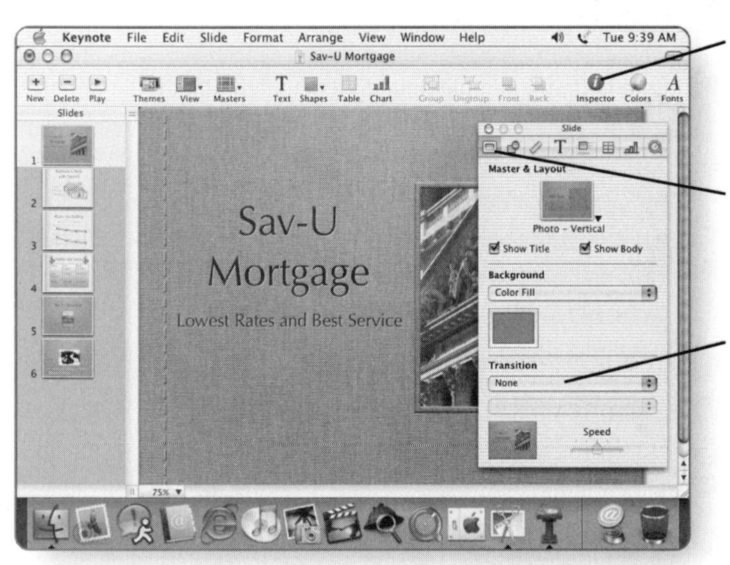

1. Click on **Inspector** on the toolbar. The Inspector window will open.

2. Click on **Slide Inspector**. The Slide Inspector settings will appear.

3. Click on the **Transition pop-up menu**. The available transitions will appear in the menu.

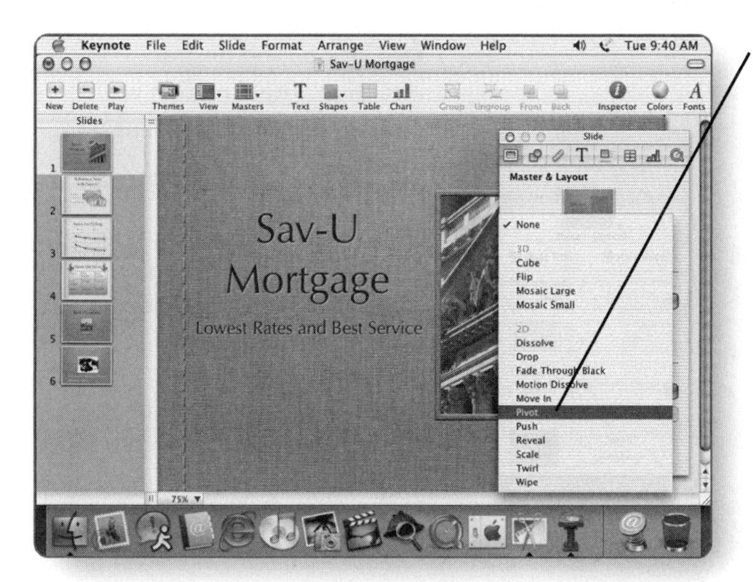

4. Click on the **desired transition**. The transition will be selected for the slide.

A blue triangle will appear in the lower-right corner of the slide thumbnail in the slide organizer to indicate that the slide now includes a transition.

5. Click on the **direction pop-up menu**. The transition directions will appear in the menu.

6. **Click** on the **desired direction**. The direction will be selected for the slide transition.

> **NOTE**
>
> Each time you change a transition setting, the small preview in the bottom left corner previews the transition with the latest settings.

7. **Drag** the **Speed slider**. The specified speed will be applied to the slide transition.

8. **Click** on **Inspector** on the toolbar. The Inspector window will close.

Animating a Single Object

If desired, you can animate any single object on a slide by choosing a build-in or build-out setting for the object in the Build Inspector. For example, if you want to build only the slide title or a graphic inserted on a slide, you can do so.

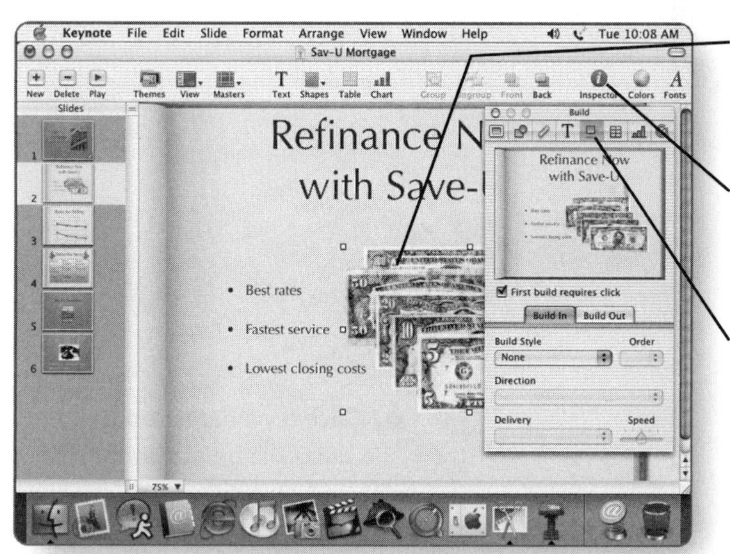

1. **Click** on the **object to animate**. Selection handles will appear.
2. **Click** on **Inspector** on the toolbar. The Inspector window will open.
3. **Click** on **Build Inspector**. The Build Inspector settings will appear.

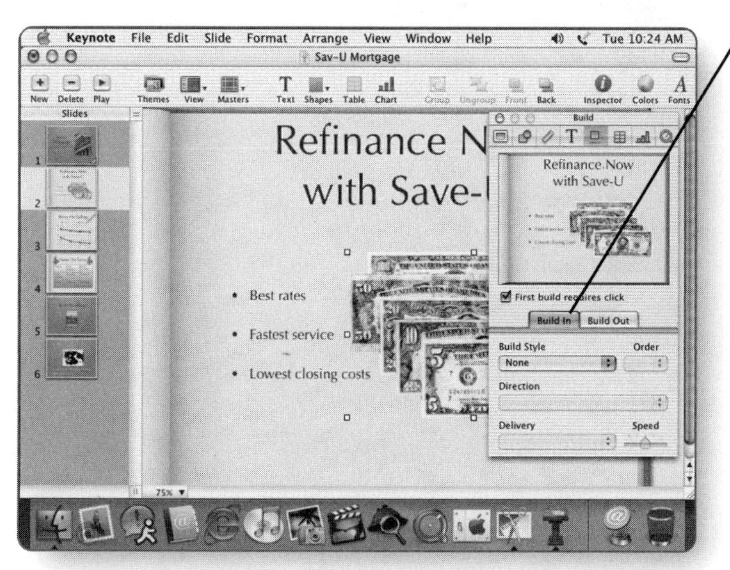

4. **Click** on **Build In** or **Build Out** as desired. The settings for building in or out will appear. You can choose animation settings for the object on either or both tabs.

> **TIP**
>
> If you want the animated item to appear without clicking the mouse, clear the First Build Requires Click check box.

5. Click on the **Build Style** pop-up menu. The build choices will appear in the menu.

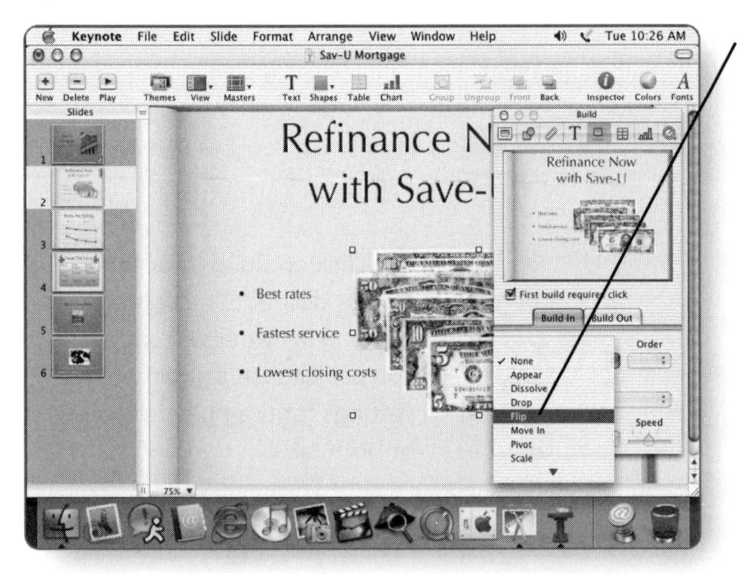

6. Click on the **desired build.** The build will be assigned to the selected object.

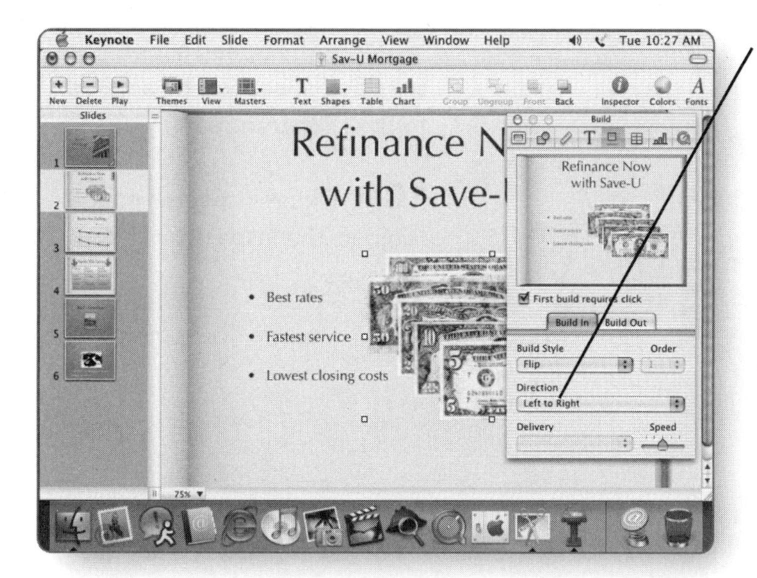

7. **Click** on the **Direction pop-up menu**. The build directions will appear in the menu.

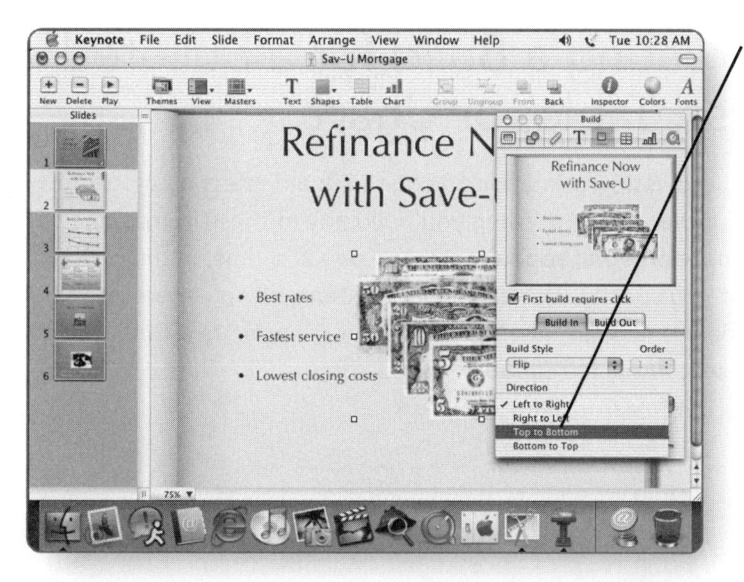

8. **Click** on the **desired direction**. The direction will be selected for the animation.

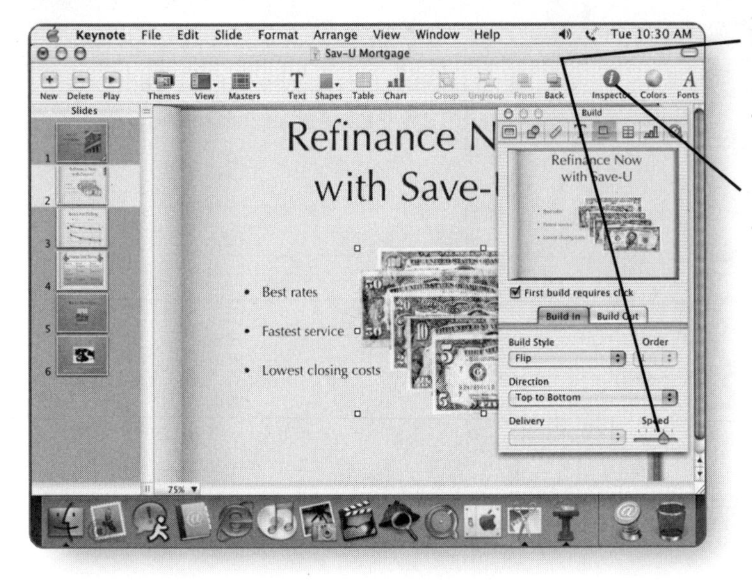

9. Drag the **Speed slider**. The specified speed will be applied to the slide transition.

10. Click on **Inspector** on the toolbar. The Inspector window will close.

Creating a Build for a Bulleted List, Table, or Chart

You can assign animation to create a build effect on a bulleted list, table, or chart. When you build any of these items, its components will appear onscreen one at a time, in the order that you specify. (For example, the items in a bulleted list will appear one bullet at a time.) The overall process for building these items is the same.

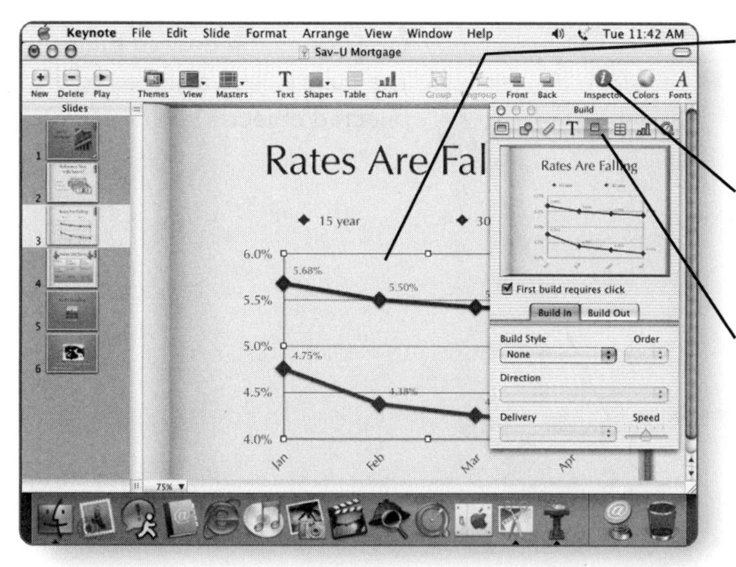

1. **Click** on the **bulleted list, table, or chart to build**. Selection handles will appear.
2. **Click** on **Inspector** on the toolbar. The Inspector window will open.
3. **Click** on **Build Inspector**. The Build Inspector settings will appear.

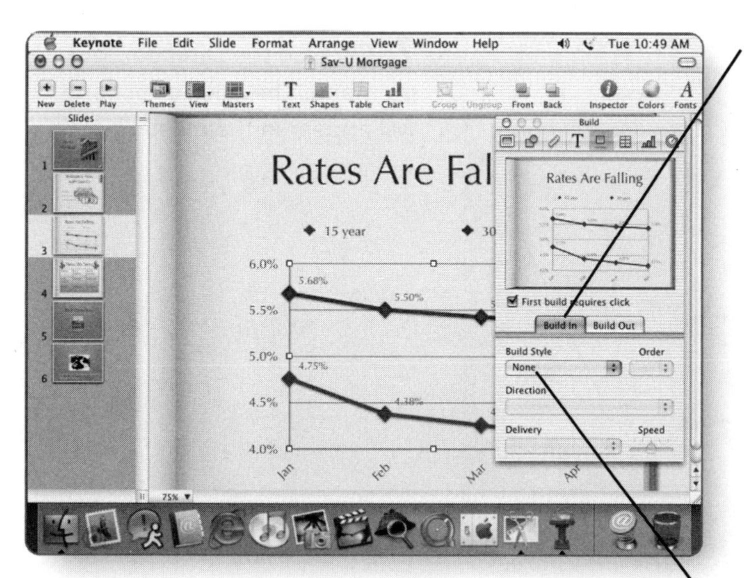

4. **Click** on **Build In** or **Build Out** as desired. The settings for building in or out will appear. You can choose build settings for the object on either or both tabs.

> **TIP**
>
> If you want the first build item to appear without clicking the mouse, clear the First Build Requires Click check box.

5. **Click** on the **Build Style** pop-up menu. The build choices will appear in the menu.

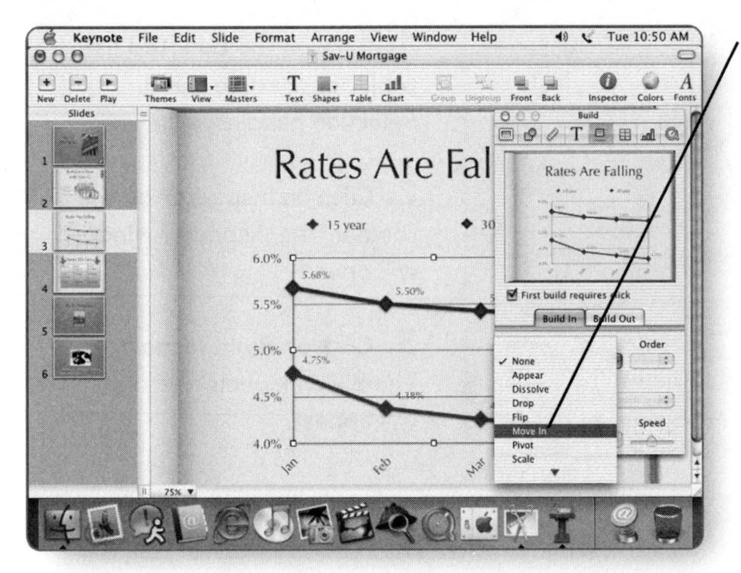

6. **Click** on the **desired build**. The build will be assigned to the selected object.

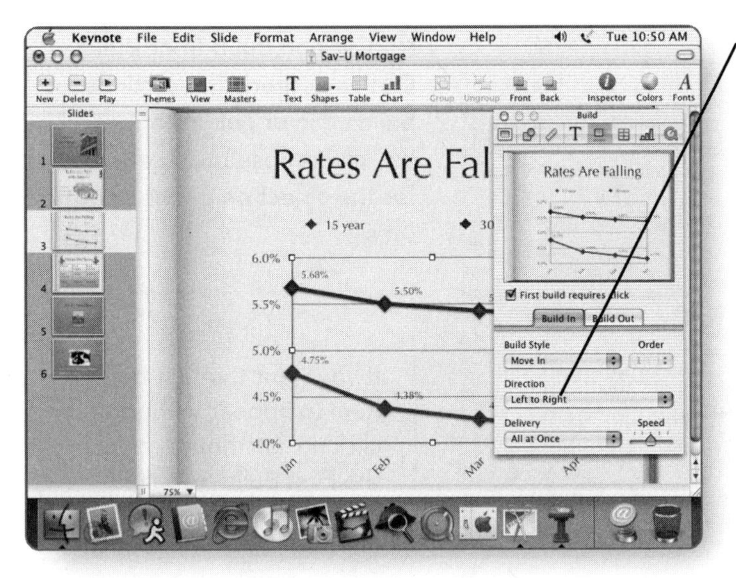

7. **Click** on the **Direction pop-up menu**. The build directions will appear in the menu.

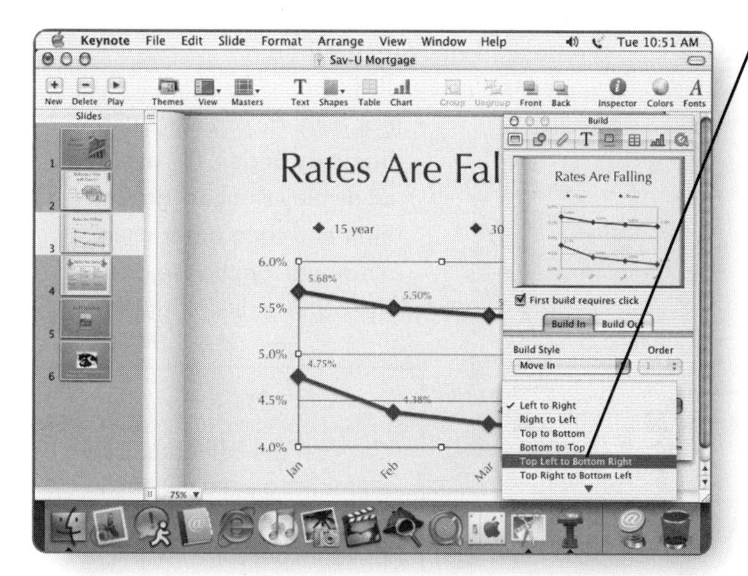

8. **Click** on the **desired direction**. The direction will be selected for the build.

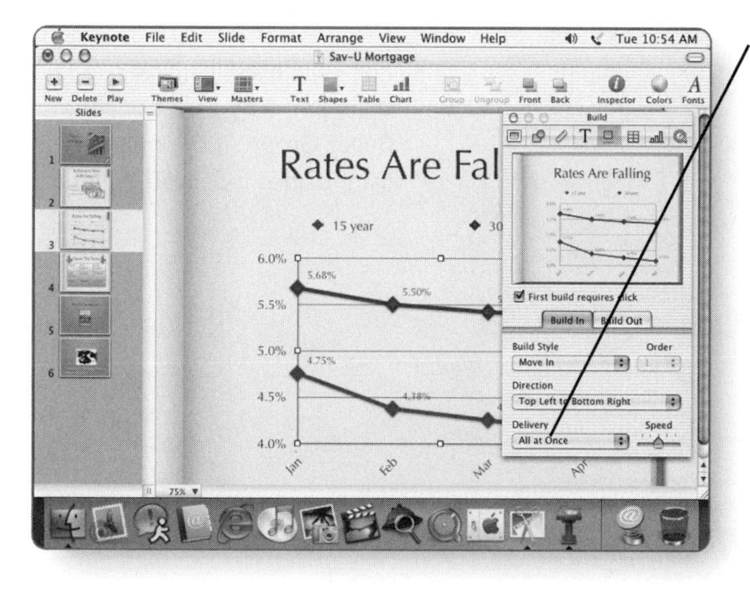

9. **Click** on the **Delivery pop-up menu**. The choices for how to build the parts of the object will appear.

10. Click on the **desired delivery method.**

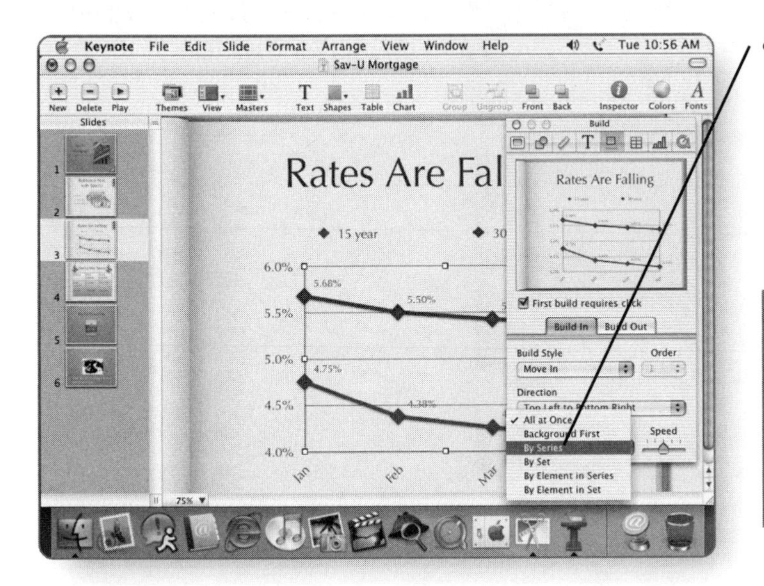

- For a chart, you can build items By Series, for example, or display the Background First and then other chart elements, or choose one of the other delivery methods.

> **TIP**
>
> Click on the selected slide element to preview each part of the build in the Build Inspector.

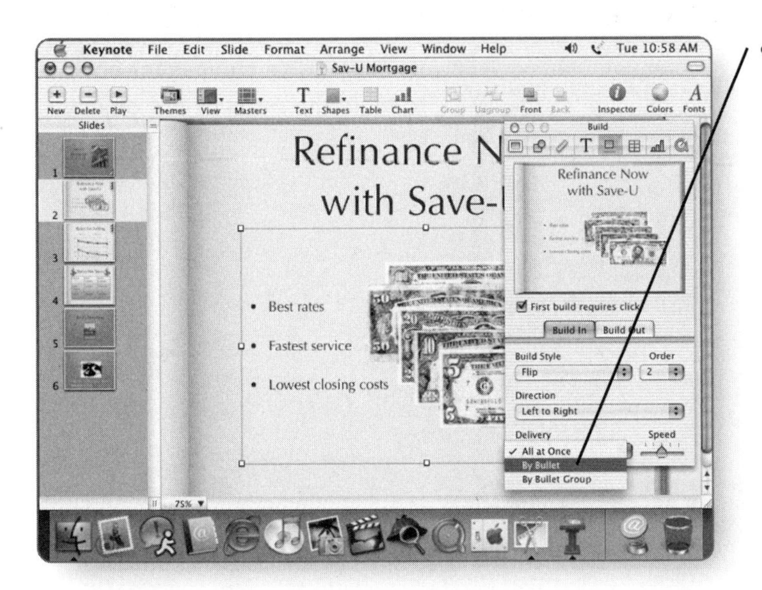

- For a bulleted list, you can build items By Bullet or By Bullet Group (if the bulleted list includes indented bullets).

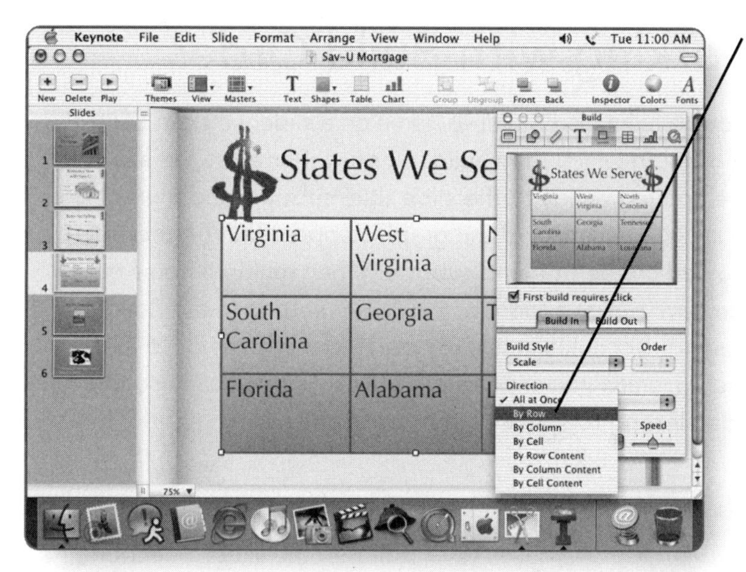

- For a table, you can build items By Row, By Column, By Cell, or according to one of the other delivery styles.

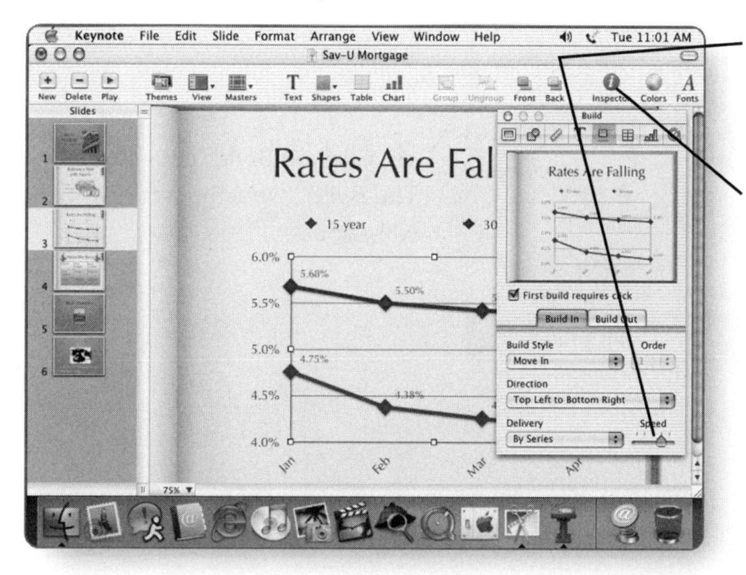

11. **Drag** the **Speed slider**. The specified speed will be applied to the build.

12. **Click** on **Inspector** on the toolbar. The Inspector window will close.

Working with Build Order

If you've animated multiple items on a slide, you can control the order in which they build in or out. For example, say you have applied builds to the slide title, subtitle, and a graphic on the slide. You can have the graphic appear first on the slide, followed by the title and subtitle. When multiple items on a slide have builds assigned, the Order setting in the Build Inspector becomes active. By default, the items build in the order in which you applied the builds, but you can use the Order setting to specify a new build order.

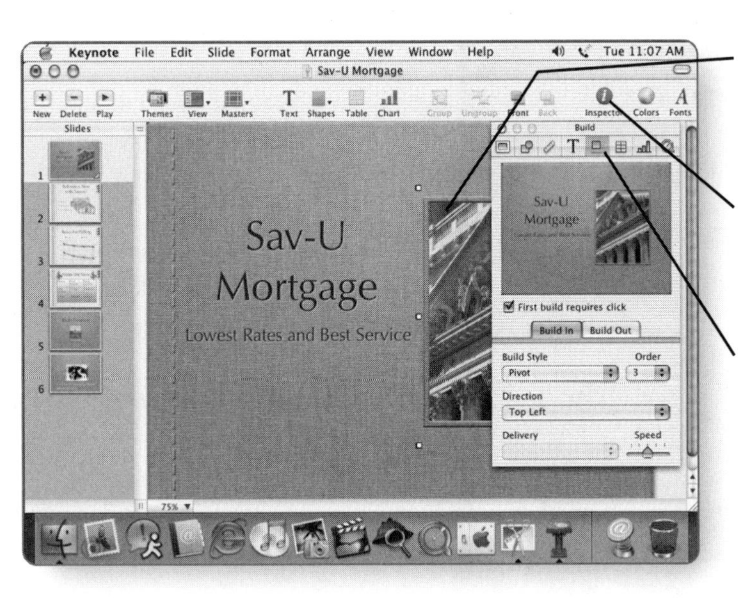

1. **Click** on the **first item to build** on the slide. Selection handles will appear.
2. **Click** on **Inspector** on the toolbar. The Inspector window will open.
3. **Click** on **Build Inspector**. The Build Inspector settings will appear.

4. Click on the **Order pop-up menu**. The order choices will appear.

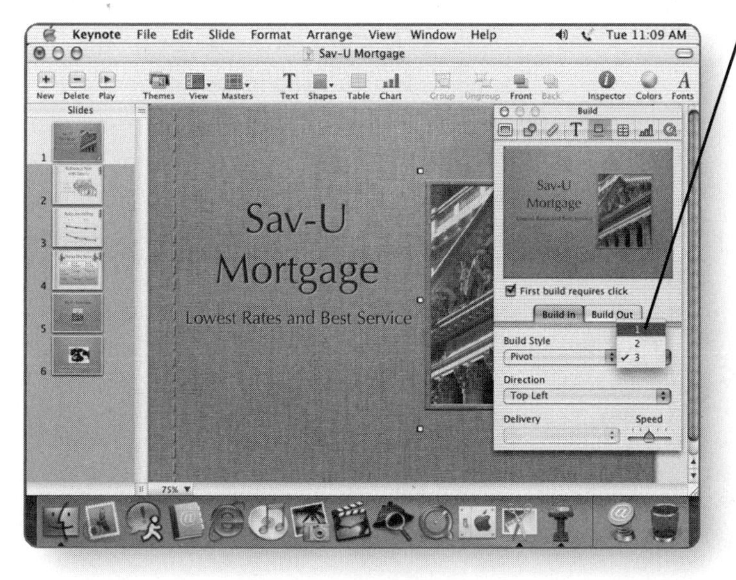

5. Click on the **desired Order setting**. The new order choice will be applied to the selected object.

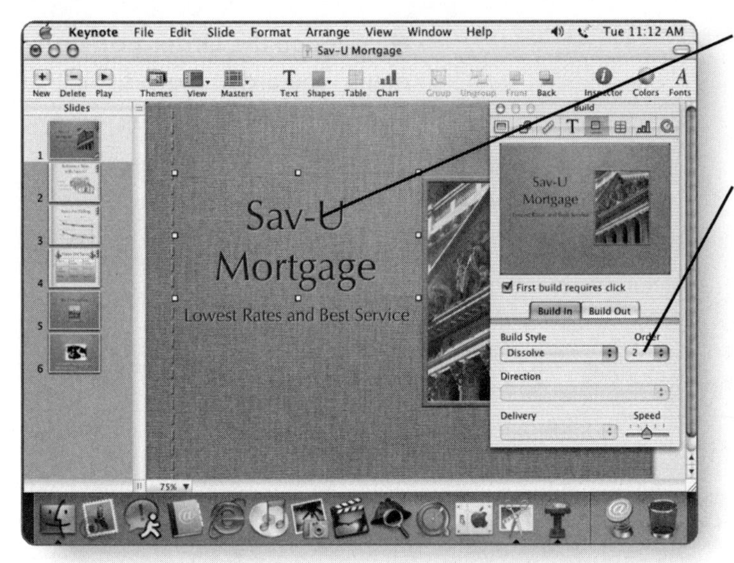

6. Click on the **next animated object** on the slide. Selection handles will appear.

7. Assign the **desired Order setting**. The new order choice will be applied to the selected object.

8. Repeat Steps 6 and 7 to apply the appropriate build order to each of the slide objects. The objects will build as specified during the on-screen slideshow.

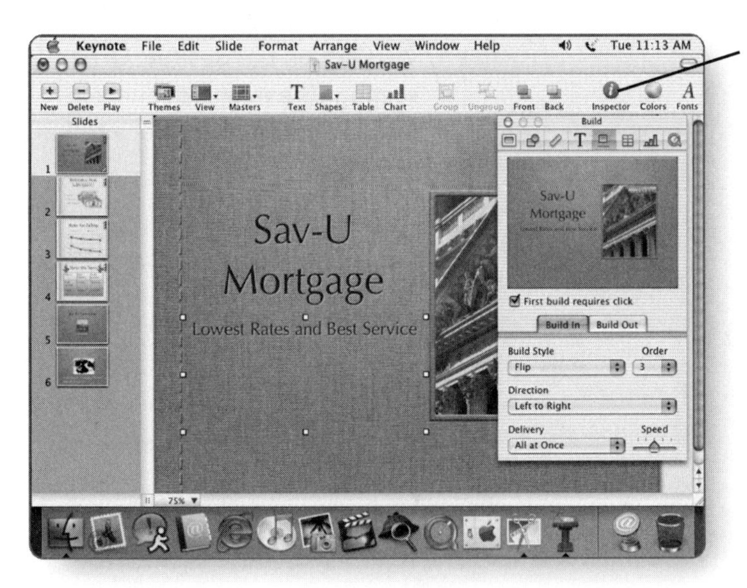

9. Click on **Inspector** on the toolbar. The Inspector window will close.

9

Adding Multimedia Elements

Early presentation graphics programs enabled you to place only simple text and graphics on slides. Today's more sophisticated presentation graphics programs enable you to incorporate a variety of multimedia elements to enhance a slideshow. In this chapter, you will learn how to:

- Insert a QuickTime movie, animation, or song file into a presentation.
- Adjust playback settings for any multimedia item.

Inserting a QuickTime Movie or Flash Animation

You can support any type of multimedia file that QuickTime supports onto a slide. The latest version of QuickTime (6.3) supports QuickTime movie (MOV) and Flash animations (SWF).

> **CAUTION**
>
> In my tests, Keynote supports only Flash animations published in Flash 5 or earlier formats. Keynote does not currently support transparency in Flash animations, nor animated GIF files.

No matter what kind of multimedia element you want to insert on a slide, the process is the same.

1. **Go to** or **select the slide** where you want to insert the movie or animation. The slide contents will appear in the slide canvas.

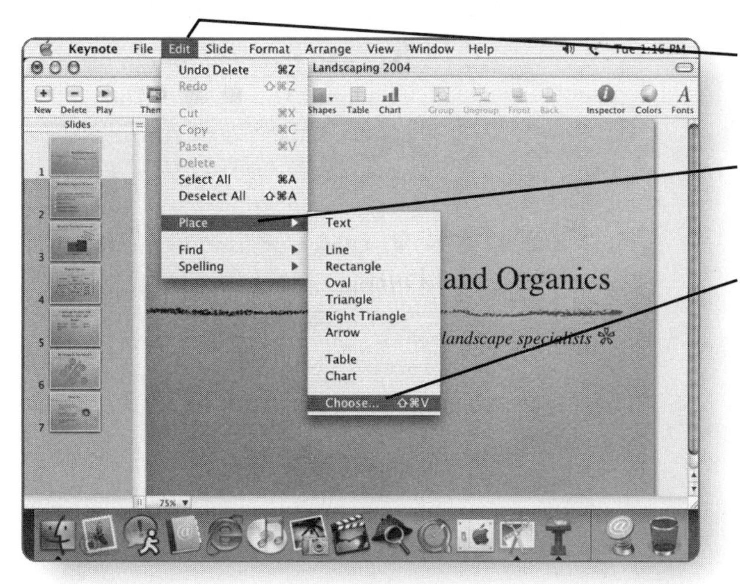

2. **Click** on **Edit**. The Edit menu will appear.

3. **Point** to **Place**. A submenu will appear.

4. **Click** on **Choose**. A sheet will open so that you can choose the multimedia element to insert.

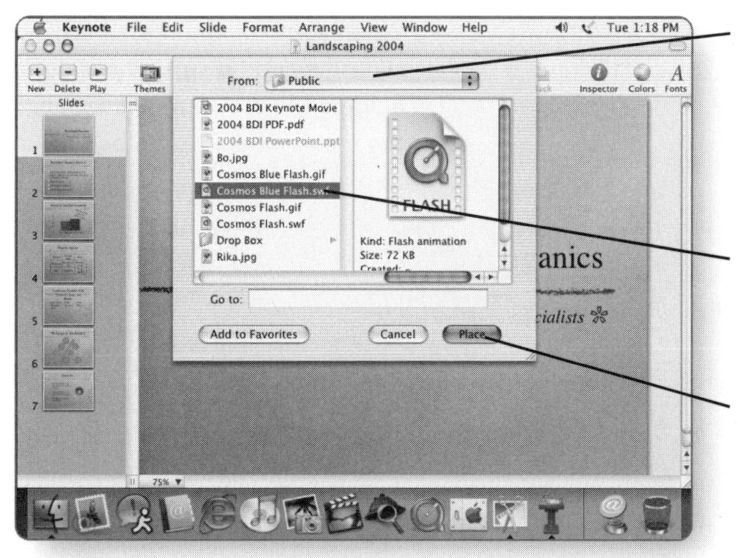

5. **Navigate** to the **folder holding the desired movie or animation**, if needed. The movie or animation file will appear in the sheet.

6. **Click** on the **desired movie or animation**. A preview icon will appear in the sheet.

7. **Click** on **Place**. The sheet will close, and the movie or animation will appear on the slide.

8. **Drag** the **multimedia object** or a **selection handle.** The object will move or resize as specified.

9. **Click outside** the **multimedia object**. The object will be deselected.

When you play the on-screen slideshow and display the slide holding the movie or animation, the movie or animation begins to play back.

TIP

You can use the Build Inspector to assign a build to the animation to enhance its effectiveness even further. See "Animating a Single Object" in Chapter 8 to learn more.

Inserting Music

Keynote also supports music file formats recognized by QuickTime 6.2 or later, including MP3 music and AAC music (M4P). Insert a music file on the slide where you want the music playback to begin during the slideshow.

TIP

iTunes 4 can convert files from your audio CDs into either MP3 or AAC files. To learn more about using iTunes 4 to create and manage digital music, consider purchasing *iTunes 4 Fast & Easy* from Premier Press.

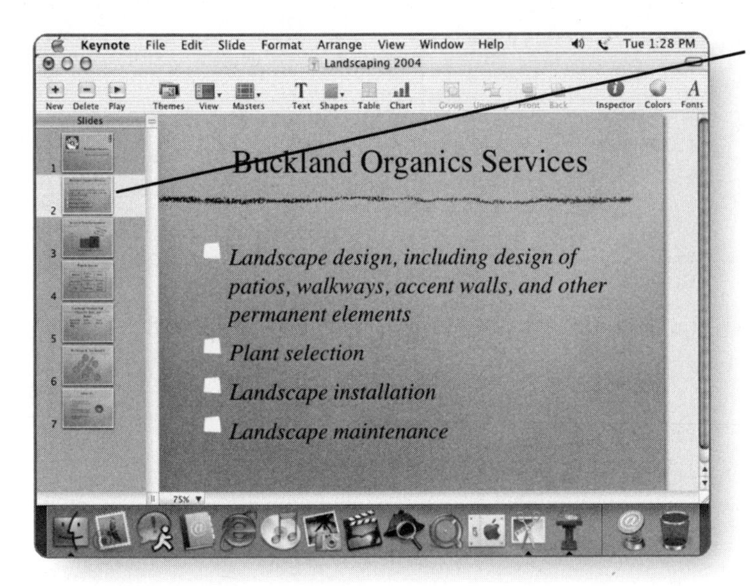

1. Go to or **select the slide** where you want to insert the music file. The slide contents will appear in the slide canvas.

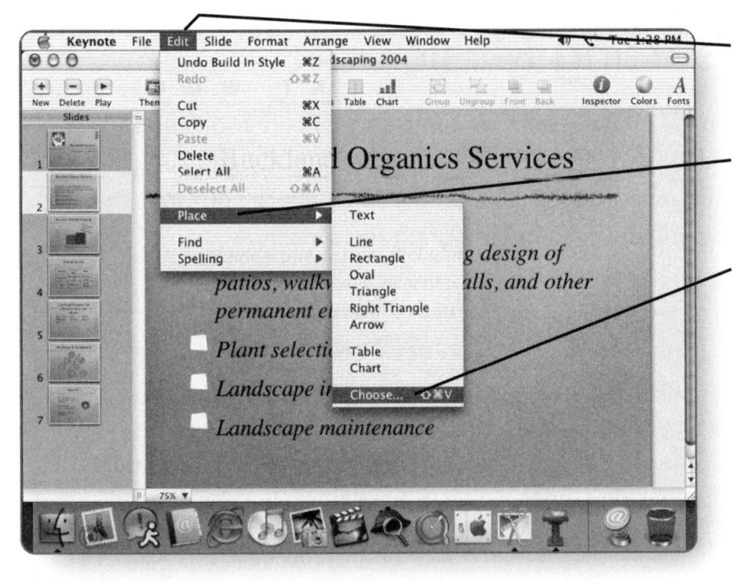

2. Click on **Edit**. The Edit menu will appear.

3. Point to **Place**. A submenu will appear.

4. Click on **Choose**. A sheet will open so that you can choose the music file to insert.

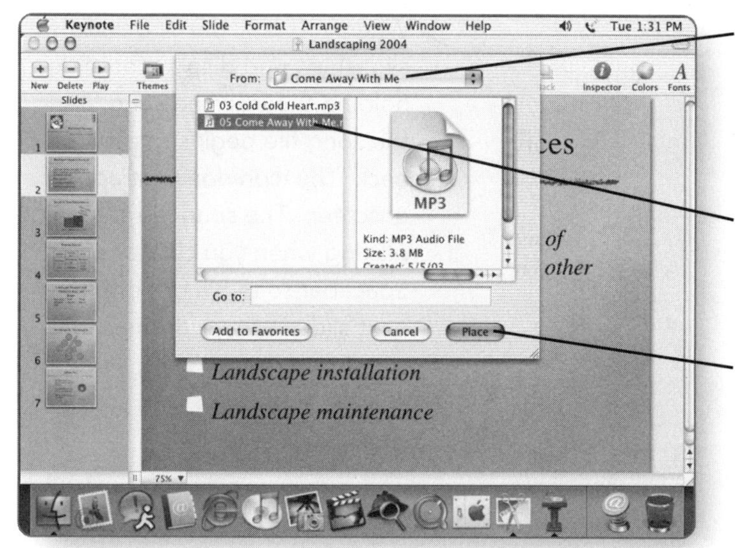

5. Navigate to the folder holding the desired song file, if needed. The song file will appear in the sheet.

6. Click on the **desired song file**. A preview icon will appear in the sheet.

7. Click on **Place**. The sheet will close, and an icon for the song file will appear on the slide.

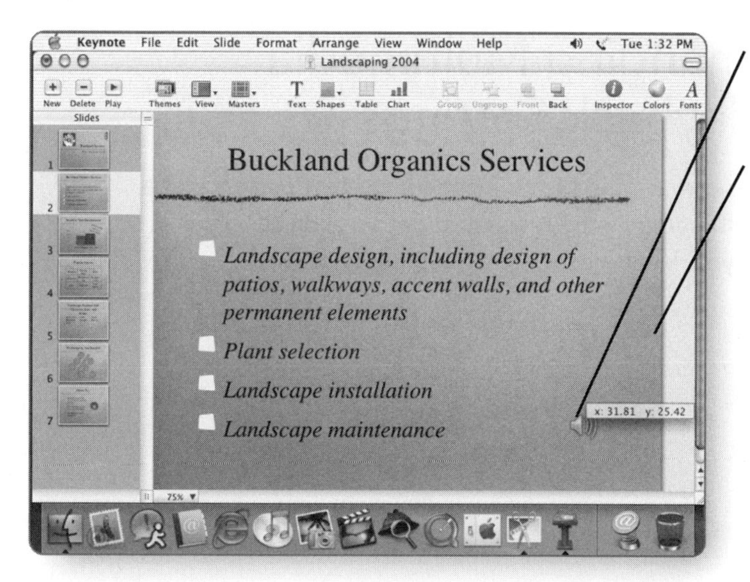

8. Drag the **music file icon**. The icon will move as specified.

9. Click outside the **icon**. The icon will be deselected.

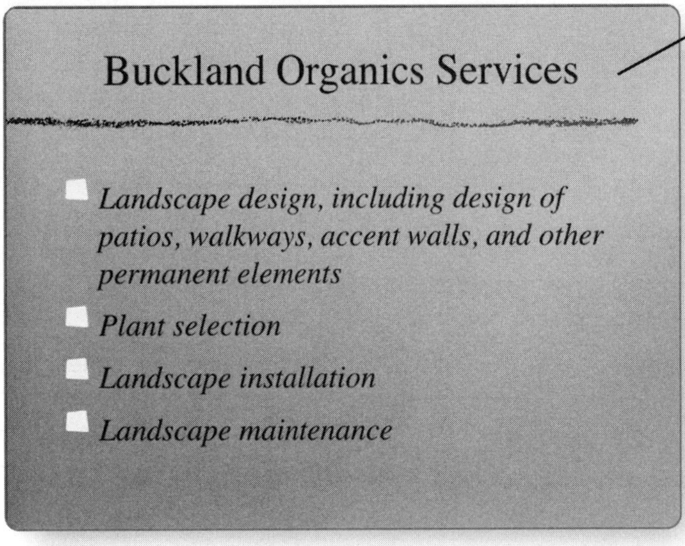

Buckland Organics Services

- *Landscape design, including design of patios, walkways, accent walls, and other permanent elements*
- *Plant selection*
- *Landscape installation*
- *Landscape maintenance*

When you play the on-screen slideshow and display the slide holding the inserted song file, the song file begins to play back. The icon does not appear onscreen. The song file stops playing when you click or press Spacebar to move on to the next slide in the slideshow.

Changing Multimedia Playback Settings

You can use the Media Inspector to test playback of a multimedia element inserted onto a slide or to adjust playback settings for the multimedia element.

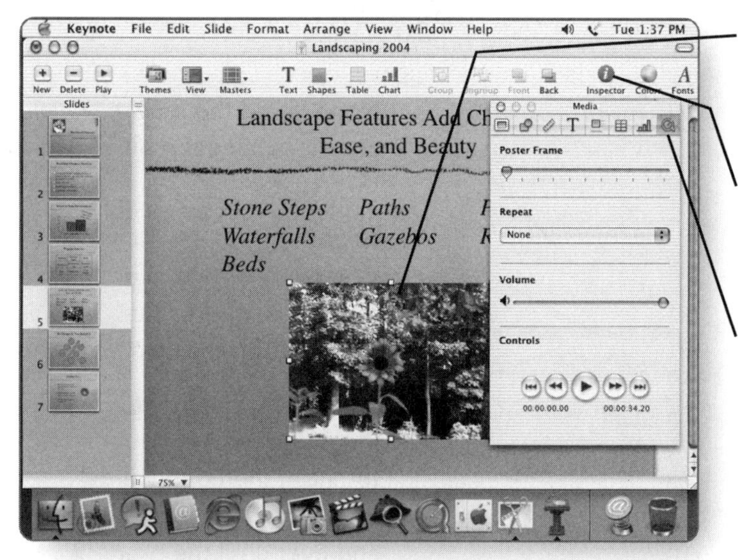

1. **Click** on the **multimedia object or icon**. Selection handles will appear.

2. **Click** on **Inspector** on the toolbar. The Inspector window will open.

3. **Click** on **Media Inspector**. The Media Inspector settings will appear.

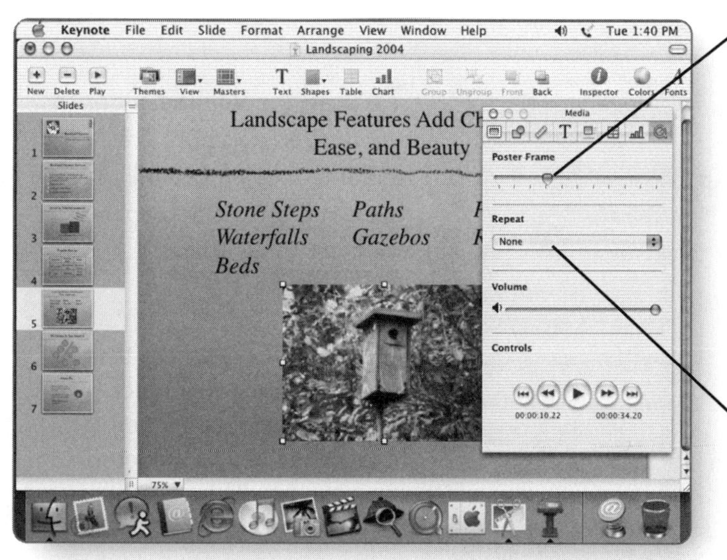

4. **Drag** the **Poster Frame slider** to the desired position. This setting applies to movies and animations only. The frame you specify with this slider will appear on the slide when the movie or animation is not playing, such as on printouts of the slide.

5. **Click** on the **Repeat pop-up menu**. The available repeat settings will appear.

6. Click on the **desired repeat setting.**

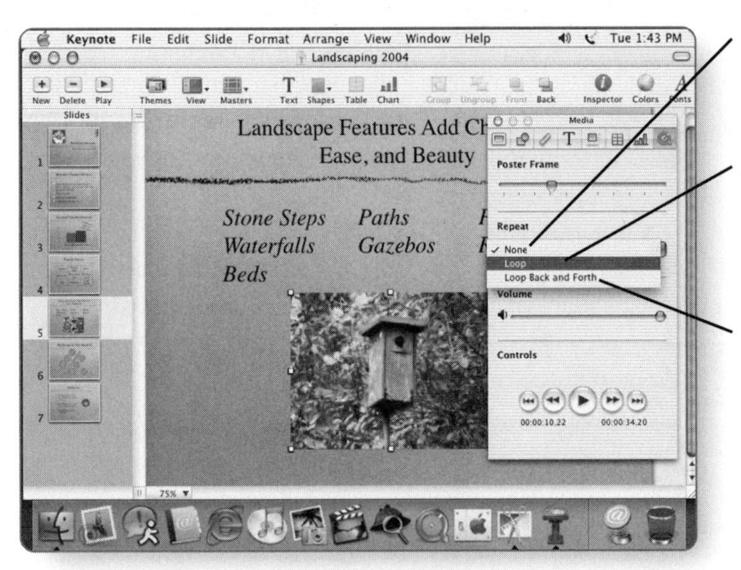

- **None.** Plays the movie, animation, or song once, and then stops it.
- **Loop.** Plays the multimedia element over and over until the user advances the slideshow to the next slide.
- **Loop Back and Forth.** Plays the multimedia element start to finish, then backwards, repeating the process over and over until the user advances the slideshow to the next slide.

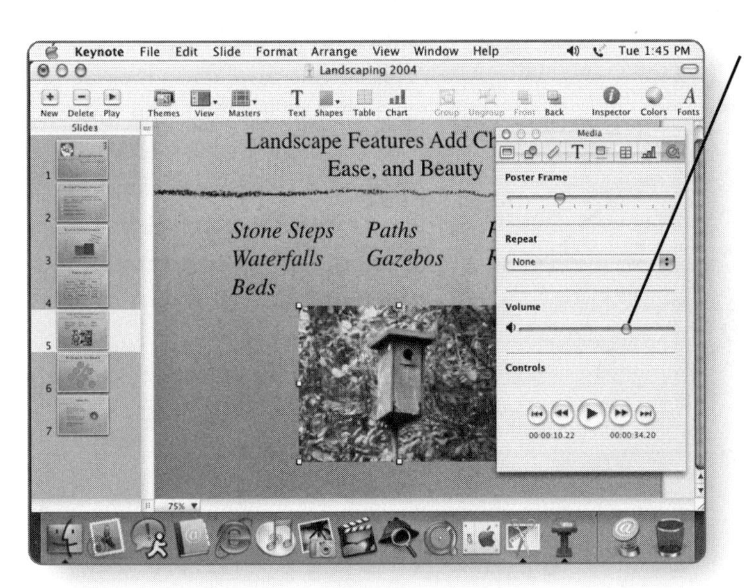

7. Drag the **Volume slider** to the desired position. The multimedia element will play back at the specified volume.

> **TIP**
>
> Use the Controls to test the multimedia object playback with any new settings you've selected in the Media Inspector.

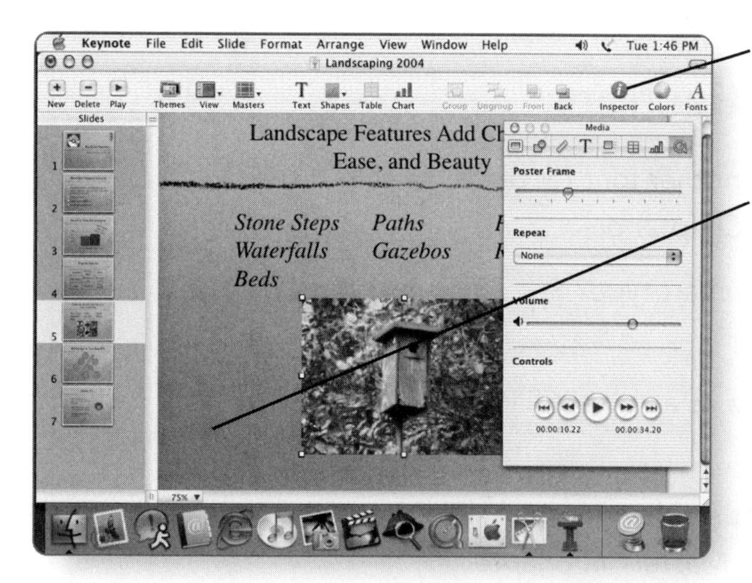

8. Click on **Inspector** on the toolbar. The Inspector window will close.

9. Click outside the multimedia object. The object will be deselected.

Part II Review Questions

1. How do you choose another font for text on a slide? *See "Formatting Text" in Chapter 6.*
2. How can I change the chart type? *See "Formatting a Chart" in Chapter 6.*
3. Can I use an image file as an object fill on a slide? *See "Working with Fills" in Chapter 6.*
4. I don't like my formatting changes on a slide. Can I undo them? *See "Reapplying the Slide Master" in Chapter 7.*
5. I need a jazzier slide background. *See "Formatting the Slide Background" in Chapter 7.*
6. My friend told me I can get other themes. Got any ideas? *See "Finding More Themes Online" in Chapter 7.*
7. My slideshow is boring. Can I change how slides appear? *See "Specifying a Slide Transition" in Chapter 8.*
8. Can I set up bullets to appear one by one during a slideshow? *See "Creating a Build" in Chapter 8.*
9. How do I add a movie to a slideshow? *See "Inserting a QuickTime Movie or Flash Animation" in Chapter 9.*
10. The movie needs more volume during playback. *See "Changing Multimedia Playback Settings" in Chapter 9.*

PART III

Viewing and Distributing Your Slideshow

10

Playing the Slideshow

Ladies and gentlemen, allow me to introduce… the on-screen slideshow! When you've refined the presentation appearance and have checked (and rechecked) all your text, you're ready to deliver it onscreen. In this chapter, you will learn how to:

- Start and control the show.
- Exit the show when desired.
- Mark a slide to be skipped.
- Work out the kinks when you're delivering the slideshow.

Playing the On-screen Slideshow

Playing back an on-screen slideshow enables the viewer to see the animation effects and hear any music that you've included on a slide. As well, movies and animations that you've placed on a slide will play automatically when you reach the slide (unless you've assigned a build to the slide object). Use the following steps when you want to play your slideshow for an audience.

> **NOTE**
>
> On-screen slideshows in Keynote require that you advance each slide manually. See "Exporting the Slideshow as a QuickTime Movie" in Chapter 12 to learn how to create a self-playing QuickTime movie of your presentation.

1. **Display or select** the **slide** from which you want to start presentation playback. The slide will appear on the canvas.

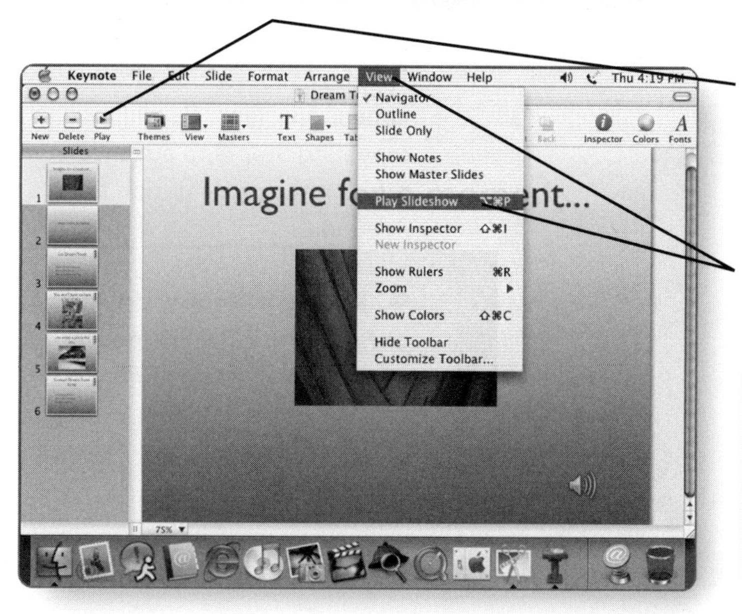

2a. Click on **Play** on the toolbar.

OR

2b. Click on **View**, and then **click** on **Play Slideshow**.

> **TIP**
>
> You also can press Option+⌘+P to start the slideshow.

Slideshow playback will begin.

3. Press Spacebar, Right Arrow, Down Arrow, or **Pg Dn,** or **click** the **mouse.**

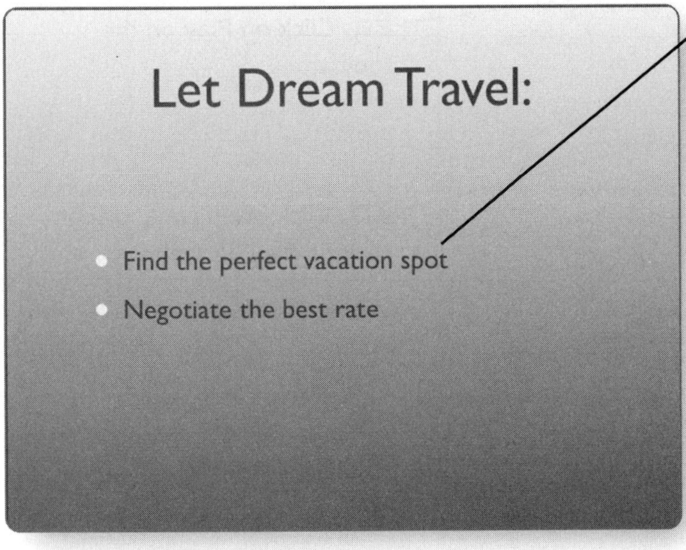

Let Dream Travel:

- Find the perfect vacation spot
- Negotiate the best rate

The next slide or build item will appear onscreen. Continue repeating Step 3 to advance through the presentation as needed.

4. **Press Left Arrow, Up Arrow,** or **Pg Up**, or **click** the **mouse**.

Let Dream Travel:

The previous slide or build item will appear onscreen. (A bullet list that builds will be treated as a single build item in this instance.)

5. **Press Home** or **End**.

NOTE

Some systems, such as iMacs, do not include an End key on the keyboard.

The first slide (Home) or last slide or build item (End) will appear onscreen.

CAUTION

If you've burned a copy of your slideshow file to a CD-R or DVD-R in order to take it on the road, be sure to copy the slide-show (.pkg) file to the hard disk of the playback system. CD and DVD drive access times really are still too slow to play back a presentation effectively, especially if the presentation file contains abundant graphics and movies.

Exiting the Show

Rather than truly pausing the slideshow, you can display a black screen at any time. To do so, press the B key on the keyboard. To return to the regular view of the slideshow, press the B key again.

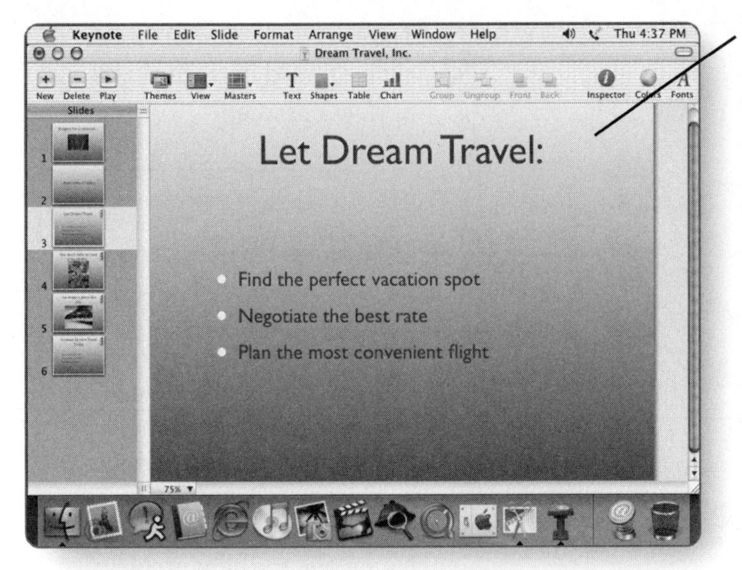

If you instead want to stop playing the slideshow at any time, press Esc, Q, or ⌘+. (period). The Keynote window will reappear and show the slide you last viewed in the slideshow.

Skipping Slides

The latest upgrade to Keynote, Keynote 1.1, adds the ability to skip slides during presentation playback. You can download the upgrade for free from the Keynote Website at http://www.apple.com/keynote. You need to mark the slide in the presentation that you want to skip. This technique comes in handy when you need to adapt a presentation "on-the-fly" for multiple audiences. You can skip and stop skipping particular slides as needed, without having to delete them from the presentation and rebuild them later. The following steps show how to skip and unskip a slide in the Navigator view.

> **TIP**
>
> In Slide Only view, use Pg Up or Pg Dn to display the slide to skip (or not), and then choose Slide, Skip Slide or Slide, Don't Skip Slide.

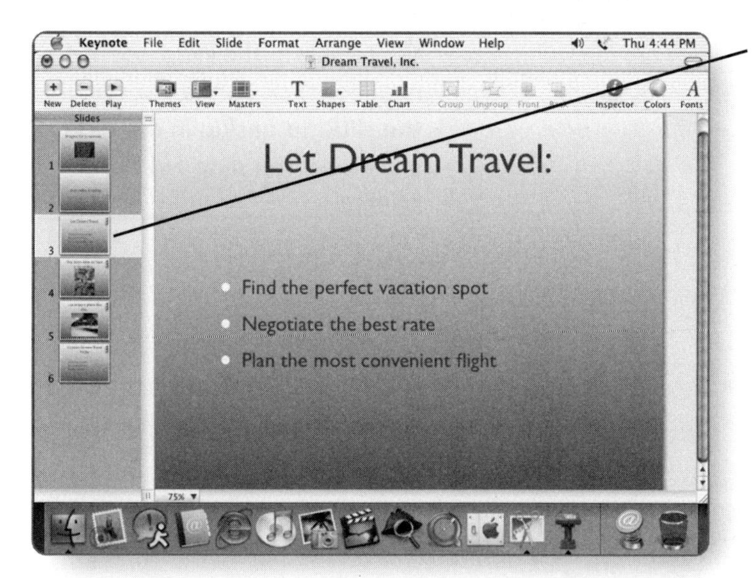

1. Click on the **slide to skip** in the slide organizer. The slide will be selected.

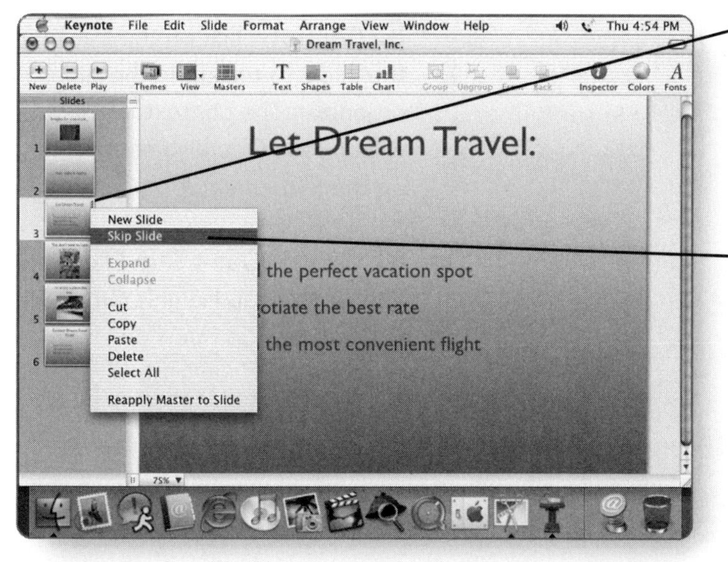

2. Control+click on the **slide to skip** in the slide organizer. The contextual menu will appear. (You also could click on the Slide menu.)

3. Click on **Skip Slide**. The skipped slide's thumbnail will be reduced to a narrow bar in the slide organizer.

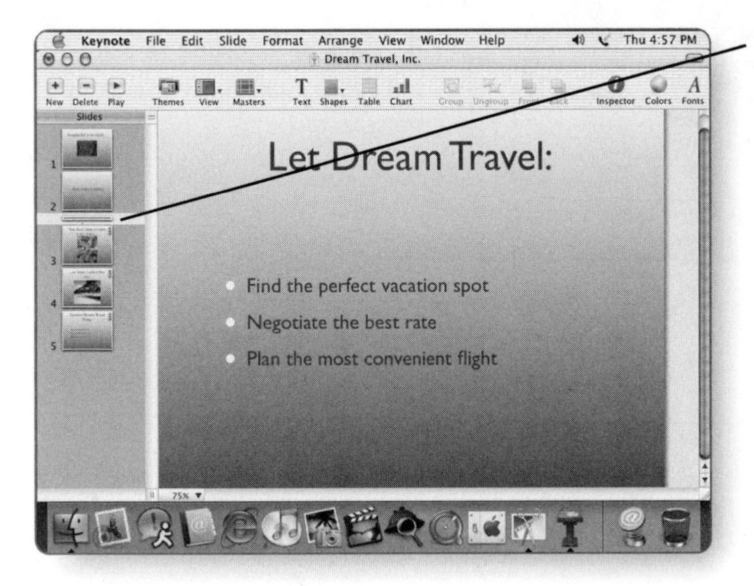

4. To unskip the slide when needed, **click on** the **bar for the slide to unskip** in the slide organizer. The slide will be selected.

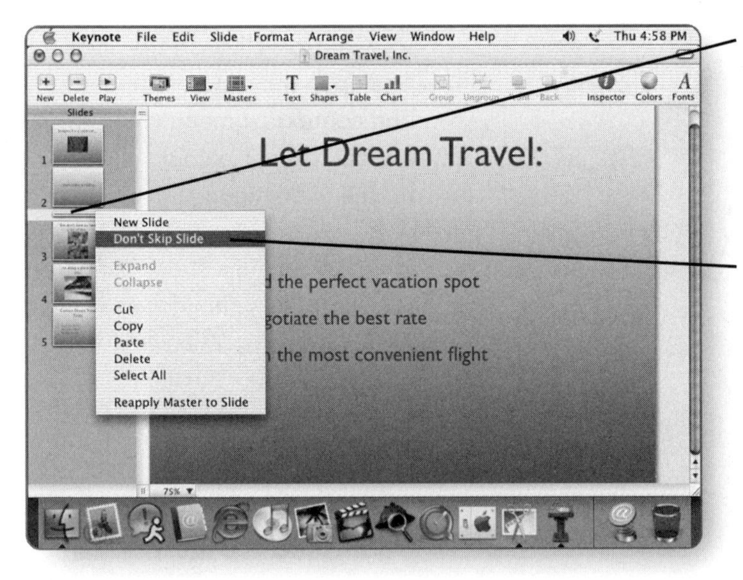

5. Control+click on the **bar for the slide to unskip** in the slide organizer. The contextual menu will appear. (You also could click on the Slide menu.)

6. Click on **Don't Skip Slide**. The skipped slide's thumbnail will reappear in the slide organizer.

Tips for a More Successful Presentation

Chapter 14 discusses setting preferences for Keynote, including how to work with settings for displaying the presentation on one monitor and speaker notes on another. Because the Keynote documentation gives a good description of these procedures, and the actual connections and settings to be used will vary greatly depending on the type of external display (monitor, VGA or DVI projector, TV) being used, I won't cover the details here. I will, however, pass along a few pointers and troubleshooting hints here to help you avoid those little "uh-ohs" that often occur when you have to deliver a slideshow:

- Always call ahead to make sure your presentation site has an external display and screen, if needed.
- If possible, test your presentation on similar equipment before you leave your office to ensure that everything is working correctly.
- Virtually all Macs support use of an external display of some type. For example, my iMac has a separate VGA port that enables me to plug in a second monitor or VGA projector. I can't show different content on the second monitor, but it does display the presentation nicely. (On the other hand, most PowerBooks and iBooks also can output to various displays using various types of connections.) If you're working with one of these systems, click on System Preferences on the Dock and then click on Displays. The Displays tab will include an Arrange tab that you can use to show the same thing on both displays (mirroring) or to show different information on each display (dual-monitor). (Note that you can only mirror the displays on iBooks.)

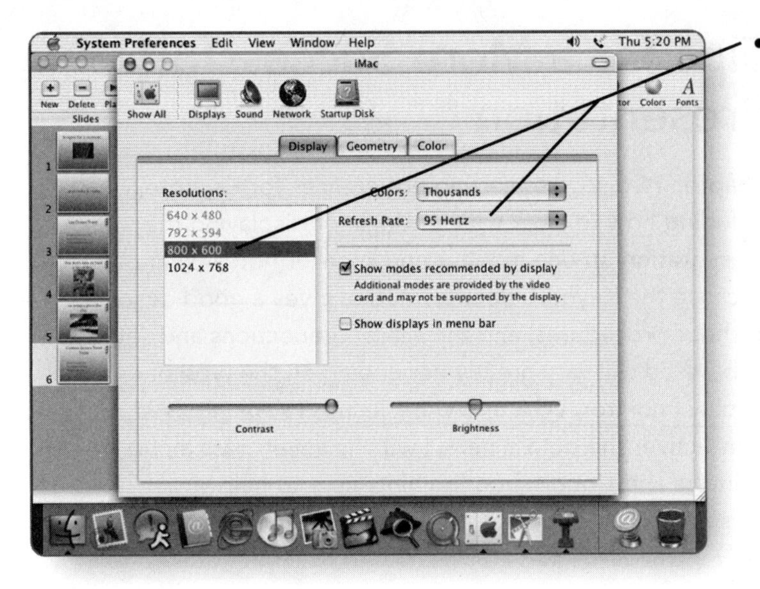

- If you connect an external display and it doesn't work immediately, click on System Preferences on the Dock, and then click on Displays. Change the Resolution and Refresh Rate settings on the Display tab until the picture appears on the external display.

- If transitions look choppy on a low-end VGA projector that you've connected, open the Displays pane of System Preferences, and try another Refresh Rate setting. DVI projectors generally don't have this issue.

- If your presentation stutters heavily or has artifacts (fuzzy or blocky spots), the problem could be due to insufficient VRAM (video RAM) in your system. The system must have at least 8M of VRAM to play animation, but 32M of VRAM is preferred. Try adjusting the display settings to use fewer colors or a smaller resolution.

> **TIP**
>
> To make more resolutions and other choices available on the Display tab of the Displays pane in System Preferences, clear the Show modes recommended by the Display check box.

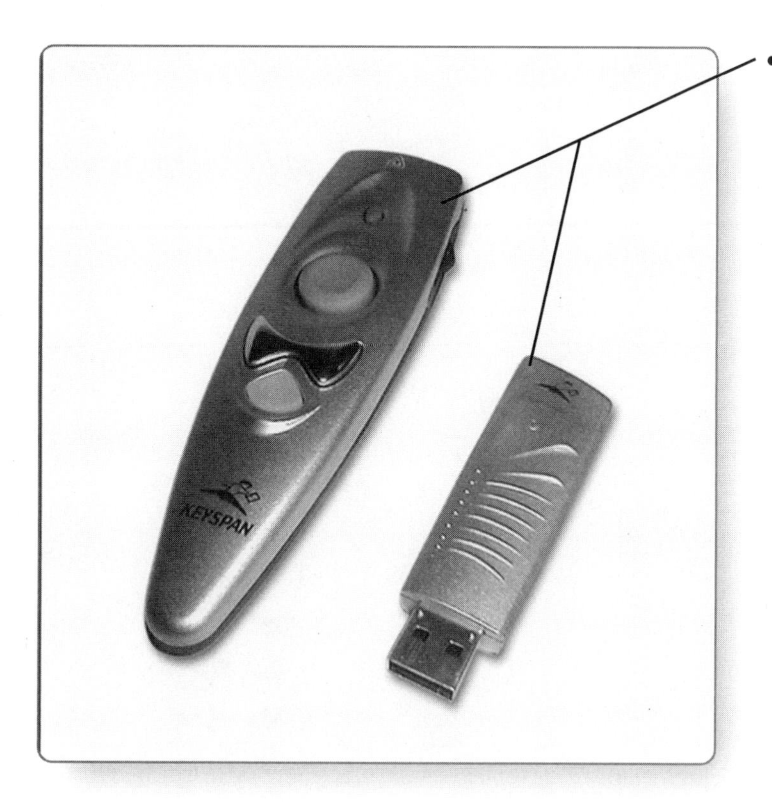

- If you like to "work the room" while you deliver your presentation, consider purchasing a wireless remote control. These devices have two pieces, a wireless controller that plugs into a port on your Mac (usually the USB port), and the remote control itself (which often incorporates a laser pointer). Mac OS X compatible wireless remote controls include the Keyspan Presentation Remote (http://www.keyspan.com), the Power Presenter (http://www.powerremote.com), the RemotePoint (http://www.interlinkelectronics.com), and the Logitech Cordless Presenter (http://www.logitech.com).
- Export a backup version of your slideshow as a QuickTime file (see Chapter 12), and take it with you to your presentation location. This way, if you experience difficulties playing back the Keynote presentation, you can try the QuickTime version instead.
- If QuickTime video is playing back in a jerky fashion on a second display, choose Keynote, Preferences in the Keynote application. Check the Present on Secondary Display check box.

11

Printing the Slideshow

In an ideal world you would skip working with paper and deliver your presentation only onscreen. In the real world, you will likely need to print your presentation for a variety of reasons: to seek feedback from colleagues, to deliver the information to someone with whom you can't meet directly, or to prepare handouts for your audience. In this chapter, you will learn how to:

- Change the page setup.
- Choose other print settings, including setting up for printing handouts and speaker notes.
- Print your slides or the slideshow outline.

Changing the Page Setup

To print to a particular type of paper or rotate the slides on the paper, you need to work with the page setup choices. You can change the orientation, choose a paper size, and even scale the printout.

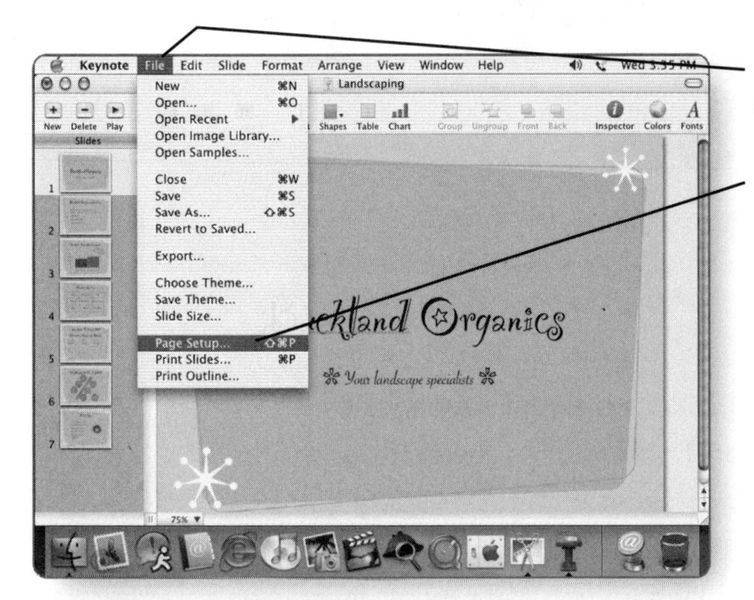

1. **Click** on **File**. The File menu will appear.

2. **Click** on **Page Setup**. The Page Setup sheet will open.

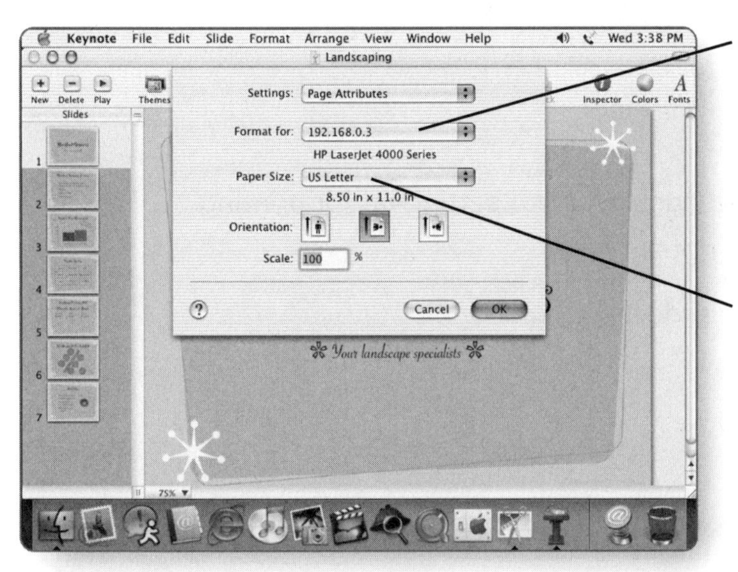

3. **Click** on the **Format for pop-up menu** and then **click** on the **printer you want** to use for the print job. The Page Setup dialog box will display your choice.

4. **Click** on the **Paper Size pop-up menu** and then **click** on the **paper size you want** to use for the print job. The document will be reformatted for the specified paper size, if required.

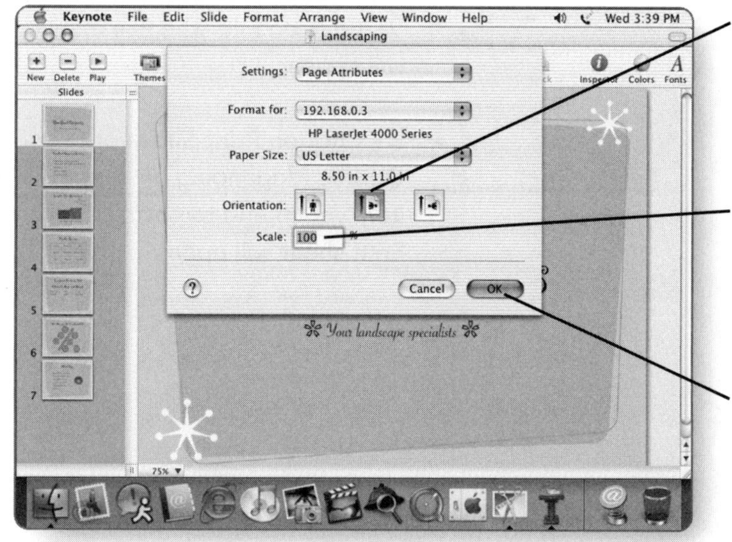

5. **Click** on the desired **Orientation button**. Keynote will print the pages in a rotated orientation, if specified.

6. **Edit** the **Scale setting,** if necessary. Keynote will print the document with the specified scaling.

7. **Click** on **OK**. Your page setup choices will be applied to the slideshow, and the sheet will close.

Changing Print Settings

In addition to choosing the page settings found in the Page Setup sheet, you also can change a variety of print settings in the Print sheet before you send the job to the printer. Follow these steps to open the Print sheet, choose a printer, and display additional print options. The remainder of this section details the choices available in each of the print settings categories, including such topics as how to print speaker notes or handouts. The available categories of advanced printing options will vary depending on the capabilities of your printer.

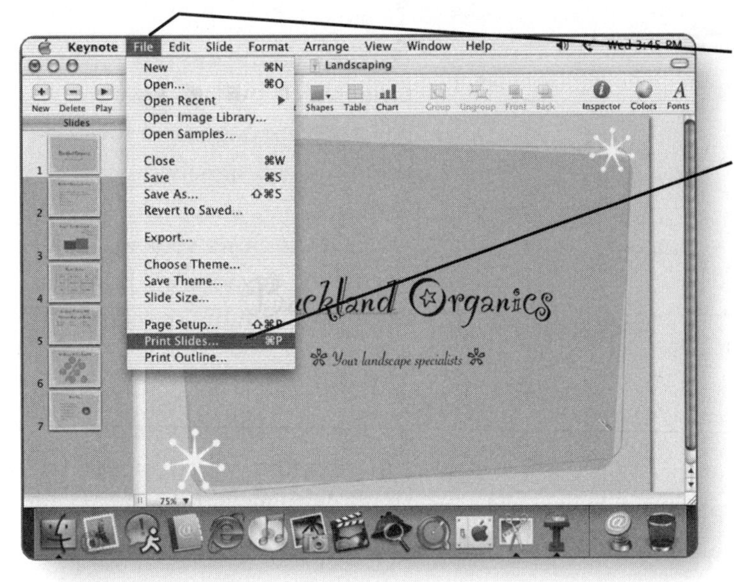

1. Click on **File**. The File menu will appear.

2. Click on **Print Slides** or **Print Outline** (depending on which item you intend to print). The Print sheet will open.

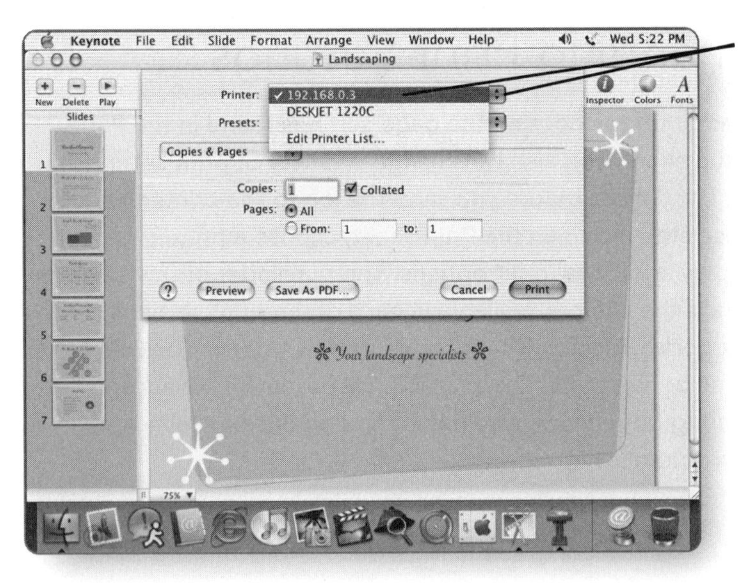

3. Click on the **Printer pop-up menu** and then **click** on the **printer** to use for the print job. (This should be the same printer that you chose in the Page Setup sheet.) The Print sheet will display your choice.

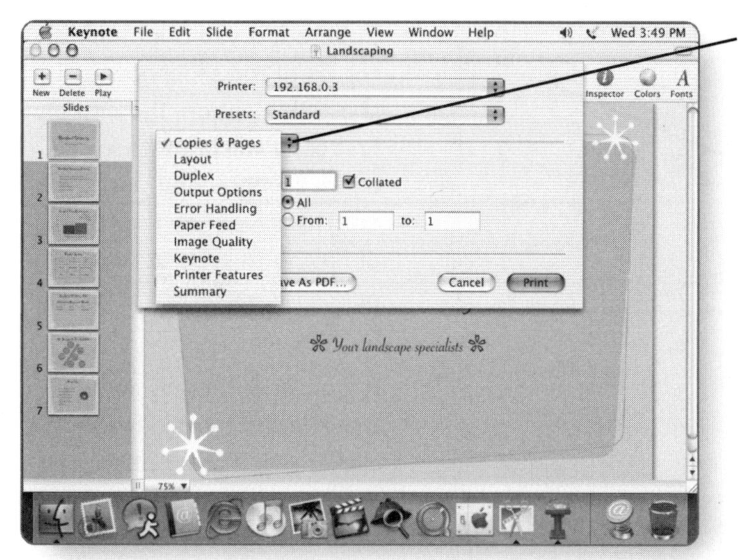

4. Click on the **category pop-up menu** at the center left of the dialog box, and then **click** on the **desired category**. The available printing option categories for your printer will appear.

> **TIP**
>
> If you want to print a quick draft copy of your slides, choose File, Print Slides. In the Print sheet, click on the Presets pop-up menu, and then click on Draft 4 Up. Click Print to send the draft job to the selected printer.

Specifying Copies and Pages

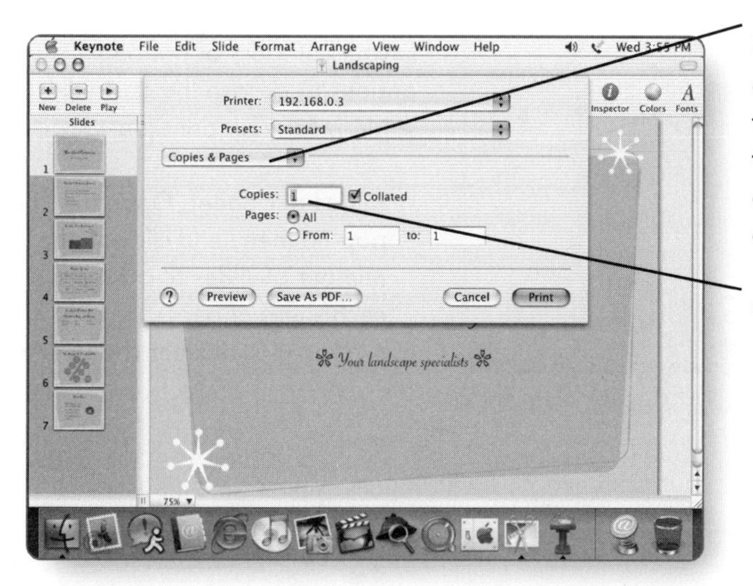

Use the Copies & Pages category of printing options as follows if you want to print more than one copy of your slideshow or if you want to print only certain pages:

- **Copies.** Edit this setting to print more than one copy of the slideshow.

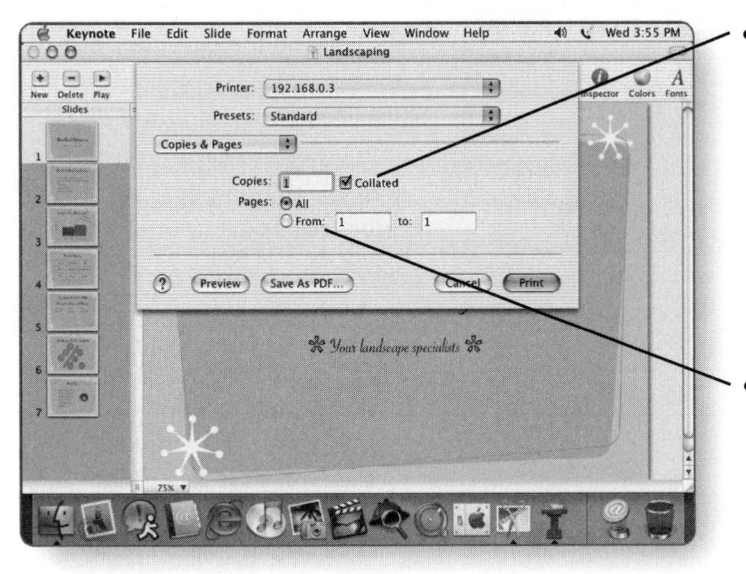

- **Collated.** If you print multiple copies of the slideshow and check this option, the entire first copy will print, then the entire second copy, and so on. This saves you the trouble of having to separate the pages for each copy after printing.
- **Pages.** To print only some of the slides in the slideshow, click on the From option, and then enter the page numbers for the range of pages (slides) to print in the accompanying text boxes.

Adjusting the Layout

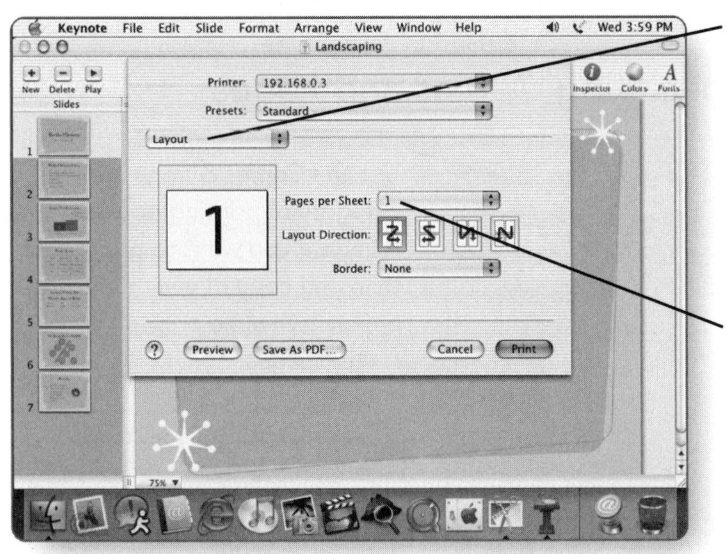

If your printer supports special capabilities, such as printing multiple document pages on each piece of paper, use the Layout category of printing options to choose the desired settings for your print job:

- **Pages per Sheet.** Open this pop-up menu and click on the number of slides to print on each sheet of paper: 1, 2, 4, 6, 9, or 16 slides per sheet.

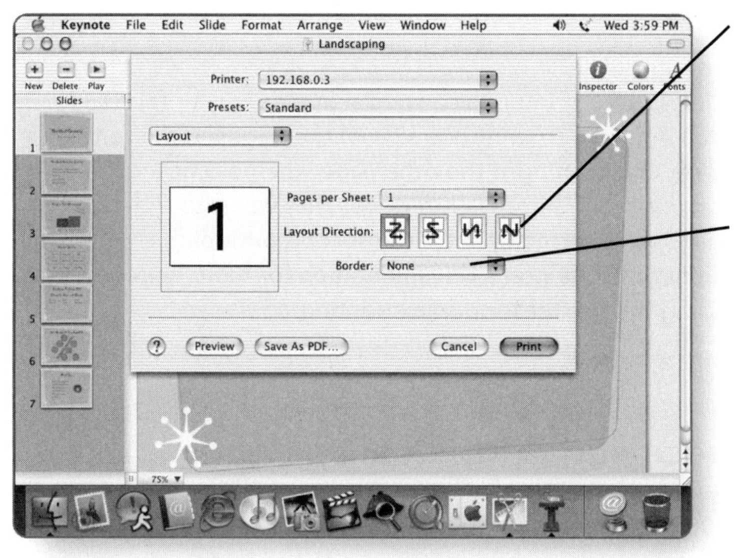

- **Layout Direction.** Click on one of the thumbnails here to control the order in which the printer prints multiple slides on each sheet of paper.
- **Border.** If you want to include a border around each slide—whether or not you're printing slides per sheet—choose the desired border style from this pop-up menu.

Printing Duplex Pages

Some printers support *duplex printing*—printing on both sides of each sheet. If the printer you've selected supports duplex printing, use the following printing options to enable and control duplex printing:

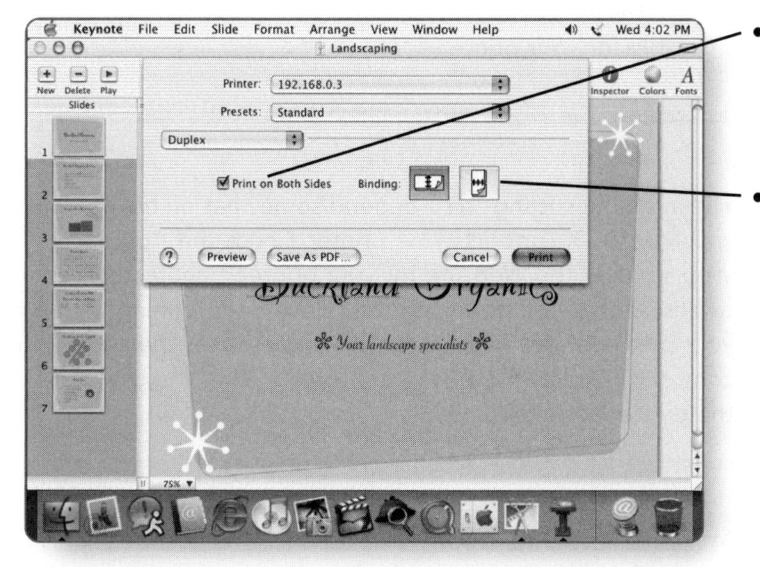

- **Print on Both Sides.** Check this option to turn on duplex printing and enable the Binding choices.
- **Binding.** Click on the appropriate thumbnail to specify whether you want to bind the duplexed slide pages along the sides or top. Your printer will shift the page contents slightly to the sides or down to accommodate the selected binding style.

NOTE

Unless your printer has a special duplex tray or feeder, you will have to print one side of the pages, turn them over, and then print the other side when prompted. This can be tricky, because it requires that you rotate the pages in a certain way for the second print pass. Consult the printer's documentation for more help on using the printer for duplex printing.

Specifying Print Quality, Paper Feed, and More

The category of settings that controls the quality of a print job, specified paper tray, and so on will use a different name, depending on the selected printer. For example, for my laser (black and white) printer, this category is called Image Quality. (And I have to choose the paper type in a separate category called Printer Features.) When I select my color inkjet printer to print a slideshow, the category becomes Paper Type/Quality. In addition, the settings in the category vary dramatically depending on the selected printer. The following examples enable you to review some of the settings that may be available for your printer.

NOTE

The available settings also depend somewhat on how well Mac OS X supports your printer. Check the Apple Web site and the Web site for your printer manufacturer to ensure that you have the latest drivers for running your printer under Mac OS X. This ensures that the best control possible will be available to you when you use the printer under Mac OS X.

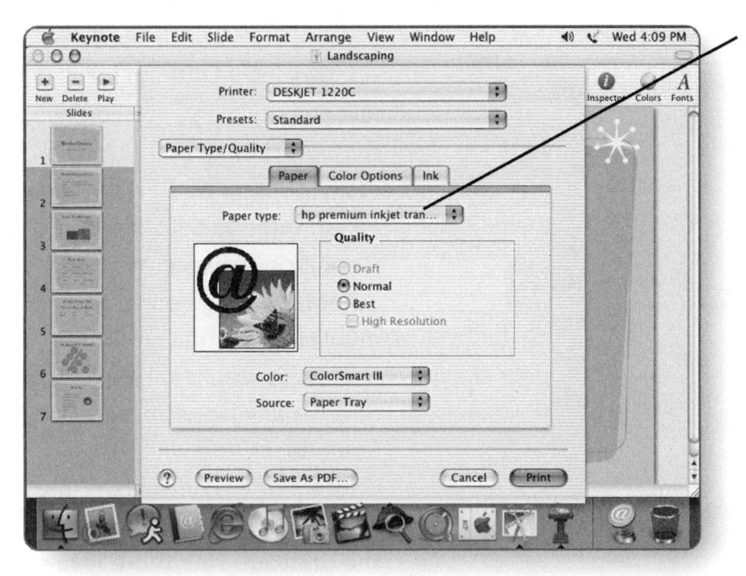

- **Paper type.** If your printer offers a pop-up menu for choosing a paper type, be sure to make the appropriate choice. Inkjet printers will automatically adjust the amount of ink applied to best saturate the selected paper type. Use this setting to select a transparency film paper type when you want to create overheads of your slides.

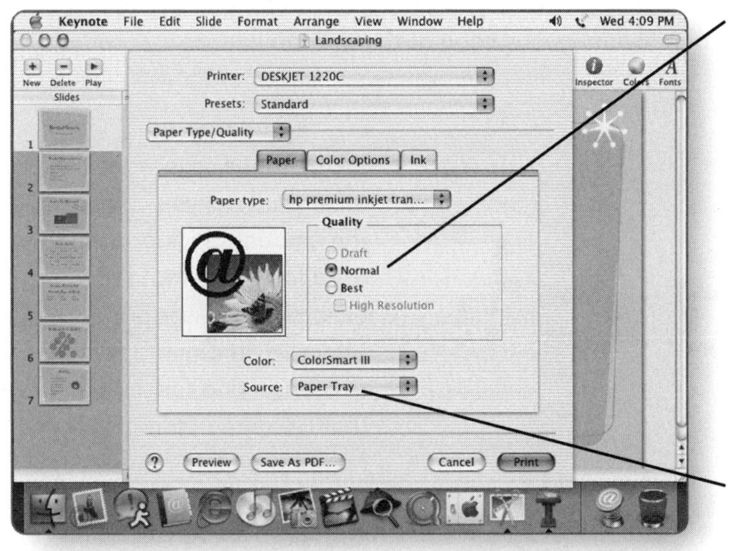

- **Quality or resolution.** Choose the desired print quality setting from among the choices presented. If your printer instead presents a resolution choice, note that a higher resolution setting (with a larger dpi number) results in a higher-quality printout. Keep in mind that a better quality printout also requires longer to print.
- **Paper source or tray.** If you've placed the paper for the print job in a particular tray or feeder, be sure to choose the appropriate location.

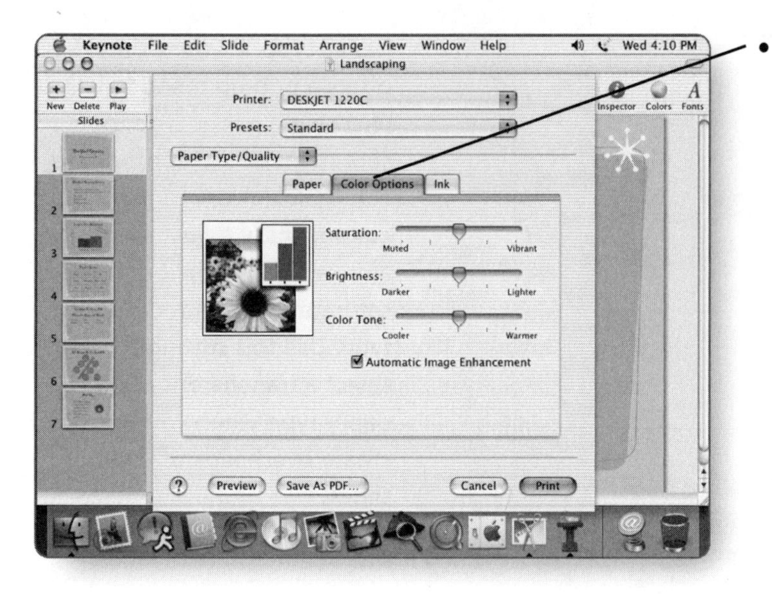

- **Color or tone options.** Some printers offer settings for fine-tuning image appearance during printing. For example, many printers (both laser and inkjet) offer an automatic resolution enhancement (or automatic image enhancement) feature that smoothes angles, curves, and edges to remove any jaggedness. Some black and white laser printers offer control over the number of levels of gray in the printout, with more levels providing smoother tonal transitions. As shown here, many color inkjet printers give you the ability to adjust the color saturation, brightness, or tone (warm versus cool) of the printed images.

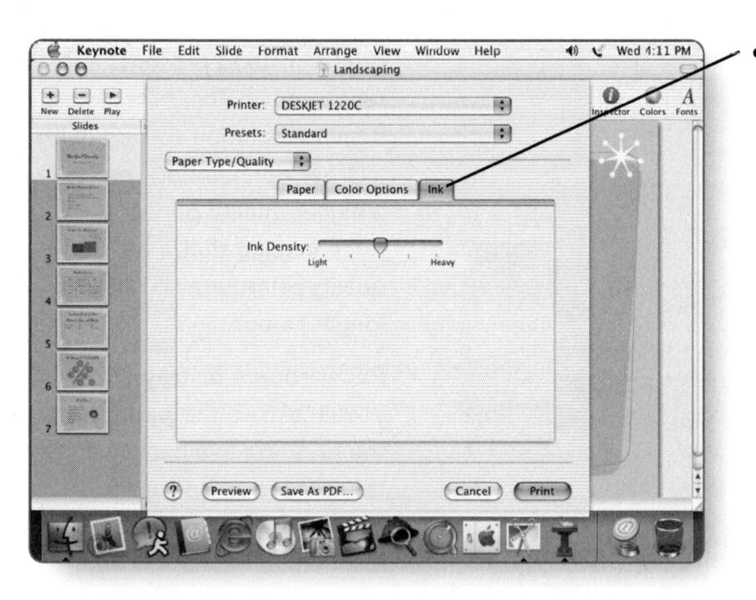

- **Ink or toner coverage.** For most printers, you can adjust the amount of ink or toner used for the printout. For example, my laser printer offers an automated feature for conserving toner. Note that uncoated (non-glossy or non-photo) papers typically have a more porous surface and require more inkjet ink for satisfactory results.

TIP

If you have any doubts about the printing settings you've chosen, print a single page of the slideshow as a test. Because slideshow printouts can take several minutes, a single page test will save you time and supplies.

Printing Speaker Notes and More

When you need to print speaker notes you've added for slides or would like to create handouts for your audience members, choose the Keynote category of settings in the Print sheet.

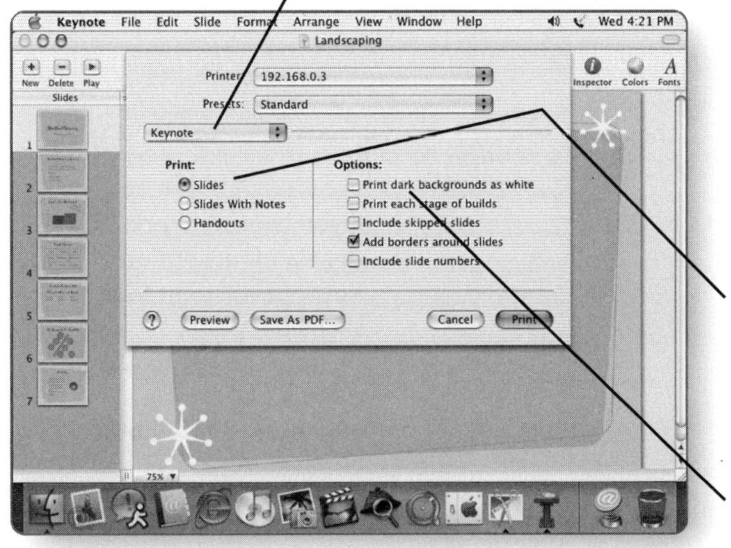

NOTE

The Keynote category is not available when you choose File, Print Outline.

- **Print.** Click an option here to choose whether you want to print the Slides in the slideshow, Slides with Notes, or Handouts.
- **Print dark backgrounds as white.** Many of the backgrounds for the themes available by default in Keynote are very dark. Because printing such dark backgrounds consumes a lot of toner and causes the printout to take longer, you can enable (check) this option to skip the background printing, which will print only the text and other objects on the slide.

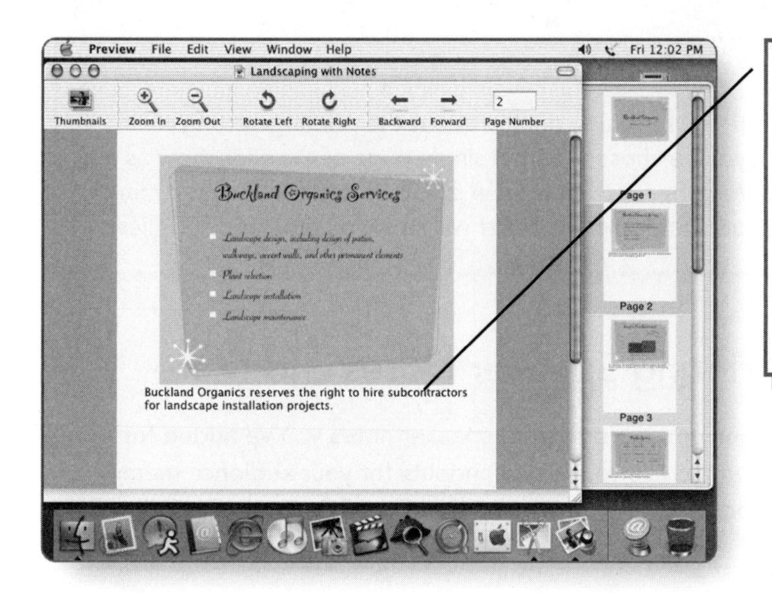

NOTE

If you choose to print the Slides with Notes option, Keynote will print a single slide per page, with the notes below the slide, as shown here in a presentation saved as a PDF file.

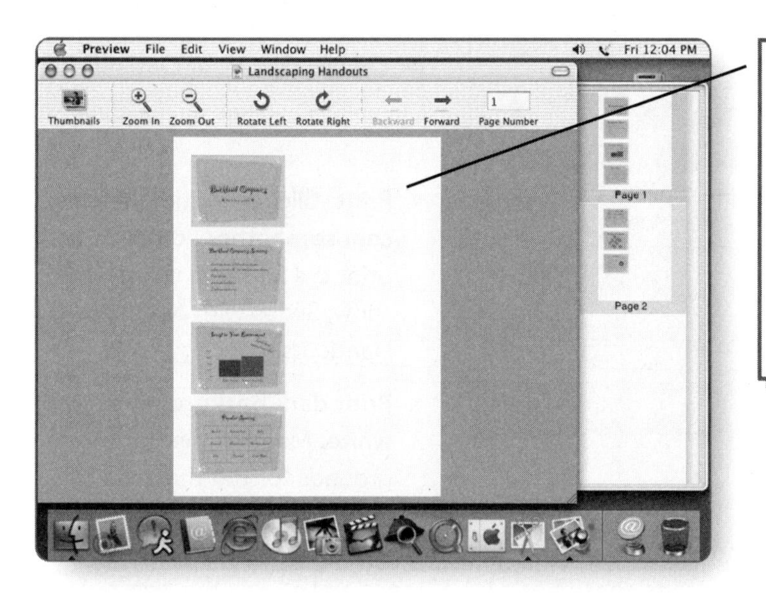

NOTE

If you choose to print the Handouts option, Keynote will print four slides per page, aligning them to the left to allow room for audience members to take notes.

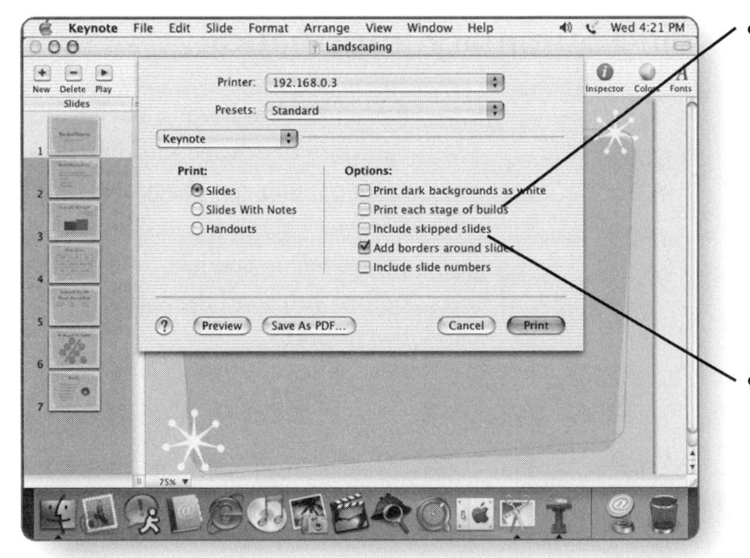

- **Print each stage of builds.** Check this check box if you want the printout to include a separate page each time a build item would be displayed for the slide onscreen. This achieves printout pages that "build," as well.
- **Include skipped slides.** In "Skipping Slides" in Chapter 10, you learned that the Keynote 1.1 upgrade (downloadable for free from Apple) includes the capability to mark a slide as skipped in the presentation. If you want the printout to include any slides that you've specified to be skipped during an on-screen show, click on this check box to check it.

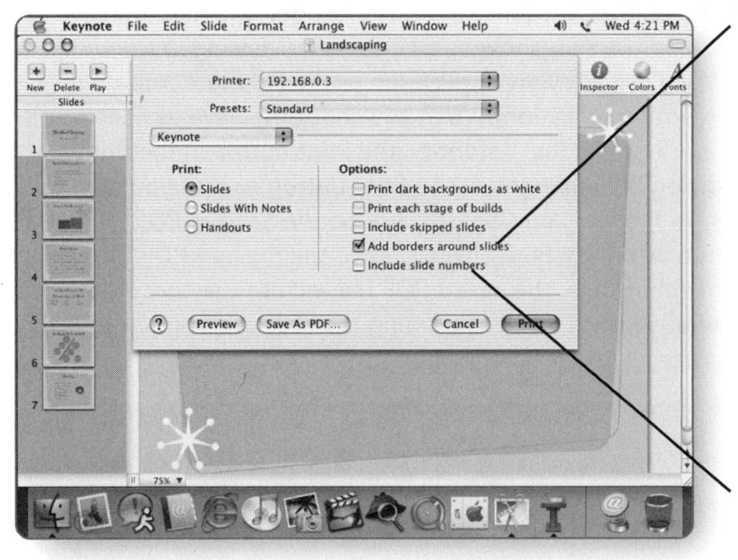

- **Add borders around slides.** Check this check box to include a printed border around each slide. You definitely should enable this feature if you opt not to print dark slide backgrounds or if your slides use a white background; otherwise, the slides will not have boundaries on the printout pages.
- **Include slide numbers.** When this option is checked, the slide number prints for each slide in the printout.

Viewing Summary Information

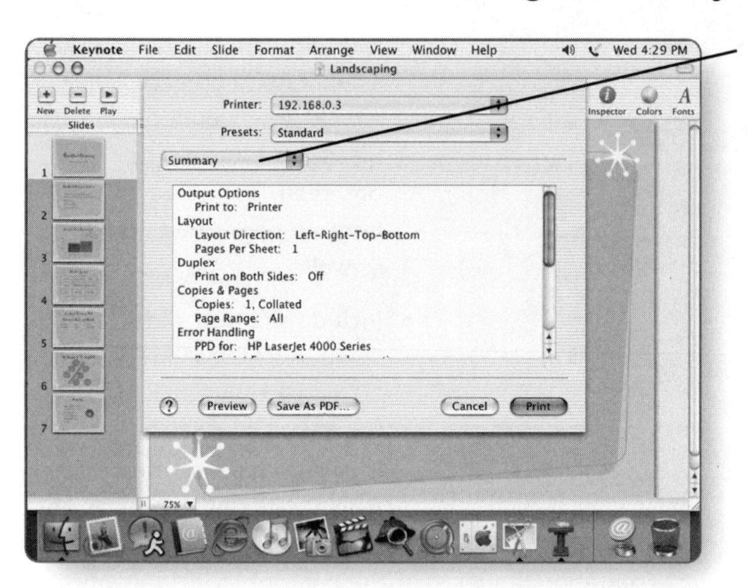

Rather than reviewing each category of advanced printing settings, you can check the Summary category to check your choices one last time before you send the job to the printer.

NOTE

The Output Options category provides one method for saving the slideshow as a PDF file for viewing in the Mac OS X Preview application or the Adobe Acrobat Reader application. When you check the Save as File check box in that category, the Print button in the Print dialog box changes to the Save button so that you can save the file. You also can click on the Save as PDF button on the Print sheet to save the file as a PDF file. In either case, the saved PDF file will use the specified print settings, such as printing the slides with speaker notes.

Printing Slides

When it's time to print your slides, here's the overall process to follow:

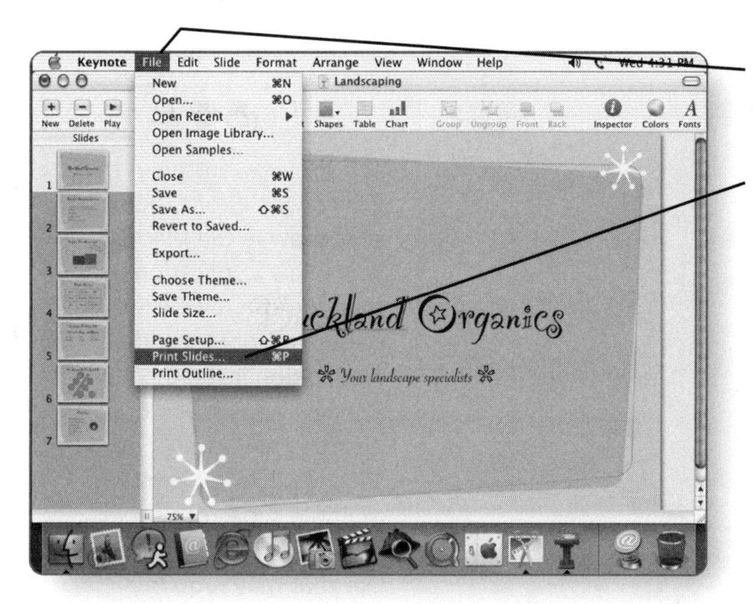

1. **Click** on **File**. The File menu will appear.

2. **Click** on **Print Slides**. The Print sheet will open.

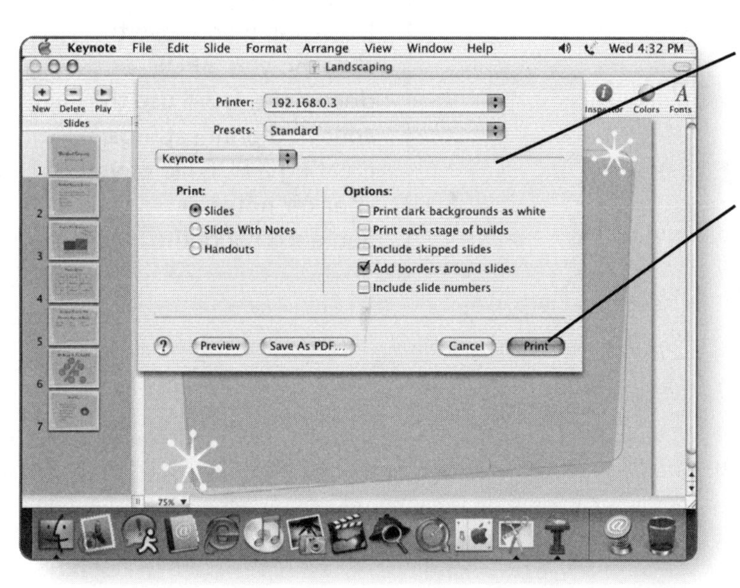

3. **Choose print settings** as needed. The settings will be used for the print job.

4. **Click** on **Print**. The Print dialog box will close, and the Mac OS X Print Manager will send the slides to the specified printer.

Processing a print job, sending it to the printer, and the actual printing may take several minutes, depending on the number of slides and images in the presentation, the amount of memory in your system, the print settings you chose, and your printer's speed.

NOTE

The Preview button in the Print sheet opens the slideshow in the Mac OS X Preview application so that you can review the pages or print from that application instead. The Preview application does not preview unusual print settings, such as printing multiple slides per sheet of paper, so a print job like that may require a little trial and error. However, if you save the slideshow as a PDF document, it will use the specified print settings, creating a PDF file of your speaker notes or audience handouts.

Printing the Outline

If you're not worried about seeing the slides themselves, but you want to review slide text on paper, you can print the presentation outline by using similar steps.

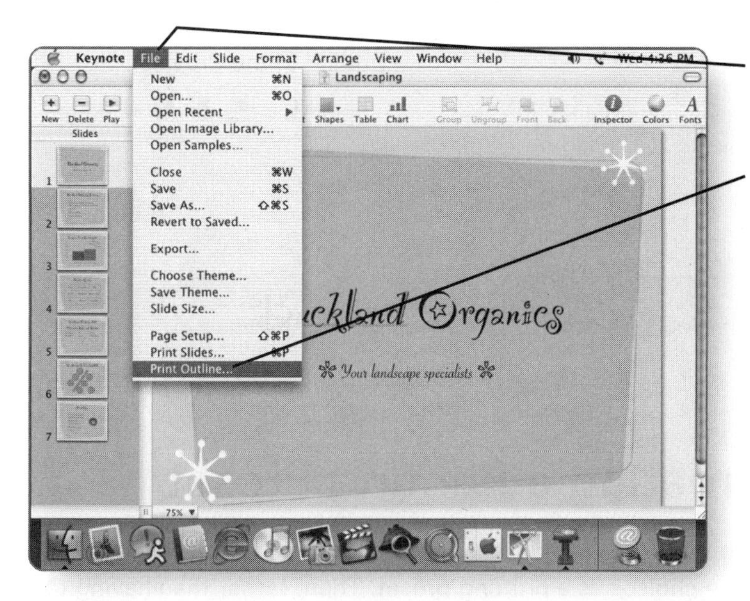

1. **Click** on **File**. The File menu will appear.

2. **Click** on **Print Outline**. The Print sheet will open.

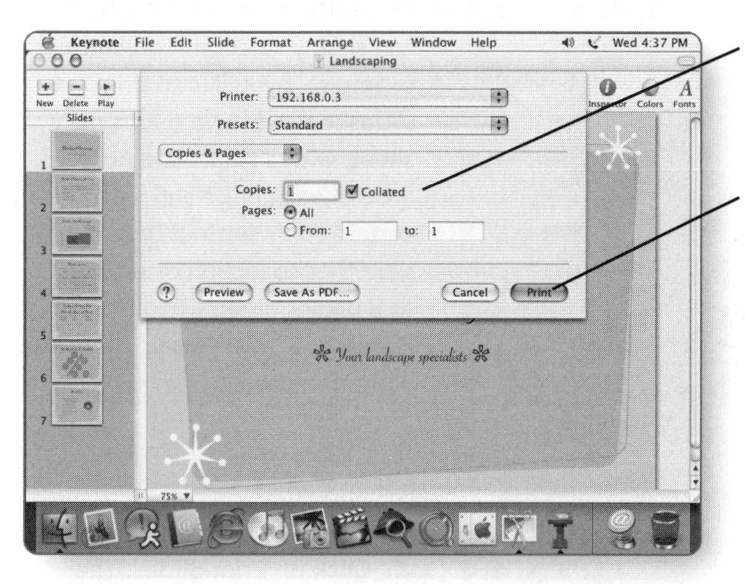

3. **Choose print settings** as needed. The settings will be used for the print job.

4. **Click** on **Print**. The Print dialog box will close, and the Mac OS X Print Manager will send the slideshow outline to the specified printer.

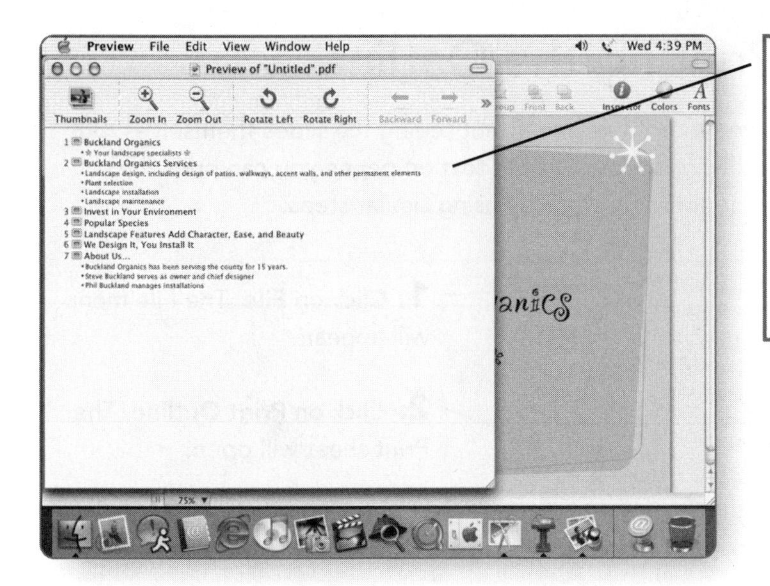

> **NOTE**
>
> When you're printing the slideshow outline, you also can click on the Preview button in the Print sheet to view the outline in the Preview.

Creating a Printing Preset

If you use certain printing options frequently, you can save those choices as a printing preset. Then, rather than having to choose the desired group of print settings for a print job, you can simply select the preset. For example, if you like to print your slideshow with two pages per sheet, with a single line border around each page and with certain color settings, you can save that collection of settings as a preset called "Two Up." Here's how to save and choose a printing preset.

1. **Click** on **File**. The File menu will appear.

2. **Click** on **Print Slides**. The Print sheet will open.

3. Choose the **desired printer** from the Printer pop-up menu. The printer will become the selected printer.

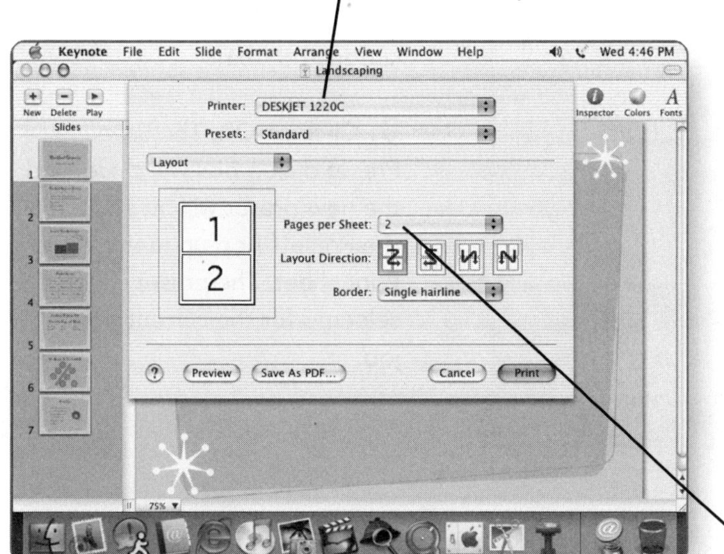

NOTE

Step 3 is necessary to ensure that all the desired advanced printing options will be available. As is indicated later, you need to select both the desired printer and preset for each print job that uses a preset.

4. Choose print settings as described in the section called "Changing Print Settings." The settings you choose will be saved as the preset.

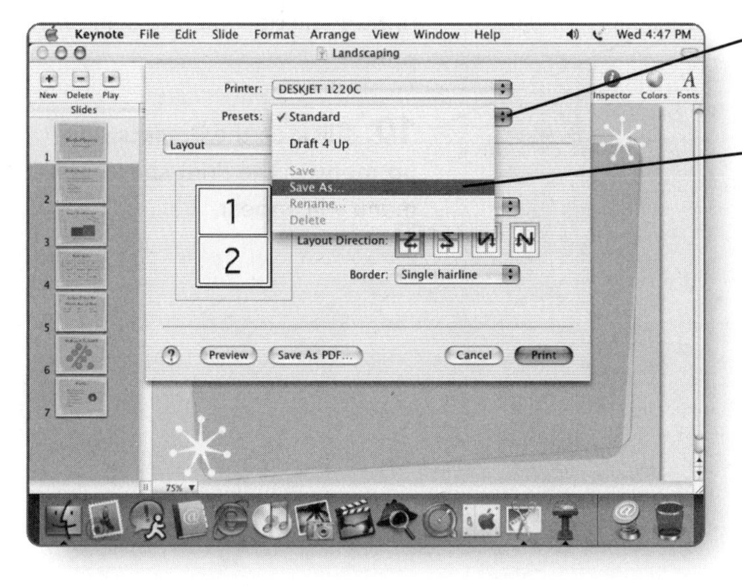

5. Click on the **Presets pop-up menu.** The menu will appear.

6. Click on **Save As.** The Save Preset dialog box will open.

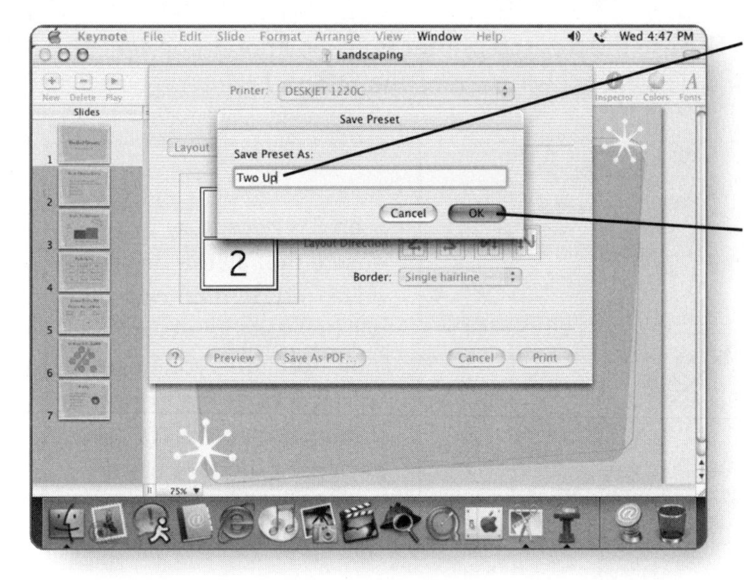

7. Type a name for the preset in the Save Preset As text box. The name will replace the suggested text.

8. Click on **OK**. The Save Preset dialog box will close, and the new preset will be added to the Presets pop-up menu in the Print sheet. The preset will be selected for the current print job.

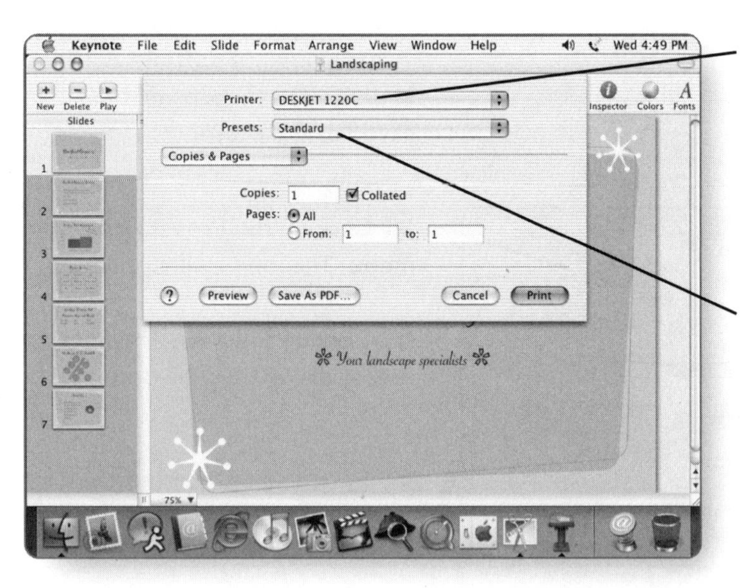

9. To select a preset for the current print job, first **choose** the **desired printer** from the Printer pop-up menu. The printer will become the selected printer.

10. Click on the **Presets pop-up menu** in the Print sheet. The menu will appear.

11. Click on the **desired preset**. The Presets pop-up menu will display your choice.

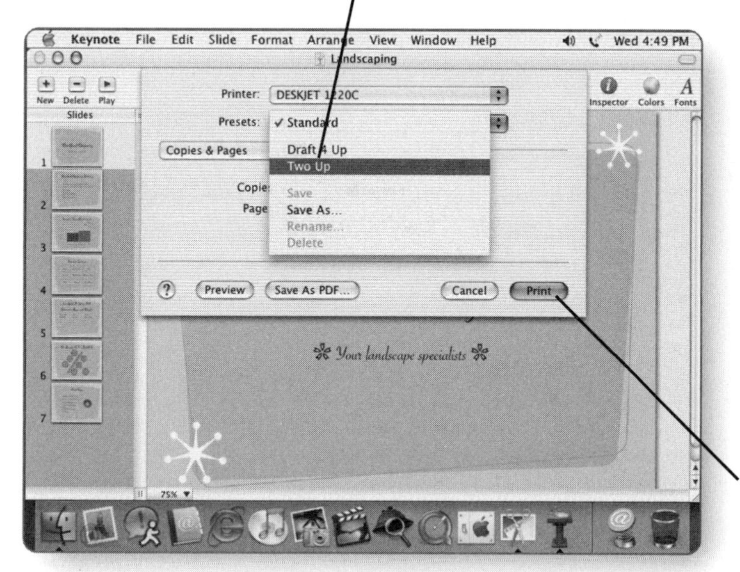

NOTE

Unfortunately, saving printing presets does not save a specified range of pages or copies for the print job. You'll need to choose those settings for every print job, even if you apply a preset.

12. Click on **Print**. The job will be sent to the specified printer using the printing options defined by the preset.

NOTE

To delete a preset, first choose it from the Presets pop-up menu in the Print sheet. Then, open the Presets pop-up menu again, and click on Delete. The preset will be deleted.

12

Importing and Exporting Presentation Information

Business partners increasingly collaborate by exchanging documents electronically. Software makers have had to facilitate this process by increasing the capability of software programs to use data from other programs. Keynote serves as a good example of this trend. It can share data in a number of ways that will save you an abundance of work when you need to share presentation information. In this chapter, you will learn how to:

- Import a slideshow created in PowerPoint or AppleWorks.
- Create a QuickTime movie from a slideshow.
- Save your slideshow for PowerPoint.
- Create a PDF file of your slide show.
- View a presentation file on a Windows-based system.

Importing Slide Content

You've probably created a presentation or two (or two hundred) before switching from another application to Keynote. Is all that work lost? Nope. Keynote can import presentations that you've created in either PowerPoint or AppleWorks. The steps resemble opening a file, which you learned about in the section called "Opening an Existing File" in Chapter 5.

When importing a file, keep these points in mind:

- When you import a PowerPoint slideshow into Keynote, you will be able to edit charts and tables in Keynote as usual. However, importing an AppleWorks presentation converts charts and tables to graphics that you can't edit.
- Keynote keeps the slide design for the imported slideshow. However, you can apply another theme as desired, especially for PowerPoint presentations. After you do so, you may have to readjust the formatting for certain chart elements, such as reducing the size of a chart to help it better fit on the redesigned slide.
- Master slide designs are not imported for an AppleWorks presentation, even those created from an AppleWorks starting point. As such, the "design" for slides will be composed of graphic objects. Applying a new master will change only the slide background. You'll have to update the rest of the slide design manually by deleting or reformatting objects.
- Don't forget to save your presentation after you import it.

1. Click on **File**. The File menu will appear.

2. Click on **Open**. The Open dialog box will open.

3. Navigate to the **folder** holding the slideshow file you want to open. The file will be displayed in the file list. You may need to do one or more of the following steps to locate the folder:

- **Click** on the **From pop-up menu**; then **click** on the folder that holds the file.
- **Click** on the **scroll arrows** below the folder and file list; then **click** on the desired **folder** or **disk name**.

4. Click on the **file** that you want to open. A preview icon will appear at the right side of the Open dialog box.

5. Click on **Open**. The file will appear onscreen.

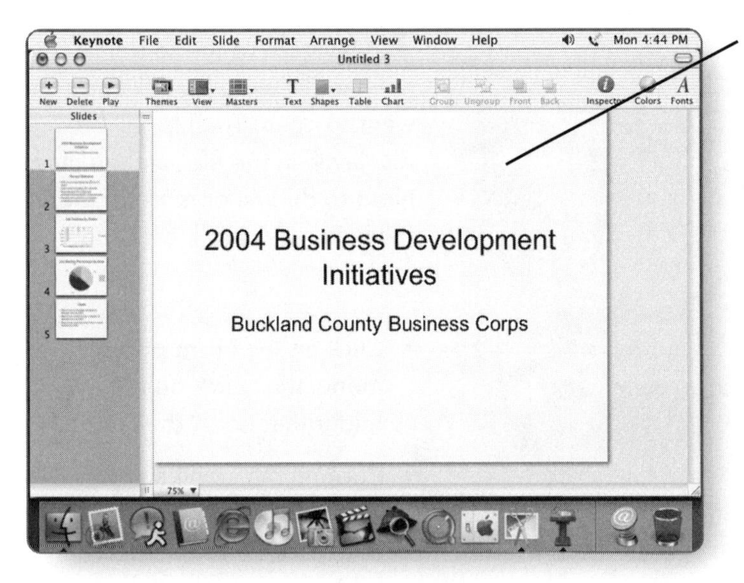

Here's a PowerPoint 2002 for Windows presentation imported into Keynote. In this case, the presentation used a blank design, so applying a theme would dramatically improve its appearance.

This example shows an AppleWorks 6 presentation imported into Keynote.

> **TIP**
>
> Control+click a slideshow file icon in a Finder window to both launch Keynote and open the specified file.

Exporting the Slideshow as a QuickTime Movie

Converting your slideshow file to a QuickTime movie enables you to share the show with perhaps the broadest spectrum of computer users. Even if a user's system didn't ship with software for playing QuickTime movies, most users have probably downloaded and installed the free QuickTime Player (for either Mac or Windows operating systems) by now. Use this process when you want to convert your slideshow file to a movie.

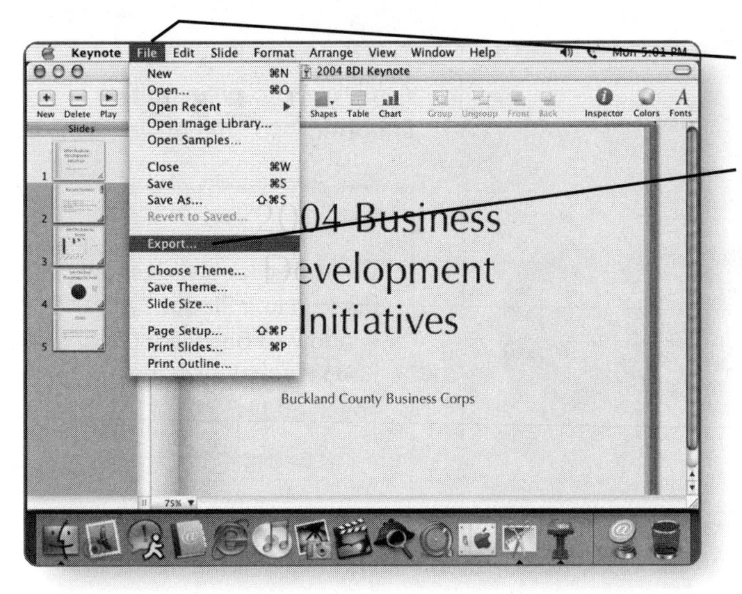

1. **Click** on **File**. The File menu will appear.
2. **Click** on **Export**. A sheet will appear to prompt you for the type of export to perform.

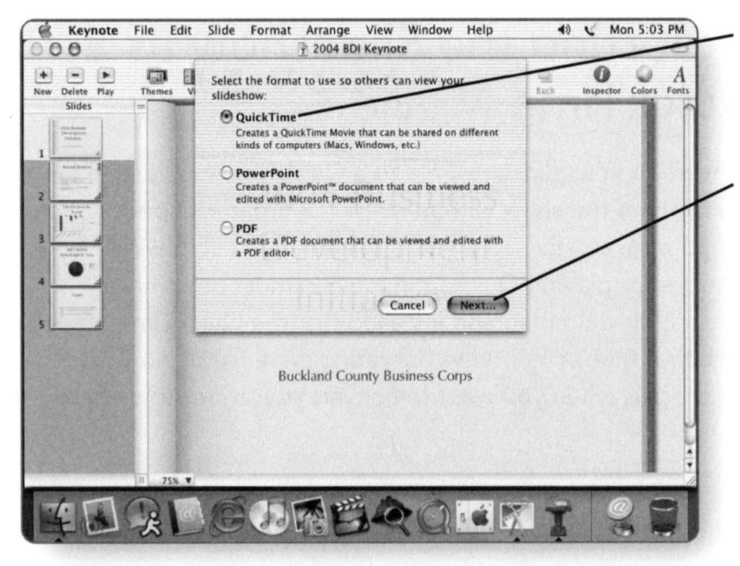

3. **Click** on **QuickTime**, if needed. The QuickTime export format will be selected.
4. **Click** on **Next**. The next sheet will present options for the export.

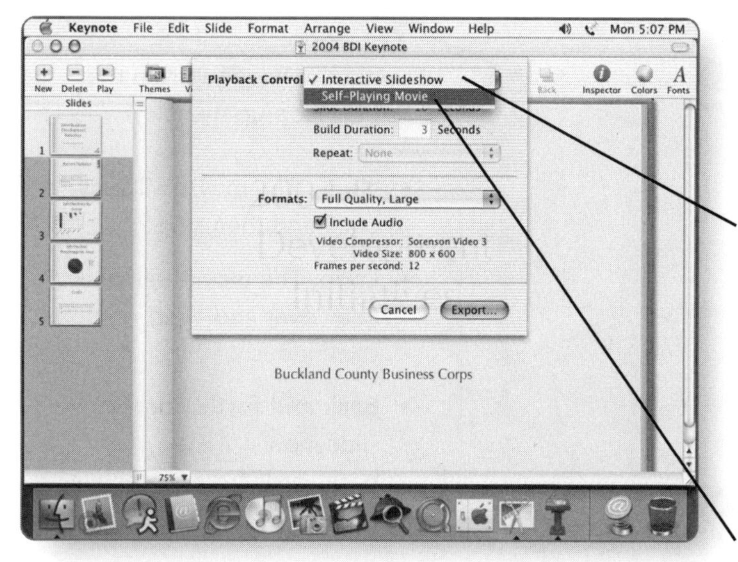

5. Choose another **Playback Control** type, if needed, from the Playback Control pop-up menu:

- **Interactive Slideshow.** When you choose this option, Keynote will create a movie with controls so that the users can start and stop playback. If you choose this playback control type, skip to Step 8.
- **Self-Playing Movie.** Choose this option to specify that the slideshow will play itself automatically once started.

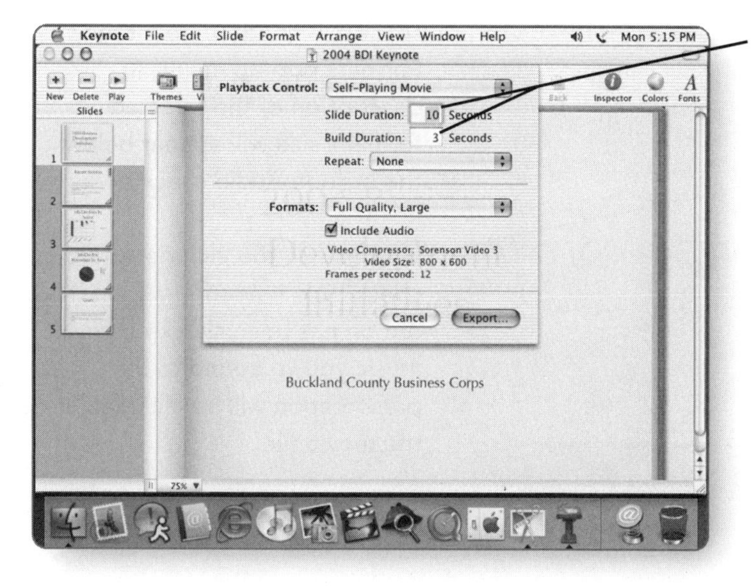

6. Enter Slide Duration and **Build Duration values.** The durations you enter will control how long each slide appears onscreen and the time between build items in a self-playing movie.

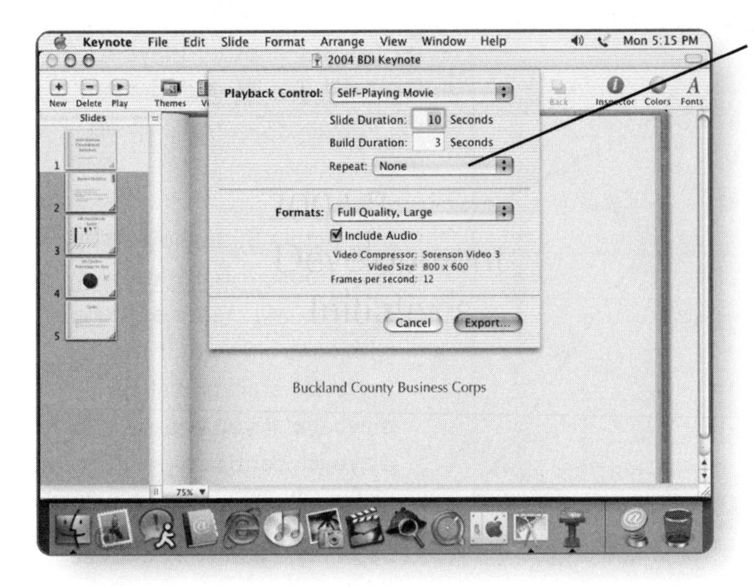

7. Choose another **Repeat setting**, if needed, from the Repeat pop-up menu:

- **None.** The movie will play once and then stop.
- **Loop.** The movie will loop (play over and over) continuously.
- **Back and forth.** The slideshow will play, play backwards from the end, play forward again, and so on.

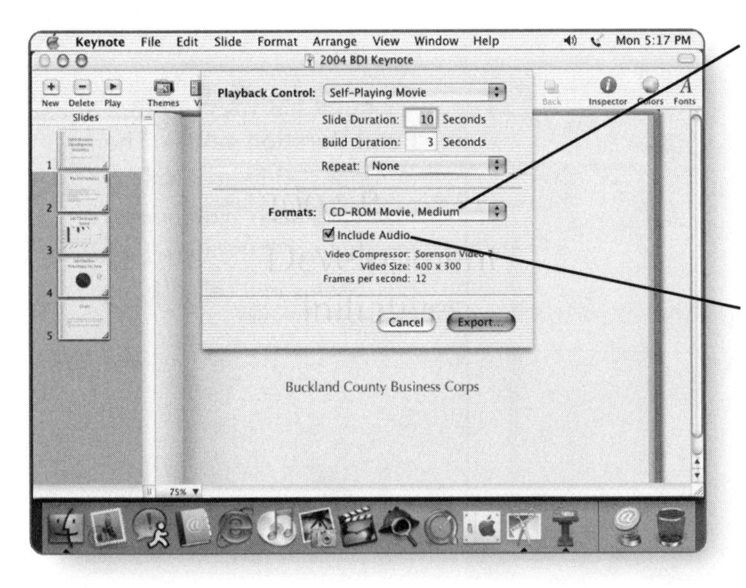

8. Choose another **Formats setting**, if needed, from the Formats pop-up menu. A description of the selected format's size will appear below the Include Audio check box.

9. Click on the **Include Audio check box**, if needed. When this option has been checked, any music you've added to the presentation will be included in the movie file.

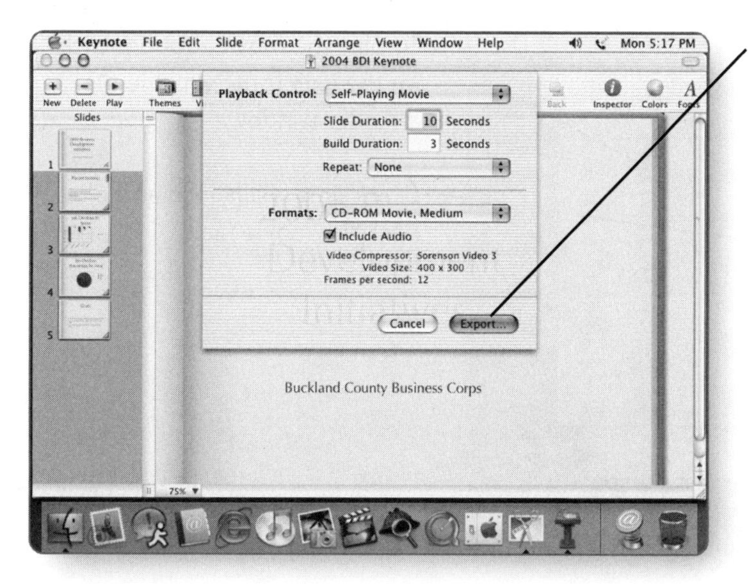

10. Click on **Export**. The next sheet will present options for saving the file.

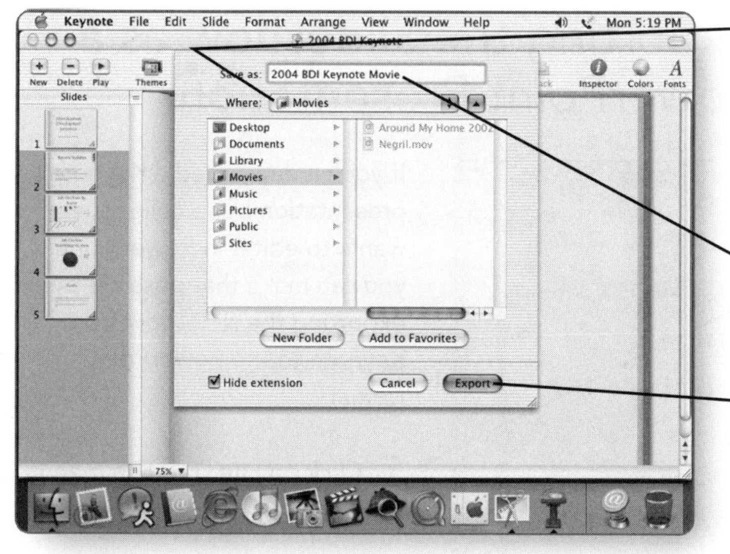

11. Navigate to the **disk and folder** where you want to save the slideshow file, if needed. The folder will appear in the Where box.

12. Type a **file name** in the Save As text box. The name will appear in the Save As text box.

13. Click on **Export**. A dialog box will display the movie during the export process. Keynote will save the movie file in the location you specified. The original Keynote file will remain open onscreen.

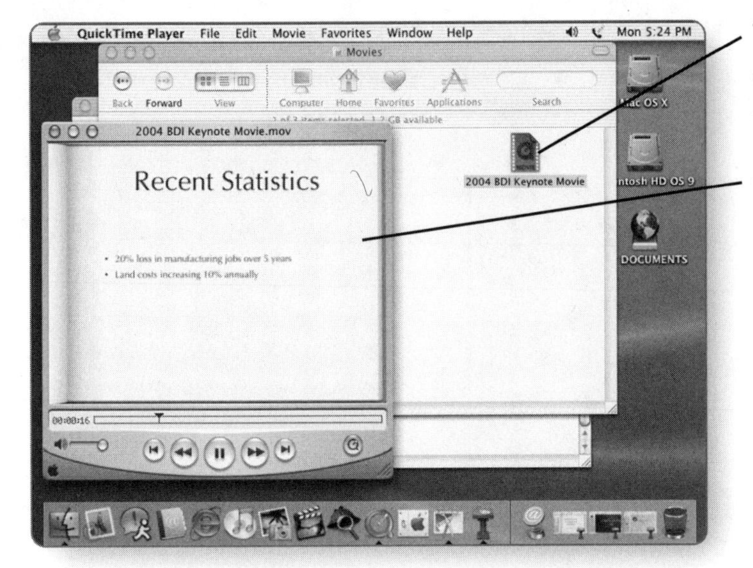

To play the movie, double-click on the icon for the movie file in a Finder window.

QuickTime will launch and play back the movie file.

Exporting the Slideshow as a PowerPoint Presentation

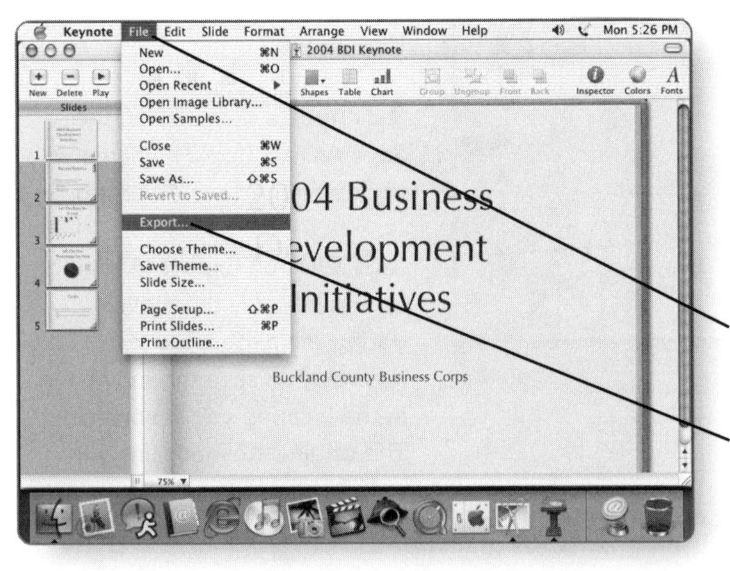

If you've developed a Keynote presentation but a colleague wants to edit it in PowerPoint, you can make that possible by exporting the slideshow from Keynote to the PowerPoint format.

1. Click on **File**. The File menu will appear.

2. Click on **Export**. A sheet will appear to prompt you for the type of export to perform.

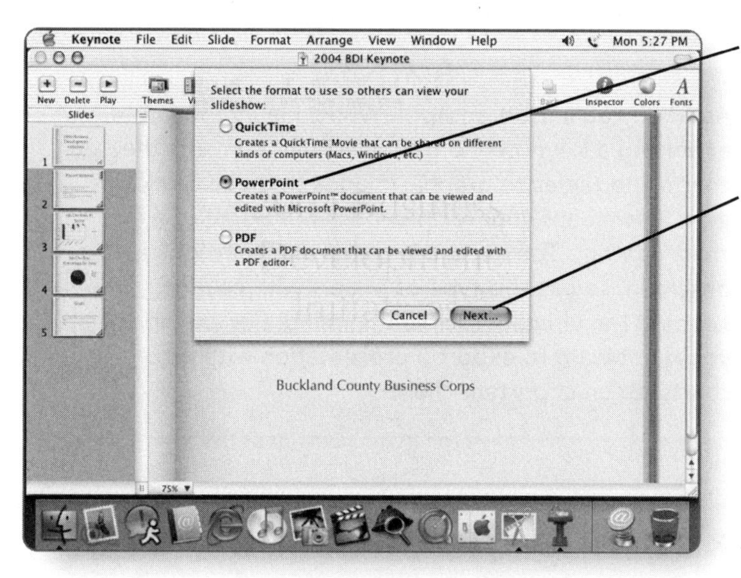

3. **Click** on **PowerPoint**. The PowerPoint export format will be selected.

4. **Click** on **Next**. The next sheet will present options for saving the file.

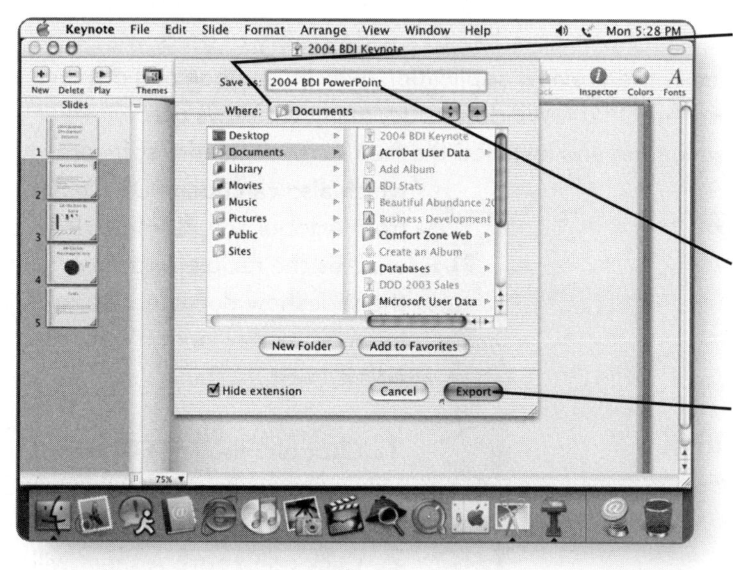

5. **Navigate** to the **disk and folder** where you want to save the slideshow file, if needed. The folder will appear in the Where box.

6. **Type** a **file name** in the Save As text box. The name will appear in the Save As text box.

7. **Click** on **Export**. A dialog box will display the export-process progress. Keynote will save the PowerPoint file in the location you specified. The original file will remain open onscreen.

CAUTION

As when you import an AppleWorks file into Keynote, exporting a Keynote file to PowerPoint converts the charts and tables to graphic images that you cannot edit. This means your recipient will not be able to edit chart content. The exported charts also may look fuzzy onscreen, so use this type of export with caution, keeping the ultimate recipient in mind. For example, you don't want to export a presentation with fuzzy charts for an important client.

Exporting the Slideshow as a PDF Document

The Adobe PDF (Portable Document Format) also can make your slideshow accessible to a wide variety of users. Mac OS X includes the Preview application, which can open and display PDF files. On the Windows side, many Windows users have downloaded and installed the free Acrobat Reader software, which also can open PDF files, from Adobe. The PDF format enables the recipient to view the slideshow document page by page, and to print it but not edit it.

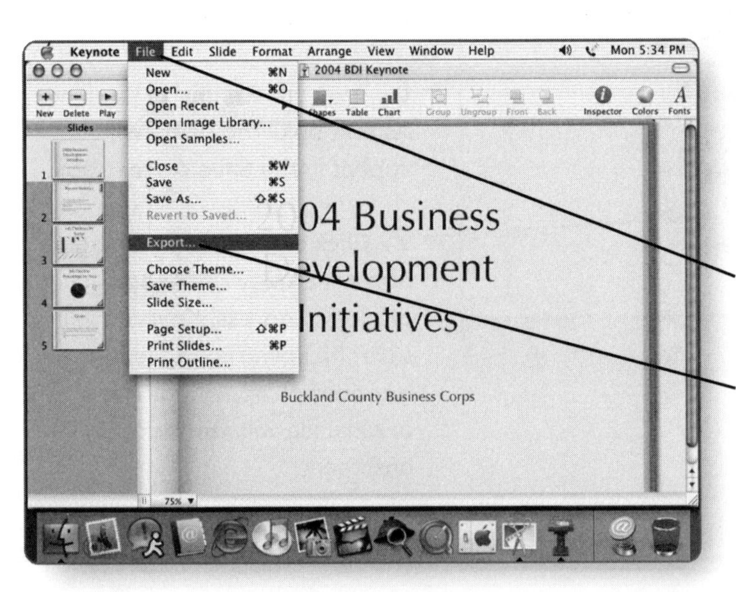

1. **Click** on **File**. The File menu will appear.

2. **Click** on **Export**. A sheet will appear to prompt you for the type of export to perform.

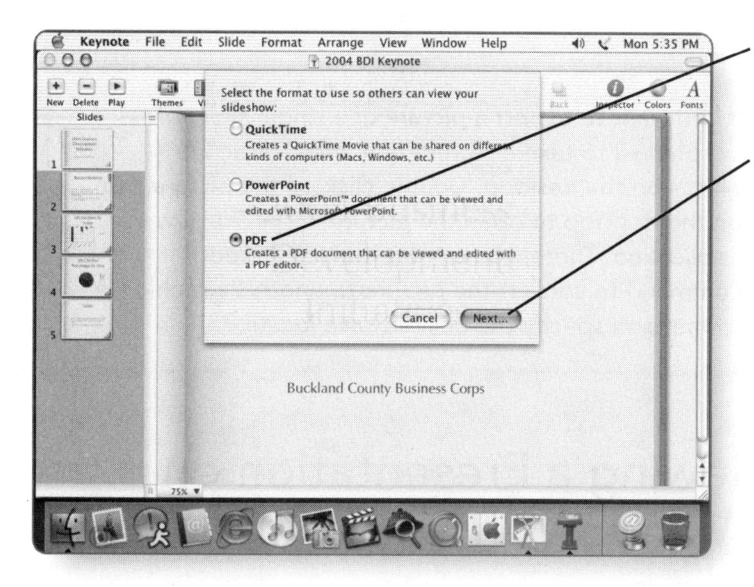

3. **Click** on **PDF**. The PDF export format will be selected.

4. **Click** on **Next**. The next sheet will present options for saving the file.

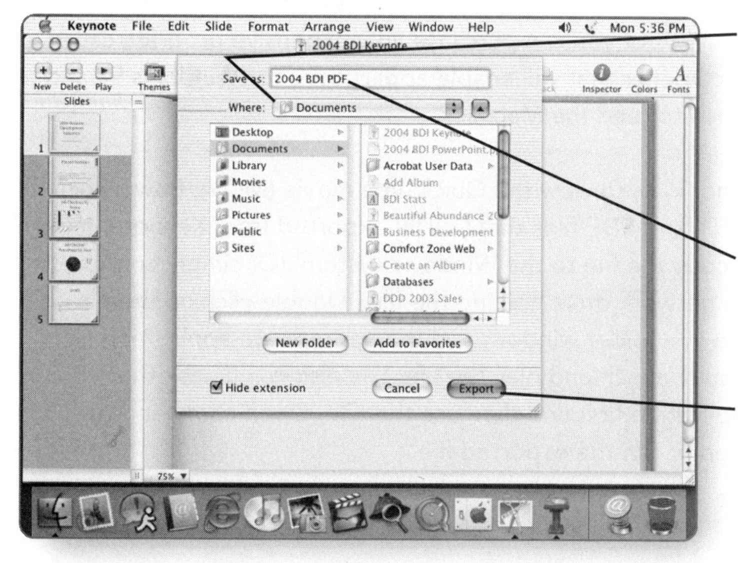

5. **Navigate** to the **disk and folder** where you want to save the slideshow file, if needed. The folder will appear in the Where box.

6. **Type** a **file name** in the Save As text box. The name will appear in the Save As text box.

7. **Click** on **Export**. A dialog box will display the export-process progress. Keynote will save the PDF file in the location you specified. The original file will remain open onscreen.

TIP

If you want to export a picture of a single slide, press ⌘+Shift+3 to take a picture of it, which Mac OS X places on the desktop. Double-click on the picture icon on the desktop to open the picture in the Preview application. There, you can use the File, Export command to convert the picture to another graphic file format and specify the desired save location.

Viewing a Presentation on a Windows PC

Windows XP applications generally can read files from comparable Mac OS X applications directly. Pre-XP versions of Windows and its apps may not be able to read Mac files directly, but you can purchase an inexpensive program called MacOpener that will enable applications for Windows 98 and above to read the Mac files.

Either way, to view the QuickTime movie (MOV), PowerPoint (PPT), and PDF files that you've exported from Keynote, move or copy the file to the Windows system. (Or simply connect to the network drive holding the file.) Double-click on the file icon in a folder window, and the appropriate application should launch and play the file. You also can launch the application first and then use the File, Open command to open or run the exported file.

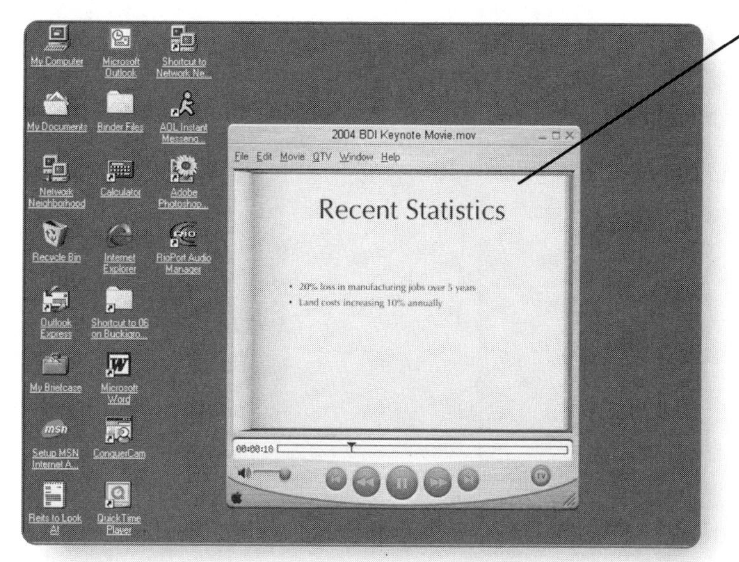

For example, here's a Keynote presentation exported as a movie file. It's playing back on a Windows 98 system with an older version of the QuickTime Player.

> **TIP**
>
> Some media players, such as Windows Media Player, may need to connect to the Internet and download a new video codec to play the QuickTime movie.

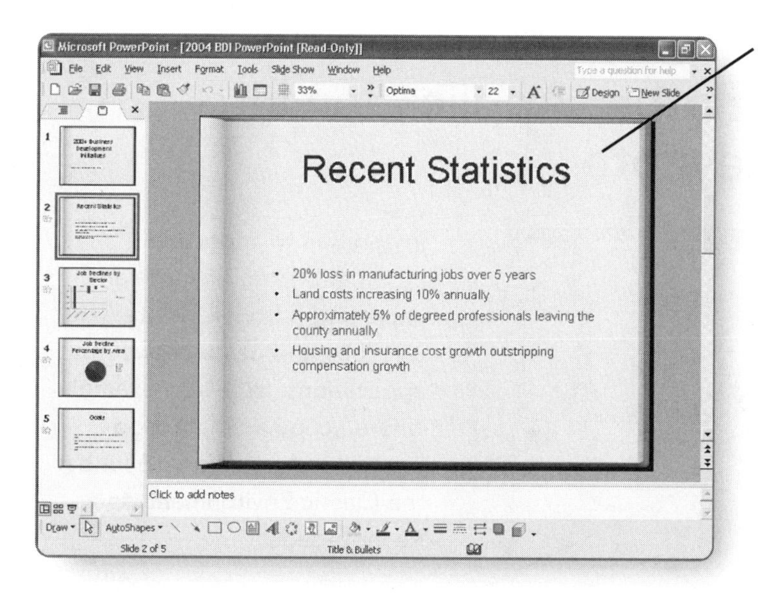

This example shows an exported Keynote presentation in PowerPoint 2002 on a Windows XP system.

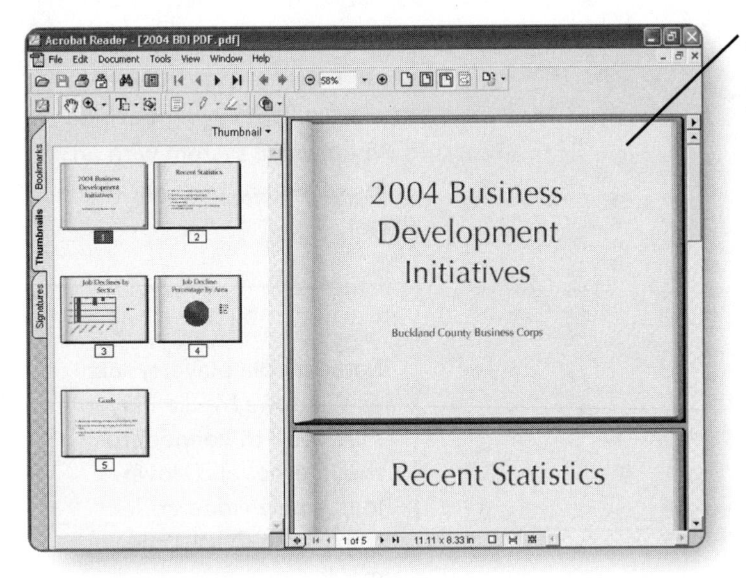

And finally, here's a Keynote presentation exported in PDF format, viewed in Acrobat Reader on a Windows XP system.

Pasting Information from Another Application into Keynote

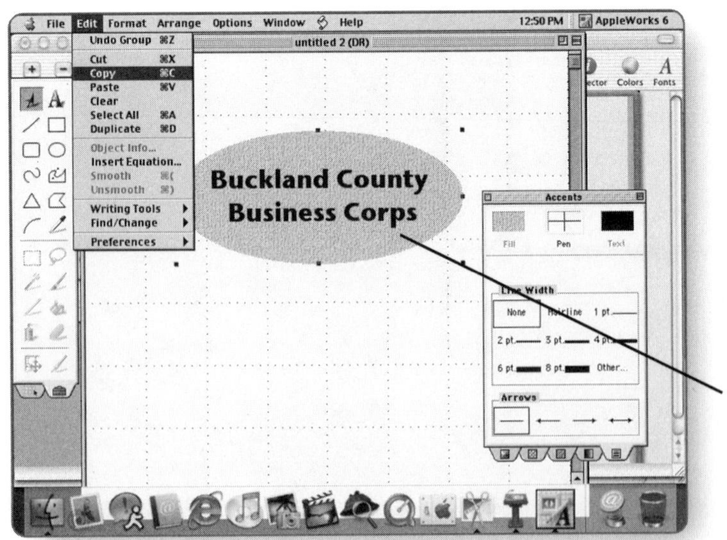

In addition to importing information into Keynote and exporting it from Keynote, you can copy and paste between applications. Here's an example where I copy a simple logo created in AppleWorks 6 (under the Classic Environment) to a Keynote slide:

1. **Select** the **text or object to copy** in the source application. A selection highlight or selection handles will appear.

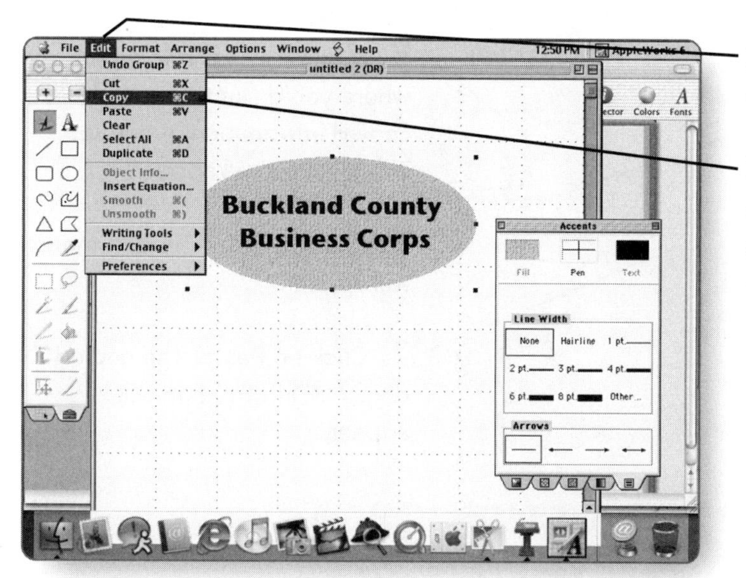

2. **Click** on **Edit**. The Edit menu will appear.

3. **Click** on **Copy**. The selection will be copied to the Clipboard, a holding place in memory.

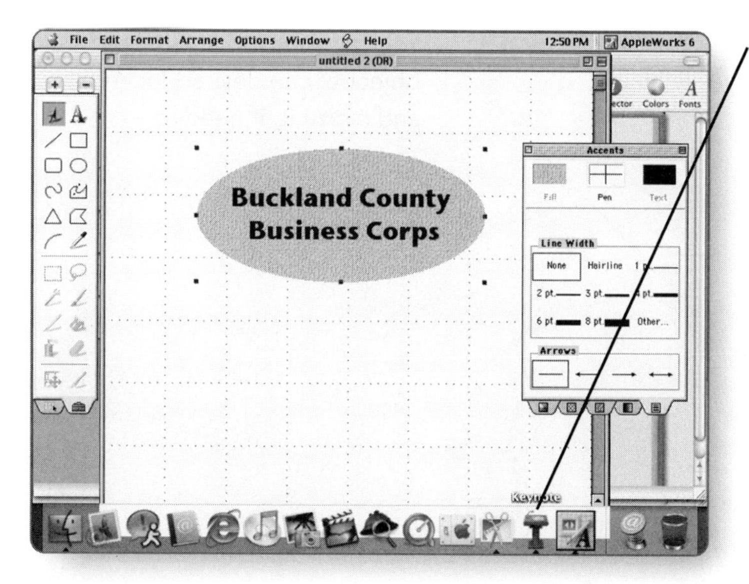

4. **Click** on the **destination application's icon** on the Dock. The destination application will become active.

5. Navigate to the location where you'd like to paste the copied information, if needed. The location will appear.

6. Click on **Edit**. The Edit menu will appear.

7. Click on **Paste**. The copied object or information will appear.

You can then move a pasted object to the desired location and resize it, if needed.

Here are just a couple of additional hints to help you with cutting and pasting:

- Copying and pasting procedures don't always work perfectly, but they're always worth a try. For example, if you paste a piece of clip art copied from Word onto a slide, the clip art content disappears. If you paste copied WordArt from Word, its appearance may be altered so that it's not readable. On the other hand, I could copy and paste an AutoShape or text box from Word without a problem.
- Copying and pasting an outline from a Word document doesn't automatically create separate slides in Keynote. All the content is simply pasted to the destination location, such as a text frame. Here's a tip, however. Change to the Outline view in Keynote, click in the slide organizer pane, and then paste. You can then click on a pasted line and press Shift+Tab to convert it to the title for a new slide.

Part III Review Questions

1. How do you start slideshow playback? *See "Playing the On-screen Slideshow" in Chapter 10.*
2. How do I quit the slideshow? *See "Exiting the Show" in Chapter 10.*
3. Can I prevent a slide from playing without deleting it from the slideshow file? *See "Skipping Slides" in Chapter 10.*
4. How do I rotate the slides on the printed pages? *See "Changing the Page Setup" in Chapter 11.*
5. How do I work with color settings for a printout? *See "Specifying Print Quality, Paper Feed, and More" in Chapter 11.*
6. How do I print speaker notes or handouts? *See "Printing Speaker Notes and More" in Chapter 11.*
7. Can I print just the slideshow outline? *See "Printing the Outline" in Chapter 11.*
8. I've got a PowerPoint file with content that I want to use. Do I have to rebuild it in Keynote? *See "Importing Slide Content" in Chapter 12.*
9. My client wants a QuickTime movie of my presentation. Can Keynote do that? *See "Exporting the Slideshow as a QuickTime Movie" in Chapter 12.*
10. A colleague doesn't have Keynote, but wants me to e-mail my presentation for printing. Is that possible? *See "Exporting the Slideshow as a PDF Document" in Chapter 12.*

PART IV

Making Keynote Your Own

13

Working with Themes and Masters

The more you use Keynote, the more you'll be itching to create new looks for your slideshow. While Chapter 7 showed you how to find some low cost and free themes on the Internet, you can test your own creativity by making your own themes for Keynote. In this chapter, you will learn how to:

- Start a new theme.
- Add a master slide.
- Make changes to a master slide.
- Copy or delete a master slide from the theme.
- Save the finished theme.

Creating a New Theme File and Viewing the Masters

Creating a new theme file works like creating a regular slideshow file. In the case of creating a new theme, however, you want to choose a theme that resembles the theme you will ultimately create. Or choose the White theme if you want to create a new theme from the ground up.

Once you create the theme file, you develop the theme by adding, editing, and deleting masters for the theme, as needed. To handle this operation, you need to view the slides in the slide organizer.

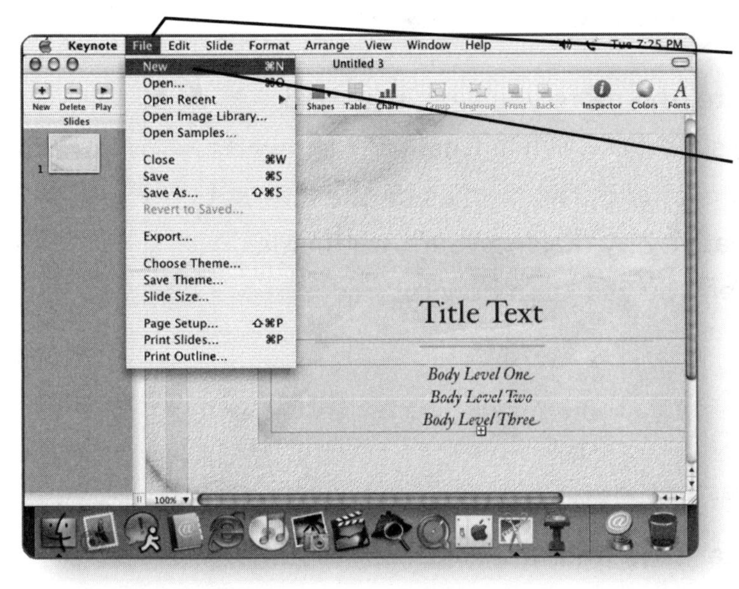

1. **Click** on **File**. The File menu will appear.

2. **Click** on **New**. Keynote will display a sheet for you to choose the theme that most resembles the theme you want to create.

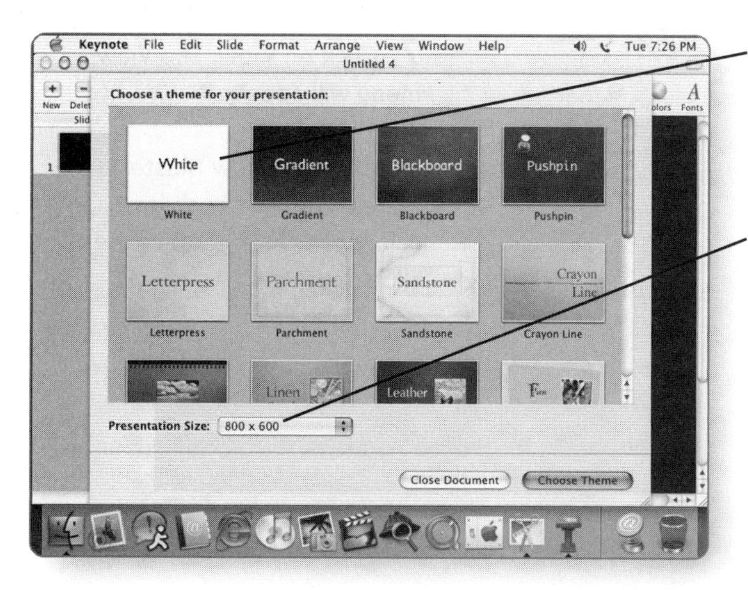

3. Scroll down, if needed, and then **click** on the **theme you want**. The theme will be highlighted in the list.

4. Click on the **Presentation Size pop-up menu**. The menu choices will appear.

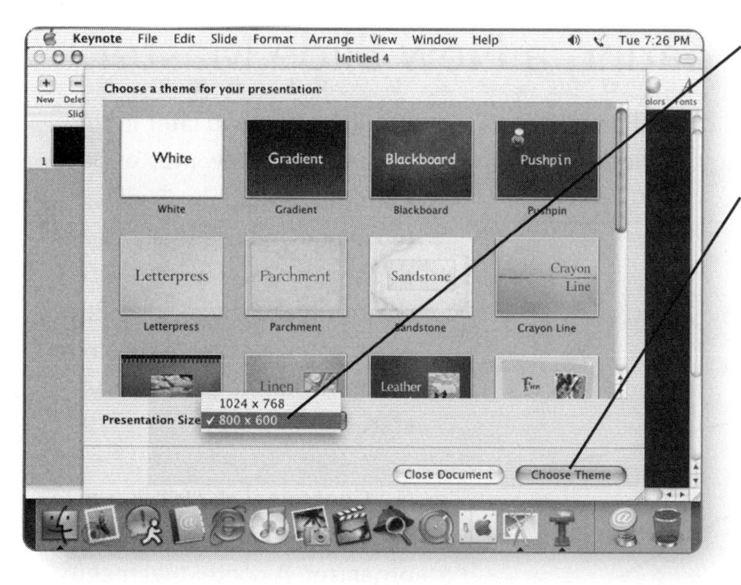

5. Click on the **size you want**. The new presentation will be set to the specified size.

6. Click on **Choose Theme**. A new presentation using the designated theme will appear.

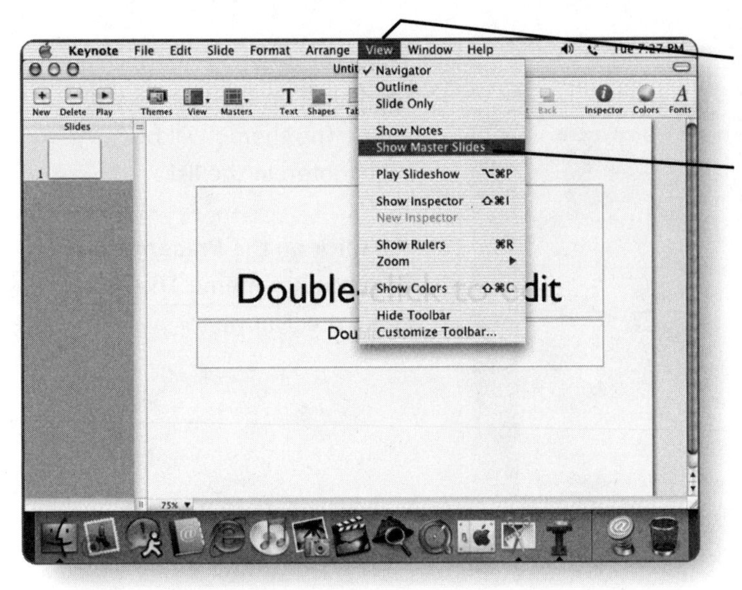

7. **Click** on **View**. The View menu will appear.

8. **Click** on **Show Master Slides**. The master slides pane will appear at the top of the slide organizer.

Creating a New Slide Master

You can either copy a slide master (as explained later in the chapter) and then edit it, or you can build a new master page from the ground up. The technique you use really depends on how unique you want to make the master. But when you want to create a new master from the ground up, start here.

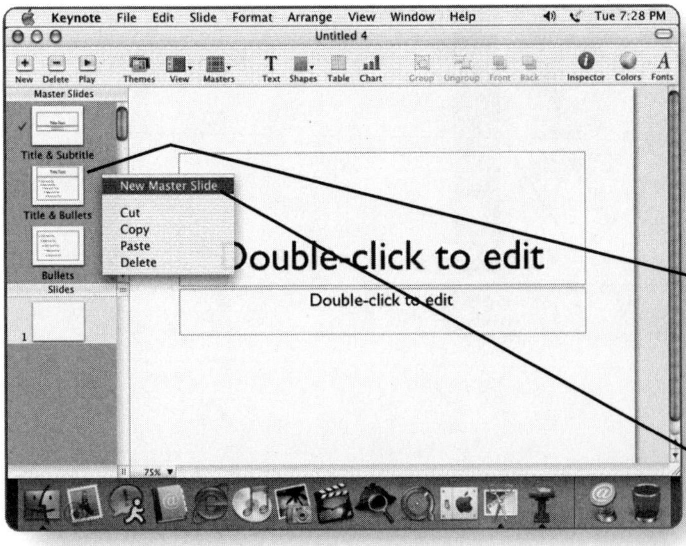

1. **Control+click** on the **master slides pane** in the slide organizer. A contextual menu will appear.

2. **Click** on **New Master Slide**. Keynote will add the new master in the master slides pane.

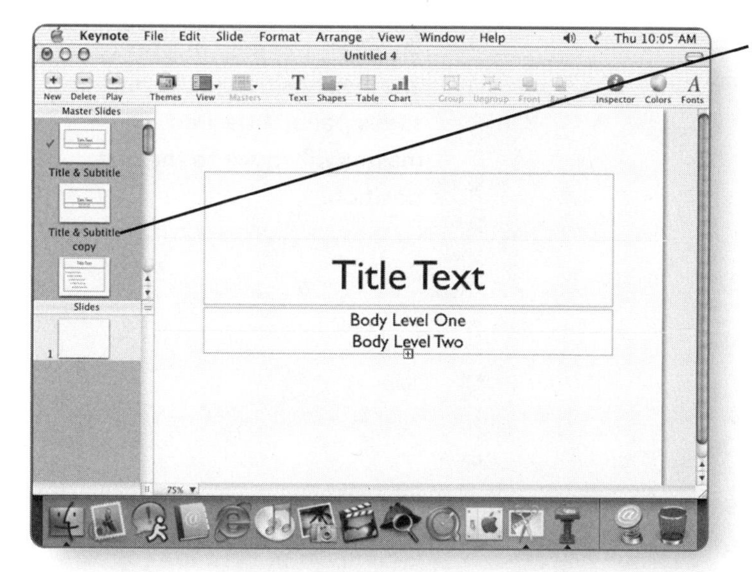

3. Double-click on the **new master name**. The name will be selected.

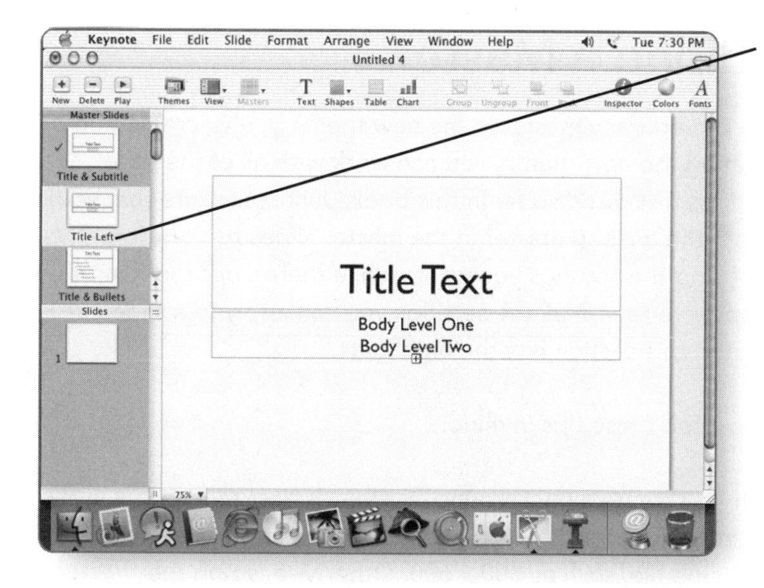

4. Type a **new name**, and then **press Return**. The new name will appear below the master.

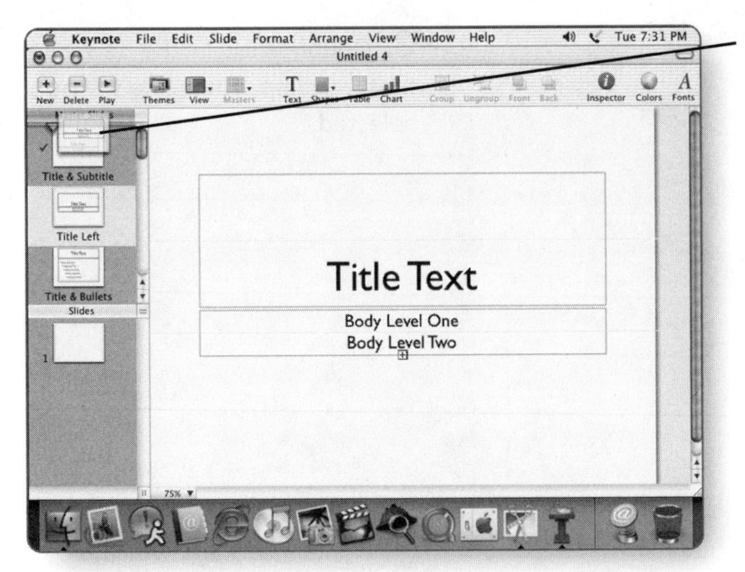

5. **Drag** the **new master** to another position in the master slides pane, if desired. The master will move to the new position.

Editing a Master

You can edit any master in the new theme you've created. In creating the new theme, you can work with all of the slide settings discussed so far in this book. Just make sure that you select the desired master in the master slides pane before choosing the settings you want. While there's not room in this chapter to rehash all the settings you can apply to a slide master, this section hits the highlights.

Also keep these tips in mind:

- If you create a background image, it's best to create it in the same size that you specified when you created the new theme file, such as 800 x 600. Otherwise, sizing the background image can distort it or degrade its appearance.

- Also be sure that any graphics or images you insert use the same number of colors as you'll be using for playing back the presentation onscreen. If an image has millions of colors but you set your display to thousands of colors, the image may not display correctly.
- If you'll be sharing the theme file with other users, be sure to use common fonts. Otherwise, you'll need to distribute the fonts you use along with the master.

Adding a Background

You can add a background color, gradient, or image to any master slide. You also can control which basic items appear on the slide.

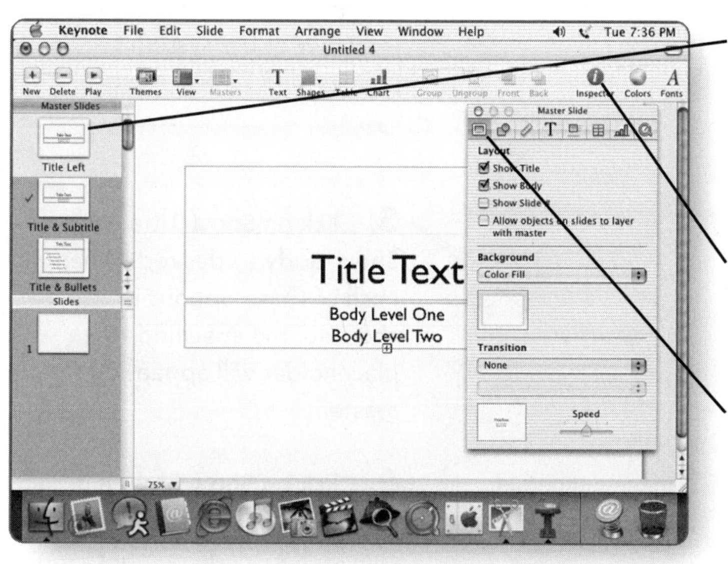

1. **Click** on the **master to edit** in the master slides pane in the slide organizer. The master's content will appear on the slide canvas.
2. **Click** on **Inspector** on the toolbar. The Inspector window will appear.
3. **Click** on **Slide Inspector**. The Slide Inspector settings will appear in the Inspector window.

4. Change the **Background fill** as desired. (Refer to "Working with Fills" in Chapter 6 to learn more about choosing a color, gradient, or image fill.) The new fill will appear immediately on the master.

> **TIP**
>
> If you don't have any background images handy, you can use some of the desktop pictures that ship with Mac OS X. Look in the Library:Desktop Pictures folder of the system's hard disk to find them.

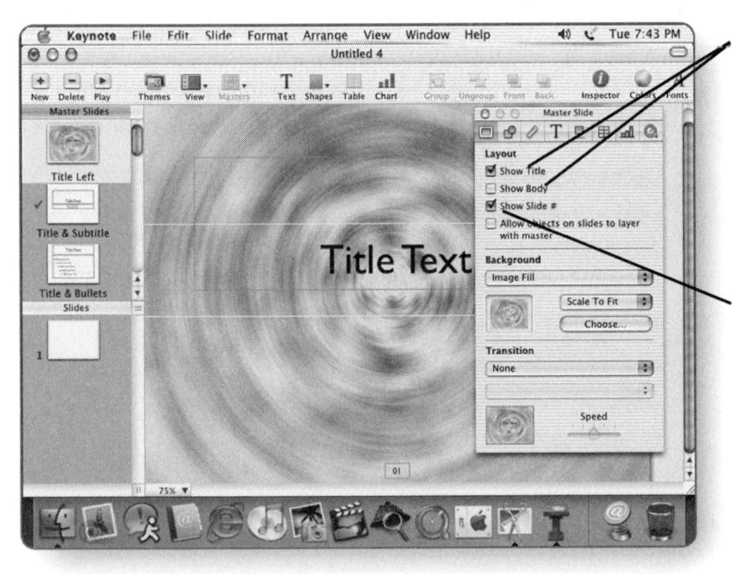

5. Click on **Show Title** and **Show Body** as desired. When each of these options is checked, the specified text placeholder will appear on the master.

6. Click on **Show Slide #** if desired. When this option is checked, a "page number" will appear on the slide master.

7. **Click** on **Allow objects on slides to layer with master**, if desired. When this option is checked, you can send objects you add to the slide behind objects placed on the master, such as picture-frame graphics.

8. **Click** on **Inspector** on the toolbar. The Inspector window will close.

Adding Objects

You can add any other type of object that you'd like to a slide, as described in Chapter 3, "Enhancing Slides." Any item you add will appear on all slides to which you apply the master.

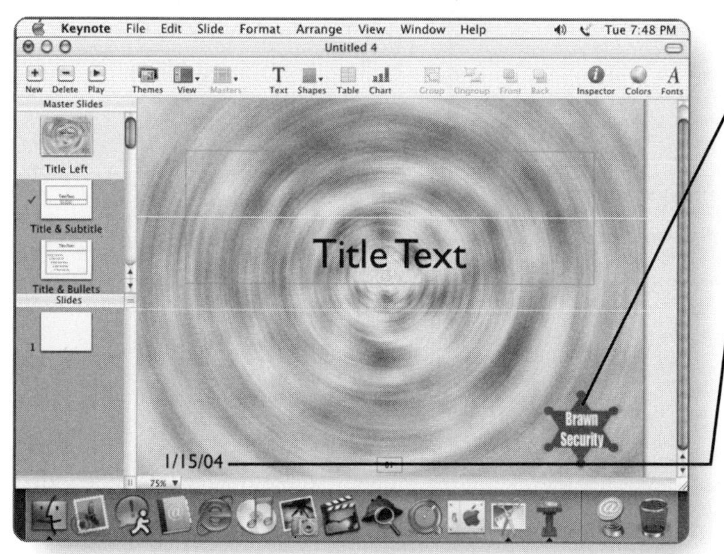

For example, the logo graphic I've inserted here will appear as a background object on all slides to which I apply the master that I'm creating.

Or if I want to include the date or some "footer" information, I can add a text item with those contents to the slide master.

TIP

Don't forget that you also can copy and paste slides between different masters in the theme that you're creating. You also can drag and drop masters between the master slides panes in separate slideshow or theme files.

Specifying Chart and Other Defaults

As you're creating the master, the settings you apply to text and other elements in the master become the defaults for that item for all slides based on the master.

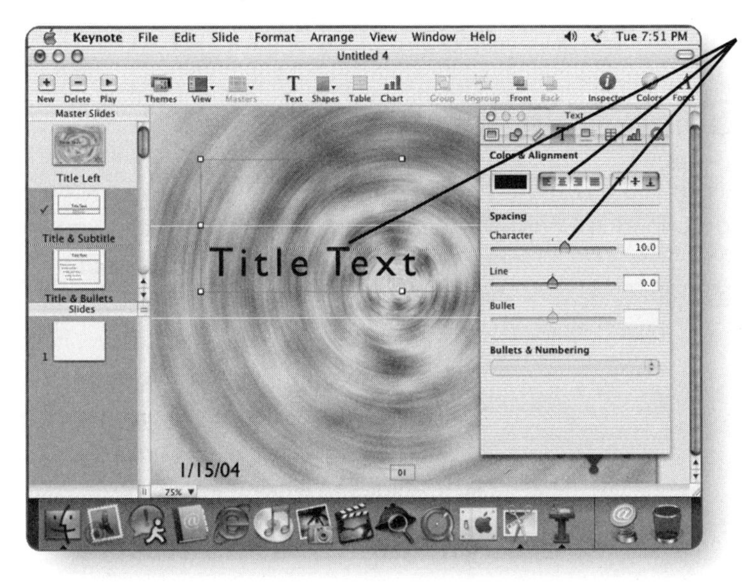

In this instance, I've used the Text Inspector (as described in "Formatting Text" in Chapter 6) to apply left alignment and increased character spacing to the title placeholder on the master I'm creating. Also use the Text Inspector to format bullets for bulleted lists.

You also can use the Slide Inspector to add a transition for the master so that you won't have to specify the transition each time you apply the master. Or you can use the Build Inspector to create builds for bulleted lists or other elements on the slide.

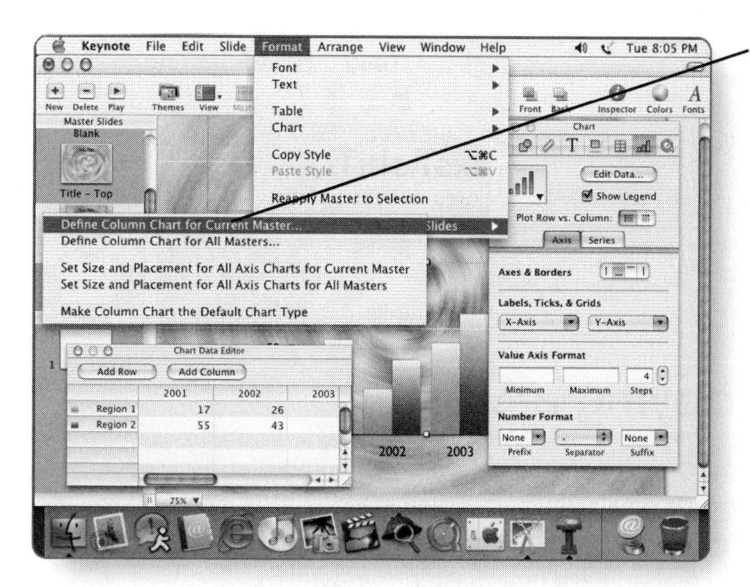

One exception to this basic process occurs when you're formatting a chart on a master. Once you've used the Chart Inspector to change the default settings for the chart, click on Format, point to Define Defaults for Master Slides, and then choose one of the commands there to further establish the chart defaults.

Define Column Chart for Current Master and Define Column Chart for All Masters display a sheet so you can specify the initial number of series and total number of series. The next two commands—Set Size and Placement for All Axis Charts for Current Master and Set Size and Placement for All Axis Charts for All Masters—establish the current chart sizing as a default. Finally, Make (chart type) Chart the Default Chart Type sets the current chart type as the default within the theme.

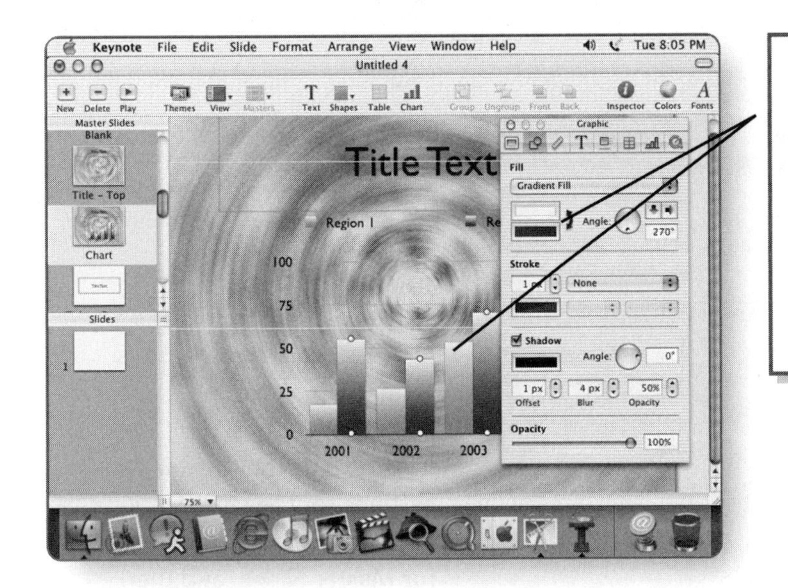

> **TIP**
>
> Click on a series marker on a chart such as a column chart, or on a wedge in a pie chart; and use the Graphics Inspector to change its fill and other formatting.

Copying a Master

If you've spent some time placing a number of background elements on a slide master, you may find that it's faster to create a copy of that master and then edit the copy rather than creating each new master from scratch.

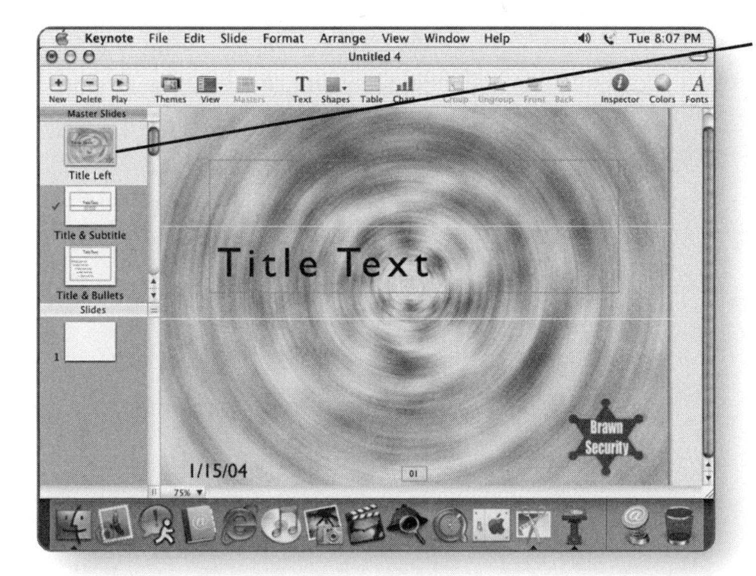

1. Click on the **master to copy** in the master slides pane in the slide organizer. The master's content will appear on the slide canvas.

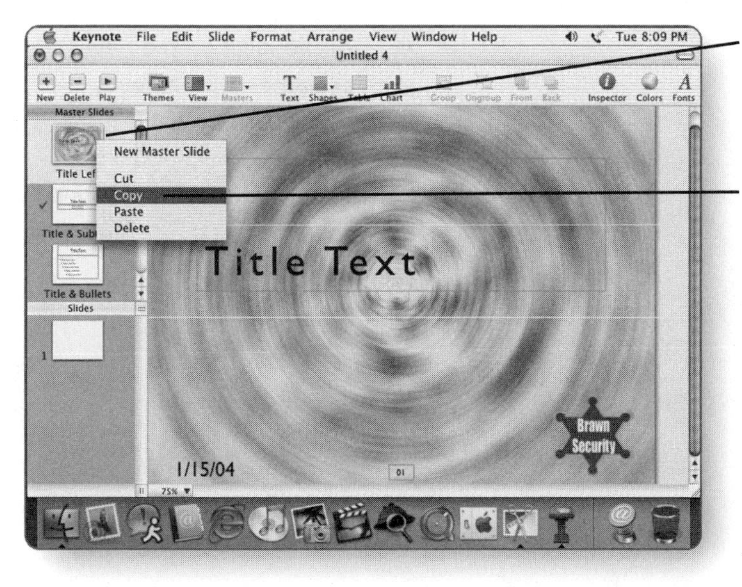

2. Control+click on the **slide to copy** in the master slides pane. A contextual menu will appear.

3. Click on **Copy**. Keynote will copy the master slide to the Clipboard.

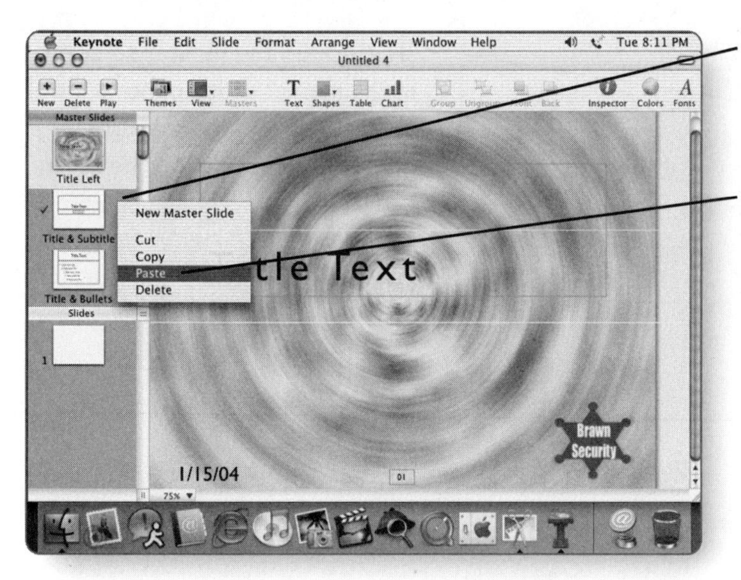

4. **Control+click** on the **master slides pane**. A contextual menu will appear.

5. **Click** on **Paste**. The master copy will appear below the original you copied.

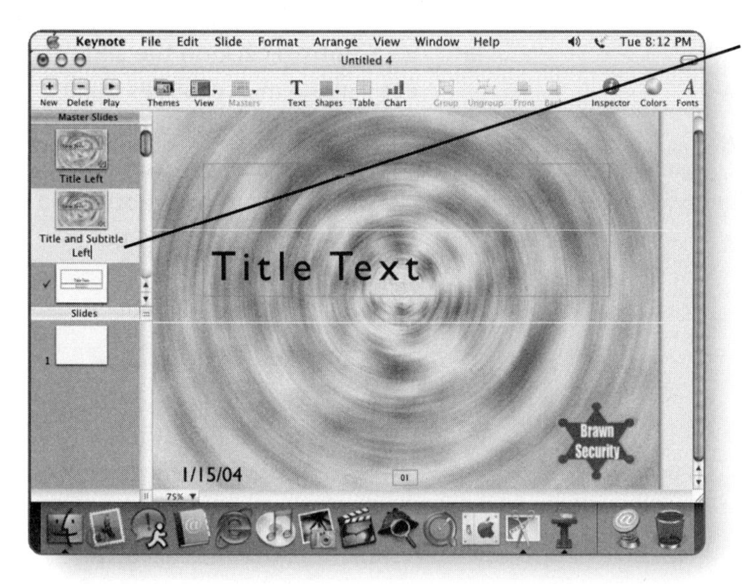

6. **Double-click** on the **new master name, type** a **new name**, and then **press Return**. The new name will appear below the master. You can then make changes to the copied master as desired.

Deleting a Master

If you decide you no longer need a particular master in your theme, you can delete it. Work in the master slides pane to do so.

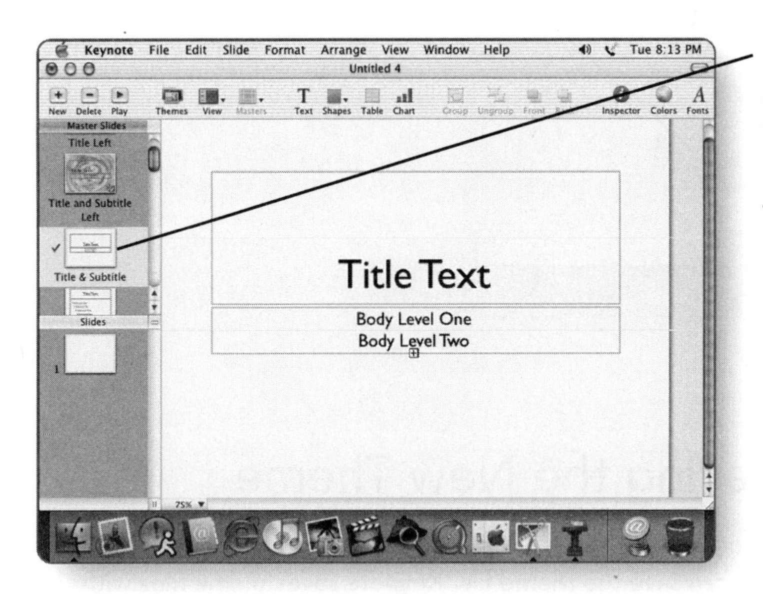

1. Click on the **master to delete** in the master slides pane in the slide organizer. The master's content will appear on the slide canvas.

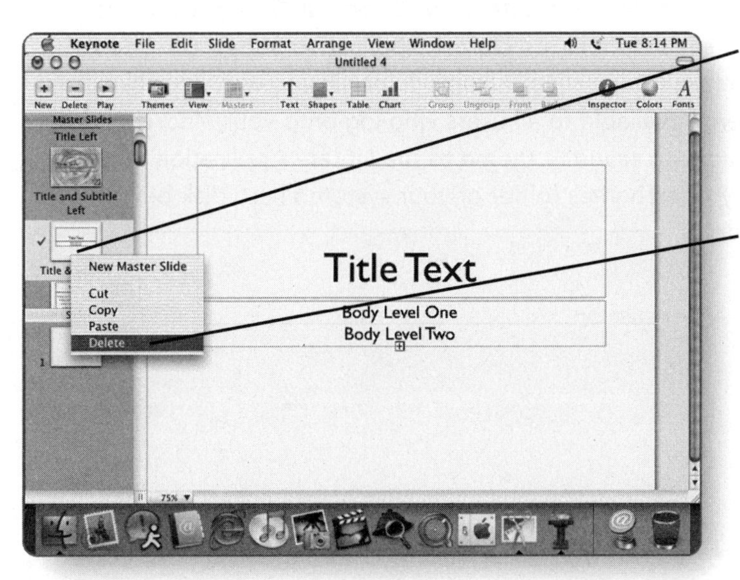

2. Control+click on the **slide to delete** in the master slides pane. A contextual menu will appear.

3. Click on **Delete**. A sheet will prompt you to choose a replacement master to apply to the slides using the master being deleted.

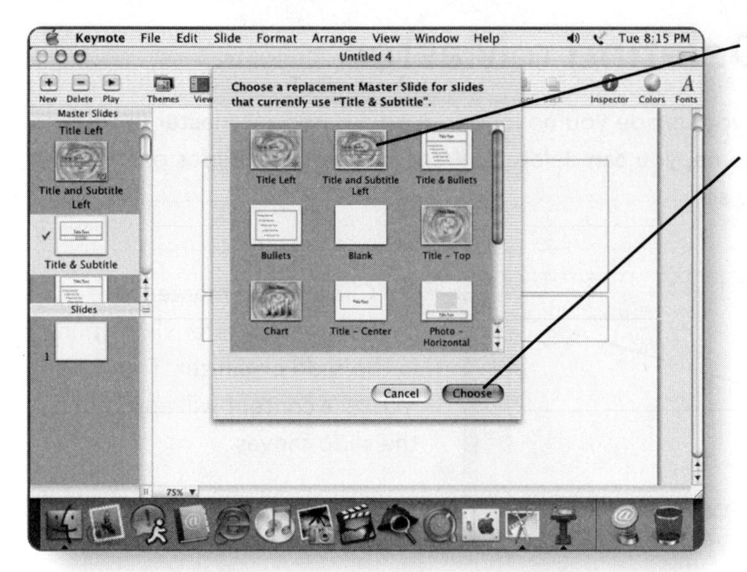

4. Click on the **desired master.** A selection border will appear.

5. Click on **Choose.** Keynote will delete the master you selected in Step 1.

Saving the New Theme

Once you've created all the masters you want for your theme, you can save the theme file. Keynote saves theme files with the .KTH file name extension. By default, it suggests that you save them in the Library:Application Support:Keynote: Themes folder of your Home folder. If you want to make the theme available to all users who log onto your Mac, instead choose to save the theme to the Library:Application Support: Keynote:Themes folder of your system's hard disk before Step 3.

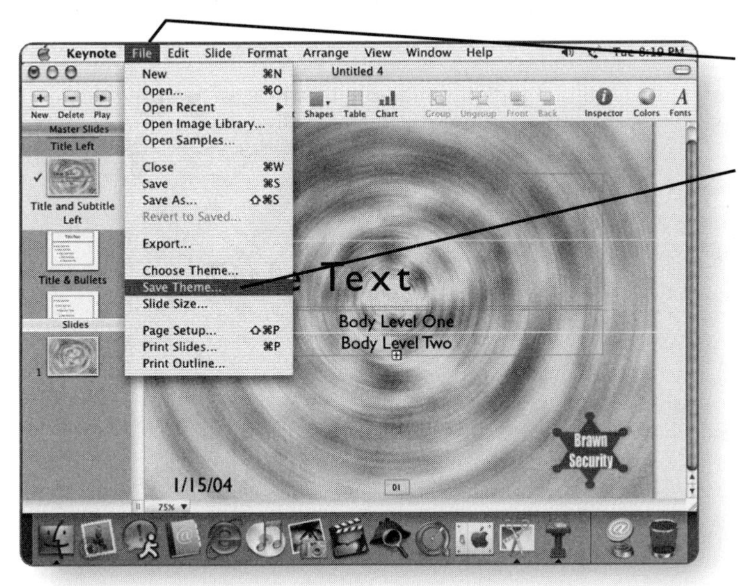

1. **Click** on **File**. The File menu will appear.

2. **Click** on **Save Theme**. A sheet with save options will open.

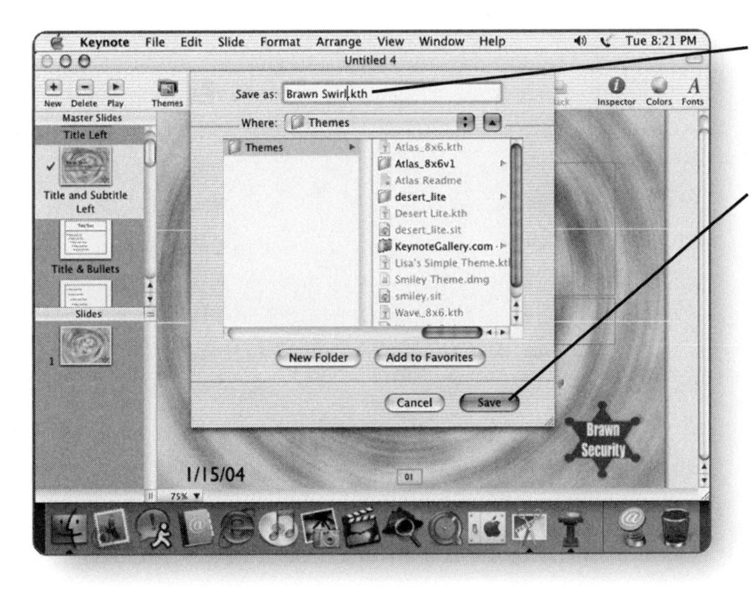

3. **Type** a **file name** in the Save As text box. The name will appear in the Save As text box.

4. **Click** on **Save**. Keynote will save the theme file in the location you specified.

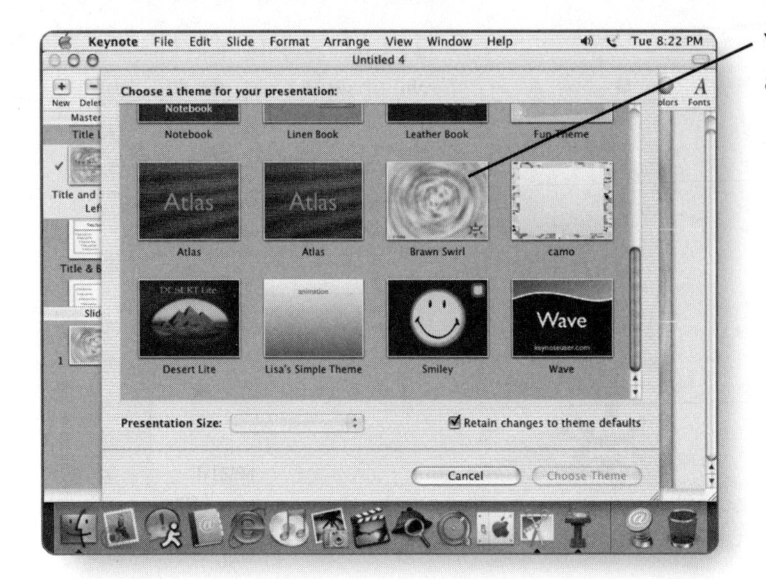

Your theme is now available to apply to other slideshow files.

14

Customizing Keynote

Different users prefer different ways of working and have differing hardware that affects slideshow playback. To adjust for varying needs, Keynote offers a variety of Preferences settings and the ability to customize its toolbar. In this chapter, you'll learn how to:

- Register Keynote.
- Use Keynote's Preferences settings to set up your working environment.
- Change display preferences for optimal slideshow playback.
- Make changes to the Keynote toolbar.

Registering Keynote

The first time you start the Keynote program, it prompts you to register the software with Apple. While you may not think of this process as "customization," it does ensure that you will be able to take advantage of available technical support options. Follow these steps to register Keynote:

1. **Connect** to the **Internet**, if required. To do so, you can use the modem status icon on the Finder menu bar or the Internet Connect application in the Applications folder. Your Internet connection will become active.

2. **Click** on **Applications** on a Finder window toolbar. The Applications folder contents will appear in the Finder window.

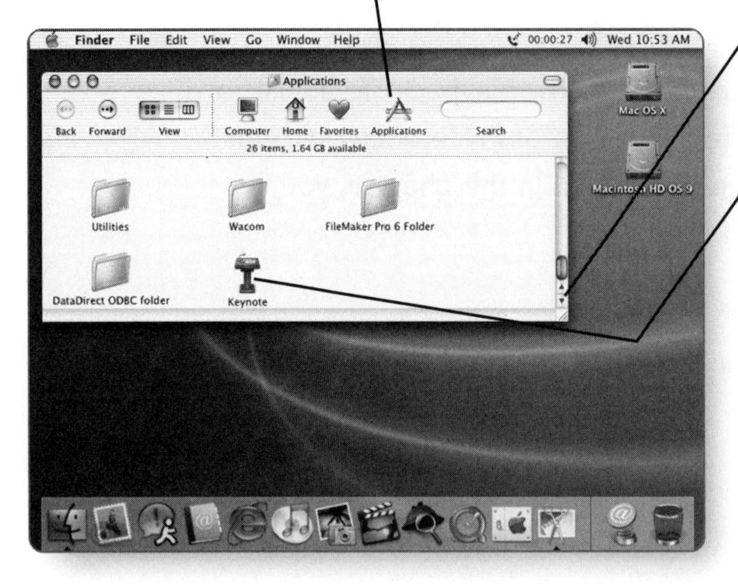

3. **Click** on the **down scroll arrow** as needed. The Keynote icon will appear.

4. **Double-click** on the **Keynote icon.** Keynote will launch and display the Registration dialog box.

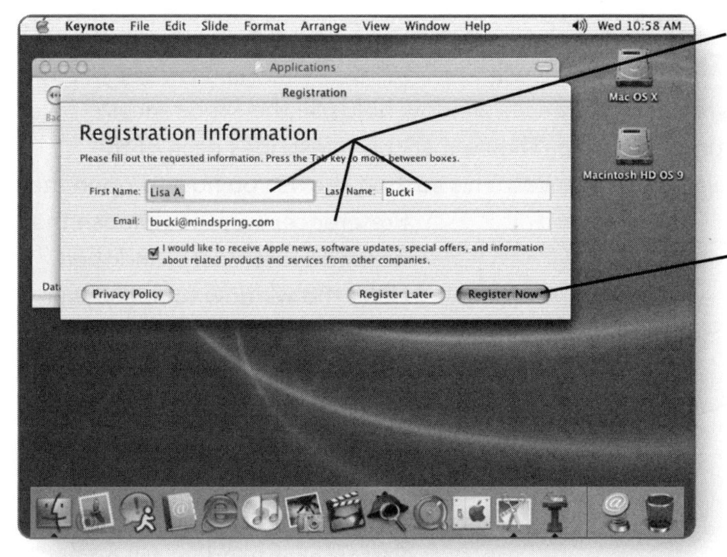

5. Enter your **First Name, Last Name,** and **Email** address, pressing Tab after each entry. Your information will appear in the dialog box.

6. Click on **Register Now**. Keynote will connect with Apple over the Internet and send your registration information. When the process finishes, a message sheet will appear.

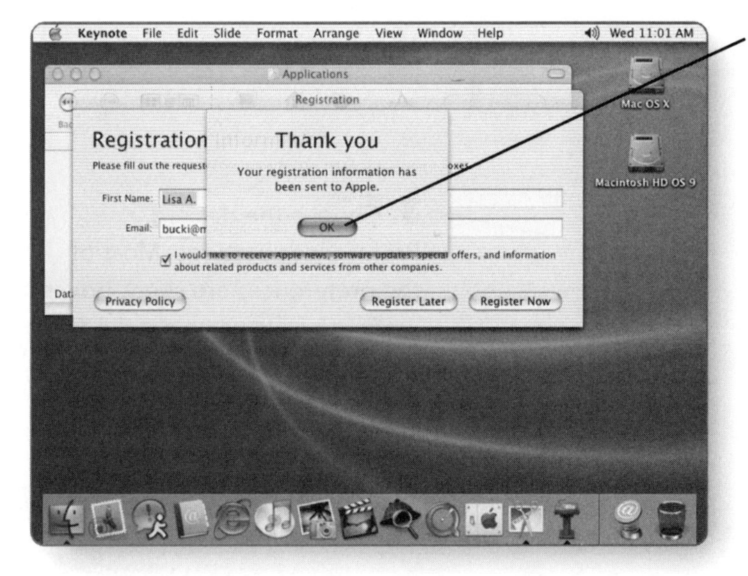

7. Click on **OK**. Keynote will finish opening. You can then disconnect from the Internet and finish working.

Setting Keynote Preferences

Keynote's Preferences window holds all the Preferences settings available. The next section describes each of the available preferences. This section shows you how to open the Preferences window, choose the desired preferences, and then close the window to apply your choices.

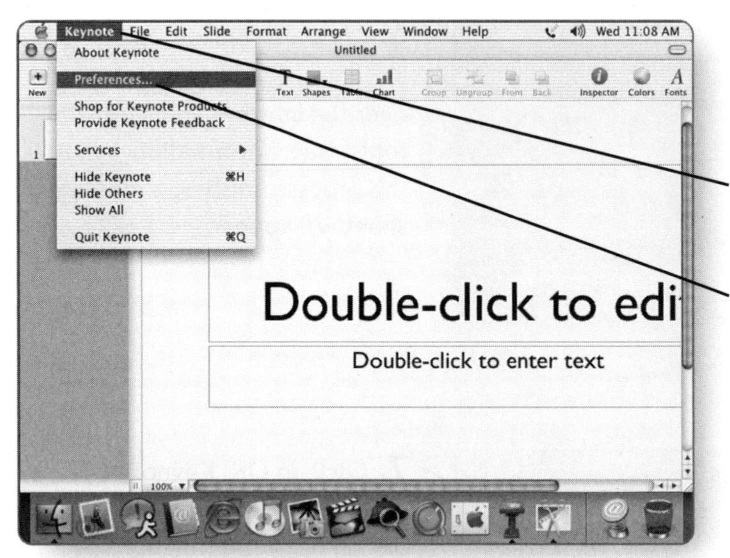

1. **Click** on **Keynote**. The Keynote menu will appear.

2. **Click** on **Preferences**. The Preferences window will open.

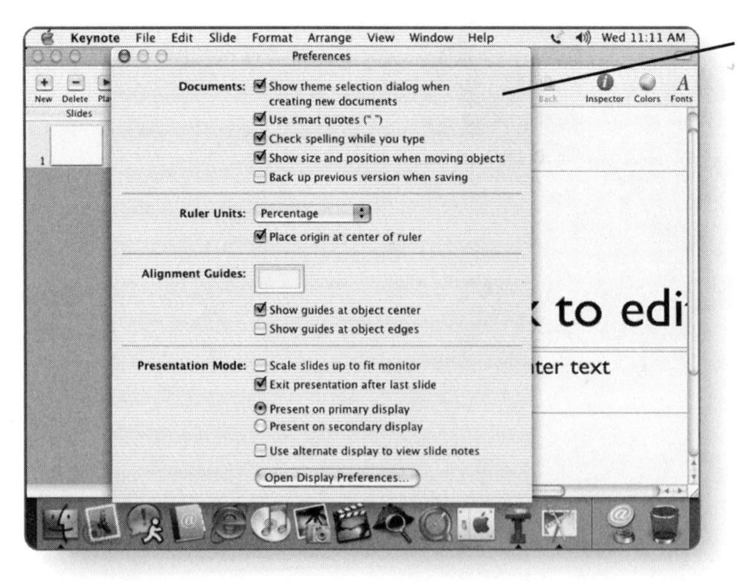

3. **Choose** the desired **Preferences settings**. Most of the preferences are check boxes that are active when checked and inactive when not checked. Your choices will appear in the window.

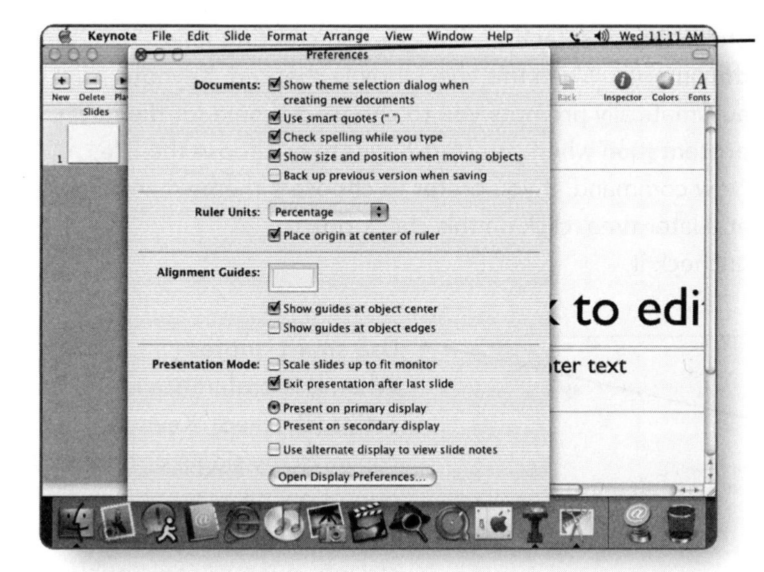

4. Click on the window **close button**. The Preferences window will close, and your settings will take effect.

Understanding the Available Preferences

The Preferences window groups available preferences into four categories for easy reference: Documents, Ruler Units, Alignment Guides, and Presentation Mode. Following is a description of each of the available preferences so that you can more easily find the setting you need.

- **Show theme selection dialog when creating new documents.** When this check box is checked, Keynote automatically prompts you to choose a theme for the new presentation when you start Keynote or choose the File, New command. If you prefer to choose a theme manually at a later time, click on this check box to uncheck it.

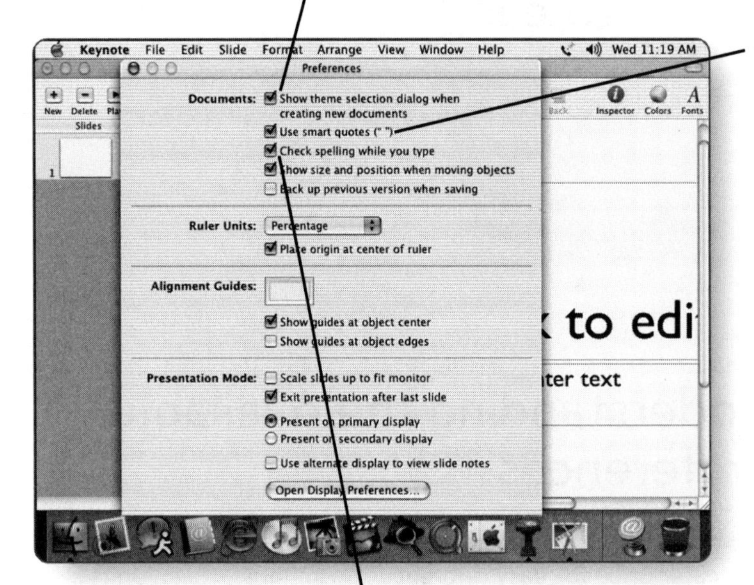

- **Use smart quotes ("").** When this preference is active (checked), Keynote converts any single or double quotation marks you type into curly quotes rather than straight quotes (single primes or double primes). Deselect this option if you need to type in primes instead, such as when you're entering measurements in feet and inches.

- **Check spelling while you type.** When this option is checked, Keynote automatically spell checks each word you type. Keynote displays a red dotted underline under unrecognized words to prompt you to make a correction. Clear this check box if you prefer to spell check at a later time.

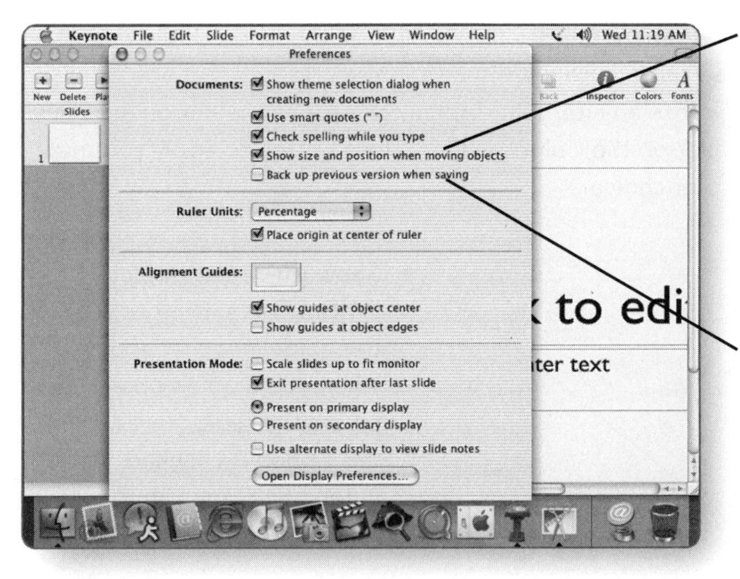

- **Show size and position when moving objects.** When this check box is checked, Keynote displays an outline when you move any slide object. If that causes Keynote to perform too slowly on your system, clear this check box.
- **Back up previous version when saving.** Check this option to have Keynote save the previously saved version of the slideshow file as a backup copy. If the original slideshow file is named "New Product," Keynote names the backup copy of the file "Backup of New Product."

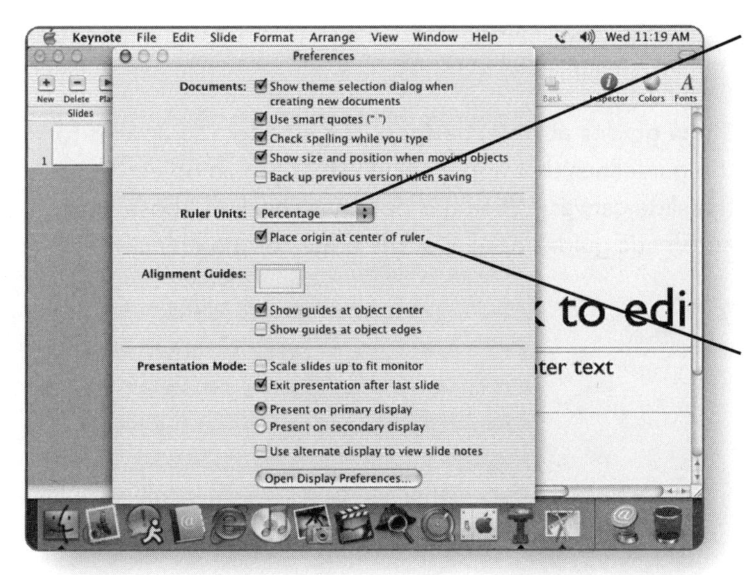

- **Ruler Units.** Choose the type of ruler measurements you prefer from this pop-up menu. The rulers can display measurements in Pixels, Centimeters, Inches, or a Percentage (of the slide dimensions).
- **Place origin at center of ruler.** When checked, the starting (0 point) measurement appears at the center of each ruler. Clear this check box to place the 0 point at the left end of the horizontal ruler and the top of the vertical ruler.

- **Alignment Guides (box).** Click on the colored Alignment Guides box to open the Colors window so that you can choose an alternate display color for alignment guides. Click on the Colors window close button to apply your new color choice.

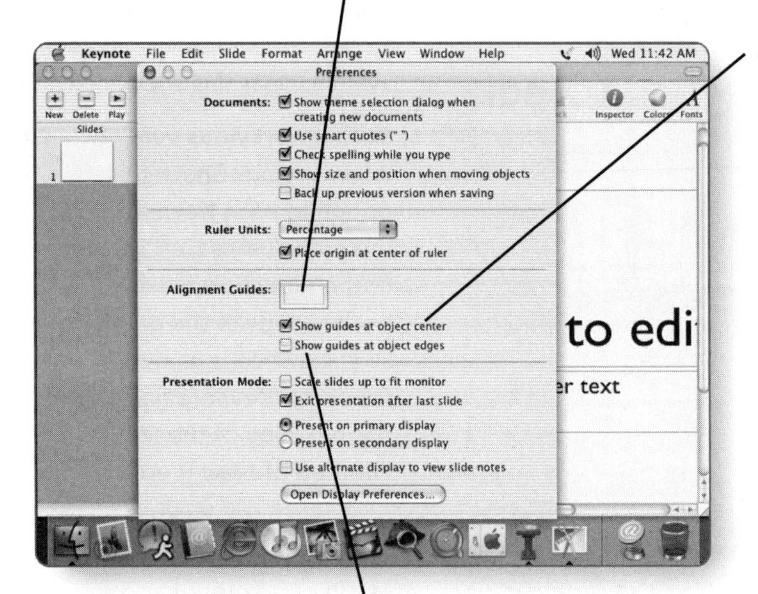

- **Show guides at object center.** This setting applies to the guidelines that appear when you drag an object across the slide canvas. When this option is checked, those automatic guides appear at the center of the object.

- **Show guides at object edges.** This setting also applies to the guidelines that appear when you drag an object across the slide canvas. When this option is checked, those automatic guides appear at the edges of the object.

- **Scale slides up to fit monitor.** If you created your slide show using the default size of 800 x 600 pixels, you can check this check box to have Keynote automatically increase the slide size if you display the slideshow on a monitor set to a higher resolution, such as 1024 x 768.

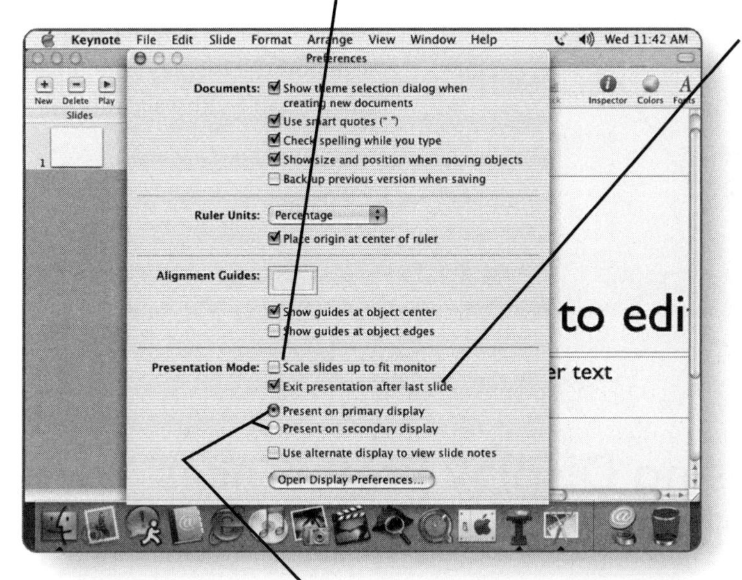

- **Exit presentation after last slide.** This setting is checked by default and tells Keynote to stop displaying slideshow and return to the Keynote application after the last slide. Clear this check box if you'd prefer to continue displaying the last slide onscreen at the presentation's conclusion—a nice alternative in a professional setting.

- **Present on primary display** or **Present on secondary display.** Click on the desired option button to specify whether to play the slideshow on your system's main display, or on a larger secondary display, such as a projector, if your system supports a dual-monitor configuration.

> **NOTE**
>
> For your system to support a dual-monitor configuration, it must have a video card installed for each monitor. Otherwise, your system supports only mirroring—also playing the presentation on a second monitor that you've connected. If your system supports a dual-monitor configuration, the Display preferences pane will include an Arrange tab.

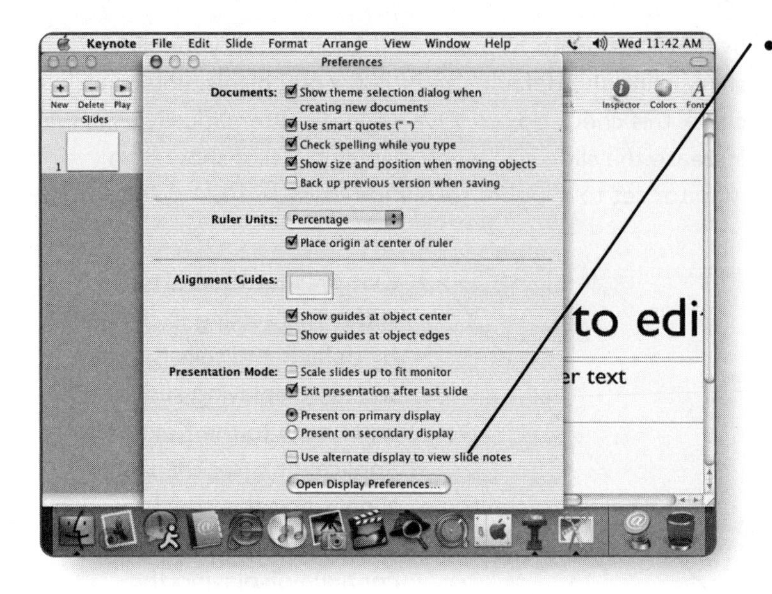

- **Use alternate display to view slide notes.** If your system supports dual-monitor configuration and you're using two displays, then when this option is checked, Keynote will display slide notes on the display not being used by the slideshow.

Using Display Preferences with Keynote

To optimize playback of a slideshow, you may also need to work with the Display preferences in System Preferences for Mac OS X. For example, if you're displaying your slideshow on an external projector, you may need to change the display resolution to 800 x 600 to ensure that the projector can show the slideshow. Or if you set up your slides to a larger size, such as 1024 x 768, then you will need to set your display to at least that resolution. You also may need to change the number of colors used by the display for better viewing, or you may need to adjust the refresh rate to ensure that an external display can function correctly. If you're having slideshow playback problems, working with these display settings is an essential troubleshooting technique.

NOTE

If your system supports a dual-monitor configuration, use the Arrange tab in the Display preferences pane to set up the monitors to display different content, such as playing a slideshow on the secondary display rather than the primary display.

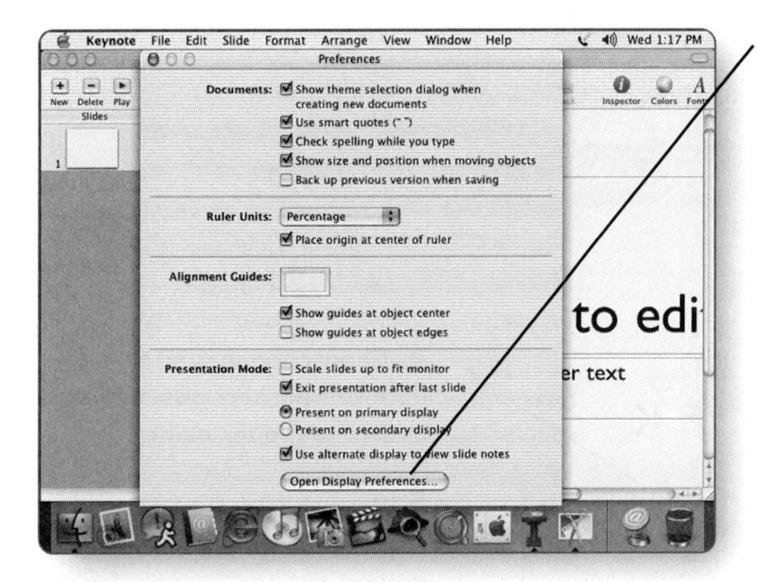

1. **Click** on **Open Display Preferences** in the Preferences dialog box in Keynote. System Preferences will start and display the Display preferences.

TIP

Alternately, you can click on the System Preferences icon on the Dock, and then click on Displays.

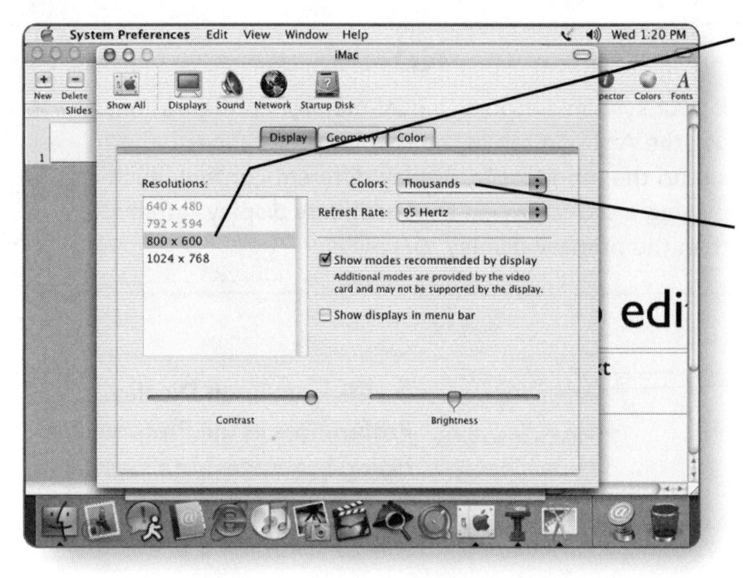

2. Click on the desired **Resolutions** setting. Your display(s) will update to the new resolution.

3. Choose the **desired Colors setting**. Your display(s) will update to use the new number of colors.

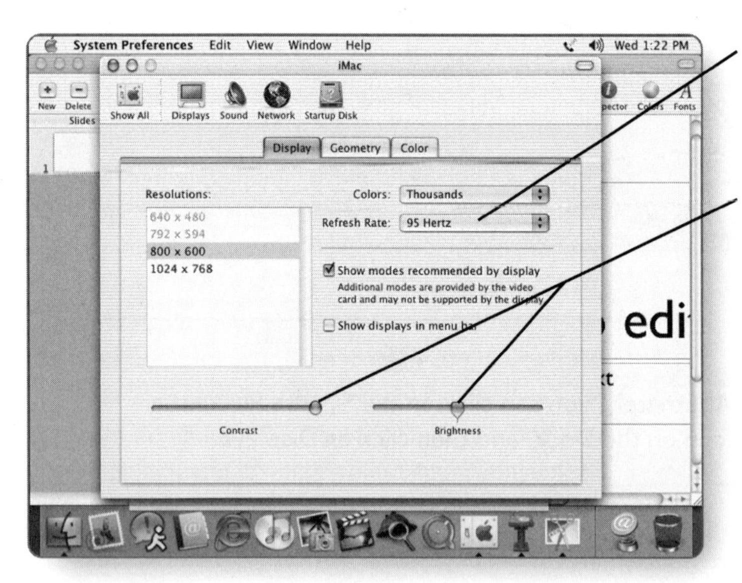

4. Choose the **desired Refresh Rate setting**. Your display(s) will update to use the new rate.

5. Drag the **Contrast and Brightness sliders** to the desired settings. Your display(s) will update to use the settings.

TIP

Often, an external projector will have a washed out appearance. Increasing the Contrast setting and decreasing the Brightness setting can help with this problem.

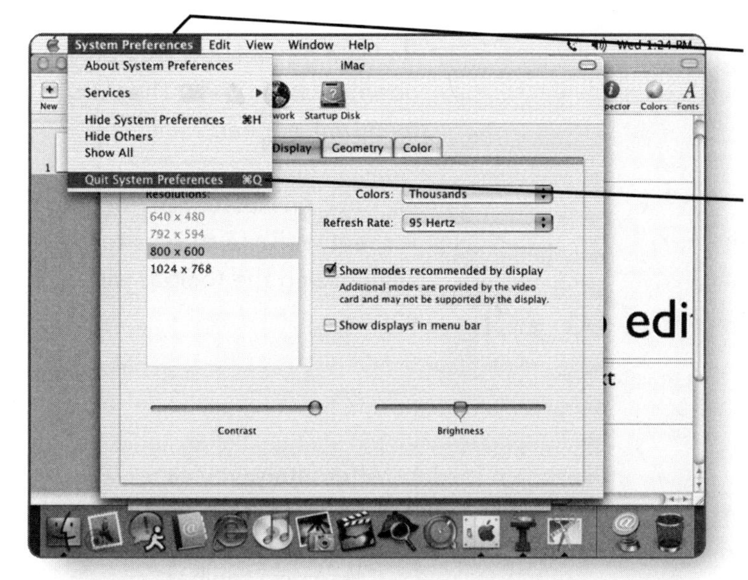

6. **Click** on **System Preferences**. The System Preferences menu will appear.

7. **Click** on **Quit System Preferences**. The System Preferences menu application will close, applying your new display settings.

Customizing the Toolbar

The toolbar on each slideshow window in Keynote offers handy access to the commands you use most. A toolbar becomes even more useful when you can customize it to include the tools you want. In Keynote, you can customize the slideshow window toolbar to add and remove tools as needed. The toolbar changes you make apply to all slideshow windows.

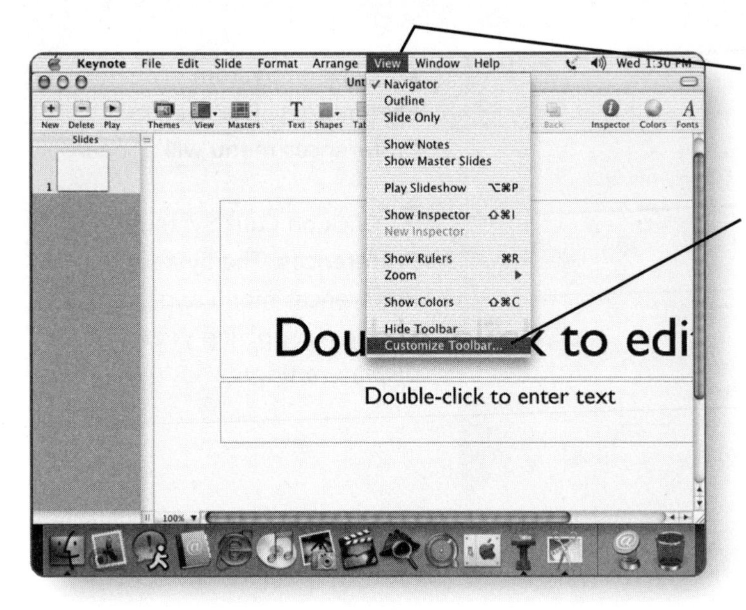

1. With a slideshow window open, **click** on **View**. The View menu will appear.

2. Click on **Customize Toolbar**. A sheet with the choices for customizing the toolbar will appear.

> **TIP**
>
> Alternately, you can Control+click on a toolbar, and then click on Customize toolbar.

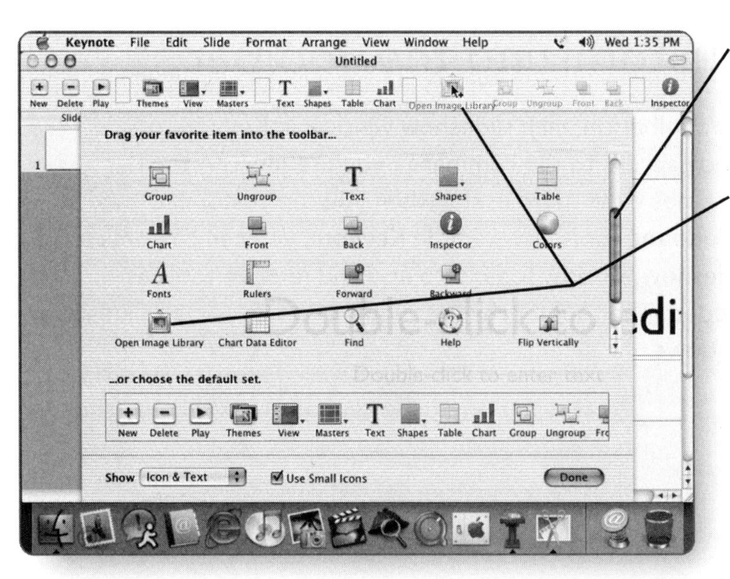

3. Scroll the **list of available icons**. Additional icons will appear.

4. Drag an **icon** to the desired toolbar position. When you release the mouse button, the icon will be added to the toolbar.

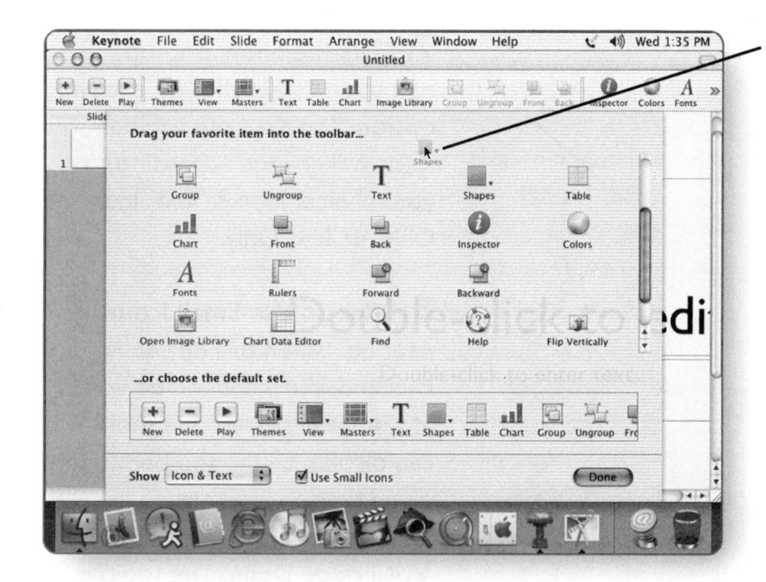

5. Drag an **icon** off the toolbar. When you release the mouse button, the icon will be removed from the toolbar.

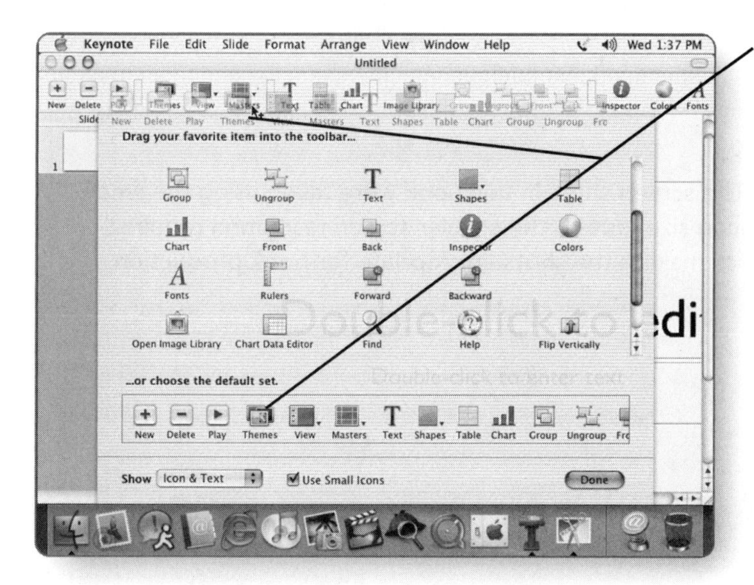

6. Drag the **default set** onto the toolbar. When you release the mouse button, the toolbar will redisplay the default set of buttons.

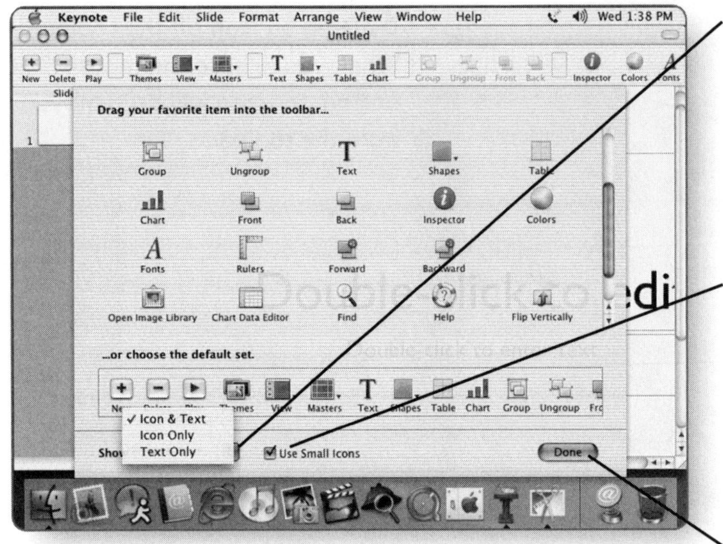

7. Click the **Show pop-up menu,** and then **click** on a **menu option**. The Keynote toolbar icons will change according to your choice: Icon & Text, Icon Only, or Text Only.

8. Click on **Use Small Icons** as needed. When this option is checked, the icons will be sized at a smaller size so that more can display on the toolbar at any given time.

9. Click on **Done**. The toolbar choices will disappear, and the changes will appear on the toolbar.

NOTE

The screen shots in this book were taken using the small icon size, due to the smaller screen resolution required for making the shots appropriate for book production.

Part IV Review Questions

1. How do I start a new theme file? *See "Creating a New Theme File and Viewing the Masters" in Chapter 13.*
2. How do I add a new master to a theme? *See "Creating a New Slide Master" in Chapter 13.*
3. How do I add a background to the new master? *See "Adding a Background" in Chapter 13.*
4. How do I turn on slide numbering? *See "Adding a Background" in Chapter 13.*
5. I want a master that's similar to another one. *See "Copying a Master" in Chapter 13.*
6. I no longer need a particular master in my theme. Can I nuke it? *See "Deleting a Master" in Chapter 13.*
7. How do I store the theme? *See "Saving the New Theme" in Chapter 13.*
8. Where can I find a preference setting I need? *See "Understanding the Available Preferences" in Chapter 14.*
9. I can't get the picture to appear on a projector I've connected. Help! *See "Using Display Preferences with Keynote" in Chapter 14.*
10. Can I change the Keynote toolbar? *See "Customizing the Toolbar" in Chapter 14.*

Installing Keynote

The Mac OS X version 10.2 Jaguar operating system features the Quartz Extreme graphics system at its core, making it the perfect platform for a presentation graphics program. Naturally, Apple built on this foundation by developing the Keynote presentations graphics program. You can obtain Keynote from the Apple Store Web site and install it at any time. In this appendix, you'll learn how to:

- Purchase Keynote from Apple.
- Install Keynote on your Macintosh.

Purchasing Keynote from the Apple Store

You can purchase Keynote from the Apple Store on Apple's Web site at any time. The software costs $99 plus shipping. To run Keynote, your system must be running Mac OS X version 10.2 or later. Your Mac also must have a G3 or G4 processor running at 500MHz or faster. If your Mac has only 128M of RAM, upgrading to 512M or more will be useful because presentation files tend to include large, memory-gobbling graphics.

1. Connect to the **Internet**, if required. Your Internet connection will become active.

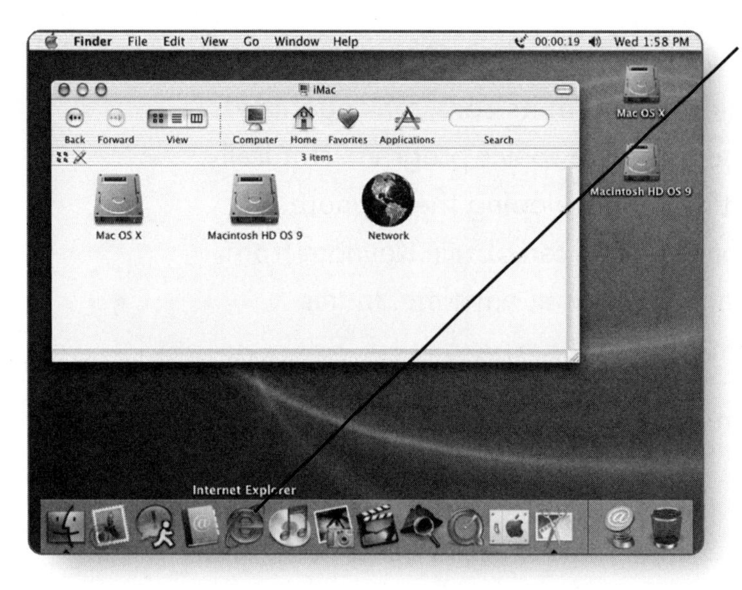

2. Click on the **Internet Explorer icon** on the Dock. Internet Explorer will open and display the home (start) page that you've specified.

> **NOTE**
>
> Of course, if you've installed another Web browser, launch it instead.

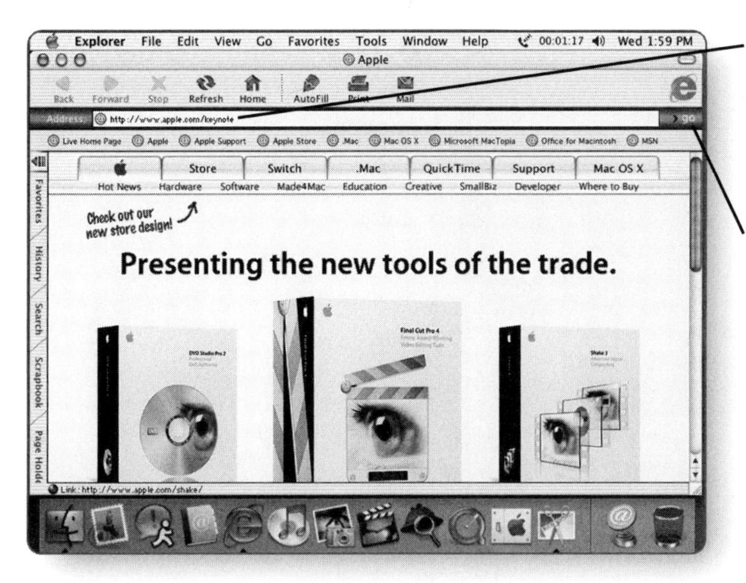

3. Enter www.apple.com/ keynote in the Address box. The Web address will appear in the box.

4. Click on **Go** or press Return. The Keynote download page will load.

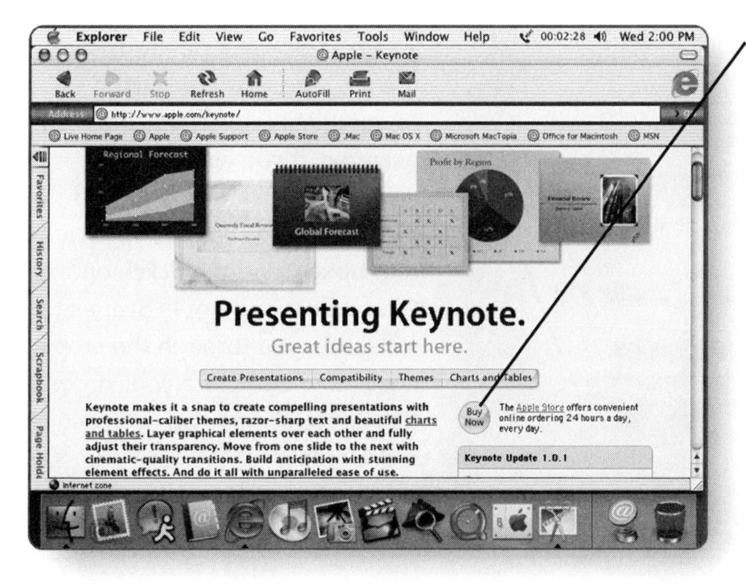

5. Scroll down, if needed, and **click** on **Buy Now**. The Apple Store Web page for ordering Keynote will load.

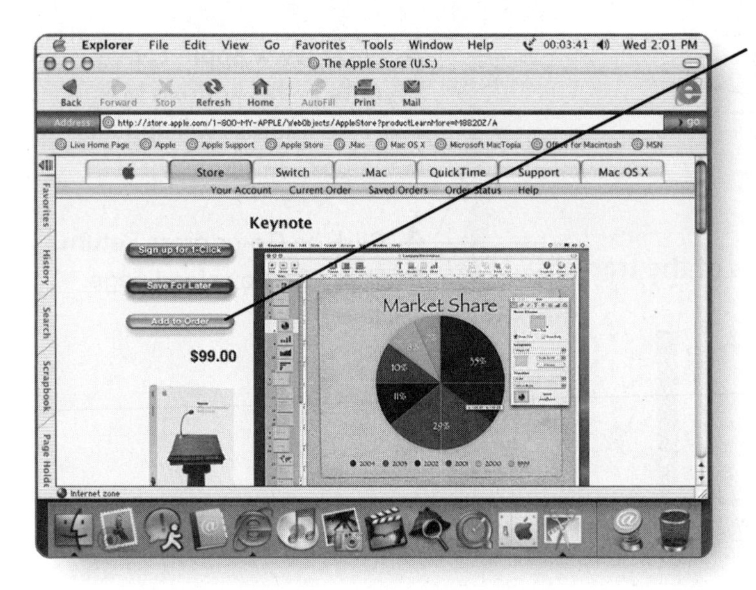

6. Click on **Add to Order**. The Review Your Order page will appear.

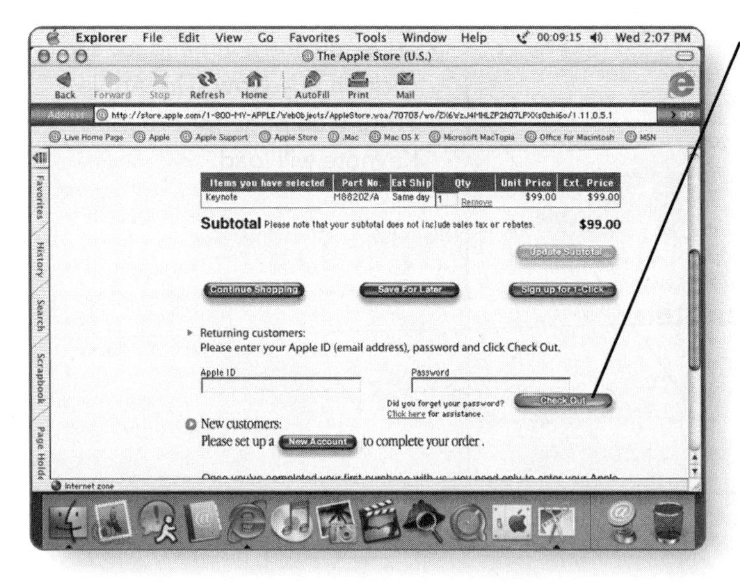

7. Scroll down, if needed, and **use** the **appropriate button** to complete your order. For example, if you already have an Apple ID, enter the ID and password into the appropriate text boxes, and then click on Check Out. The Apple Store site will guide you through the steps needed to complete your order. Be sure to print a copy of your order receipt.

> **NOTE**
>
> If a Security Notice message box opens at any point, click on Send or OK to continue.

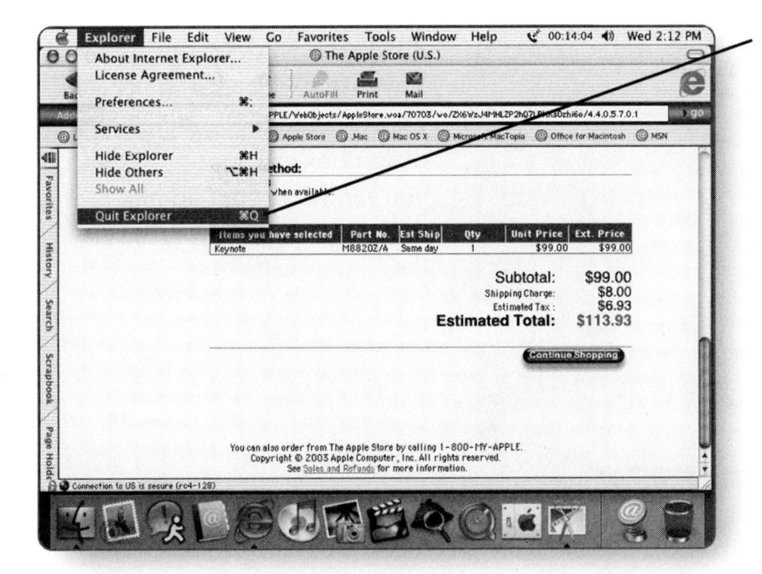

8. After you finish the order, **quit Internet Explorer** and **disconnect** from the **Internet**. The Web browser will close.

Installing Keynote

As when you install any software for Mac OS X, you must be logged on as an administrator to install Keynote. After you've logged on as an administrator, use the following steps to perform an easy (basic) installation of Keynote.

1. **Insert** the **Keynote CD** into your Mac's CD-ROM or DVD-ROM drive. An icon for the CD will appear on the desktop, and a Finder window for the CD will open.

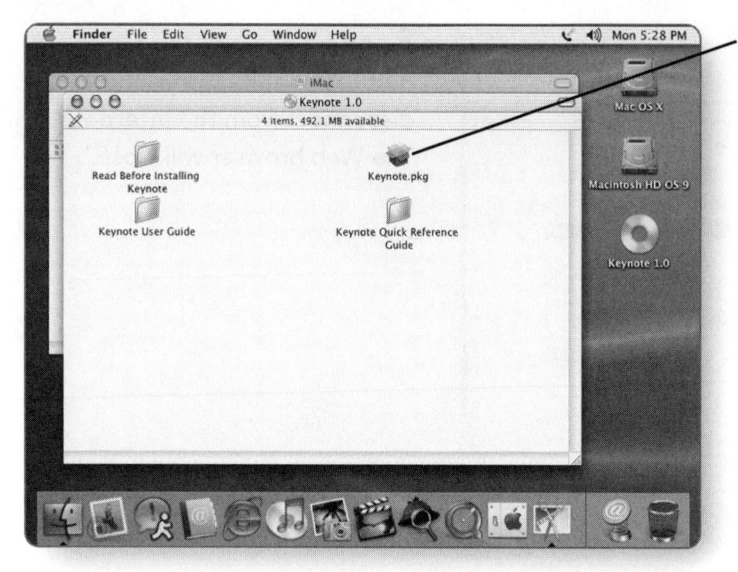

2. Double-click on the **Keynote.pkg icon**. The Installer will start and the Authenticate dialog box will appear so that you can verify your administrator information.

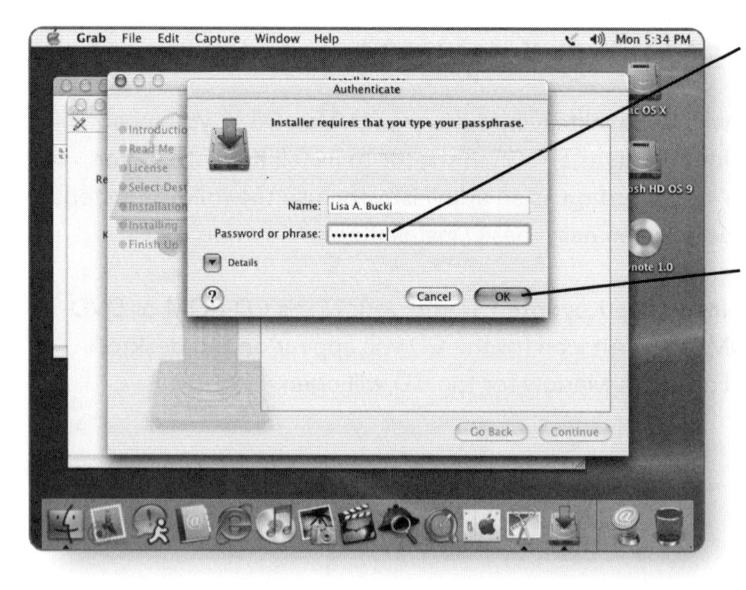

3. Type your **administrator password** in the Password or phrase text box. A black dot will appear for each letter in the password.

4. Click on **OK**. The Authenticate dialog box will close, and a Welcome message will appear.

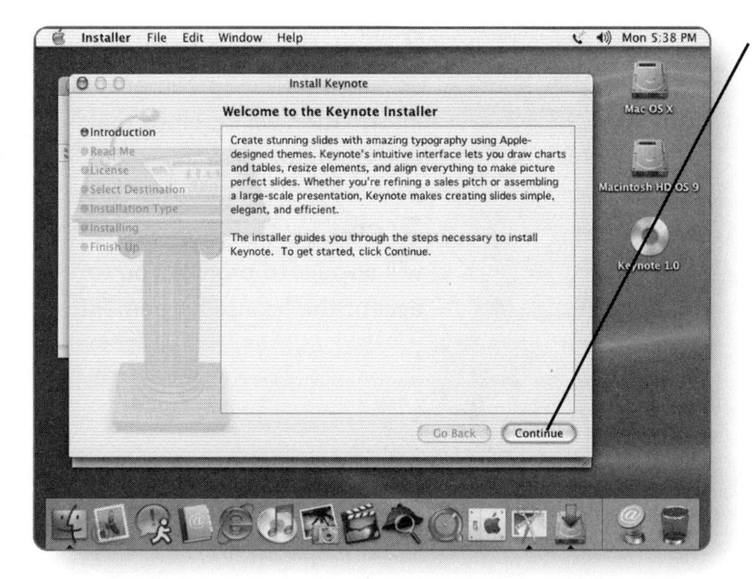

5. Click on **Continue**. Important installation information will appear.

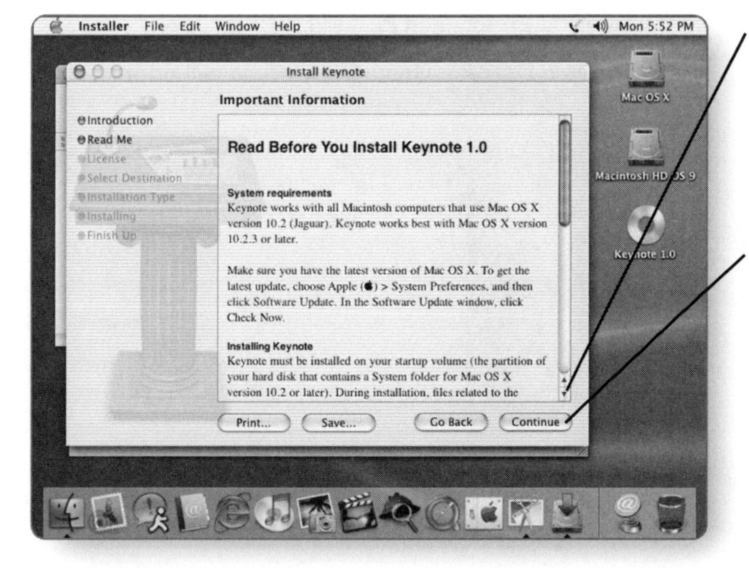

6. Click the **down scroll arrow** as needed. The installation information will appear, so that you can read it before continuing the install process.

7. Click on **Continue**. The license agreement will appear.

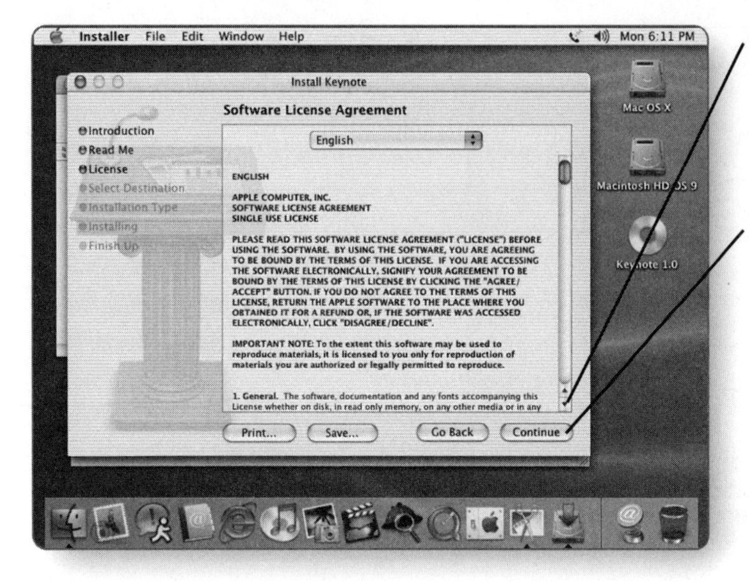

8. Click the **down scroll arrow** as needed. The agreement information will scroll so that you can read the full agreement.

9. Click on **Continue**. A sheet will appear to prompt you to accept the license agreement.

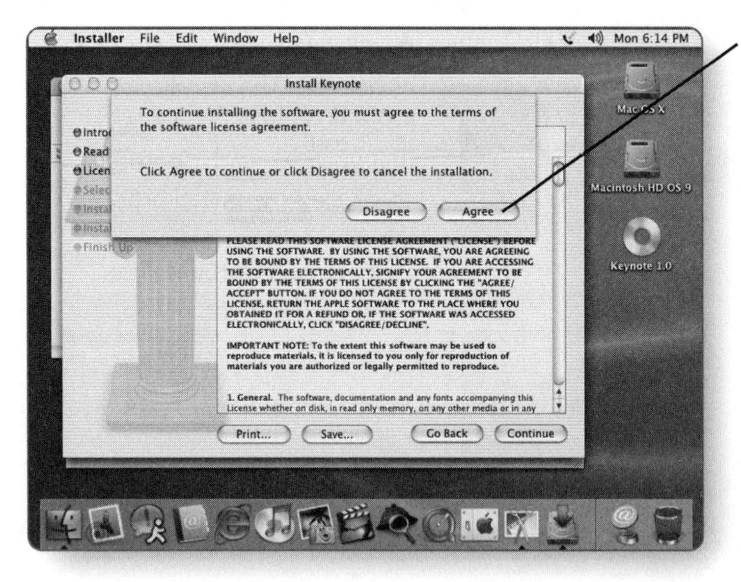

10. Click on **Agree**. The next Installer window will open.

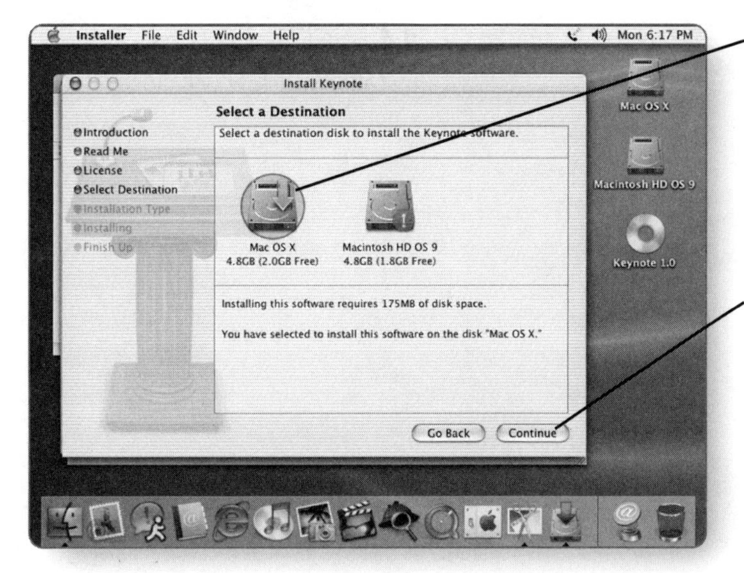

11. Click on the **icon** for your **system's startup volume** (disk where Mac OS X is installed). The startup volume will be selected as the destination for the Keynote software install.

12. Click on **Continue**. The Easy Install screen will appear.

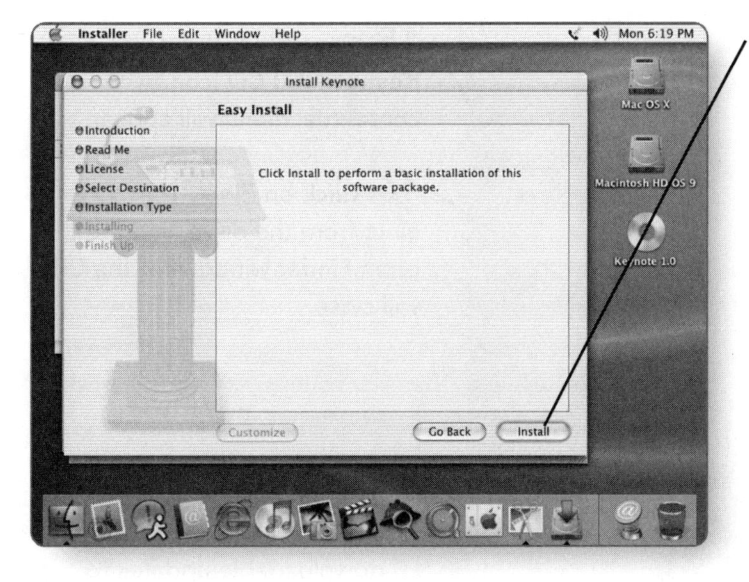

13. Click on **Install**. The Installer will write the program files to your system's startup volume. The Installer will inform you when the right process finishes.

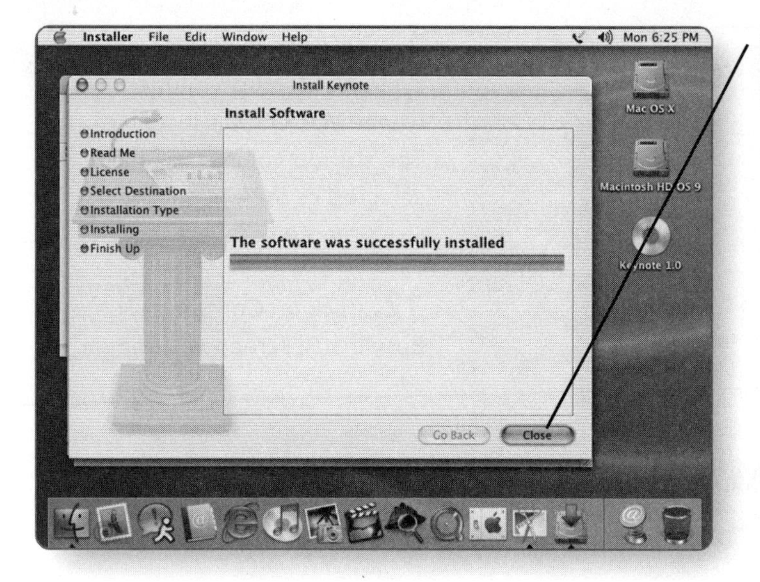

14. **Click** on **Close**. The Installer window will close.

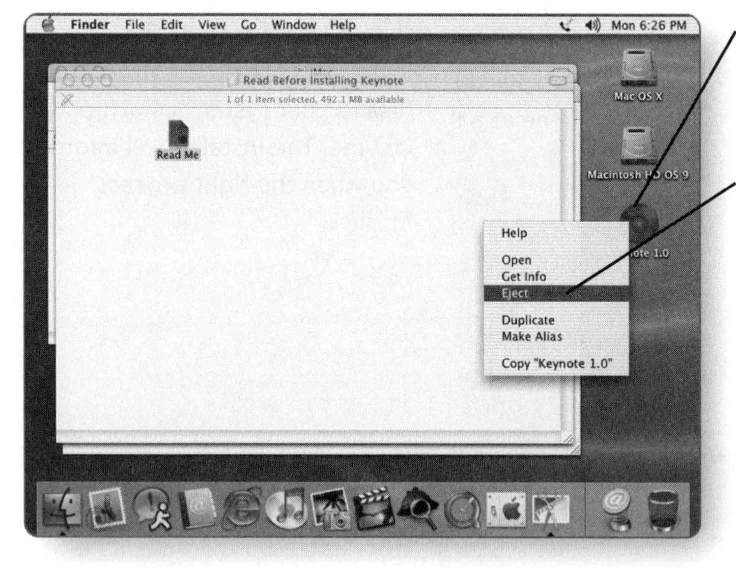

15. **Control+click** on the **Keynote 1.0 CD icon.** A contextual menu will appear.

16. **Click** on **Eject**. The CD will eject from the drive, and the open Finder window for the CD will close.

> **TIP**
>
> Visit http://www.apple.com/keynote/download/ periodically to check for downloadable updates to the keynote software.

B Glossary

Active. The currently selected file or object.

AAC. Also called simply "MPEG-4 AAC," this is a new audio encoding format that (according to Apple) delivers higher sound quality at a lower bit rate, creating digital files with a smaller file size. iTunes 4 (with QuickTime 6.2 installed) supports the AAC format. You can embed AAC files on slides in a slideshow.

Alignment guides. Yellow guidelines that appear by default to help you position objects on a slide relative to other objects. You also can add your own alignment guides.

Alpha channel image. Also called a masked or clipped image, this is an image file that has transparent areas.

Animation. A graphic that includes movement. The most common type of animation file is a Flash (.SWF) animation.

Automatic resolution enhancement. A feature offered by some printers. When enabled, this feature automatically smoothes angles, curves, and edges.

Build. A style of animation that you can apply to a list on a slide or a series of objects on a slide. A build makes the objects appear one at a time when you play the on-screen slideshow.

Bulleted list. A list of items where each is set off by a small dot or graphic.

Chart. A graphical representation of how data changes over time on a slide.

Clipboard. A storage area in a Mac's memory that can hold a copied or cut item until it's pasted in a new location.

Contrast. The overall difference between the lightest and darkest tones on a slide. A slide with little difference between text and background areas has low contrast and is called "flat." Flat slides are less readable.

Disclosure triangle. A triangle that appears beside the top slide in a group of indented slides in the Keynote slide organizer. Click on the disclosure triangle to collapse (hide) or expand (redisplay) the slides in the group.

dpi. Dots per inch. The number of dots a printer can print per inch, or the number of pixels a photo includes per inch. Higher dpi values yield a better quality printout or image.

Dual-monitor configuration. The capability of some Mac systems to display one image on the main screen and a separate image (such as a slideshow) on a second display attached to the system.

Duplex printing. Printing on both sides of each piece of paper. Not all printers offer duplex printing capabilities. Unless the printer is equipped with a duplex feeder, you must manually print one side of the pages, and then turn the paper over to print the other side.

Export. To save a slideshow file in another format to make it viewable in another application or under another operating system. For example, you can export a slideshow as a QuickTime movie or a PowerPoint file.

Font. A design of lettering you can apply to text.

Landscape. A format for slides (printed and on-screen) where the slide is wide rather than tall.

Locking. To prevent changes to the object on the slide.

Loop. To play a movie, animation, or song over and over during an on-screen slideshow.

Masked image. *See Alpha channel image.*

Master slide. The layout that defines the placement and formatting for elements on a slide. You can apply a master from a theme to multiple slides in a slideshow file.

Mirroring. Displaying the same image on the main display and a secondary display connected to a Mac.

Movie. A digital video, typically in the QuickTime format.

MP3. A digital music format. You can insert MP3 files on slides in a slideshow. The music will play when you run the on-screen show.

Navigator view. The default view in Keynote that displays the slide on the slide canvas and a thumbnail of each slide in the slide organizer pane at the left.

Notes. Speaker notes that you can print along with a slide image to use as prompts while delivering a slideshow presentation.

Notes field. A pane that you can display onscreen in Keynote in order to enter speaker notes.

Opacity. A setting in the Graphic Inspector that enables you to make text or an object more transparent.

Outline view. A view that includes the slide canvas and slide organizer. Rather than displaying thumbnails in the slide organizer, this view displays the text of the slides in the presentation so that the user can edit and organize the slideshow content in the slide organizer.

PDF. The Adobe Portable Document Format file format extension. PDF files can include text and graphics and can be viewed in the Mac OS X Preview application or in Adobe's free Acrobat Reader application. You can export a slideshow as a PDF document.

Pixel. Another name for picture element—a single dot of light or color in an image. More pixels onscreen yield a higher-quality image.

Portrait. A format for slides (printed and on-screen) where the slide is tall rather than wide.

Presentation graphics. A type of program for developing presentation content delivered via handouts, overheads, on-screen, or electronic presentation display via QuickTime or PDF.

Preset. A saved collection of print settings that you can apply to any print job.

Resolution. The size of the displayed slide or screen in pixels. For example, at an 800 x 600 display resolution, a monitor displays an image 800 pixels wide by 600 pixels tall. Many projectors used for presentation display require that you set the display resolution for the source computer to 800 x 600. May also refer to the print resolution in dpi (dots per inch).

Revert. To discard all changes to the slideshow file, returning the file to the contents it had when you last saved it.

Series. A set of related data points in a chart.

Slide. The equivalent of a "page" in a slideshow or presentation.

Slide canvas. The large area that displays the contents of each slide. Use the slide canvas area to position and format objects added to a slide.

Slide organizer. A pane at the left side of the Navigator and Outline views that you can use to organize content order in the slide show.

Slideshow. Also called a presentation, this is a Keynote file that includes information to be delivered to an audience page by page (slide by slide). Also refers specifically to a presentation delivered on a computer screen or projector.

Stroke. Another name for the outline or border of a graphic in Keynote.

Table. An object that enables you to arrange information in rows and columns on a slide.

Theme. When designing a slideshow, choose a theme to determine the overall look, size, and arrangement of the photos on the pages.

Transition. An animation effect applied to a slide. When you move to that slide during an on-screen slideshow, it appears using the specified animation effect.

Transparency film. A clear plastic on which you can print slides for display via an overhead projector. Not all printers support the use of transparency film.

Typeface. A specific set of characters (such as all the italic characters) for a font.

Value axis. The axis (usually the vertical or y-axis) on a bar, column, line, or area chart that identifies the value range for the data series being charted.

View. A screen appearance within Keynote that provides particular features or capabilities. For example, use the Outline view to build a slideshow by entering its text content first.

Zoom level. The setting that determines how large or small the slides appear on the slide canvas.

Index

D

E

F

G

H

N

O

P

T